D1352342

The Advertising Handbook

2nd edition

'The book is excellent. It is the only text I know that looks beyond the theory to the practical application of advertising strategy and is not afraid to challenge long-held beliefs . . .' *John Egan, Middlesex University*

The Advertising Handbook is a critical introduction to the practices and perspectives of the advertising industry. Sean Brierley explores the structures of the profession and examines the roles of all those involved in advertising including businesses, agencies, consultancies and media owners.

The Advertising Handbook traces the development of advertising and examines the changes that have taken place from its formative years through to today's period of rapid change: the impact of new media, the rise of the ad agency, industry mergers, the Internet and digital technologies, and the influence of the regulatory environment.

The Advertising Handbook offers a theoretical understanding of the industry and it challenges many assumptions about advertising's power and authority. Thoroughly revised and updated, it examines why companies and organisations advertise, how they research markets, where and when they advertise, the principles and techniques of persuasion and how companies measure performance.

The Advertising Handbook includes:

- Illustrations from a range of high-profile campaigns including Budweiser, Barnardo's, Benetton and Club 18–30
- New and detailed 'workshop' exercises accompanying each chapter
- Case studies and profiles of ad agencies and key media players
- A revised and up-to-date glossary of key terms
- A guide to useful websites and online resources

Sean Brierley has been Deputy Editor of *Marketing Week* and Editor of *The Lawyer* and a lecturer in mass communications at Liverpool John Moores University. He is currently head of new product development at Centaur Communications and a columnist in *Marketing Week*.

Media Practice

Edited by James Curran, Goldsmiths College, University of London

The *Media Practice* handbooks are comprehensive resource books for students of media and journalism, and for anyone planning a career as a media professional. Each handbook combines a clear introduction to understanding how the media work with practical information about the structure, processes and skills involved in working in today's media industries, providing not only a guide on 'how to do it' but also a critical reflection on contemporary media practice.

Also in this series:

The Advertising Handbook

2nd edition

Sean Brierley

London and New York

First published 1995, reprinted by Routledge
11 New Fetter Lane, London EC4P 4EE

Reprinted 1996, 1998, 2002

Second edition first published 2002 by Routledge

Simultaneously published in the USA and Canada
by Routledge
29 West 35th Street, New York, NY 10001

Routledge is an imprint of the Taylor & Francis Group

© 1995, 2002 Sean Brierley

Typeset in Times by
Florence Production Ltd, Stoodleigh, Devon
Printed and bound in Great Britain by
Biddles Ltd, Guildford and King's Lynn

British Library Cataloguing in Publication Data
A catalogue record for this book is available from the British Library

Library of Congress Cataloging in Publication Data
A catalog record for this book has been requested

ISBN 0–415–24391–2 (hbk)
ISBN 0–415–24392–0 (pbk)

In memory of my dad,
Brian Brierley

Contents

....

Figures

....

Tables

....

Acknowledgements

Extra special thanks to Kerry, my wife, who put up with more than any reasonable person should have to, while I was completing this book, which would not have been written without her devotion and support. Special thanks too for my former colleague Paul Caplan, who against all odds managed to teach some excellent courses. And Jenny Holgate and Clare Renn, David Pugh, and Phyllida Onslow. Also Jon Leech, Patrick Crawford, Caroline Mills, David Brook, Godfrey Mann and Kirk Macpherson, Alan Strang, Mark Maddox, Camilla Honey, George Islip, Paul Butler, Chris Hughes, Jo Thomas, Billy Howard, Rebecca Barden, Simon Waldman, Susannah Richmond, Tom O'Sullivan, Stuart Smith, Al Deakin, Margaret Marshment, Nickianne Moody, Adrian Mellor, Dimitrius Elefethriotis, Davenport Lyons, Stuart Lockyear, Philip Conway, Martin Shelley, Grant Harrison, Lucy Hayward, Chris Cudmore, The Advertising Association, Philip Spink, my copy-editor John Banks and my colleagues at *Marketing Week*. The others are my numerous advertising contacts who in one form or other contributed to the form of the book, but are not to blame for the content.

Introduction

A t every point of the day you are bombarded with commercial messages. Ads are everywhere. When you are woken in the morning by your bedside radio, when you pick up junk mail from the doormat, when you stand at a poster-laden bus stop, when you sit on the bus itself, when you read a newspaper, when you send and receive faxes and emails, log on to the net, and when you watch TV at night, the commercial assault on your senses seems relentless.

Researchers in the United States have estimated that by the age of 18 the average American will have seen around 350,000 commercials (Law 1994: 28). Love them or hate them, you cannot avoid them. Aside from advertisements being viewed, read and listened to, advertisers try to get us to practise advertising as well as consume it – and they often succeed. When I was a child my parents and neighbours were compelled to indulge in a commercially inspired ritual: when I burst through the door in a cowboy outfit brandishing a cap gun, they had to shout, 'It's the Milky Bar Kid!' Thirty years later my two-year-old nephew was amusing family and friends by sticking his tongue out and growling 'Wassup?', the advertising slogan of beer brand Budweiser. There is nothing new in this. In the late nineteenth century Victorians replied to 'Good morning' with the advertising slogan, 'Have you used your Pears Soap today?' Though some may claim that this displays the power of advertising to influence our behaviour, there is little evidence that such acts resulted in increased sales of Milky Bars, Budweiser, or Pears Soap for that matter. Though advertising practitioners encouraged the view that single-message advertising is powerful – Saatchi & Saatchi's 1979 general election poster campaign for the Conservative Party which used the slogan, 'Labour Isn't Working' and a photograph of a dole queue is still perceived to have placed Margaret Thatcher in Number 10 – this popular perception is flawed. Saatchi & Saatchi would be the first to admit that elections are not won on single posters or slogans. Advertisers hedge their bets. They usually use many media and in most cases several messages to appeal to consumers. This is almost always accompanied by a whole host of other commercial messages in the form of sponsorship, sales promotion, merchandising and public relations.

Advertising can be used for a number of reasons: to motivate consumers to buy goods, or certain consumers not to buy goods, to change attitudes or to encourage retailers to stock produce. But the structure of the modern advertising industry has its roots in the Industrial Revolution. Technological progress improved production techniques, thus making possible mass production of goods and services. Producers had to find new consumer markets and expand existing ones to maintain profits and keep control over prices. They branded goods and advertised the brands to consumers to appeal over the heads of retailers and wholesalers. Manufacturers identified the mass media as a vehicle to stimulate demand. The promotional efforts of large firms focused almost exclusively on mass-media advertising, increasing promotional costs and pricing potential competitors out of more concentrated markets. The term 'advertising' came to be defined as paid-for mass-media communication, rather than all promotional activity. It became a means to the marketing ends of managing and controlling the consumer markets at the least cost. Up to the 1980s advertising agencies also focused almost exclusively on high-revenue mass-media advertising. However by the turn of the twenty-first century advertising agencies were transforming into their pre-mass media organisations. In 1991 43 per cent of ad agencies continued to describe themselves as traditional full-service ad agencies, providing account handling, creative work and media planning and buying. By 2000 there were virtually no traditional full-service agencies, media buying had been hived off from the main ad agency.

Though there are thousands of academic studies of advertising texts and their interaction with audiences, there are very few that examine the production of advertising from the advertiser's perspective.

Though it in no way attempts to provide a 'missing link' in academic analysis, this book is intended as a contribution to a wider debate about the role of advertising in society, enhancing understanding and knowledge of a part of advertising practice that has, unlike journalistic practice, been generally ignored. The purpose of this book is to examine the organisational structures and professional practices governing the production of advertising. There are four broad areas covered. First, the advertisers: who advertises? Why do they advertise? What do they advertise? Second, the economic and social relations between the producers of advertising practices; companies, agencies, media owners and government. Third, the theoretical approaches and professional discourses governing research, production, media planning and buying: how is advertising put together? Where and when does advertising appear, and why? Fourth, the book examines the historical changes to the advertising industry from its formative years to the period of rapid change at the turn of the century. Universities and colleges generally teach advertising practice from two perspectives; for those on business courses wishing to go into advertising and marketing, and for those on arts and humanities courses who seek to examine advertising in its widest cultural context. Ironically, many of the students on arts and humanities courses also end up in the advertising industry and find that much of the social or semiotic analysis they performed at college bears little relation to everyday practice. It is tempting to suggest that the very real uses of social and semiotic analyses are often rejected or misappropriated by those in the industry. This is not an attempt to make advertising 'more approachable' to students and academics: as will be revealed in following chapters, advertisers are extremely adept at arguing their own case.

Though this book does not seek to right the wrongs of the industry, there is an underlying wrong that this book does seek to address: the ghettoisation of academic life from real-life practices. Students are aware that when they leave college or university they will enter an unfamiliar world which bears little relation to what they have been taught in class or read in books.

This book aims to examine industry practices critically, offering people within the industry a fresh insight into how they work, dealing with moral and ethical issues as well as the inevitable social and political questions that always arise. It aims to bridge the gap between practice and theory. It offers a theoretical understanding of the industry from a historical, cultural and economic perspective to those who are involved in the industry, practitioners and students of advertising and it offers an understanding of industry practices and discourses to students of mass communications and cultural studies. It is not a guide to best practice. The aim of this book is to produce not better advertising but better understanding of advertising.

It examines what advertisers themselves regard as 'best practice' and why, and the repercussions of this for society. Unlike most books for practitioners, it is not a 'how-to' guide. It has a linear structure, beginning with the economic context of advertising: the economic rationale for advertising within companies, examining the relationships between manufacturers, retailers and companies and the imperative to control prices and stimulate demand (Chapters 1–4). The book shifts in Chapters 5, 6 and 7 to an examination of the formal organisation of the advertising industry: how agencies came to dominate advertising, and how advertising came to dominate the mass media. Chapters 8 to 12 examine the mechanics of the advertising process: the buying and selling of buying media and when creating advertisements. Chapters 13 and 14 examine not only the relationships between advertising and consumers from the perspectives of practitioners and regulators but also theories of advertising effectiveness, consumer behaviour and the regulations governing the industry. The advertising industry is undergoing radical change and restructuring. In recent years, a crisis has emerged. The hegemony of the advertising agency has been shattered and new forms of paid-for communication have emerged to challenge old practices.

The second edition has updated most of the figures and improved the content of some of the chapters. Since the first edition it appeared to many, including advertising practitioners themselves that the advertising industry was undergoing a fundamental revolution around the explosion in new media. However, five years is a long time in advertising and the move into the brave new world of interactive media came and went.

The destruction of the traditional mass media such as television and news-papers did not happen and a number of dot.com companies and their fellow travellers floundered as the limitations of the new media became apparent.

What did happen was an acceleration of a trend highlighted in the first edition of this book which is an increase in media clutter and fragmentation brought on by the web and digital media.

A further trend highlighted in the first edition has also accelerated. In 1992 37 per cent of total advertising expenditure was generated by packaged goods manufacturers, by 1999 it had fallen to 27 per cent as a large amount of promotional spend was diverted towards sales promotions and direct marketing in an attempt to avoid media clutter and fragmentation in their fight against retailers.

The advertising world has also continued to concentrate with a large number of high profile mergers and takeovers in London including WPP's takeover of Young & Rubicam – making it the group's third agency network alongside J. Walter Thompson and Ogilvy & Mather – and Omnicom's purchase of well-known London agencies Simons Palmer and Gold Greenlees Trott.

The very definition of advertising has changed from the traditional 'use of media to inform consumers about something and/or to persuade them to do something' (Economist Books 1993: 25) to a much wider definition which includes all paid-for publicity. The Postscript at the end of the book indicates the features of the crisis, and some of the new changes that advertisers and their agencies have made in response. Because of the dual focus of this book, 'workshop exercise' suggestions are provided for each chapter, and a glossary of terms is located at the back for lecturers and students. As advertising industry commentator Adam Lury pointed out, 'There is no formal industry-wide training scheme and very little knowledge is formalised. The most powerful influences are myth and oral history. Any study of advertising . . . needs to take this "invisible history" into account' (Lury 1994). In practice, advertising people bring their own experiences and histories to their work. They act on a mishmash of industry folklore, past research findings, intuition and the need to meet tight deadlines. They also work in a hierarchical environment, competing with others for status and money, which can inform practices. Around these practices are all kinds of competitive discourses mediated by award systems, the trade press, conferences and exhibitions, and books and manuals with which they negotiate. This book is an examination of those discursive debates and practices. It critically examines the practices and perspectives of people working in the industry – in businesses, agencies, consultancies and media owners – analyses key themes and debates and examines the wider societal context.

1 Why businesses advertise

....

Modern companies are very complex organisations with very diverse business needs. But whether they are involved in printing newspapers, refining sugar, baking bread, brewing beer or developing personal digital assistants (PDAs) the fundamental reasons why they advertise today are essentially the same as they were for businesses three hundred years ago. These reasons are to do with the micro-economic needs of business and primarily the need to stimulate demand.

The roots of mass advertising are embedded in the industrial revolution.

The new factory system – which for the first time provided enormous volumes of cheaply produced goods – resulted in over-production. There were simply too many goods and not enough consumers buying them. Industrialists were faced with the problem of having to shift these surplus items by either getting existing consumers to buy more of them or finding more consumers to buy them.

As the first industrial nation Britain was also the first country to introduce mass advertising techniques.

One of the first mass advertisers was Josiah Wedgwood. He began to manufacture luxury pottery for the upper classes in the mid-1700s. He used factory production to mass-produce household items. But because of this mass production the UK market rapidly became saturated. To get around this problem Wedgwood used new markets abroad. By the late 1780s, 84 per cent of Wedgwood's total annual production was for overseas markets (McKendrick *et al.* 1983: 136). He also tried new techniques to stimulate demand at home. These techniques would be very familiar to modern day marketing people. He segmented his range of products: from labelling doors and bins to kitchen products, bathroom ware to chandeliers, crucifixes and christening fonts, brooches, snuff boxes and ornaments.

And he targeted new consumers as separate groups: middle classes and merchants, women, men and children (especially with toys). Wedgwood used a variety of techniques to target his consumers, including money-back guarantees, free delivery, almost every form of advertisement available (newspaper ads, posters, handbills), shop signs, auctions and give-away sales promotions. He organised public relations (PR) stunts to generate publicity and developed a classical, upmarket brand image for Wedgwood produce. He produced a copy of a Roman vase which became the focus of a PR roadshow for Wedgwood's new 'Jasperware' collection (Wernick 1991) and generated press coverage. He was at the centre of the classical revival, part of a nostalgia for a mythical, idyllic past. Wedgwood even called his modern mass production factory Etruria.

Wedgwood's use of advertising has many parallels with today, especially in new technology markets.

When a market becomes saturated and supply outstrips demand, the producers often merge and concentrate their businesses and try to expand the market in other ways. Sometimes this means finding new geographical markets by exporting abroad, or to find new consumer markets by segmenting their products and targeting them at different types of consumer.

One way of stimulating consumer demand is to make it easier for consumers to pay. In 1858 Singer developed a domestic sewing machine, but it was too expensive for the market to take, so the company introduced a hire purchase scheme to expand the demand for the market. This was one of the first consumer credit schemes to try to cope with a restricted market. They also offered free trial of their machines for one-month periods. Singer's US sales quadrupled in a year (Forty 1986: 94–99). It brought the same formula to the UK in the 1860s and came to dominate the UK market. But there were still prejudices against home use to overcome. Singer used extensive advertising to promote home use of the machine and change consumer behaviour, encouraging acceptance of the new machine as a domestic appliance. It promoted the machine as a labour-saving device which could free mothers to look after the children and allow women into employment. It also changed the design of the machine, adding gilded ornamentation to make it a furniture feature.

Though the fundamental reasons why businesses advertise are to do with the company's micro-economic needs to stimulate demand and generate profits, it is the state of the macro-economy which determines how successful they will be.

It is no accident that the first mass advertisers of the nineteenth century were from industries using cheap colonial labour from the British Empire: Lipton's (tea), Cadbury, Fry's and Rowntree (cocoa), Pears and Lever (vegetable and animal fats for soap), Tate and Lyle (sugar). All these relied on cheap labour from plantations, estates and farms in the colonies, partly because of the destruction of agricultural production during Britain's industrial revolution. The supply of cheap raw materials helped to keep prices down and expand the domestic consumer market. As the consumer market grew in the late nineteenth century (along with real wages), competition from overseas also increased. But in Britain, unlike markets such as the USA, the class system prevented advertisers from targeting potentially the biggest market of all: the working class.

Consumer markets were able to expand only so far because of the impoverishment of vast numbers of workers. These markets soon became 'saturated'.

Most of the heavily advertised goods of the late nineteenth century were aimed at middle-class, not working-class, consumers. the nineteenth-century advertisers needed to stimulate demand, just as Wedgwood had done earlier. They also turned to advertising. Advertising emerged as a tool to try to stimulate the consumer markets to pay for over-produced goods. But the problem was not so much one of over-production as one of under-consumption. US manufacturers who came to the UK in the 1920s and 1930s targeted working-class consumers with low-priced goods. But with low levels of housing, health, education and wages, US manufacturers faced a particularly restricted market. During the inter-war years manufacturers introduced a system of consumer credit through hire purchase to try to encourage working-class families to consume more.

Advertisers lobbied hard after the war for the removal of rationing and the re-establishment of hire purchase. But it was only with the development of the welfare state – which provided a safety net for working-class consumers in free health, education and cheap housing after the Second World War – that consumer markets began to open up for mass advertisers. However, by the 1960s markets became saturated again, the welfare state contracted and to stimulate demand advertisers had to revert to traditional techniques such as interest-free loans, credit cards, cash-back and special schemes whereby consumers were encouraged to trade-in old goods for new and carry previous loans over. They also encouraged multiple purchase of goods.

Controlling markets: concentration and oligopoly

In the USA, advertisers were also preoccupied with the problems of saturated consumer markets. A US ad man, E. E. Calkins, said in the 1920s that products had been so heavily advertised in the USA that they might be 'scratching gravel from the bottom of consumer demand. The grocer and the chemist look despairingly at their crowded shelves when asked to find places for another breakfast food or a new toothpaste . . . advertising is almost at the point where it must find new worlds to conquer' (Bradshaw 1927: 492). One technique that manufacturers used to stimulate demand was developed by car manufacturer Henry Ford. He inflated the real wages of his own workers, thereby raising the disposable income of a whole class of manufacturing workers (C2s – see Chapter 4), and brought car ownership within the expectations of the American working classes.

The other response that manufacturers made was to expand into overseas consumer markets. US firms had already arrived in the UK in the late nineteenth century. Whereas before the First World War US manufacturers such as Kodak and American Tobacco simply exported goods, in the 1920s they started to set up branch plants. Other US companies followed, see Table 1.1.

Other US companies who came to Britain at this time included Colgate Palmolive, General Motors, Ford, Procter & Gamble, Sun Maid Raisins and American Walnuts.

Table 1.1 US businesses open UK factories

Company	Year
Kraft	1920
Kellogg's	1924
Wrigley's	1927
Heinz	1928
Hoover	1932
Mars	1932

British markets became saturated and, in order to compete with the US consumer goods industries, British industries concentrated. Some of the first mergers occurred at the turn of the century. In 1905 as a response to a fierce marketing campaign by American Tobacco in the UK, twelve British tobacco manufacturers formed Imperial Tobacco. The extent of merger activity can be seen in Table 1.2 which shows the mergers that have taken place to form Anglo-Dutch household goods giant, Unilever.

Another household name in Britain, Beecham, bought up many competitors in the 1920s and after the Second World War. It was eventually bought by US drug company SmithKline in 1990 which in turn merged with Glaxo Wellcome in 2000. Such big mergers were increasingly made not only to defend markets but also to rationalise the higher costs of advertising and marketing goods.

Such merger activity created oligopolies, where three or four of the largest companies control the market. Most mature advertising markets are dominated by oligopolies. The top two spending UK advertisers are oligopolists in their sectors: Unilever £183m and Procter & Gamble £165m (*Marketing*, 2 March 2000). They operate in the fast-moving consumer goods sector: Unilever and Procter & Gamble dominate in soaps, food, detergents, toothpastes and beverages. Companies use distribution, pricing and patents to prevent competitors from entering markets: by controlling distribution outlets (such as car dealerships), pricing the goods too cheaply for smaller competitors to enter the market and controlling the patent for the product to prevent any imitators (as in the pharmaceuticals sector). But advertising is also used as a method of preventing new competitors entering a market.

Oligopolies are able to maintain high advertising and marketing expenditures to make the high costs of entering a market prohibitive. As the industry concentrates, as with the confectionery market this century, so the amount spent on advertising has increased. In the 1930s high levels of advertising expenditure helped to concentrate the confectionery, beer and tobacco markets. Of eighty-one firms in the confectionery market in 1936, two were responsible for 60 per cent of the confectionery advertising in newspapers, three beer companies out of 114 accounted for 49 per cent of advertising, and three tobacco companies

Table 1.2 A short merger history of Unilever

Year	Bought/merged
1911	Lever buys Pears Soap
1919	Crosfield bought (the owners of Persil)
1929	merged with the Dutch Margarine Union to form Unilever
1960s	Elida Gibbs bought
1980s	Birds Eye Wall's and Brooke Bond Oxo bought
2000s	Bestfoods bought

out of eighty spent 35 per cent of the total (*Economist*, 27 February 1937). In the early years advertising provided a clear advantage for mass production manufacturers, as one contemporary observer said, 'the advertiser profits by selling his goods more cheaply; for not only are his factory costs reduced thus, but the path of competition is made harder' (Russell 1924: 138).

In this sense, the prohibitive cost of advertising can be anti-competitive.

Media inflation was one of the factors which caused J. Lyons to move out of chocolate manufacture in the 1960s. The major chocolate manufacturers – Mars, Cadbury, Rowntree and Nestlé – all massively increased their advertising spend in a move to TV advertising. In 1958 Mars increased its ad spend by two-thirds, the following year Rowntree increased its by 86 per cent, Nestlé by 60 per cent and Cadbury, the market leader, increased by 40 per cent. Lyons dropped out of confectionery altogether (Birch 1962: 115). Media cost has been a decisive factor in helping the further concentration of advertiser power.

The restricted TV market in Britain, which for almost thirty years was dominated by the ITV monopoly, had helped to force up advertising costs. This meant that new entrants into a market had to find extra capital to compete with the big-brand advertisers. Whereas in the past there were cost advantages in advertising, now manufacturers had to engage in advertising to maintain market share against competitors. Oligopolists invest so much in advertising that they make it prohibitive for anyone to enter the market. In Britain the average age of the top grocery brands is over 40. It has been estimated that in some markets, such as packaged goods, 90 per cent of new products fail partly because of the prohibitive advertising and marketing costs needed to sustain them. The greater size and concentration of an advertiser in a market, the greater power it has to control distribution, prices, and advertising and media costs. This makes it more difficult for a new entrant to come into the market. The small number of large companies who dominate a market can prevent new entrants from coming into a market by keeping prices low. Rupert Murdoch used this strategy in 1993 by cutting the price of *The Times* and *Sun* newspapers (the *Telegraph* followed suit: see Chapter 14) to try to squeeze competitors out of the newspaper market. He charged low prices for newspapers and supplemented the income from advertising revenue.

When the *Sunday Correspondent* newspaper was launched in 1989 it needed a high promotional spend to enter the national newspaper market. All the established newspapers also increased their advertising and marketing spends, and within a year the *Correspondent* was forced to close, with some of its competitors owning a share of it. Swiss chocolate manufacturer Suchard suffered a similar fate: they tried to launch Lila Pause into the UK in 1989. The attempt was made via its main chocolate bar, Milka. It used a heavy advertising and merchandising campaign, doing deals with retailers to make sure that the brand had good in-store positions. The main confectionery manufacturers – Cadbury, Rowntree and Mars – did nothing, and then they all launched heavy promotional campaigns. Milka and Lila Pause disappeared (Griffiths 1992: 39). Since the 1950s world advertising expenditure per person has doubled in real terms. Greater concentration of the industry often leads to greater ad spend and higher advertising to sales (A/S) ratios. These measure the money spent on advertising as a proportion of the sales revenue for the brands. In 1999 the sectors with the highest A/S ratios (%) were as in Table 1.3.

The rise of brands

'Advertising as the handmaid of distribution' was the subhead in a 1924 article about advertising in the *Illustrated London News*.

The mass movement of the rural population to the towns and cities of the north and midlands in nineteenth-century Britain meant that distribution patterns had to change. To distribute their goods, manufacturers needed guaranteed retail and distribution outlets. Some manufacturers simply bought up retail outlets. Boots, Timothy Whites, Freeman Hardy Willis and Sainsbury's all bought and expanded their retail business in the late nineteenth century and early twentieth century to try and control distribution. Tea importer Thomas Lipton had no branches in 1870 but by 1899 he had 500 retail outlets across the country. Other manufacturers, such as Lever, Bird's and Cadbury, reduced costs by moving out of retail and using the savings to produce heavily branded and advertised goods. In 1884 W. H. Lever copied US advertising and marketing techniques by branding his soap as Sunlight and selling it in one-pound tablets in imitation parchment. 'Sunlight' was imprinted on the soap (Forty 1986: 76).

Because of problems with the large number of retail outlets, manufacturers used wholesaler intermediaries to distribute their goods. Vince Norris argues that national advertising and brand-naming was developed by manufacturers to go over the heads of wholesalers and get the retailers to demand certain brands (in Leiss *et al.* 1990: 140–141). Wholesalers had been able to sell products in cheap bulk orders by offering retailers whichever manufactured soap was cheapest. Branding added value to the products over and above their use value: it restricted the power of wholesalers and re-asserted the manufacturer's power to control prices. The wholesaler was forced to stock certain brands because the manufacturer had developed a relationship with the retailer and the consumer

Table 1.3 Advertising to sales ratios

Top ten A/S ratios by product category	(%)
Hair colourants	34.5
Indigestion remedies	21.9
Denture cleaners	18.6
Shampoos	18.4
Soap	16.6
Nail make-up/care	16.5
Dishwashing liquid	14.1
Asthma/hayfever remedies	13.4
Cough remedies	13.1
Analgesics	11.4

Note: This means that for every pound spent on hair colourants, for instance, you are contributing 34.5p to the advertising of that product. These figures are taken from the *Advertising Statistics Yearbook* 2000.

through the new mass media. Wholesalers virtually disappeared from many business sectors. Big retailers were able to spread their costs and create economies of scale by dealing direct with the manufacturer, rather than through the wholesaler. In the twentieth century, the growth of retailer power meant that the manufacturer's branding strategy had to concentrate more overtly on stimulating consumers. Guinness launched its high-profile 'Guinness is Good for You' campaign in 1928 because it did not own any pubs and needed to appeal directly to the consumer to encourage pubs to stock it. During the inter-war years, many manufacturers rushed to package their goods, eroding the power of the retailer. One example of this was Anchor butter. In 1924, the New Zealand Dairy Company started to pre-package butter to encourage customers to choose its brand. Retailers had previously measured out the butter, along with other items, such as tea, sweets, chocolate and medicines (in pharmacies). Pre-packaging cut shopping time and reinforced the relationship between brand and consumer.

Manufacturers gave their products added values to establish difference in the marketplace. Difference was established in terms of price – cheap or premium (more expensive implied higher quality) – or by some other added values to the product that the competition did not provide. Brand values were sustained through continuous advertising. Advertisers believed not only that brands added value to products but that they created 'brand loyalty'. In 1988 Nestlé paid six times Rowntree's reported asset value (£2.5 billion) solely because the brands added value in terms of customer loyalty (or good will). The other major sales environment for advertisers is the home. Sears Roebuck & Co. started mail order catalogues in 1893 in the USA for jewellery and watches as a way of cutting out retailers and dealing directly with consumers. Catalogues have proved to be a very popular form of merchandising and advertising: they have managed to cut out the retailers and deal direct with the consumer. In the late 1990s a number of manufacturers also opened their own stores such as Nike, Levi's and Doctor Martens. Others also moved into media launching their own websites and even launching their own magazines such as *Sony Magazine*. In 2000 Unilever launched a website called www.myhome.co.uk which offered home cleaning services to customers in South West London using Unilever cleaning products such as Persil and Jif (*Marketing Week*, 24 August 2000: 21).

Summary

Mass advertising grew from the need to stimulate consumption to meet the demands of mass production. Manufacturers used mass-media advertising to appeal to consumers over the heads of wholesalers and retailers. Advertisers were also able to use the high cost of advertising as a prohibitive mechanism to keep out potential challengers in their markets. Ownership and control of markets became more concentrated and consumers had to pay more for their goods.

2 Making and segmenting markets

....

Pre-industrial markets operated in clearly defined geographical spaces (market towns), at clearly defined times (market day). However, after the Industrial Revolution markets were no longer controlled and regulated in such a way. Road, rail and air transport and the mass media helped to break down spatial and temporal boundaries, bringing individuals and communities into wider consumer markets. If a modern-day hypermarket wished to advertise the opening of a new store in East Kilbride, for instance, it would advertise not just in the immediate geographical region, but also in towns and villages up to forty miles away which had easy access to motorway routes. Regional media planning became as much concerned with the time it took to reach a retail outlet as with the physical space.

If you lived only two or three miles away and you didn't have a car it might take you longer to reach the supermarket than if you lived twenty miles away in a more affluent area. Because modern markets are wider and more open than pre-industrial markets, advertisers try to make communication easier and cheaper by fixing the market in a specific place and time. They also attempt to control their business environment by classifying, measuring and 'mapping' their product and consumer markets. They use market information to predict future behaviour, and to gain advantages over competitors. The geographical market includes its regulatory boundaries which can be local, national or regional (such as the European Community).

The consumer market involves classification into 'types' of consumers. This can include all adults, all car enthusiasts, all women, all young women, all young northern women, all young northern women who are independent and ambitious, etc. (this is explored in Chapter 4). The product market includes the goods or service that the business is trying to promote. Marketers identify similarities in products and services and classify according to type such as all consumer durables, all vehicles, all cars, all saloons, or all Y-registered saloons, for instance.

However, product and consumer markets are not self-contained, they overlap. A car manufacturer's competitors include other car manufacturers, and other forms of transport: vans, fleet cars, train, plane, bicycle. It is therefore in the car manufacturer's interest for consumers to prefer car travel to other forms, as well as their brand to others. Part of the success of US car manufacturers in the inter-war period was the destruction of public transport (trams) in cities. In the British meat industry in the 1980s and 1990s, manufacturers came together to launch generic advertising campaigns, with a 'Meat to Live' theme, featuring slim meat-eaters in various sporting and outdoor pursuits leading active lives, to counter claims that high-fat diets are unhealthy and lead to heart disease. In the media industry, magazines and newspapers responded to the competition for enter-tainment and news from TV: they increased advertising spends, launched generic campaigns to their advertisers to support their medium, increased the coverage of TV stars, lifestyle features and provided TV listings.

The advertiser's market may also be affected by its dependence on another, such as tyres and cars, sauces and meat, video cassettes and video recorders.

Though marketers talk in terms of their product's market, they are aware that it is not enclosed but overlaps with many others. There is no such thing as a simple family car market; it is merely a convenient classification to base marketing decisions upon. Modern marketers do not accept the narrow defini-tions of a single market and constantly try to find new niches and ways of exploiting overlaps in markets to gain advantage over competitors. Broadsheet newspapers try to woo tabloid readers, bitter brewers target lager drinkers and cosmetics companies try to encourage men to use cosmetics. One other way is for the brand advertiser to move the brand into a different product field alto-gether, such as chocolate bar brands moving into ice cream (Mars, Bounty, Milky Way), liqueurs (Cadbury and Terry's Chocolate Orange), soap powders moving into washing-up liquid (Persil) and spirits manufacturers moving into 'soft' drinks ('alcopops' such as Hooper's Hooch).

Because of the need to manage markets in a cost-effective way, businesses define and delineate markets in terms of the way consumers use their products or services.

Consumer markets

Packaged and fast-moving consumer goods

Packaged and fast-moving consumer goods (FMCGs) are goods which are frequently bought and used, including confectionery, toiletries (toothpaste, tissue paper, shampoo), alcoholic and non-alcoholic drinks, cigarettes, newspapers and magazines. These goods are often bought at shops and supermarkets and are very often categorised as convenience and shopping goods. A 'convenience' good is one that does not involve much thought on the part of consumers and is purchased without bothering to make a comparison (as with toilet paper). The 'shopping' good, on the other hand, involves the consumer spending some time comparing the brands on the market for price, quality and brand image. An example of a shopping good may be meat or vegetables. Because of the heavy reliance on the retail environment, a large part of the marketing budget for FMCGs goes on sales promotion (competitions, money-off coupons), and packaging and design. Because these goods are bought and used daily and weekly, advertising is used to remind the consumer that the brand is available and to encourage repeat purchase. Some packaged goods, such as magazines, chocolates, beers and many packaged supermarket goods, are also often the subject of impulse buying, where people decide on the spur of the moment to buy them. Because of this, such goods are often prominently displayed to catch the consumer's attention. In 1992 packaged goods accounted for 37 per cent of total advertising expenditure, by 1999, however, it had fallen to 27 per cent of total advertising expenditure. Though packaged goods manufacturers had increased advertising spend in real terms, the rate of increase was nowhere as high as other categories. They also diverted a large amount of their advertising money towards sales promotions and direct marketing because advertising was seen as less effective in the fight against retailers (see Postscript).

Consumer durables

Consumer durables are bought occasionally. They include 'white goods' such as washing machines, fridges, driers, dishwashers and freezers, and 'brown goods' (a phrase which comes from the days when these goods had wooden boxes) which include hi-fis, TVs, video recorders and camcorders. Also in this sector are gardening tools, bicycles, personal computers, vacuum cleaners, furniture, carpets and cars, which, on average, consumers buy every three years. Marketers believe that, because of expense, consumers take more time gaining information before making buying decisions. The consumer would be expected to travel distances to get a good deal, or to see a particular brand at showrooms. Consumer durables manufacturers provide more detailed information through brochures and sales staff. They also tend to offer more credit schemes (such as hire purchase) and incentives. Consumer durables manufacturers have massively increased their advertising spend. According to the Advertising Association, durables accounted for 19 per cent of advertising expenditure in 1992, by 1999 its proportion had risen to 21 per cent. This was largely fuelled by the growth of mobile phones, games consoles and personal computers.

Services

Service industry advertisers include the travel industry, tour operators, airlines, railways, restaurants and fast food chains, leisure parks, health clubs, water companies, electricity, gas, telecommunications, solicitors, accountants, hairdressers and breakdown services. They try to offer the emotional benefits of service such as quality, reassurance, security, expertise, comfort, subservience, style, leisure and fun (in the case of McDonald's). They provide services to customers rather than products or commodities, though they often promote goods to consumers. The most important influence on service industries is the consumer's time. Advertising either emphasises taking 'time out' from normal routine – relaxing on a train, at the hairdresser's or at the health club – or it may emphasise speed and efficiency, as in fast food restaurants and breakdown services (RAC and AA). Services accounted for 12 per cent of advertising expenditure in 1999.

Financial advertisers include banks, building societies, insurance companies, and financial and institutional investors such as pension funds. Financial advertising tends to emphasise security and convenience. In recent years the high-street banks have begun to shift their attention away from attracting new customers and towards trying to retain existing ones. Banks have difficulty in differentiating from each other. They tend to offer the same services. The rare exception is the Co-operative Bank which advertises its 'ethical' banking as a main selling proposition. Others have tried to emphasise the personal nature of their banking services by featuring bank workers in commercials, to emphasise personal service and encourage people to come into branches. Financial advertising accounted for 8.7 per cent of the total in 1999. According to the Advertising Association, between 1980 and 1990 financial service advertising grew by 199 per cent as a consequence of deregulation and competition.

Business-to-business and trade

Business and industrial advertising used to be generally restricted to a controlled market: providers of printing machines, office and factory equipment, components and business services all had a tightly defined sector to market to. This often meant that advertising was confined to the business press and the sales-force, giving incentives such as travel vouchers, taking business consumers on trips, organising conferences, exhibitions and trade shows. Though this is still the major feature of business-to-business advertising, it has expanded. There has been a movement of business out of the public sphere and into people's private and personal lives (especially with the aid of the computer, which crosses over from business to personal use, telephones and cable). Business-to-business advertisers target this wider market in the business pages of national newspapers, and in business programmes on TV. One example of this is the *Daily Telegraph* using sponsorship of American football to gain the attention of ad agency people (see Postscript).

Packaged and consumer durables manufacturers advertise their goods to retailers and distributors. This trade advertising often includes targeted incentives such as a higher cut of the retail price of the brand (the retail margin). Or it may include competitions with prizes for those retailers who managed to sell the most products. Most trade advertisers use trade magazines such as *The Grocer*, *Confectionery and Tobacco News* (*CTN*), *Travel Trade Gazette* or *Chemist & Druggist*. But trade advertising can also be disguised. The main aim of a trade ad, as opposed to a business-to-business ad, is to secure distribution. Trade ads tell retailers when to expect a large demand of the brands from customers, especially if there is an expected price decrease, or a special promotion. Many manufacturers aim consumer advertising (in local papers and outdoor media) at retailers rather than consumers to persuade them to stock the product in the mistaken belief that there is a large consumer ad campaign occurring. Trade and business-to-business advertising accounted for 9.1 per cent of total advertising expenditure in 1999.

Consumer advertising campaigns can be aimed also at the distributors, or retailers. Britvic's campaign for boxed orange juice ('we squeeze 12 oranges into every box') in the early 1990s was aimed at just five retailers, to get them to put the brand on the shelves. Poster sites were bought near to supermarkets; this was backed up by a heavy sales and merchandising campaign. The campaign may also be intended to give a boost to sales representatives who are trying to open distribution channels. This happens particularly with the pharmaceuticals industry, where reps use a current advertising campaign to persuade chemists to stock more of their brands. Advertisers can also use advertising to tell consumers where to get the product ('only available from your local pharmacist', etc.). A direct response campaign may also provide the salesforce with names and addresses to follow up. This happens a great deal with double-glazing firms. Mail order firms will also use advertising to build up their list of names and addresses (such as Kays catalogues).

Recruitment advertising has grown with the demand for highly skilled workers and business executives. In the 1980s recruitment consultancies became substantial advertisers in some sectors. This has been tipped as one of the growth areas for the next century. Recruitment advertisers use a variety of media, usually the national and local press and business magazines. In the 1980s national newspapers carved substantial niches in recruitment advertising. Other classified ads include business services, and the local advertising market of personal columns, 'buy and sell' columns, which make a substantial part of local newspapers' advertising revenue. By 2000 a substantial amount of this advertising was forecast to move on to the web.

Geographical markets

Marketers have traditionally used political–geographical boundaries as the basis for their own market maps. Because of the different regulatory levels (local, national, regional, international), state boundaries constructed an idea of the market as fixed in space and time. But people and markets do not fit into these finite geographical boundaries. Fixed markets are inherently unstable. Faster channels of communication and transport have transformed political boundaries and undermined traditional regulatory controls (tax, pricing policy and self-regulatory codes and standards).

The widespread ownership of private cars in the post-war period has transformed local markets. Retailers who set up in retail parks judge their consumer markets in terms of the length of time it gets to reach the market, rather than in terms of space. A supermarket may have a catchment area of up to forty miles if it is near a motorway.

E-retailing has also transformed these boundaries where dot.com retailers such as Tesco.com and Amazon.com has threatened traditional retailing by offering direct mail via the web.

Though national markets are limited in terms of the legal and political boundaries, there are very few brands which have the same weight and strength across the country. 'National' advertisers tend to have heavy concentrations in certain cities and regions of the country and sections of the population. National campaigns are often marketed regionally. A 'national' brand such as John Smith's Bitter had to run two separate advertising campaigns for its brand in the Yorkshire region and the south of England in the late 1980s. The Southern campaign included stereotypes of 'typical' Yorkshire men (flat caps and funny accents), the Yorkshire campaign associated the brand with hard-working, hard-drinking men. 'National' advertisers have been squeezed on two fronts, first from more ethnically diverse 'local' advertising markets and second from regional or international markets.

International advertisers plan and direct advertising campaigns across national boundaries. Though many international advertisers such as Nestlé, Unilever and Procter & Gamble tailor their individual brand and campaigns to national and regional markets (Elida Gibbs's Lynx men's deodorant is called Axe in Germany), some advertisers have standardised their brands across frontiers. Coca-Cola, Marlboro, Gillette, Elida Gibbs's Impulse all developed advertising campaigns and marketing strategies which would operate across frontiers. Though very few advertisers can be said to be a significant force in almost all markets, like Coca-Cola, the main imperative for standardisation has been to minimise costs. In 2000 Unilever announced that it would drop two-thirds of its brands – a total of 1,400 worldwide – to focus on what it called 'global power brands (*Marketing Week Brand Saviours* 22 June 2000).

Standardised advertising through global brands gave rise to the global slogan: Nike, 'Just do it'; Coke, 'The Real Thing'; Marlboro Country; Gillette, 'The best a man can get'. These campaigns have been criticised for reducing the sales message to a minimum to appeal to all cultures through a 'lowest common denominator'. Advertisers have tried to get around the problem by using multi-language packaging to keep costs down.

The opening of the Single European Market in 1992 facilitated the growth of Euro-brands such as Gillette's Natrel Plus, and the change of 'national' brands such as Mars Marathon towards an international brand such as Snickers. However, in Europe there are differences not only in taste and culture but also in terms of disposable income and approaches to consumption. Though Natrel Plus was a standardised Euro-brand, it had to have different formulations in European countries; some with anti-perspirant, and some without. And though all cars are the same across Europe, they have to run different advertising campaigns to appeal to different cultures. Some markets prefer smaller cars (Italy), some larger performance cars (Germany), some buy on the basis of national cars (Italy, France and UK), others on safety. Volvo attempted a pan-European campaign in 1990 with a car morphing into a horse, but it soon dropped the campaign and went back to focusing in the UK on safety (it did this in Switzerland as well, in France on status, in Sweden on economy and in Germany on performance). The problem that Volvo had was not only in terms of the different types of consumers, but of the differences in terms of competitors in each market and the historical precedents and situations in each 'national' market.

Markets and the problem of media access

Markets are about access. There is no point in having a market if nobody can get to it. Traditionally, markets have been defined in terms of geographical areas: local, national, regional or global. Media markets became the main advertising and marketing environments, rather than political boundaries.

Because media do not generally organise in terms of geographical markets, advertisers have had to rearrange their markets to suit the availability of media. Geographical markets overlap when advertisers consider media and communications markets. The ITV regions formed the basis for marketing regions. After 1955 marketing departments no longer referred to the Lancashire region when advertising but to the Granada region. Part of the language of the advertising world involved talking about the Granada region as a geographical space rather than just as a transmission area.

The biggest problem with international co-ordination of campaigns has been the expense of matching the media market to the geographical and political distribution market. For international advertisers, media has to be selected on a regional basis. There are variations in regulations, size, and cost of media across boundaries. Satellite TV does not go into all homes, only a small proportion; advertisers are not able to conduct a pan-European campaign on TV, only a pan-European satellite TV campaign. Local advertisers also have the problem of commanding prices in local media. The local media's advertising rates are set by competition not only in the local market but also in the national and international market. One of the reasons why local hairdressers are not able to advertise on regional radio or TV, for instance, is the high prices governed by national and international advertisers on the medium.

With the explosion of the Internet and TV home shopping facilities, many consumers are now able to access worldwide markets via computer terminals or via digital television, or via mobile phones using WAP technology and are able to mail order goods and services across different markets. This has meant that some markets are being defined more in terms of time than of space.

Regulated markets: pharmaceuticals

Because of regulations, pharmaceutical products are divided into three categories: prescription-only medicine, pharmacy only, and general sales list (GSL). Prescription-only drugs are controlled by general practitioners, and can be bought only on prescription; pharmacy-only medicines can be sold only in pharmacies under the guidance of trained pharmacists; and GSLs can be sold anywhere. Painkiller Distalgesic is an example of a prescription-only drug; the painkiller Panadeine, which includes codeine, is an example of a pharmacy-only drug, and in small quantities painkiller Panadol (which includes paracetamol) is an example of a GSL. In 1985 the British government used a World Health Organisation recommendation to limit the number of drugs available on prescription as an opportunity to cut costs by banning certain branded drugs from being prescribed; cheaper generic drugs were available when GPs were prescribing the heavily marketed branded variety. As a concession to the drugs industry, the government agreed to move a number of prescription drugs to over-the-counter. This allowed drug companies to market directly to consumers drugs which were previously mediated by trained GPs. Two examples of this are cough mixture Benylin and more recently the herpes treatment Zovirax. The government further compensated drug companies by allowing wider distribution through drug stores, supermarkets and even newsagents. In the past most OTC drugs were allowed to be distributed only through pharmacies with highly trained professionals. According to the Advertising Association, between 1980 and 1990 pharmaceutical advertising grew by 119 per cent as a consequence of deregulation. Branded drugs still remain on prescription, and drug companies spend a great deal of money marketing to GPs to make sure their branded goods appear on prescriptions.

Marketing in the company

The size and scale of an organisation is a major influence on the form of its marketing and advertising activity. Large multiple-brand manufacturers like Nestlé, Unilever and Ford tend to launch products to markets in order to defend the market share of their brand leaders, for example Unilever's launch of Radion soap powder in 1989, launched to protect leading brand Persil at a vulnerable end of the market. They have the resources to do this and to gain favourable rates with the media. Whereas most local advertisers would have to pay for advertising at the set price (rate card price), a huge regular advertiser can arrange volume deals which will guarantee income for the medium, and give it more prestige to other advertisers. These deals will often involve substantial discounts being offered to the big advertiser, which a small advertiser could not achieve because it could not guarantee volume over a certain period of time.

Marketing departments have grown considerably in the past thirty years. In the 1960s marketing was largely controlled by the managing director or chairman, who would not have any formal qualifications in marketing. In the 1990s marketing departments were usually staffed by marketing graduates and there are more likely to be women in positions of authority. However, by 2001, of the top 100 advertisers in the UK, only 14 had women marketing directors.

The structure of the marketing department usually reflects the size of the organisation. Larger organisations with many brands may well have special teams looking after dedicated areas of the brand's management, with a market-ing manager who looks after all aspects of marketing for a single brand; others may have separate departments looking after the sales promotions of all brands in the portfolio, and a separate advertising team looking after them. Smaller organisations usually have a team or (in some cases) an individual who looks after the entire marketing and communications output of the brands (including PR, sales promotion, merchandising and the advertising of the brand).

The marketing manager and/or the brand manager deals with all aspects of the brand's management: liaising with the advertising agency and other commu-nications services and with other departments in the firm such as sales and distribution. She or he also helps to set the budget for the coming year, though the ultimate decision is made by the marketing director and the board.

In small organisations where the advertising market is local or very specialist, as with estate agents, the advertising will be controlled by the chief executive of the company. But even small organisations will have a separate section that looks after the marketing, sales and distribution of the company and the need to co-ordinate the brand imaging in some way. Often this may be through a sales and promotions department or through the PR and advertising department.

Marketing as a discipline has been engaged in a struggle for legitimacy: not only with the state and consumerists in terms of legislation and regulations against advertising but also within the firm. One study showed that, despite the success of marketing in the 1980s, only 49 per cent of the top thousand British firms had marketing directors on the main board, compared with 89 per cent of finance directors (Whittington and Whipp 1992: 53).

The business community on the whole still does not see advertising as an essential investment. Marketers have found themselves in a constant struggle with accountants and finance directors because of its unmeasurable, abstract nature and confusion over the precise role of advertising for companies. Advertising and marketing are substantial costs to a firm and are always the first to go in a recession because they are the areas where the firm has least control. Many of the decisions are outside the controlled environment of the firm. Nevertheless advertising benefits from being included as an expense, which is therefore tax-deductible.

Saturation and segmentation

Research conducted in the late 1980s into 1,096 brands, including Kellogg's, Unilever and Procter & Gamble, in twenty-three countries, found that 90 per cent of the sales in those markets showed very little growth, and they tended to be dominated by oligopolies. The markets are saturated and static (no move-ment in demand) and the A/S ratios tend to be between 4 per cent and 8 per cent (Jones 1990: 39).

There has been a growth of the number of brands, but a concentration of them in a small number of big advertisers. Whereas in the past an advertiser might have three or four brands in a market, the concentration of power among big advertisers through mergers and acquisitions has meant that companies now have multiple brands and the ability to control entire markets. This is the case with Nestlé, Cadbury, Unilever, Procter & Gamble, Allied Lyons, Rank Hovis McDougall, British American Tobacco. It is not unusual for big-brand advertisers to have a portfolio of hundreds of brands in related markets. Firms tend to use brand proliferation and advertising support to occupy all market niches where they may be vulnerable. This is especially true of the FMCG sector such as cereals, margarines, chocolates, but also now of consumer durables such as cars and electrical goods. Retail and financial services, banking, etc. aim at different sectors to prevent other financial services occupying their niche, for example First Direct's phone banking and insurance service.

Manufacturers have responded to saturated markets by fragmenting existing ones. One example is the toothpaste market. In the 1950s there were fifteen toothpaste products, in the 1990s there are over a hundred. This is because the four main brands, Colgate, Gibbs, Macleans and Crest, have all developed multiple varieties of the same brand to segment the market: tartar control, smoker's, children's, different mint flavours and bicarbonate of soda. Marketers call these brand segments 'line extensions'. The toothpaste brands also have own-label competition to fight for market share.

Multi-brand manufacturers launch line extensions of the brand in segments of the existing market. Line extensions, or stretching, can also move a brand into other product areas. Advertisers often use the authority of existing brands to enter another product area. Unilever extended its Persil laundry detergent brand into a washing-up liquid in the early 1990s. Mars also diversified its brand into milk and into ice cream in the late 1980s, Ovaltine into chocolate bars, Cadbury into chocolate and liqueur, Nesquik into chocolate drink and cereal, and Virgin records into an airline, vodka, cola, mobile phones, pensions and train services. There is little genuine innovation in these developments. They also run the risk of diluting the brand-name and if one of the products or services is inferior to the others it could possibly damage the main brand. Many of the 'new' products launched in the 1980s were actually more about launching old brands into new markets than developing new brands and products (see Postscript).

Another tactic is to launch new brands into other segments of the market to prevent competitors stealing market share, or launching a new product. This is called 'line filling'. Procter & Gamble has twenty-four brands of fabric-washing products such as Ariel, Bold and Tide, which all differentiate from each other (Economist Books 1993: 111). Unilever also did this in 1989 with Radion, which was launched as an odour-attacking soap powder at the younger end of the market. The intention was to try to eat into the rival brands Ariel and Bold owned by Procter & Gamble, rather than Unilever's own brands Persil and Surf. Line filling usually occurs where established brands are vulnerable to competitors, especially in markets where the brands are relatively new, such as computers or electronics. Line extensions usually occur where an old brand needs to develop variants to keep up sales and market share (e.g. new flavours), or where a manufacturer wants to exploit the established name of an old brand to introduce a different product.

Some do this expecting the brand to last only for a short time. This happened in the London newspaper market when Robert Maxwell tried to launch the *London Daily News*, and Associated Newspapers (publishers of the *Evening Standard*) relaunched the *London Evening News* to protect its monopoly position. The result was that the *Daily News* and *Evening News* closed and the *Evening Standard* remains the only evening newspaper for London. Such defensive new brand launches happen all the time in the mature markets of soap, confectionery, soft drinks and toiletries. The risk with brand filling is that a manufacturer may erode the market of its own brand: this is called 'cannibalisation'.

However, line filling is more expensive and more risky than line extending. For instance, extending Coca-Cola into diet and caffeine-free lines in a market which already has high awareness of the Coca-Cola brand-name would cost less and need much less awareness-raising advertising than launching a new brand such as Tab Clear (Lannon 1993: 19). Unilever's Radion was also scrapped in 2000.

If a market is segmenting, old and conventional brands often have to re-position themselves, from being mass-market (general) brands towards a niche brand, to try to maintain sales. This has occurred in most markets (women's weekly magazines, for example). If a brand is not in a lead position it can still differentiate by occupying a niche; this is often done by using a luxury pricing policy, as with Stella Artois beer, or maintaining a regional, demographic or lifestyle advantage as with Old Spice with older working-class men, or Body Shop by providing 'green' cosmetics and toiletries.

Because advertisers in mature markets seek to maintain market share, much of their strategy is focused on encouraging existing users and buyers to consume more, rather than trying to win new consumers to the market (see Postscript). Part of the campaign can be to try to prevent the medium and light users of a brand from switching to a rival, or to try to encourage people to switch from a related competitor in an adjacent product market, for example from razors to depilatory cream.

Summary

Markets are constructed according to three main criteria: the political boundaries which demarcate rules and legislation, the size and organisation of producers, and the availability and access of media. Because of the communications revolution, markets are no longer geographically limited. Marketers need finite markets in order to plan and co-ordinate campaigns in the most profitable and cost-effective way. Finite markets are constructed and classified in terms of the product category and consumer usage. However, though marketers constantly try to fix and manage markets, they are, by their very nature, hetero-geneous and unstable. Most marketers perceive markets to be saturated and in decline. To keep the overall market share of the company up, they segment the market into niches, repositioning existing brands and launching new brands against rivals. To gain an advantage, marketers often try to work outside the constructed world of the fixed markets to undermine the competition, bringing consumers in from other markets and moving their brands into others.

3 'Finding' consumers

Classifications of one kind or another are fundamental to understanding the market and taking action to change them. It is only by putting similar people together in groups, labelling the groups and then observing how the behaviour that interests us varies between them that we can work out the reasons why people behave the way that they do.

(Cornish 1990: 28)

The marketing concept

In the 1920s, when US advertisers and agencies brought research techniques to Britain, one commentator wrote of the new techniques, 'Such research will include a study of the product, its purpose, the consumer, the trade, and general business conditions . . . firstly . . . to cut out, as far as possible, the gamble in advertising; secondly, to discover a definite objective; thirdly, to find the quickest way to that objective and to tie up the advertising to marketing distribution' (Bradshaw 1927: 86).

All aspects of planning, the marketing mix and the idea of targeting the consumer arose in this period. From as early as the 1920s books such as Claude Hopkins's *Scientific Advertising* tried to make marketing and advertising into a professional discipline.

This was attempted through the development of professional organisations, standards of training and the rise of the marketing concept. Marketers and advertisers needed to make the unmeasurable and unmanageable consumers as measurable and controllable as the production assets of the firm. Controlled consumption was offered to balance controlled production. Marketers offered captive consumers to the boards of their firms (even though the consumers were not as captive as they asserted). The use of research statistics and figures on consumers gives legitimacy to a profession which previously relied on 'common-sense' notions of how the market works.

The marketing concept was first articulated after the Second World War by the General Electric Company. This concept assumed that buyers were rational and chose and preferred those brands that best met their wants. This meant that firms should try to identify wants and then try to satisfy them (Dickinson *et al.* 1986: 18). Part of the ideology of the marketing concept is to assert that, in the bad old days, producers produced the goods and then advertisers in the firm devised ways of selling them to the public. With the marketing concept, the story is supposed to start with the consumer. Consumers have the power to shape their own wants without influence or persuasion.

The manufacturer researches the consumer market and develops products to meet and match consumer expectations. The marketing concept asserts that markets already exist in the real world, the purpose of research is to go out and find them. But markets are made, not discovered.

The multiple-brand advertisers launch products because of competition and market conditions, not because consumers' needs are not being satisfied. An advertiser needs to have a reason to advertise: it is not simply to satisfy consumers. As Dickinson *et al.* state, 'the marketing concept understates the power of corporation to shape wants. . . . Marketing academics often see no inconsistency in promoting the marketing concept as the basic posture for all marketing, while simultaneously agreeing that it is consumer perceptions that count and such perceptions can be greatly influenced' (see Hopkins 1966).

Consumer research gave a perceived advantage in markets where there was no product difference, such as jeans, so the supposed lifestyles of consumers replaced the sales message. In the 1980s one of the criteria for repositioning brands was to conduct research to find out the ways in which segments of the existing markets were using the brand to find a niche. Very few genuinely new products are researched in this way, because there is no way of knowing how popular they will be. So it is usually in established product categories that this occurs. That is why so many me-too products appear, aimed at slightly different segments of the market.

The marketing concept has been refined from the bold statements of authors such as Peter Drucker, 'True marketing . . . does not ask, "What do we want to sell?", it asks, "What does the consumer want to buy?"' (from Randall 1993: 2), to more recent marketing commentators to 'Marketing tries to match the firm's resources and capabilities to customers' changing needs and wants, at a profit' (ibid.). This more restricted definition still asserts that marketing begins with the consumers but recognises that the parameters are set by wider factors, such as cost, the nature of competition, the availability of technology and so on. But the ideology of profitably satisfying the needs and wants of consumers has never been realistic. A huge part of advertisers' marketing activity is aimed at trying to change consumers' behaviour and wants. As an article in an advertising industry magazine *Admap* pointed out, 'The role of the modern Marketing Communications department (or "Marcom") . . . is to affect behaviour, not just to increase awareness. The emphasis is not on things (ads, brochures, direct mail pieces) but on results' (McQueen 1992: 43).

Markets have refocused from a consumer-led to a competition-led approach. Marketers in most major product sectors have their eye more firmly on what their competitors are doing than on what the consumers are doing (Schudson 1993: 24). The marketing concept is used on two levels, first as ideology to defend marketing against consumerist attackers, and second to defend marketers against attackers in their own firm, the technologists and the accountants. An ideology helps to legitimise the interests of certain groups, in this case advertisers and marketers. Part of the ideology of marketing is to assert that business is not powerful, but under the control of consumers. Using market research techniques, marketing people are able to know their markets and know their consumers by claiming scientific status and backing it up with statistical evidence.

The marketing concept cannot work in practice; if it did there would be little or no innovation and no new products would be launched. Most new product marketers adhere to the shotgun principle of shoot first (promote), ask questions (research) later.

Targeting predisposed consumers

Though advertisers since the time of Wedgwood had classified and segmented consumers to target their advertising, it was not until the 1920s that systematic 'scientific' market research became established. This was largely as a response to the growth in advertiser competition and a perception by many advertisers that markets had become saturated. Advertisers needed to find 'scientific' reasons why their markets were not growing. They needed to find out both what was wrong with their existing market and whether any new ones could be found. Many manufacturers and companies in Britain and the USA such as Unilever and Guinness commissioned research to try and discover how consumers consumed their products and what they felt about them.

Because of the nature of the communications process, advertisers deal in masses, not individuals. The purpose of classifying and positioning consumers is to measure those things that consumers have in common, to target advertising and marketing campaigns at them and to measure and predict human behaviour. Many classification systems were developed for large national and international advertisers who needed to plan advertising across diverse cultures. They needed regulated and measurable markets to organise their campaigns. Advertisers needed to find an 'essence' – a single measurable reason for consumer motivation, what makes the consumer tick.

In the USA theories such as Maslow's hierarchy of needs offered clients the possibility of targeting the same needs of different people. This involved the belief that 'consumers anywhere in the world have the same basic needs and desires and can, therefore, be persuaded by universal advertising appeals' (Kanso 1991: 134). More recently, US ad agency Young & Rubicam developed a planning method called Four Cs (Cross-Cultural Consumers Characteristics) which assessed lifestyle and values statements across different markets and matched them across countries. Whether the basis is your age, sex, attitude or personality, all these systems suppose that there is a behavioural link between these common traits and your predisposition towards buying brands. This issue will be explored more fully in Chapter 13.

The main reason is money. If advertisers are to pay millions on mass-media advertising, they need to know whether their money is being properly spent. Advertisers believe that their money has been wasted if the advertising is received by people who are not in their brand's market. Most consumer classifications systems in Britain came out of media research. This is largely because of the need to match the brand's potential customers with media usage. Research provides a yardstick by which they can measure the value for money of their spend on advertising media. Because of this, some of the biggest power struggles in advertising are around the issues of who controls research, who classifies it, and the methods employed in developing it. Demographics were used in the inter-war years for research into media consumption. Advertising agencies J. Walter Thompson (JWT) and the London Press Exchange used demographic classifications in readership research during the 1930s.

But demographics began to be common currency and a central part of the advertising process only after the Second World War. The advertising and media markets expanded rapidly, helped by the welfare state; there was more disposable income and a perceived increase in the size of the available market. Media consumption also expanded; huge circulation newspapers (in 1939 the *Daily Mirror* had a circulation of 1.5 million; by 1948 it was 4 million), mass women's weeklies (by the mid-1960s *Woman* had reached a circulation of 3.2 million and *Woman's Own* 2.2 million) and commercial TV in 1955 meant that the media could offer to advertisers much wider audiences than could be previously delivered. There was a new need to match consumer markets to media markets. Because of this, the most common form of classification for advertisers was and still is demographics. The practice of classifying consumers arose out of the National Readership Survey (NRS), which established the use of demographic classifications in the 1950s.

Demographics

Demographics measures the population in terms of occupational class, age, sex and region. Advertisers build up a demographic profile of their target market to indicate consumer behaviour. These classifications arose out of media research and were a convenient way of discriminating different elements of the target audience. Social class is based upon the occupational status of the head of the household (generally the man) and falls into six categories (Table 3.1).

Demographics were used to read off certain values, such that DE men are more likely to be Labour voters, or that C1C2 women aged over 45 are more likely to be more interested in romance fiction. 'More likely' is the tentative link that the advertisers make when using classification, such as that

Table 3.1 Social class categories

A	Upper middle class	Higher managerial, administrative or professional
B	Middle class	Intermediate managerial, administrative or professional
C1	Lower middle class	Supervisory or clerical and junior managerial, administrative or professional
C2	Skilled working class	Skilled manual workers
D	Working class	Unskilled manual workers
E	Lowest subsistence levels	State pensioners or widows (no other earnings), casual workers

25-year-old single women are four times more likely to be readers of Cosmopolitan than 25-year-old married women with children (Bird 1990: 26).

The expansion in production and consumption in the 1950s gave marketers new working-class consumer markets to target their brands at. In particular, marketers identified and targeted the growing C2 consumer group in their advertising campaigns. They were identified by marketers as those who 'drink lager instead of beer, smoke tipped instead of plain, eat plain chocolate instead of milk' (Pearson and Turner 1965: 29).

One example from the 1970s was *Cosmopolitan* magazine, which used demographics to show that the average C2 woman would have a baby at 22, and the 'average' AB woman would have a baby at 28 (Bird 1990: 26). The problem with these measurements is their fixed nature. A 'B' university lecturer in cultural studies may have different interests from a 'B' accountant. The problem is compounded by the fact that not all cultural studies lecturers (or accountants for that matter) have similar interests or spending patterns.

But by the early 1960s consumer markets were also faced with static markets. Demographics is also unable to identify much difference, or only negligible difference between some brands and products (brands in the same product category of, say, soap powder, toothpastes and paper tissues will usually have similar demographic profiles). The demographic classifications were unable to suggest ways in which advertisers could expand markets or stop their markets declining. Advertisers began to look at new forms of research to find new ways of expanding markets.

By the 1980s changing work patterns and changes to the nuclear family has also resulted in reclassifications; the population of C2s declined from 38 per cent in the early 1960s to around 27 per cent of the adult population in the 1980s, and 22 per cent in 1999 reflecting Britain's decline in manufacturing. Demographers have reclassified people according to not only their occupational status but also their role in the family: divorcees, one-parent families, teenage mums, single-person households. They have added categories such as 'lifecycle' stages, like 'having a baby', 'buying a house', 'about to retire' (added to the NRS in 1991). As we grow up we are meant to progress through certain 'stages'; baby, toddler, infant, teenager, young and single, married no kids, married kids and mortgage, thirtysomethings, empty nesters, retirement pension. At these different stages advertisers believe that people are more susceptible to certain consumer habits.

Motivation

Since the turn of the twentieth century advertisers have tried to explain consumer behaviour with the help of psychological theory, seeking to unlock advertising effectiveness with the key to individual motivations and desires. Between 1943 and 1954 7,000 psychologists joined US advertising agencies.

In the post-war era two psychological approaches became popular; the first, based on Freudian psychoanalysis, sought the motivations of consumers as repressed within the subconscious and looked for hidden needs and desires; the second carried the view that people are motivated by certain biological, psychological and social needs. Both these models are still used today to determine the fundamental motivations of consumers.

In 1954 Maslow developed a hierarchy of human needs, stating that humans have a rational basis for needs starting with the basic: sleep, food, warmth, thirst, then later safety, security and fairness, trying to assert control over our environment. Other needs then arise, such as the need for belonging, love, status and esteem. These motivational and behavioural assumptions have formed a 'common sense' about what makes consumers tick.

The model supposed that the lower level needs such as warmth and food have to be satisfied before higher level ones such as status and esteem are achieved. These are basic determinants of consumer behaviour. Going to a football match, watching TV in a family setting or having a family meal, or even people's 'need' to be entertained or to feel that they are 'informed' and well educated, are part of psychological behavioural reasons for belonging, security and assurance. Advertising in this behavioural psychological framework starts by seeking to match and satisfy consumers' needs and desires. To unlock consumers' spending, advertisers needed to appeal to the higher levels of human need, especially love, status, esteem and belonging.

In the 1940s a team of US psychoanalysts headed by Ernest Dichter developed a less rational view of consumer motivations and desires. Motivational research suggested that the 'real' motives of consumers lay in the untapped subconscious. The motivational researchers held that we do not know the real reasons for our actions in buying things, so we invent reasons for doing it which fit in with our world-view (Colwell 1990: 15). All that an advertiser needed to do was to use a psychologist to tap into the subconscious. Consumers could be persuaded by images that hooked into their psyche, into their self-perceptions (anxieties, fears, frustrations), by relieving their anxieties through brand values and brand images. Consumers were depicted as more interested in the form of advertising than the content, the emotional sell rather than the logical, rational reason-why of advertising.

According to motivationalists, this kind of research revealed irrational buying habits of certain sets of consumers such as those who tend to pick up a wine bottle with scenes from rural France on it rather than a plain label. They sought the answer in individual psychology, rather than in cultural differences.

The personality of the consumer had to be matched by a personality for the brand. Consumers were meant to self-identify with brand personalities. The brand now had a complex 'brand image', and the advertisers were told that people would actually identify with this brand image. In 1960 Unilever launched a campaign for a detergent soap called Breeze. The brand featured a naked woman. This was one of the first campaigns in which an ad aimed at women included a sexually alluring woman. The intention had been 'that women of any class will identify themselves with a model provided she is beautiful enough' (Pearson and Turner 1965). Dichter and the motivationalists believed that consumers self-identify with advertising and brands: 'she is me'. Vance Packard's book *The Hidden Persuaders* (1957) took the motivational researchers at their word and fuelled a great deal of publicity for their technique and their power. Advertising agencies willingly embraced this powerful view of their own abilities. It is still held by many in advertising today: the idea that a person matches her or his own personality to that of the brand, or the person in an ad.

Psychographics

Though motivation research lost some credibility throughout the 1960s and 1970s, it underwent a revival in the 1980s, with the re-emergence of psychographics and lifestyle research. Clients were faced with declining markets, and demographics was widely criticised as an unwieldy and crude basis for predicting consumer behaviour. The first system to be developed in the early 1970s was Values Attitudes and Lifestyles (VALs). It was adapted to the UK market only in the 1980s when advertisers perceived accelerated changes in consumer markets. Lifestyle categories, based in psychographics (the study of personality types) put people into categories. These 'types' were branded by market researchers to make them more amenable to clients. If you prefer to stay at home, tend your garden and want security and children in the future, your personality type is a 'nest-builder'. This means that you are more susceptible to advertising of pension plans, house insurance, DIY, etc. Advertisers also used the new lifestyle analysis to segment their brands. This became particularly prevalent in the 1980s where brands were launched to target specific personality and lifestyle 'types'.

Though most major markets were saturated, in order to maintain profitability manufacturers needed to make consumption grow by segmenting the market (see previous chapters). They were less able to do this technologically, because the merging and concentration of industry meant that competitors were at similar stages of development; as a consequence, products were easily and quickly copied. Manufacturers were less able to differentiate products. Therefore, to try to gain an advantage and locate 'new' markets, they needed to identify 'difference' among consumers. They replaced product difference with consumer difference. As a consequence of many of the theories of consumer behaviour, advertisers in the 1980s started to launch products to try and match the attitudes, personalities and values of target consumers. Through the use of new technology they were able to produce goods targeted at 'lifestyle' segments which included elements of the target groups' 'self-image'. This form of product segmentation, based on the supposed identity of the consumer, is also informed by the Marketing Concept idea of satisfying consumer wants. However, it is the straightforward result of the need to protect market share and to find new markets for similar products.

One example was the government's anti-drugs campaign in the 1980s in which the images of drug users were glamorised by young people, opposite to the campaign's intention. 'Far from countering the reasons people have for trying drugs, it actually mimed and re-enforced them. . . . The agency had actually managed to brand heroin . . . succeeded in promoting the junkie's self image' (Davidson 1991: 157–158). The agency had used lifestyle advertising, which involves the use of the social context of advertising. Rather than focusing on the product, it focuses on consumers, their lifestyle, values and beliefs. Lifestyle advertising involves the reinterpretation of the consumer's self-image.

Lifestyle 'types' are categorised on the basis of a specific personality trait. People can be virtuous, admiration seekers, pleasure seekers, security and stability seekers, anti-authority rebels who want everything their way, joiners who want to be accepted and follow others, those who don't want any responsibility or commitment, those who haven't got a clue what they want and don't really care (Generation X), materialists who want fast money and lots of it, complainers, do-gooders, survivors, achievers, belongers, experimentalists, succeeders, working-class puritans, struggling poor, resigned poor. If you are someone who likes to leave their mark and likes new things all the time, new gadgets, computers, hi-fis and new food and drink, you are an 'innovator'. This means you are more susceptible to new products and new launches and to make a trial of a product. Advertisers do not particularly like 'innovators' because they are not supposed to be very 'brand-loyal'. However, they are supposed to be good surrogates if you want to target the 'followers': these are people who are supposed to be loyal and to copy the fashions of the innovators and fashion-setters. 'Followers' are the lifestyle advertiser's favourite consumers. 'Empty nesters' are also favourites of the advertising world. They are usually middle-aged couples whose children have grown up and left, are at a high point in their career, are coming to the end of their mortgages and have more disposable income as well as inheritance from deceased parents.

Lifestyle, as with all the other types of classifications, tried to fix consumers' personalities and identities, make them stable and measurable. Most of these 'types' identify traits in our personality and turn the traits into totalising definitions of our character. The greatest problem with these types, as with the demographic types, is that we can probably see all of these traits in ourselves at different times and in different contexts. Advertising people have condemned lifestyle analysis for its 'illiterate static caricatures'(York 1988: 35). Reading-off buying habits from an objective personality 'type' was no more useful than reading-off from an objective social class. However, at the same time, agencies have also used lifestyle analyses along with demographics to plan campaigns and act as bench-markers for targeting consumers.

However, as Randall points out, 'Since we know that consumers can describe brand personalities and describe differences between brands (frequently, of course, feeding back previous advertising campaigns), it is tempting to specu-late that people buy brands which somehow match their personality, or that in some way different brands appeal to differing personality types' (Randall 1993: 69). And as Judie Lannon pointed out, 'researchers often labour under a major misconception: that user personalities and brand personalities will be/should be the same and that the task of consumer research is to match the two' (Lannon 1992: 12). Many people buy a variety of brands. Single brand purchasing is very rare. The idea of matching assumes that the buyers of brands are brand-loyal and buy brands that match themselves. Brand loyalty is a myth of adver-tising that sought to ascribe power to advertising's ability to build brand values. 'Most people buy most brands at some time or other' (ibid.). Just as there is no such thing as a typical consumer, there is also no such thing as a typical brand, or a definite meaning to a brand. A chocolate bar eaten in bed has different kinds of meanings to a consumer from the same chocolate bar eaten at work, in front of the TV or at the cinema. Brands try to attach preferred meanings to the mode of consumption, such as sharing a pizza, or 'Have a Break', but there is no reason why consumers should only eat Kit Kats as convenience goods at work, or why pizza cannot be eaten on your own. These meanings are not fixed. Lannon calls these preferred meanings of the brand, the brand personality.

Sagacity

Some research companies offer a combination of the main categories of demo-graphics, lifestyle, media usage, income and expenditure and life-stage. This method of combining income, occupation and 'cultural' categories is known as 'sagacity'. Sagacity classification involves four 'types': Dependant (those adults not head of households – teenagers, students); Pre-family (adults who are head of households or housewives); Family (those with children); and Late (all others whose children have grown up and left home, or are over 35 and have no children) (Chisnall 1992: 260). Income and occupation and lifestyle are then considered. Banks and financial institutions may be some of the most interested parties when it comes to sagacity measures, because they perceive life-stage to be significant and important for making major financial decisions, such as weddings, first car, mortgage, pensions, life insurance and so on.

Geodemographics

Geodemographics is based upon the principle that people tend to live by people with a similar outlook and spending patterns as themselves, and that where they live significantly influences their lifestyle; where you choose to live reflects the 'type' of person you are. There are over twenty different geodemographic systems in operation in the UK. One of these, ACORN, includes fifty-four neighbourhood 'types' according to lifestyle, demographic and life-stage criteria. For example type C18, urban neighbourhoods populated predominantly by singles living in flats. It is highly likely that the people here live in rented accommodation and read broadsheets such as the *Guardian*, the *Independent* and the *Observer*. The lifestyle type is an avid wine drinker, has a high phone bill, is probably into telephone banking and has a passion for skiing holidays. They are unlikely to have kids, dogs, own a satellite dish and give to human rights charities such as Amnesty International. If a brand advertiser for an Internet bank wanted to target a direct mail campaign at this market, ACORN could give a breakdown of where those C18s live. The *Guardian* may identify them as its core/target market of possible brand users, and they may use ACORN to back up a current promotional or advertising campaign. Equally pet food manufacturers would not bother mailing to this neighbourhood.

Retailers and FMCG manufacturers use geodemographics for door-to-door distribution of coupons, samples and leaflets and can test products in very localised areas to see which groups respond better to trial. Money-off vouchers and samples usually get a good response rate. This type of direct advertising is often used in sales promotions to promote packaged goods such as tea and coffee and detergents. Geodemographics companies compile their research from census data, and electoral roll and postcode data, and use county court judgments to find out the debtors for finance and insurance companies.

Users and buyers

Because of the flaws in demographic and lifestyle analyses in predicting behaviour, advertisers tend to concentrate on the purchase and use of the brands by consumers. Advertisers make a distinction between buyers and users: those who buy may not always be the users. This is especially the case for children, but also for some adults who buy for partners and the household. According to the National Readership Survey in 1999, women are still the biggest food shoppers by a ratio of 2:1.

In the early 1970s in the UK 70 per cent of watches and 90 per cent of toys were bought as gifts (Schudson 1993: 142). Often the advertisers target the people who make the decision. In some cases it is the user, not the buyer, that advertisers aim at – a child would pester a parent to buy the latest toy. In other circumstances, where the child could not care less what was being bought, as with underwear, the target would be the parent. The advertiser needs to know who is making or influencing the buying decision.

This category of research is used mostly for established brands in mature and saturated markets (see Postscript). It tends to separate existing users of brands into light, medium and heavy. Advertiser research shows that a small percentage of the users of brands account for a huge proportion of the total consumption. In 1985 8 per cent of Guinness drinkers accounted for 35 per cent of all Guinness sold (Douglas 1984: 118). This may affect the advertising strategy, encouraging medium users to become heavy users and heavy users to become even heavier, for instance.

When a new product or brand extension is launched, knowledge of the market is limited. Marketers use a shotgun launch, whereby the campaign is scattered over the widest possible range of consumers. The market settles down and research is conducted to find which types of consumers have been 'hit'. Most new products are launched in this way, even some brand extensions. This technique is often used in direct mail. Research is used less as a prescriptive tool and more as a post-scriptive tool to analyse the market. One marketing executive from a major FMCG company said that pre-launch consumer research for new products is useless, new products are launched 'because you think there is a need for it. You research after the campaign to see how well it goes and who is buying it. None of the things we have developed are due to research. They were research-supported' (interview). But as a post-scriptive tool, there is little competitive advantage to be gained, so advertisers will constantly try to find a way to predict how the market will react; that is why some have turned to other methods such as econometrics. Advertisers do not want to be told that advertising is hit and miss, they want to be told that if A is done, B will happen. Or, at least the range of possibilities will narrow.

Methods

The first place that marketers often go when doing research is to established surveys. These include the government's Social Trends, the National Readership Survey (NRS) and the Target Group Index. TGI was launched in 1969 by advertising agency J. Walter Thompson's market research arm, British Market Research Bureau (BMRB). It is a year-long survey which matches brand purchase to media habits, and indicates light and heavy usage. It reports on the characteristics of groups within universes: how many C1C2s eat muesli (penetration) and how many muesli eaters are C1C2 (profile). It includes hundreds of lifestyle statements in the survey, from which TGI makes out a number of 'outlook' groups: trendies, social spenders, pleasure seekers, working-class puritans, moralists and indifferent. TGI also has stablemates such as Youth TGI, and ABTGI, which researches upmarket consumers. The surveys can indicate trends over time. For instance Youth TGI, which began in 1993, revealed that in seven years the number of 7- to 10-year-olds claiming to have a TV in their bedroom had grown from 30 per cent to 60 per cent. It also revealed that among 15- to 19-year olds mobile phone ownership has increased from 15 to 40 per cent, and that among all age 'groups' between 7 and 19 there has been a steady decline in concern about future employment prospects and a decline in concern about the environment and pollution in particular (*Marketing Week*, 'Signs of Premature Ageing', 2 December 1999).

Advertisers and representatives of the direct mailing organisations rely most heavily on databases and try to gain access and control over a variety of information sources. They gain lists from private companies (customer databases) and the national census survey (1991) to the Royal Mail post codes, county court judgments (for debtors) and the electoral register.

Quantitative research: demographics, users and lifestyles

Quantitative research is used to find out the composition and size of consumer markets in an easily recordable way. The method involves teams of researchers using questionnaires to gauge the opinions and buying habits of a cross-section of the population. The methods involved in gaining data like this are usually straightforward direct response questions. Which brands do you use? How often do you use them? When developing quantitative tests advertisers first identify the target consumers. The tests usually include two or more of the classification systems: demographics, lifestyles/psychographics or brand/product users. Once the 'universe' has been established, for instance all product users, the advertiser then needs to establish the profile of the universe. This includes the proportion of men to women, the class profile, the lifestyle and age/life-stage profile. This is often done by using the single source data of TGI, NRS, Social Trends, etc., to try to find the main discriminators in the market. An advertiser may find that the main discriminators in the product market are not class or sex but age. Or that none of the demographics show sharp differences, but lifestyle does; 'nest-builders', for instance, may be 'more likely' to buy the product than other groups. This would be useful to know for the creative treatment of the campaign.

A quota sample involves a researcher, going either to a place were the target population congregates, or door to door. It will be very difficult for a researcher to hit each of the quotas. Towards the end of the researchers' work they often have to find the most elusive groups, such as male 25-year-old ABs to fill the quota. The more statistically valued (and more expensive and time-consuming) method of sampling is the random sample, which means that there is a probability of all the members of the universe in question being surveyed. The sample size is determined by how many are interviewed in a given time period. The interviewer is given names and addresses of potential respondents. For the random sample names are usually taken from the electoral roll or the customer list.

Qualitative research

Qualitative research is concerned not with measurement but with interpretation: no statistical analysis is used, only views and opinions of the respondents and the observer. The report is usually a highly selective account of the discussion, which is edited to illustrate the main thesis of the research.

In the 1960s, qualitative research gained wide acceptance as a methodology. First it purported to give the advertiser an insight into why the consumer bought the product, not just how many of them did. Second, it was a much quicker process than the field surveys of quantitative research. Third, qualitative research appealed to advertisers because it was cheaper than the expensive quantitative field surveys. Marketing and advertising costs were already spiralling because of the increased costs incurred with the launch of commercial TV in 1955.

Qualitative tests take two general forms: the focus group discussion, and the one-on-one depth interview. Focus groups generally consist of a 90-minute session with a group of around eight interviewees. The agencies will usually run around eight groups and try to present a cross-section of the consumer base (they may well conduct half in the south and half in the north, depending on the brand). It involves a small group of people sitting with a researcher and responding to detailed questions about why and how they use the brand, their feelings, attitudes and values and the language consumers use to describe it. Advertisers try to locate the context in which the products are consumed, and how advertising adds meanings to products. Researchers may use a general questionnaire to help with discussion.

The respondents fill in the questionnaire and discuss it as they go along. Respondents can be videoed or observed through one-way mirrors, but most often they are tape-recorded. Videoing is often used if the respondents have to do something such as using the products or examining a range of them. The respondents would also tell the interviewer what the most important factors in buying a product are: price, value for money, image, status, colour, taste, texture, after-sales service, availability of parts, safety, performance, reliability, impressing the neighbours. However, there are problems to this method as well. Consumers may say that they buy a brand for specific reasons but they may not be telling, or probably cannot remember, the exact reason why they bought a specific item.

To try to get around this problem, another qualitative research method is the empathy approach. The researcher tries to take on the consumer's role to share the experiences and interpretations of respondents. This form of 'method acting' research is intended to get the client even closer through the medium of the researcher. However, it is questionable whether researchers can ever truly empathise or understand a group of people they are not members of.

These methods deal with the 'surface' answers of the respondent. However, in the 1950s, psychoanalysts claimed that the true motivations for consumers buying and using brands were hidden inside the consumer's subconscious. A psychoanalyst was needed to probe the anxieties and fears within the subconscious through one-to-one 'depth' interviews with chosen consumers to reveal the deeper emotions that underlay buying decisions. Using techniques from psychoanalysis, the unconscious part of the mind can be reached only by drawings and acting out ('Be a shampoo bottle!') (Tuck 1976: 46). Psychoanalytical research tries to find the other reasons why people eat, drink, play and fantasise. For instance, drinking lager for escape, for social pleasure, success, to appear desirable, to relax, to release tensions/inhibitions, to refresh (hardly ever to savour the taste). These individual psychotherapy techniques involve repeated interviewing of respondents to develop a rapport and get them to reveal more information (psychotherapy). Other methods involve psychodrawing (if this chocolate bar was a plant, what kind of plant would it be? if this car was a part of your body, which part would it be?) and photo-sorting (Colwell 1990: 19).

Other qualitative researchers use semiotics and look for the way signs and sign systems are decoded by consumers. They try to examine the way consumers negotiate with the meanings conveyed by the signs.

In all these approaches, the client company is very reliant on the interpretations of the researcher to mediate the signals from the consumers. It is in the interpretation of the results where the greatest controversy arises. This depends entirely on the researcher and whatever she or he is looking for. Qualitative research has been attacked for producing wildly different results from different focus groups and from depth interviews. One of the main criticisms of the use of psychoanalysis is that it attaches wild generalisations about human psychology to behaviour.

Mapping the consumer

Consumer research is a way of trying to communicate with an external reality. Like journalism, it tries to negotiate with what goes on in an outside 'real' world. The purpose of developing these methods is to try and construct a map of human behaviour. Though advertisers consult widely they are not examining actual experience, only consumers' highly stylised representations of what goes on in the consumption process. Similarly, with quantitative research advertisers are looking for tendencies in order to predict the behaviour patterns of consumers and be able to assert that sets of consumers are 'more likely' to do certain things rather than others.

Creating audience and consumers is a simple process. It involves taking somebody who has bought a product, say a car, then turning her into a car-owner. Or taking somebody who watches television and turning her into a viewer. It is apparent that we all occupy several hundred and probably thousands of these categories and identities that the advertising and media industry construct for us. When advertisers examine and use the maps of consumer behaviour in Social Trends, TGI, NRS and their own quantitative and qualitative research, they are either using tables of statistics to represent consumer behaviour, or sets of quotations and researcher interpretations. They are not dealing in people's real lived practices, only in representations of them.

Though advertising is about creating brand difference, whether there is one or not, when it comes to consumers, advertisers look for sameness to make communications cheaper and more effective. Advertisers need to identify and address 'typical' consumers in their advertising and marketing campaigns. The 'typical' consumer is the one 'most likely' to be predisposed towards the brand.

However, others in the advertising industry reject such totalising definitions of consumer behaviour. Advertising planner Kay Skorah claimed that advertisers should not be misled into thinking that research can predict that consumers will behave in a certain way and that they will be most likely or more likely to do so than other sets of consumers (in Cowley 1989: 9). Research is used to try to narrow the range of possibilities, rather than eliminate uncertainty altogether. But because marketers try to eliminate uncertainty from the market and try to manage and control consumer markets, they use demographics and lifestyle analysis to predict behaviour by asserting that consumers 'will' act in this way and 'will' respond to this market. It gives marketers a sense of security that they are able to read off behaviour from these classifications.

Summary

Market research arose in the 1920s as a response to clients' perception that markets were saturated and the way to gain an advantage was to unlock the mysteries of the consumer. Before then there was little need to research consumer markets which were still expanding. Marketing rose as a discipline to provide businesses with manageable and controllable consumer markets. The traditional marketing concept suggested that the way to do this was to go out and 'discover' consumers, classify and measure them, and produce products aimed at these consumers, giving consumers what they want. Consumers are constructed as sets of statistical data, tendencies and frequencies that are mapped in order to find out who the 'most likely' and 'predisposed' groups to buy and use the brand are. For this reason, they construct different classification systems which all need 'typical' consumers, people who will act in a predictable and manageable way.

4 Advertising and marketing

....

Advertising strategy

....

For years marketers have identified the components of the marketing mix as the four Ps: price (of the brand), product (including service, packaging, brand-name and design), place (distribution) and promotion (including advertising, public relations, personal selling, gifts, exhibitions, conferences and sales promotion). The terms and conditions of the market are set by the costs, nature of competition, product category, regulations, time and space. The firm tries to make elements of the marketing mix work together to support the brand.

Price

Price includes the costs of production and a margin for retailers, and is most often set in terms of the brand's relationship to other brands in the product category. Price can be used as a promotional tool. The price of a product can be discounted to increase sales, or it can be kept artificially high to suggest to consumers that the product is high-quality. Marketers use this perception to make pricing central to their promotional strategy. They have a policy of premium pricing. The best market for this is the perfume market. Consumers expect perfumes to be expensive, so manufacturers play up the exclusive and 'high-quality' aspects of the brand to justify the expense. Premium pricing goes on in most markets. Stella Artois's promotional strategy is heavily reliant upon its 'reassuringly expensive' pricing strategy. When Tesco tried to cut the price of Stella lager in their supermarkets in 1993 a dispute erupted: this move had undermined the whole premium pricing strategy of the brand. Pricing can also be used to deliberately confuse consumers. The technique, dubbed 'confusion pricing', has occurred in markets where there is a great deal of competition from low priced rivals such as financial services (especially credit cards), utilities (especially gas and electricity), and telephony (especially mobile phones). It involves placing the promotion of special and limited offers at the centre of a company's marketing strategy. It can also involve elaborate pricing structures and adding incentives such as Air Miles or membership rewards. The objective is to confuse consumers about price, making comparison with rivals extremely difficult. The consumer is confused and resorts to making a buying decision based on the emotional feeling towards the brand rather than the price ('Dazed and Confused', *Marketing Week*, 24 January 1997).

Product and service

The product includes the brand-name and design, the after-sales service, customer relations and packaging.) Packaging and pack design has become increasingly important in the FMCG sector. Branded goods have to impress even more to compete with own-label products. The packaging of goods such as coffee in jars, lager in bottles, washing-up liquid in squeezy bottles and toothpaste in dispensers is as significant as the substances they contain. Packaging indicates the type of product, and can be used to differentiate the brand. Boxed chocolates are set on plastic trays, liqueurs and spirits are in specially designed bottles. Tea bags are made round instead of square to differentiate them from the others. Sanitary towels have wings and are supposedly specially shaped to fit more snugly. These elements all influence the branding of the product.

One technique of advertisers is to get us to buy something that needs something else, for instance sauces. Whereas before we may have bought goods ready packaged, now it is in the manufacturer's interest to get us to buy the parts separately. Apple Macintosh and other computer companies do this with software, as do the games manufacturers: once you have bought the base (the hardware), you have to buy more in order to run the computer. You have to keep coming back for more. Toy marketers are adept at this: they sell separately collectable items such as the Batman characters or Pokemon cards. Kids need a complete set, but they wouldn't sell it that way. They also enlarge pack sizes to make consumers believe that they are getting more for the price increase. This, known as 'packaging to price', is done by many grocery and pharmaceutical producers.

Place

The distribution environment is also an extremely important promotional medium) In some markets where marketers believe impulsive buying decisions are made, the retail environment is significant: 'Beer is a cheap, ill-differentiated product. Accordingly, purchasing is largely impulsive as opposed to considered. Good packaging and the bar countermount are therefore important in prompting purchase. Advertising is also important in providing a point of difference' (Ring 1993: 17). (See Chapter 12.)

Advertisers also need to secure prominent positions on shop shelves. Availability and a constant presence on retail shelves helps to guarantee brands such as Coca-Cola and Pepsi continued success. When Rolling Rock launched its bottled cider campaign with Naked Gun star Leslie Nielsen, the company completely underestimated the demand for the product. Red Rock was sold out within three days. It was an advertising success, but a marketing flop.

Campaigns can be launched with the main aim of stimulating the salesforce. In September 1994 Pearl Assurance launched a £2m TV advertising campaign aimed at motivating their five thousand salespeople to feel good about their relationship with customers. It was also intended to challenge people's attitudes towards salespeople generally and defend Pearl Assurance's core business from banks and building societies by contrasting their personal home-service to the competitors' impersonal shop service.

Distribution is also decisive in the development of oligopoly and in some cases monopoly positions. The car industry in particular has assisted sales growth for main brands and concentration in the industry by control of dealer networks.

The Internet has hugely affected the whole notion of 'place' in marketing. As a buying environment it has become a crucial area of control in the battle between retailers and manufacturers in trying to secure prominent advertising and sales promotions on the net.

Promotion

From Wedgwood to the present day, advertisers have always used advertising as part of the complete marketing and distribution package of the firm. During the Boer War Bovril supplied grocers with display boards headed 'Bovril War Cables', on which Bovril messengers placed despatches. They also ran national sandcastle competitions for children.

With the growth of mass media, advertising became divided into two broad camps: above-the-line, which means all those media for which an agency gained commission (see Chapter 6), and below-the-line, all those areas for which an agency received a fee. Above-the-line media include TV, cinema, radio, news-papers and magazines, and posters. Below-the-line include direct mail, sponsorship, public relations, sales promotions or merchandising. The terms come from where the different media appeared on the agency balance sheet; as we have seen, the agency received a commission for above-the-line spending from the mass media, and were paid a separate fee by the client for below-the-line work. Below-the-line activity represents around 35–40 per cent of total advertising costs in most western countries. On the 1999 figures, around £5 billion would have been spent on sales promotion, sponsorship and PR.

Sponsorship also works with advertising and sales promotion activity. The value of the sponsored event or body is supposed to add value to the brand through association, for instance Nescafé and *Friends*, Cadbury and *Coronation Street* and Tizer and *CDUK*. All of these brands sponsor these programmes because they reach the target market and add to the brand values, for instance coffee drinking as a social activity, shared by friends, Cadbury's is a national brand with heritage and tradition and Tizer as a youth brand associating with pop music. Sponsorship of editorial in newspapers, magazines, TV and radio associates the brand with the authority of the editorial. Sponsorship is often used to help reposition a brand, for example Kit Kat and youth radio programmes, or Coca-Cola and football, or to get the company better known, as with the electrical goods company NEC sponsoring Everton or Candy sponsoring Liverpool football clubs. Mars sponsored the London Marathon, a fitting association of an energy product with a stamina event – health and fitness, winning and achieving – and ultimately the company was associating with a 'national' event. Companies also provide corporate sponsorship to charities and worthy causes to undermine consumer perceptions of selfish big business. McDonald's, for instance, sponsors educational projects. Sports are chosen to enhance brand awareness among those groups that advertisers are not allowed to advertise to; Embassy sponsored snooker, alcohol brewers such as Carlsberg and Newcastle Brown Ale sponsor football teams, and Rothman's produces football annuals, all of which have a high following among young people.

Public relations includes publicity such as in-store leaflets, press releases, engaging the company in political and moral affairs lobbying for legalisation on behalf of companies, promoting the financial affairs of the company, and promoting the company or organisation as a brand to investors and the public. PR also involves supplying 'experts' to journalists to comment on stories. Daytime TV and radio shows are given people paid by the companies to present, demonstrate and offer advice. Generating extra publicity makes campaigns last longer and gives them the authority of the 'trustworthy' editorial coverage. PR helps to fight the negative publicity in the editorial columns which enjoys more legitimacy. PR tries to influence opinion formers, such as journalists, where paid-for mass-media advertising is less appropriate, as in the leisure industries (film, theatre and TV) and magazines dealing with cars, fashion, hi-fi and music. Anita Roddick of the Body Shop used PR without advertising to target opinion formers about her policy of not testing products on animals and gained a great deal of free editorial publicity.

Sales promotions, including free samples, money-off coupons, competitions and give-aways, are some of the most popular sales promotion techniques. Money-off coupons are best for inducing trial and are often part of an advertising campaign. In the store they help to improve the product's shelf position and make it more noticeable. Free samples have become increasingly popular in trying to induce trial of a product. With every free sample there is an implication that what you are trying is different and better than what you already have. Sales promotion can also be used to communicate the brand values of the product. The campaign can be targeted at specific consumers by having certain incentives such as Harrods goods or Shaeffer pens, or offering badges, balloons and stickers for kids (as well as toys and bags in cereal packs), cosmetics for women, or aftershave for men.

Companies such as Kellogg's have continuous sales promotions for all of their Ready-to-Eat cereals because of the highly competitive nature of the market and to keep sales and market share up. These promotions often involve the consumer collecting tokens and being encouraged to repeat the purchase. In many large marketing companies, sales promotion is now bigger than above-the-line media spend. Sales promotion activity is believed to be much more effective at increasing sales in supermarkets than brand advertising.

Advertisers often integrate most or all of these elements into a promotional campaign. Many advertising campaigns which were supposed to have created huge sales were underscored by public relations activity and sales promotions ('25% extra free!', '50% off', 'Win two free tickets to . . .', etc.). Similarly, direct mail can be timed to work with a campaign. It could be timed to coincide with a new report that will gain news coverage (for example, a charity releasing a report on famine in Africa for publicity in the media could send out a direct mail shot the same day). Some of the most 'successful' advertising campaigns have been those which generated extra publicity from the media, such as the Nescafé Gold Blend couple, the Benetton ads, Wonderbra. These were all backed by public relations which tried to secure additional coverage for the campaign.

Advertising aims to provide coverage and frequency via the mass media and add brand values to the product. It can be used to try and boost the morale of the salesforce, or to assist the salespeople in their job by providing materials and sales support literature around the theme of the campaign. Advertising objectives often include creating awareness, changing attitudes, etc., whereas marketing objectives often include increasing sales and profits. Advertising's role in the marketing mix generally supports the other marketing activities such as distribution, sales promotions, money-off coupons, reduced prices, competitions, give-aways, etc.

Why use advertising?

Advertising is often used to try to increase sales of a product or the use of a service. However, this is not always the most important objective of a firm: it may conflict with long-term profit goals. In one famous case (though not confirmed by the company), Chanel launched an ad campaign to discourage sales to consumers from a lower social grouping. Chanel's long-term profitability relied on sustaining its upmarket image. It wanted to sacrifice short-term sales to safeguard the upmarket brand image (Myers 1986: 50–51). In the 1960s *The Times* also tried to reduce its circulation in order to attract more upmarket advertisers and keep its exclusive readership. More recently, Sony is understood to have restricted the availability of its Playstation 2 games console in December 2000 in order to make the product more desirable.

Long-term profits are a more useful indicator of a firm's objectives than increasing sales. Achieving direct sales effect is actually one of the least effective aspects of advertising. Industry estimates suggest that the immediate response can be as little as 0.01 per cent. Advertisers have generally given up on the claim that advertising has a direct and discernible effect on sales. As Evans points out, apart from direct response ads, 'advertising cannot in and of itself cause sales. It can only help or contribute towards sales success' (Evans 1988: 6).

A related second reason for advertising is to improve the firm's 'corporate image': to persuade people that the company is benevolent and trustworthy. Most image advertising is designed not to challenge bad images but to change people's perceptions of the company. Firms such as BP or Shell try to project an image that deflects from the main purpose of their activities – petrol extraction, refinement and petrol stations – by building the company as a brand. The company adds value to it, and it also adds value to their products. Advertising focuses on certain aspects of the company to shift the agenda away from those elements they do not want publicising. British Nuclear Fuels has tried to destabilise the popular perception of the industry as extremely dangerous and damaging to health by using images of the countryside, cleanliness and youth, as well as education. In some cases the advertiser may simply want a change, rather than improvement in attitudes. Volvo may like the association with safety, but may want to change attitudes towards viewing the car as more stylish. Corporate advertisers use image advertising either to change attitudes to the company which are believed to affect long-term buying decisions, or to reposition the company to different sets of consumers. British Nuclear Fuels ran campaigns on TV and in the press to undermine negative publicity from Greenpeace and the media about the safety of their Sellafield nuclear reprocessing plant. British Telecom ran corporate campaigns aimed at older consumers, as well as trying to undermine their image as a de-personalised virtual monopoly.

A third reason for advertising, particularly applicable to government information campaigns, is social advertising, which tries to changes people's behaviour: anti-smoking, anti-drugs and healthy eating campaigns are examples of this. Though all advertising is ultimately about using information to try to influence people's behaviour, the difference with government advertising (and some forms of advocacy advertising) is that the ultimate goal is not profit-maximisation.

Some of the most famous advertising campaigns appeared in the First World War – 'Daddy, what did you do in the war?', and 'Your country needs you' – and in the Second – 'Dig for victory', and 'Careless talk costs lives'. The government had also been involved in campaigns to buy British goods in the 1930s and 1960s. At the end of the Second World War the government set up the Central Office of Information which was to act as the consultative agency for state advertising. It was to appoint agencies to run campaigns for the state. At first this included vaccination, spending restrictions and work on farms. More recent government information campaigns have covered fitting smoke alarms, drink driving, safety in the home, job clubs and health awareness. One of the highest-profile government campaigns of the 1980s was AIDS awareness. Another large area of government advertising is recruitment advertising, especially for the armed forces, the police, nurses and teachers. The wider functions of these campaigns have been to try to change attitudes towards the services concerned as well as to recruit more staff. In 2001 the government ran a recruitment campaign for the police which featured celebrities such as Joan Bakewell, John Barnes and Simon Weston saying why they couldn't be a police officer. The campaign was intended to both recruit more police officers and lift the morale of existing police officers.

Advocacy advertising often involves identifying those consumers most likely to be won to the cause. Religious advertising needs to appeal to those who are in the market for religion: those who have had an upsetting time, or are at a time in life when they might take a spiritual turn. Time is also important in the sector of consumers who would potentially donate to charity but find the process too time-consuming. Because of this, charities often emphasise the convenience and immediate effect of the donation. Blood donation is a good example; it needs to be portrayed as convenient, hassle-free, quick and painless. Charities and religious and political organisations make use of PR because of the news value of much of their work. They use reports and research findings to stimulate publicity. Though political ads are not allowed on TV or radio, they have been constrained more by the costs involved; because of this, most political campaigns, outside election time, are conducted through public relations, or through pressure groups and trade unions.

When an entire market is perceived to be under threat, competitors in the same market can come together to launch a generic campaign. In the 1960s and 1970s the wool industry did this, as did the Milk Marketing Board. In the media industry the Newspaper Publishers Association spent £10 million to try to convince advertisers that TV was not essential and that press advertising was effective. Generic advertising often occurs when the sector is under threat or when advertisers perceive that more can be gained from attacking a related market than each other. This happened in the wool trade in the 1960s when the entire industry was threatened with artificial fibres. Other forms of co-operative advertising are where different brands do a tie-up to help each other. In the 1920s Gillette and Wrigley's did joint campaigns, offering free packets of gum with razors. In publishing, the *Guardian* and *Elle* have done promotional tie-ups. And Kellogg's and milk manufacturers have run joint promotion on milk bottles and cartons to support each other's brands.

Campaigns can also be launched to reassure consumers. Advertisers believe that advertising often provides consumers with false expectations of what the brand can do for them, causing cognitive dissonance (see Chapter 13). Some advertisers believe that consumers decide to buy goods for irrational reasons and then need to justify the decisions rationally. Advertising is meant to reassure these consumers that they have made the right decision. This can be done through the use of guarantees, after-sales service and warranties that the product is not faulty or unreliable. In May 1994 Unilever had to reassure consumers of its Persil Power brand that it did not cause clothes to be shredded and eventually had to scrap the brand (see Chapter 13).

In mature advertising markets, with well-established brands, the purpose of most advertising is to remind loyal consumers to buy goods such as ubiquitous fast-moving consumer brands – for example Mars bars, Coca-Cola, Kellogg's corn flakes, Pampers nappies, Kleenex tissues, Andrex toilet tissues, Heineken lager and Guinness stout. Commercials for all of these, which frequently show new versions of familiar themes, are generally aimed at reminding consumers about the brand's values and persuading them to keep buying the goods.

The most common reason for the use of mass media is to gain coverage to generate awareness. Advertising tries to stimulate and motivate people to find out more about a product or service. This is especially so with TV advertising which generally has only thirty seconds to get a message across; get people to send off or phone 0800, for example.

The advertising industry has for many years been extremely adept at generating media chatter about campaigns; creating awareness but also creating conversation pieces that get their advertising and brands talked about. This can be done through having popular songs associated with commercials ('I'd like to teach . . .', 'Heard it through the grapevine'), writing soap opera style commercials, or just plain shock tactics (Benetton ads or the NSPCC shock ads in the 1999/2000). There is nothing new in this. Rowntree's Elect Cocoa was launched in 1897 with a budget of £250,000 in a joint scheme with the *Daily Telegraph*: coupons from the paper were exchanged for a sample packet and a penny stamp (Piggott 1975: 28). S. H. Benson made a classic statement about the main intentions of the campaign: 'We had to devise a scheme which would stock the trade, and at the same time make the public talk' (ibid.). This predates the Benetton, Wonderbra and NSPCC ads by a hundred years. The agency produced follow-up schemes using London transport, generating publicity in national newspapers who called it the 'Cocoa War'. Awareness is also important for those who will come on to the market in the future. Companies promote washing powders to keep the brands at the top of the minds of young people who will try and use the brands when they leave home and become consumers themselves. The same goes for tobacco and alcohol manufacturers who target teenagers to get their brands known (through sports sponsorship in particular) for when they come on to the market.

Some campaigns may be launched to increase awareness of a related brand. For instance for over twenty years Benson & Hedges managed to flout the IBA code on advertising cigarettes on TV by using their brand-name in Hamlet cigar commercials. The cigar commercials (which were permitted on TV) finished with the phrase 'Hamlet, the Mild Cigar, from Benson & Hedges'. High-profile TV commercials, which astonishingly asserted that the cigars could take away your worries, were aimed less at cigar users and more at buyers of Benson & Hedges cigarettes (Bell in Henry 1986: 446–447).

In some markets there is a limited time-span for use of a product, and some consumers cease to be in the market fairly rapidly: teenagers for spot cream, new mothers for nappies, and those large number of consumers of 'older' brands who shuffle off the mortal coil each year. Advertisers therefore need to encourage new trial of goods. Very often this involves sales promotions such as competitions, money-off coupons and give-aways to encourage people to switch from rival brands (getting the consumer to try the product – see the *Daily Telegraph* example in the Postscript). Advertisers need to have a constant stream of new entrants and trialists of their brands to make up for the lost ones. However, encouraging trial of products does not secure long-term sales. Advertisers in mature markets increasingly concentrate on encouraging existing buyers to buy more of the product. An alternative way of trying to keep consumers when it is used only for a limited period is to convince them that they should continue using it. The makers of Head & Shoulders shampoo had to indicate to customers that the brand should be used even when the symptoms of dandruff went away; it even brought out a frequent-use shampoo.

All markets have newcomers, and have people leaving the market as well – dying, moving out of the age range (kids' clothes, etc.). Advertisers need to make sure that the stream of newcomers balances those who are leaving the market just to maintain market share, so they have to invite trial. Often established advertisers have to appeal on all fronts: they need to develop campaigns that will stimulate trial by non-users, and get the users of rival brands to switch, as well as encourage existing users to consume more and reminding them to buy as well as trying to change long-term consumer habits. Campaigns, then, do not have single goals: very often advertisers will use different elements of the advertising and marketing mix to try to address the different goals. Below-the-line methods may be used to stimulate new trial, TV advertising to promote repeat buying and change consumer habits, press and direct mail to try to encourage brand switching. A soap powder may need to have a reminder campaign on TV, a press campaign in young women's magazines to encourage trial, a brand switching campaign on TV or radio and trial offers in the supermarket for competitions or money-offs.

In-store trial and use is important especially with perfume counters in department stores where trying the product at the point of purchase can heavily influence buying. These types of sales techniques give the consumer the chance to say that they decided for themselves, and were not persuaded. Advertisers work on the belief that the most persuasive forms of advertising communications are where consumers believe that they have decided for themselves.

Examples

Barclaycard

Barclaycard launched the first credit card in Britain in 1966 (Access followed in 1973). Visa and Mastercard networks allowed the use of credit cards abroad, but by the late 1980s the credit card market was saturated and the recession brought a different attitude towards credit. Transactions began to decline.

In 1990 Barclaycard made a loss. The problem was compounded by the introduction of annual fees on the cards. Barclaycard needed to differentiate itself from other brands in the saturated market and arrest further decline because of the introduction of fees, so they offered additional services, including a reduction in interest rate, purchase protection (for anything bought by Barclaycard lost, damaged or stolen), a cash and delivery service if the card was lost while abroad, and opportunity to apply for free Mastercard for Barclaycard holders. Barclaycard anticipated that there would be some loss of custom from people who paid off balances each month and from non-users. Profits come from people who overspend. They wanted to lose fewer than 20 per cent of the cardholders after the fee introduction, and to restrict losses to less profitable cardholders, thereby increasing turnover and at the same time winning new cardholder customers.

When the fees were introduced, many consumers cut up their cards, but often left one. Barclaycard wanted to ensure that it was their card which was left, and which would be used. They notified all cardholders by post of changes to the product before the fee was introduced, and backed it up by an above-the-line ad campaign. (The problem was that people do not like credit cards . . . they encourage you to spend money then tell you off when you do so and charge high interest rates. Therefore Barclaycard used Rowan Atkinson: respectable, worldly wise and cynical . . . important because consumers were perceived to be cynical generally. Humour also helped to break down the hostilities towards banks and credit cards generally. He softened the image and helped the brand to be more acceptable . . . used the familiar genre of the spy commercial, the bumbling secret agent (Ind 1993: 155–163).)

Figure 4.1 Barclaycard: comedian Rowan Atkinson was the bumbling star of this spoof of the James Bond spy film genre. Though the ad contains comic situations, it also reinforces the main selling points of the Barclaycard brand, that it is accepted across the globe and has insurance protection. He was replaced in 2000 by Angus Deayton. © Barclaycard. Agency: BMP DDB Needham.

Packwood

In the eighteenth century George Packwood used newspaper ads to sell his shaving products. Very often these took the form of a poem, a conversation between two people discussing his product, or a song (McKendrick *et al.* 1983: 146–194). Packwood's skill was not only to develop the use of copywriting for advertisements but also to develop a brand image for his products, to develop a sustained advertising campaign around that brand and to extend his advertising campaign towards promotion of retail outlets. His brand image was a goldfinch's nest; his razor-paste boxes and the dollops of paste in them were supposed to resemble a bird's nest. He built the identity of his brand around the nest idea and used the brand-name of The Naked Truth at his retailers' shops (this was the name of the first shop he opened in London). Packwood didn't stop there. He even collated the advertisements of his campaign and published them as a book, and then advertised his advertisement book in newspaper columns (ads about ads). His campaigns were repetitious and he managed to keep up the momentum through new executions and persistent use of the newspaper medium. Packwood used authoritative figures to give testimonials endorsing the brand, associating it with nobility (the aspirational element) and claiming it to be the best in the world and made use of the razor-paste's packaging in the campaign. His advertisements were also aimed at different occupational and lifestyle segments of the men's shaving market: sportsmen, lawyers, lovers and merchants.

Budweiser

In September 2000 Anheuser-Busch launched a world-wide advertising campaign for its main beer brand, Budweiser. The ads, which originated in the US, were launched during the final episode of TV series *Big Brother* and featured a group of men ringing each other on the phone, sticking their tongue out and shouting 'Wassup?' down the phone. The campaign created its own momentum and developed a 'viral marketing campaign' on the web and via emails with new executions featuring elderly women, Hassidic Jewish men and Marvel comic heroes. Newspapers and TV programmes took up the phrase 'Wassup?' and SMS messages were sent via mobile phones along with video clips via the Internet.

The campaign was intended to target a young media-savvy audience. It was intended to make the brand more sociable and fun. Though the TV ad was central to the campaign, it was the central theme – people shouting 'Wassup?' at each other – working across other media which helped the ad take on its momentum. The central theme cut across national press radio, postcards, badges, stickers and, crucially, on to the web.

The campaign managed to plug into an everyday social interaction – making a telephone call – and invited people to live the commercial by repeating the phrase whenever they phoned friends.

Drinkers in bars were filmed creating their own versions of the ads and the stars of the original ads were brought over to the UK for radio and television appearances. One of the most interesting aspects of the campaign was the high

Figure 4.2 Budweiser: This multi-media campaign was the most talked about campaign of 2000. It featured several friends ringing each other, sticking their tongues out and yelling 'Wassup?' to each other down the phone. The ad used the rhetorical device of repetition and invited audience participation. The TV ads were backed by a viral marketing campaign on the Internet and generated acres of extra media publicity. © Anheuser-Busch: Agency DDB Needham.

proportion of young people not legally allowed to drink who used the 'Wassup?' slogan.

Summary

Advertising is one element of the marketing mix. It works in conjunction with others such as pricing policy, distribution, and changes to the product or service, such as packaging. All these elements work together to convey the brand's values. Advertising also encompasses a range of promotional activities, from paid-for mass-media promotion to public relations, sponsorship and sales promotion. There are many reasons why marketers use advertising, but three fundamental ones: first to improve long-term profits generally by increasing sales; second to improve the image of the firm or organisation; and third to try to affect behaviour. Many companies have different objectives at the same time. For instance, they may need to target retailers to stock the product; need to motivate the salesforce; to target separate segments of the consumer market; to change the brand image; and to encourage brand switching from a rival product. The objectives can and do change over time because of market conditions.

5 Advertising agencies

M ost brand advertisers use advertising agencies to buy advertising space and time in the media and create advertisements. Unlike marketing departments, which tend to be scattered over the country, the advertising agency business is highly concentrated in London, with regional centres in Manchester, Edinburgh and Bristol. This is largely because the UK national media are based in London and a vast network of ancillary services is available within a short distance of the West End.

Agencies are in a very short-term market. Unlike lawyers and accountants, advertising agencies do not keep clients for very long periods of time. According to Media International, fewer than 25 per cent of major client accounts stay with agencies for ten years or more (Briggs 1993: 22). This is partly due to the nature of the business. If the client is unhappy with the work done by the agency it is quite easy for the client to try again or resign the account. Sometimes this can be simply because the company has a new marketing director who wants a change of strategy for the agency. Most agencies are employed on short-term contracts and have very tight margins because of high salaries and location overheads. A typical agency would spend around 60 per cent of its gross income on payroll and staff bonuses (*The Economist* 1990b: 17). Because of this, there is a strong need to attract new business. The new business director in an agency is often one of the most important members of staff. These directors trawl the trade press and seek to woo and win clients from other agencies.

When companies want to advertise, many go to the Advertising Agency Register (AAR) which holds the video 'reels' of the major agencies. The AAR is involved in about a third of all new-business reviews in the UK. It makes a charge to agencies to lodge a ten-minute reel about themselves, and charges clients to view them. This guarantees confidentiality and impartiality. The marketing department of the agency views the agency reels, which contain past commercials and statements from personalities in the agency. The marketing department draws up a 'pitch list' of agencies who are invited to make a presentation detailing what the agency would do with the client's brand(s) in terms of creative work, targeting consumers, media planning and buying etc. A re-pitch occurs when an agency already has the account and the client wants the agency to make a fresh presentation against other agencies.

When a pitch is proposed, the client eliminates many agencies automatically, because of client conflict, inadequate facilities for their brand (such as no European network, limited media buying) or lack of experience in their sector. They would whittle down the pitch list to around six, visit them and then ask three or four agencies to make a formal presentation in which they would indicate what the agency would do with the client's brand(s). Some advertisers will pay a fee to the pitching agencies for the time, effort and expense of the pitch. Most pitches will last between an hour and an hour and a half. Agencies usually use slides, videos and overhead projectors; some use computer graphics. The account handler or planner will usually start with their overview of the market and advertising needs of the client, then the creative and media director will deliver presentations on what kinds of things they might offer. The pitch usually finishes with the proposed storyboard (usually left till last). Some agencies refuse to show any of their creative ideas to clients but show them their research and buying strategies instead and reels of the best commercials. Advertising agencies are often disgruntled when clients use the pitch process as a way to get fresh advertising ideas.

Up to 1970 most business was decided on an informal agreement, rather than drawing up contracts, often over lunch at one of the media village restaurants in London's West End. However, the business relationship became much more formal in the 1980s.

Like the brands that they sell, advertising agencies actually differ very little from each other. Though they may offer some extra services, they essentially offer the same menu to clients. An agency that comes up with something orig-inal is quickly copied by others in the business. But the larger agencies are able to differentiate from the rest not only in buying but in research as well. They have been able to commission proprietorial research to augment the inad-equacies of the industry standard research. Carat and J. Walter Thompson have been key players in this (see Chapter 6).

The only real differences they have are in the people in the agency. Because agencies generally start up as small private companies, they are geared not towards making high profits but towards paying their directors and staff high wages. One way an agency makes additional money is through late payment. The longer an agency hangs on to the money it is going to spend in the media concerned, the more interest it can make. Some very large agencies were notori-ous for getting the client's money up front, booking the space and then hanging on to the money until the very last moment to cream off the interest. The agents bill the client very early and pay the media very late (*The Economist* 1990b: 5).

Copyright is often owned by the agency either because the work is created by an employee – in which case the copyright is automatically owned by the employer – or by a freelance, in which case the agency will usually insist on copyright being signed over to it. When an advertiser moves agency it usually makes an agreement to sign over copyright. The copyright laws cover work by performing artists. Though an agency can use the musical score for Beethoven's Pastoral Symphony because the music itself is out of copyright, a recording of a performance by the Halle Orchestra is covered by copyright and subject to permission and usually a large fee. The same goes for all forms of commercial recording, and most written forms. For years Paul McCartney would not allow Beatles tracks to be used in advertising. Michael Jackson bought the copyright and sold 'Revolution' to Nike Air (Evans 1988: 83–84). The copyright laws governing the reproduction of commercials and print ads apply to work for up to 70 years after it is produced. If agencies reproduce the artwork within 70 years, permission has to be sought from the author, or royalties paid. Slogans and catchphrases are generally not protected as they are too insubstantial, but artwork and more substantial written work is protected.

Agencies are not only in competition with each other, they are also in competition with other elements of the marketing mix: sales promotion, direct marketing, PR, sponsorship, Internet activity and market research. Because of this they have developed a two-track approach to this extra competition. The first is to try to undermine the client's belief that other forms of promotion are as effective. The way they do this is constantly to berate sales promotions, giveaways and competitions as 'eroding brand values' in the trade press, and to produce regular publications of Advertising Works case studies to try and show the clients how effective advertising can be. The other strategy is one of appropriating the below-the-line activities by buying in sales promotions, contract publishing, sponsorship and direct marketing companies and launching new media divisions which offer web-site development. Because agencies command large sums of client's money, and are outside the client's firm, they are often singled out for criticism and are often the first to be cut in time of recession. Agencies respond by heavily promoting their power and capacity to influence. One particularly strong advocate of the advertising cause at the turn of the century was ad agent S. H. Benson, who launched a journal for advertisers, wrote two books on best practice, and organised an international advertising exhibition in London in 1899 (Piggott 1975: 23). This was done to persuade manufacturers to use advertising as a persuasive tool to stimulate consumer demand. They often sold themselves as magicians, able to save struggling brands through the power of creative and persuasive advertising. At various times, agencies have employed the mythic status of 'art' (serendipity) and 'science' (rationality) in their arguments for mass-media advertising. Peter Mead of AMV said: 'Our aim is to destroy the view that advertising is a commodity. It is the creation of an elusive spark of originality which can fundamentally enhance a client's business' (Ring 1993: 171). They have created numerous creative awards to elevate their work to the status of art. Other agencies have supported a 'scientific' view of advertising based upon rational behavioural theories to make advertising more professional and manageable to the sceptical business world (see Hopkins (1966) *Scientific Advertising*). They triumphed the power of the expensive mass media to deliver coverage, and its ability to control and shape consumer demand.

One vehicle for this is the weekly advertising industry magazine *Campaign*, a fast-talking news magazine which carries gossip, account wins and losses, appointments and sackings. *Campaign* not only made agencies appear more glamorous (photographs including moody nasal shots and fire escapes became legendary in the 1980s) but also helped to construct and negotiate many of the myths around the business; features on the 'philosophy' of different advertising agencies, the literary tradition in advertising (1990), the weekly review of creative work usually attacked by other 'creatives' in which the common sense of 'good' and 'bad' advertising is negotiated.

Agency people also use the trade press journalists to establish their authority as experts and reassure clients that the people who handle their account and buy their media have respect in the industry.

The structure: how most agencies work

Because full-service agencies were involved in so many aspects of the advertising process they needed control departments to make sure that the different departments were meeting deadlines and that the commercials and art work would be ready on time. This department is now often called traffic or progress. It supervises invoices, and supervises the different stages of the production and media processes, makes sure that copy is ready on time, that pre-tests are complete and reports received by different departments.

The account handler in the agency prepares briefing documents and liaises with the client on behalf of the agency. This job has been replaced in some agencies by the account planner who usually has a research (or psychology) background, and is intended to be the client's contact with the consumer. Larger agencies also have account directors who look after key clients. It is their role to take charge of the strategic direction of the brand and suggest new ways of exploiting advertising opportunities.

Creative departments consist of the copywriter and the art director who usually work as a team. When creatives move agencies they usually move together. In bigger agencies the creative team may have assistants, more copywriters or graphic designers. Art directors are the people who are supposed to come up with the visual ideas for a campaign. The role of the art director is to come up with the ideas and set them down on paper for artists and photographers to produce. In the 1950s and 1960s most of the production was done by the agency who had their own photographers, illustrators, film and recording studios. But these have gradually been farmed out of the agency because of costs of maintenance. The agency may also have a TV producer who would arrange the commercials to be produced via an independent commercials production company, or negotiate with film directors for the commercials. Some agencies also commission pack design (from design agencies), sales promotion and merchandising material which may tie in with the advertising campaign (especially if it is a money-off campaign); in the past this used to be handled in-house.

In the past the client's direct contact with the agency was the account executive. This person would liaise with various members of the agency and the client to keep them informed about progress with the campaign.

Agencies had given up on expensive quantitative research in the 1960s (largely because clients refused to pay for it), and, faced with exclusion from the vital area of research (which judged effectiveness of campaigns), introduced the account planner. In the 1970s this person replaced the account executive in a number of agencies. The account planner usually came from a research background (usually psychology). The result was that agencies brought the control of research back within the agency (clients had farmed research out to market research companies) and were able to 'reassure' clients that the advertising side of the business was working. (Crompton 1987: 2).

Planners use industry standard research such as TGI, NRS, BARB and geo-demographics, and conduct qualitative study groups. The vast bulk of research, however, concerns testing creative treatments and conducting tests of finished commercials and print ads for clients. Agencies generally do not like it when clients enlist outside market research firms to conduct this research.

In the 1960s all media buying was controlled by the media departments of full-service agencies. However, by 2000, around 90 per cent of all media expenditure was handled by a separate agency (or dependent of an agency). The reasons for this development and the characteristics of it are explored in the next chapter.

Media dependants and independents are generally structured in two ways. Some departments have TV buyers who work on separate accounts in the agency all working together. TV buying is in a volume market, where deals between media owner and agencies are done on the basis of the volumes of money being spent, rather than on the basis of individual purchases. Agencies achieve greater discounts if they can pool their different clients' accounts into a single volume of business. Such deals affect the rest of the market, which becomes volume-led, rather than set by individual negotiations between a single advertiser and media owner. In TV buying, therefore, knowing what others are doing is more important in doing deals than co-ordinating individual brand campaigns with press buyers. This strategy involves trying to get the best discounts by combining the buying power of all the brands in the agency. If the agency organises its dealers on the basis of volume, by having a pool of TV buyers and a pool of press buyers all working on separate selling points, it is easier to sell on the basis of volume. The benefit is lower rates. The problem with this approach is that the possibility of placing ads strategically is diminished because the individual client is part of a pool of clients. The separation of departments is still most common, because TV buying is based on volume. Other agencies develop account teams. That is groups of TV buyers, press buyers and media planners who work on just one brand or a small number of brands. A big agency may have several of these account groups. The benefit of this system is that the client has an integrated media buying strategy because the different buying sectors are working together on the same brands. The drawback of this system is that it may lessen buying clout with the media owners. If different TV buyers from the same agency are negotiating with Granada, for instance, there is less likelihood of volume deals.

Another department which is very important to the agency's day-to-day business is the information department or library. This is where research documentation is kept, and full-time library researchers are paid to inform the account planning, creative and media research teams of developments in their area. They can be involved in supplying quantitative data on certain sectors, finding answers to puzzles and questions from creatives, and providing data on overseas markets. Finally there are the ancillary workers such as secretaries, receptionists, postroom workers and messengers who run between the different agencies and creative organisations.

Jobs

For many years there has been no formal career structure in the advertising industry. Account managers and handlers generally came from public school and universities, media buyers were generally recruited from schools, creatives came out of art schools and copywriters invariably studied English literature at university.

Advertising qualifications are organised by the Communications, Advertising and Marketing Foundation (known as the CAM Foundation). This was established in 1969 by the Advertising Association, the IPA and the Institute of Public Relations. In the early 1980s the IPA withdrew from CAM. CAM courses are available in colleges, but many large agencies employ graduates with diverse degrees and run training schemes leading to CAM qualifications. The IPA runs its own courses focusing specifically on advertising.

Advertising is still a largely haphazard profession to enter, though formal training schemes are run by large agencies. Most employment is on an ad hoc basis. Agencies do not generally employ people with advertising degrees; they prefer to train students themselves.

Part of the struggle for professional recognition was to establish formal teaching and develop a recognised training certificate. After the Second World War the Advertising Association set up a diploma for advertisers. The IPA also set up a formal certificate, called MIPA, which directors needed to pass to become members of the IPA. In 1970 a joint examining body was set up for PR, marketing and advertising. This included the AA, IPA and IPR, who combined their exams into the CAM Diploma. The Institute of Marketers declined to be involved and continued with their own Diploma. These moves introduced social regulation and control to the industry, but did little to formalise career structures. Agencies negotiate personal contracts with individual members of staff, which allows highly desirable 'names' to command extremely high salaries.

One of the other reasons for the growth of media independents in the 1970s was the disaffection of media directors in agencies who were on much lower salaries than the creatives and account handlers and had lower esteem.

There were very few media directors on the boards of agencies. In the past the directors of agencies would come from the creative or the account-handling side. In the 1980s many more media planners had joined the boards of agencies, reflecting their increased status and the greater emphasis placed on their role by clients who saw them as vital to spending decisions. The launch of *Media Week* magazine in 1985 reflected the increased importance of media buyers, and of media in general, to agencies.

In the 1960s and 1970s creatives were the most valuable commodities in agencies. They cultivated a creative mystique and through various award schemes managed to elevate their work to the status of art. They convinced clients that their work was valuable and were able to command large salaries: some in the bigger agencies achieve salaries in excess of £200,000. However, clients' concerns that attractive advertising did not mean effective advertising, increased reliance on research, increased media availability and concerns about costs have served to undermine the creative's hegemony; the common-sense notion that high production qualities equal effective advertising.

Similarly, account handlers have been undermined. Many clients saw them as ill-qualified and ineffectual; merely there to butter-up the client. In many agencies, their role was replaced or conjoined with an account planner or researcher (often trained psychologists) to give the client hard facts and data to back up the agency's assertions.

Because of the nature of the business the members of an agency board include the key members of staff. In the past the board used to consist of account handlers, but now many include planners, creatives and media directors. The membership of the board and the names of the agencies generally reflect the most important selling points of the agency. The star creative, or well-known (often quoted) media director, will often be on the board and sometimes appear in the agency name. Board membership is generally seen as a reward to staff and an incentive for them not to leave and join other agencies. Each member of the board will be responsible for a specific account (e.g. Kellogg's) or department in the agency. Though the board decides on formal policy, there is usually an executive which handles day-to-day running of the agency.

According to a report by the IPA in 2000 called , 'Women in Advertising, 10 years on', there are now significantly more female board directors in advertising agencies, and there has been a marked increase in the proportion of women in account handling, creative services and TV production, certain departments are still very much male preserves. The creative department, for instance, is still very much a closed shop, with women accounting for only 17 per cent of copywriters and 14 per cent of art directors. There were only two women with the title of creative director in any top twenty agency). There are also notoriously few women at senior levels of media buying and planning. Account-handling, information and research and planning still remain the most likely career path for women in agencies.

The 1970s included the advertising industry's first and last major confrontation with trade unionism. In October 1975 the print craft trade union, Slade, attempted to recruit new members. In some provincial ad agencies they had been successful at recruiting agency creative staff. In 1976 the union aimed for recognition in the main London-based agencies. They had formed a special branch, the Slade Art Union, and two years of bitter conflict between the agency executives and the union ensued. Slade, joined by the National Graphical Association (the main newspaper print union), put a boycott on print work from 'unrecognised' agencies. Major regional agencies such as Brunning and Harrison Cowley were boycotted by the unions.

London agencies such as Collett Dickenson Pearce, who prevented Slade from recruiting the creative department, were also threatened. The controversies died down after a rift emerged in the union.

The advertising industry also fell into dispute with the actors' union Equity in the early 1980s over the level and extent of repeat fees on Channel 4. The station was off the air for several months during the dispute which saw neither side win. Equity members have to be paid repeat fees when the commercial is broadcast more than once. The fees are paid as a compensation for subsequent loss of earnings. Those who appear in distinctive ads are so associated with the brand that they cannot work in other commercials. Celebrities are usually paid a total sum and the commercial can be shown an unlimited number of times. Celebrities can command large salaries. In 2000 TV chef Jamie Oliver was reported to have received £1 million for appearing in a series of commercials for Sainsbury's.

Process

At the planning stage, the ad agency librarian or head of information identifies source data for research (industry-wide data) in looking for wider areas of research, government surveys, company surveys, trade associations and bodies. This is much cheaper than committing resources to field surveys, and can in many cases form the backbone to qualitative research. By using publicly available research (and proprietorial research, TGI, NRS, and private research, Mintel, Euromonitor) the researcher can gain knowledge of the size of the market, its total competition and a breakdown of consumers per brand. For this, they can develop a universe for qualitative research.

A proposal for a campaign will often be approved by the marketing director. For some companies the marketing director will have to present the campaign proposal to the board of the company. At this meeting it is usual for an agency representative to be present to sell the ideas to the board. In some cases, where the client is a small company, the marketing director will also be the chief executive. In others, where the company is large, the marketing director will not be expected to provide a formal presentation to the full board. When the briefing comes back from the client the agency sets out a plan document which indicates in full how the product should be promoted.

The process will include the agreement of the media and communications strategy first because of the costs involved. If a client's budget is below £3 million a national TV strategy may not be an option. It also depends on which consumers they want to try and hit. If for instance they wanted to reach company executives, advertising on TV might not be the best option. They may make a decision to use posters, or radio. At this stage the main decision concerns the most appropriate media to use. The media planners and buyers then go to negotiate deals with TV companies, radio stations and newspaper and magazine sales operations. The meeting will also decide the campaign's weight, duration and relationship to other promotions that the client is involved in, as well as its relationship to competitor activity. This will form the basis of a media schedule. The account planner will provide a creative brief to the creative team detailing the client's requirements, the target market, the media to be used and competitor's activity.

The creative staff – which include copywriters, visualisers, artists and graphic designers – need to know which medium they will use for the campaign to design and produce storyboards and layouts. They will also use the information department for any details needed for a campaign, such as how many calories there are in an apple. The storyboards and ideas are proposed and pre-tested by the planners on selected groups of consumers for approval and then given the go-ahead for production. When creative strategies are agreed, the creative team commission production of the commercials and ads (actors, illustrators, film production company, etc.). Meanwhile the space and time would have been booked. When the advertisements are finished some will be pre-tested again using focus groups; tests are usually conducted by the agency. Then the commercials and ads are aired and printed. Other departments in the agency check that the invoices and fees are paid and that production is on time. Any further research into the effects of the campaign are usually conducted by the client, if at all.

Summary

Advertising agencies tend to offer similar services to their clients. The main differences lie in the people in the agency. Because of this, agencies try to sell the brilliance of their people, championing them as 'gurus' and 'experts'. Agencies maintain 'common sense' through awards, *Advertising Works* series and in constant references to 'good' and 'bad' advertising in the trade press, reinforcing the myths of advertising power. Salary and status for an advertising agency employee are usually dependent on how far up the 'guru' or 'expert' ladder she or he is. Agencies tend to bid up salaries to keep 'names'. Salaries are generally the biggest cost in advertising agencies.

6 Client relationships

....

The modern advertising agency structure grew with the mass media. Some
of the original advertising agents began as news agencies, selling stories
to the newspapers. In the early nineteenth century advertising agents sold
space for regional newspapers to national advertisers. In return for selling the
space, the agent would get a percentage of the sale in commission.

Advertising grew enormously in the late nineteenth century with new advertisers requiring space in newly emerging national newspapers and magazines.
Advertising agents began to switch allegiance. Before, they sold space for a
large number of newspapers to a small number of clients; now, a large number
of clients required advertising in a more concentrated media market. Instead of
representing the newspapers, the agents switched to representing the clients,
though the agency was still paid commission by the media owner. The media
owner was happy with this. Instead of the newspaper proprietor having to follow
up every advertiser for payment, the agency would guarantee this payment and
receive a commission from the newspaper for placing the ad.

It was not cost-efficient for clients who did not run advertising campaigns
all year to do their own advertising. By having a portfolio of large clients,
agents could use the combined strength of their advertising spend to gain cheaper
deals from media owners. The media owner was happy with the deal. The cost
of going directly to all the clients was prohibitively high, and the commission
system would mean that agents would still keep the price of media space up.
The agent occupied a privileged position.

In the late nineteenth century it was not unusual to find rival chocolate or
soap manufacturers using the same advertising agent to book space and create
ads. However, as advertising competition intensified, client conflict within large
agencies grew. Clients began to move their business to other agencies if their
agents took on a rival client. Agencies often have to resign clients because of
conflicting accounts. Clients have been very sensitive about having near and
direct competitors in the same agency. In the 1990s Lowe Howard Spink's
supermarket client Tesco, for instance, would not allow rival retailers, or rivals

to its own label products such as Heinz, to be clients of the agency. In many cases, client conflict has caused new agencies to emerge. Because of this, medium- and large-sized agencies need to have a range of clients in different sectors of business – retail, soft drinks, confectionery, cars, pharmaceuticals, tobacco and government, etc. – rather than specialising in one area.

Advertisers began to produce creative work for advertisers in the late nineteenth century as a way of promoting advertising. Many agencies at this time also offered sales promotion and merchandising which were paid from fees. By the 1920s an advertising agency became more clearly defined as an intermediary which managed, created and bought advertising campaigns on behalf of clients. Agencies were now 'full-service', offering sales support, creative work, research and product development in addition to the basic job of media broking. J. Walter Thompson, for instance, advised the *Daily Mirror* and Rowntree (Black Magic) on product development and positioning. Some agencies also had their own kitchens to test and try out new products for clients. Though some of this still occurs, clients have generally taken this function in-house, or farm it out to small specialist consultancies, such as market research and brand planning consultancies. The clients brought marketing in-house to wrest control back from agencies and to contain costs.

The recognition system closed shop

At the turn of the century media brokers who did not create ad copy – because clients did their own – undercut the other full-service agencies by taking as little as 1 per cent commission and passing the rest to clients. Other groups, calling themselves 'advertising consultants', were paid on a fee basis to provide information and advice and to produce copy for clients and agencies (Nevett 1982: 153). The consultants even formed a society which collapsed in the 1920s. After the First World War advertising activity intensified when US companies began launching brands on to UK markets.

It was in this context that the full-service agencies began to push for regulation and professional status. In 1917 the Association of British Advertising Agents formed and in 1927 changed its name to the Institute of Incorporated Practitioners in Advertising, later Institute of Practitioners in Advertising (IPA). It set up compulsory standards of practice and later suggested to the Newspaper Proprietors Association (the national newspaper trade association) that a recognition system should be introduced.

The recognition system was introduced in 1932 and was to dominate advertising for most of the twentieth century. It effectively squeezed out any other forms of advertising business relationship – such as media brokerage or consultancy – in favour of the full-service advertising agency.

It included a no-rebating clause, which meant that the commission could not be rebated to the client and must stay in the agency; this effectively prevented agencies who would offer only media buying. The commission system would be the standard payment method; all other forms of relationship between client and media owner were to be excluded. It was essentially a cartel agreement between full-service agencies and media owners to stop small shops and media independents from undercutting.

Agencies also had to abide by the IPA's code of practice, reinforcing the role of IPA as regulator and a closed shop with a monopoly on industry knowledge. Agencies would lose out if they were not members of this new club.

Up to the inter-war period, agencies had received as little as 2.5 per cent and 5 per cent commission. However, in the 1930s and 1940s it rose to 10 per cent. This was due to the introduction of the recognition system, the extension of agency services into research and new product development (especially the US agencies) and the newspaper marketing war.

In 1955 the TV companies introduced 15 per cent commission levels to help cover the supposed extra costs of TV commercial production for agencies. However, agencies paid not only for commercial production out of this extra income but also for market research and merchandising. In addition they charged clients extra fees for research and production. Because agencies could get higher commission from TV, newspapers also increased their commission payment to 15 per cent.

It was in the agencies, and media owners' interest to keep the negotiation of rates between media owner and agency secret. The client might not be privy to the discounting and extra deals that were done, and other clients and agencies in the same market would not know who was providing the lower discounts on volume deals. This monopoly of information further helped to privilege the agents' role. This lack of transparency in the business relationship has led to distrust and the feeling among many advertisers that agents had something to hide.

There is an implicit bias towards expensive media in the commission system, which acted as an incentive for the agencies to place ads in expensive media and not to push for discounted rates. The only check that large advertisers would have was to have several agencies buying for its different brands and compare each agency's buying performance. This system was awkward and lost advertisers revenue in terms of volume deals, but it was the only objective test they could make.

The recognition system began to break down in the 1970s when US advertisers who had produced commercials at home wanted to use UK media buyers to buy space and time. The 'media independents' as they were called took the full 15 per cent commission and 'illegally' rebated 10–12 per cent to the client for 'creative' costs. This massively undercut the full-service agencies. Many of the first media independents operated under 'flags of convenience' for established but small full-service agencies who would get a cut of the commission. This was because the media 'independents' were not recognised in their own right and they had to use the recognition of a full-service agency in order to trade.

One of the first 'independents', The Media Department (TMD), used full-service ad agency KMP. The recession of 1973 also helped the media independents to grow when advertisers were forced to cut back their media spend and use old art work through the media independents who were cheaper and could rebate some of the commission to the client (claiming that it went to creative work). Separate media buying also allowed advertisers to dip in and out of different agencies, allowing them to pick and choose services. By 1980 there were thirty media independents.

The Restrictive Practices Act 1976 and the Office of Fair Trading ruling in November 1978 that fixed commission was anti-competitive and monopolistic killed the recognition system. In 1979 the NPA and the regional newspaper trade body, the Newspaper Society, dropped traditional agency recognition.

Under the new system rebating commission to clients was allowed (though media independents had been doing this anyway and claimed that it went to pay for creative work), and all categories (including media independents, etc.) were allowed to be granted commission, as long as they could prove credit-worthiness. The current relationship still includes the role of the agency as first principal, responsible for outstanding debts for the client.

Agencies had to provide audited accounts to receive recommendation from the media owner trade bodies to their members that they should receive credit terms. The new recognition agreement missed any mention of the payment of commission, or preventing rebating, or limiting it to a certain type of agency. Commission has to be negotiated between the agency and the newspaper rather than between the agency and the Newspaper Publishers' Association or Newspaper Society. Before, it was the publishers' organisation which granted recognition and set the commission, not the individual paper.

Agencies were forced to negotiate their own commission from the media and get remuneration from their clients. This opened up the possibility of fees – payment by results – and, for the first time since the inter-war years, it also meant that agencies could compete for client business on price, though the IPA strongly discouraged the practice. On a solely fee-based system the commission is rebated in full to the client and an agreed fee is negotiated on a flat rate, or on the amount of time spent on the account, or on payment by results; that is, relating the advertising objectives to the outcomes of the campaign. In 1965 media commissions accounted for 76 per cent of agency income (Cowan and Jones 1968: 17). By 2000 a report carried out by ISBA and the Advertising Research Consortium found that the majority of the top 116 blue-chip companies (such as Procter & Gamble) were paying agencies on a fee basis or payment by results. None of them now paid the ad agency the 15 per cent commission. The report found that on average the agencies were being paid the equivalent of 11.2 per cent commission in fees. The reduction was largely due to client demands for reductions because of the soaring cost of media.

Ironically, the credit recognition system of the 1990s (guaranteeing that advertisers and agents don't default on payments) has been a source of tension between media owners and agencies. Agency failures – Yellowhammer, Charles Barker City, and Hall's Advertising – provided the incentive for NPA and the

Periodical Publishers' Association to tighten credit recognition even further in 1992. The IPA was forced to agree to this.

According to a report by Coopers & Lybrand and Media Register, between 1986 and 1991 media independents' share of business grew by over 184 per cent. The media independents won a great deal of media-only business from full-service agencies. Large advertisers were beginning to pick-and-mix their advertising services.

Full-service agencies responded by hiving-off their media departments into completely separate agencies. In the late 1980s the Saatchi & Saatchi group which then owned two advertising agencies – Saatchi & Saatchi Advertising and Bates Dorland – hived-off their media into a single, centralised media buying agency called Zenith. Zenith combined the buying power of the separate agencies under one roof, though not all clients who used the separate agencies, such as Bates, for creative work would just use Zenith for media buying. They could now pick and choose different media buying and creative agencies. The others followed: Initiative Media (Lintas), CDP Media, The Media Centre (DMB&B), Mediacom (Grey), Optimedia (Publicis and FCB). All these new set-ups aimed to take business from the media independents and from each other's account.

By the early 1990s it became established practice to have one agency to create advertising, a separate media planning and buying agency and another set of agencies (some subsidiaries of entirely different full-service agencies, other independent) to run direct marketing and sales promotion campaigns.

In the late 1990s several other mergers took place and new media dependents were created such as WPP's Mindshare which was launched in 1997, combining the media buying power of its main agency networks, J. Walter Thompson and Ogilvy & Mather.

By 1999, seven of the top ten media buyers were media dependants, the rest were media independents.

Most advertisers now choose not to spend all their money through a single full-service agency; they tend to pick and choose different agencies for different elements of their marketing mix. By 2000, there were no significant full-service agencies operating in London.

Volume buying, broking and surcommission

Buying and selling advertising space and time in the UK is mainly influenced by availability. The number and range of TV channels, radio stations, poster sites, magazines and newspapers directly affects the relationship between advertiser, agency and media owner. Where supply is restricted, media owner and advertiser use the weight of buying and selling power to negotiate price. Media owners have concentrated their selling operations and advertisers have concentrated their business in large single buying points to gain an advantageous place in the media market (see next section).

When an agency knows that in a year they are going to commit a certain amount of business to the media, they then make a forward promise to the TV contractor that the combined spend of all of its clients in that contractor will reach a certain volume of time. The contractor pays the agency a brokerage fee for putting such a large amount of advertising spend its way; this secret practice is referred to as broking.

The other main media market where this occured is in outdoor media where, in the 1990s, an additional intermediary operation – the poster specialist agency – controlled 95 per cent of roadside, and the majority of transport bookings. They agreed to spend a target amount with the contractor over the year. The specialist or agency would then receive a special discount. Large outdoor contractors were known to give poster specialists extra discounts of 3–5 per cent for guaranteed volume of business over the year in the early 1990s.

Broking is also widespread in the newspaper and magazine market. At the turn of the century a number of large agencies negotiated deals with large media owners whereby they would block-book space in magazines and newspapers at a special discount and fill the spaces with their numerous clients, this practice was called 'farming' (Nevett 1982: 103–104).

Newspapers benefited from the arrangement because they only had to deal with one agency and could keep their costs down; if the publication was struggling for advertising it could also appear that it was doing well. The agency would also promise not to run ads in rival publications, in exchange for the extra commission which it kept. Though the client would get cheaper advertising space, it could not specify where its ads would be placed in the publication, and was often committed to publications which were not read by its target market.

The agency, which was supposed to represent the client's interests, ended up more as the sellers of ad space for the media owner. This relationship benefited the big agency more than anyone else; small agents had to deal through big agents if they wanted to get space in the title. Lord Northcliffe's women's magazine, *Answers*, was known to have been involved in such deals, as were two leading London advertising agencies, Smith's and TB Browne (Hindley and Hindley 1972: 64). Advertisers campaigned at the turn of the century to stop the practice.

There are similar reservations about the benefits of broking today. Though a large media buying outfit may pass on the extra commission to its larger advertisers who are more aware of media practices, the deals also include many smaller clients whose combined volume can often effectively subsidise the bigger clients (Makin and Dovey 1991: 16).

Sometimes the extra commission is simply kept by the agency, with or without the client's knowledge. This can be a valuable source of extra income for larger agencies. Concern about such hidden income for larger agencies led many clients in the early 1990s to call for transparency in media deals (see pp. 73–74, Regulating Industry Practice). Because of these and other factors, though broking is not illegal in the UK, few admit to it. Broking and volume dealing also restrict the advertiser's choice. If its money is committed to a single station for a given period of time, it is less easy to develop targeted tactical campaigns.

Broking and volume dealing do affect the chances of smaller media owners who try to compete by offering higher discounts or combining forces with other media to offer packages, squeezing profits further. Smaller agencies too try to resist by combining forces in media buying clubs, or shifting to specialist areas of advertising.

However, one alternative practice which has been commonplace in France for many years, but is less easy to quantify in the UK, is surcommission. This involves additional payments made as a reward to agencies by media owners for placing volumes of advertising (Jacobs 1991: 287–288). These sweeteners are made to guarantee that agencies will continue to place ads with the media owner. It is often used in media markets where the media owner finds it difficult to get regular advertising and is most appealing to smaller agencies, whose revenue has been squeezed by client cutbacks.

Centralised media buying

Because of the commission system, multi-brand advertisers were not able to pay for separate creative and media services; they tended to have a roster of agencies handling the full service for separate brands. This also enabled the advertiser to monitor and compare the performance of different agencies for its different brands. It helped the agency business because accounts could be spread across a larger number of agencies. It also benefited the media owners, because advertisers and agencies were unable to volume-buy space.

To gain greater buying power, an advertiser would continue to use a number of agencies for their creative work, but the media buying for its entire portfolio of brands would be channelled through just one agency (e.g. Carat for Cadbury). They would be able to get more media coverage for their money. If they did a deal for the whole year, a confectionery manufacturer could use summer slots for chocolate ice cream, winter slots for chocolate bars and chocolate drinks, and Easter and Christmas spots at discounted rates for special brands. Nearly eighty of the top hundred advertisers in Britain, including Cadbury, Heinz, RHM Foods and Premier Brands, had centralised their media buying in this way by 1993.

Centralised buying was introduced because of four factors. The first was the deregulation of the market with the end of the recognition system (rise of separate media buying). Secondly, the centralisation and concentration of advertisers in the 1980s, via mergers and acquisitions, made even bigger portfolios of brands (e.g. Nestlé including Rowntree's brands, Unilever including Brooke Bond, Birds Eye Wall's, Van den Berghs, Elida Gibbs, etc.); it was cheaper and more effective to pool all the brands' media buying resources into one account rather than use many separate ones. Thirdly, there was a concentration of media selling points into an effective duopoly in television, which reduced from fifteen sales houses in the early 1980s to just two sales houses by 2000. Finally a consequence of media inflation in the mid-1980s and the fragmentation of the media was that media buying became more difficult and expensive.

The centralisation of media buying resulted in an even greater concentration of the agency business among a few, very big buying points. The drive was to make British media buying a volume-led buying market, with a few key players commanding large volumes of business and able to force beneficial rates for clients. This new power of big agencies and advertisers to volume-buy opened the field to broking in the UK market. Media buying is a costly business, requiring computer hardware, research tools, accounting systems and the sales-people. One of the reasons why Saatchi's and other agencies went for centralised media buying was to achieve economies of scale and the rewards that volume can bring in media broking. Like other small- and medium-sized agencies, CDP hooked up with media independent CIA because of the threat of losing Rank Hovis McDougall and Boots in 1993. GGT desperately tried to find a media independent to link with (and linked with GGK for European network) to hang on to KP, Courage and Cadbury, all of which it lost.

By 1999 the concentration of media buying points meant that the top ten agencies controlled £3.8 billion of advertising billings, one quarter of all adver-tising in the UK.

The clout that advertisers could get through centralising their media through one big agency (or 'buying point') can be demonstrated by the fact that in 1992 the top five advertisers (Unilever £167 million, Procter & Gamble £127 million, Kellogg's £61 million, Mars £59 million, Nestlé £54 million, totalling £468 million) accounted for 22 per cent of the total advertising revenue of TV (excluding satellite and S4C). But the five main buying points account for over 40 per cent of this total TV market. In TV buying the top ten buying points have almost 60 per cent share (Perris 1993: 20).

The clout of the big five advertisers has been doubled by the volume concen-tration of the big five (Zenith, Initiative, BMP, Media Centre and TMD Carat). For Carlton the big five advertisers provided 32.5 per cent of revenue, and for Time Exchange (which became Granada Media Sales) 22.6 per cent. The big five advertisers therefore have much more power in London than elsewhere to influence negotiations. On Carlton TV alone Unilever alone controlled 9 per cent of revenue.

In 1991 Unilever managed to force commercial TV company TVS to accept its own buying terms because it controlled such a volume of business in the market. Some advertisers such as Kellogg's were known to be demanding discounts from ITV companies of up to 75 per cent in 1992 for children's TV, largely because of the erosion of the audience for children's TV from satellite, videos and computer games, but also because of the recession and the com-pany's buying clout. The big clients tend to make deals around a year in advance with the sales houses, guaranteeing volume.

International agencies

Though Quaker Oats launched into the British market in 1894 via the London Derrick Agency, other advertisers, such as American Tobacco, started a trend at the turn of the century of bringing their own US agencies with them. Their agencies brought new advertising techniques such as public relations, direct marketing, market and media research. Lord & Thomas, who launched Wrigley's and Palmolive in the UK, inspected every poster position in London just after the First World War, with a breakdown of class structure, whether the site was a shopping, residential or industrial area and whether the posters were on a major transport route. The agency also had sixty-nine residential district poster inspectors across the country and three in London (Bradshaw 1927: 250). US agency JWT began campaigning for Libbys in 1923, and in 1927, the same year that McCann-Erickson came to launch Esso, it set up a formal branch to launch GM cars and later launched Kraft foods on the UK market. These new agencies soon attracted British advertisers such as Unilever and Rowntree.

British agencies reacted to the growth of US agencies by trying to offer much of the same. They expanded market research, PR and below-the-line activities, often employing Americans to run them, and offered them free of charge. One agency, the London Press Exchange, set up a market research division (later to break away and form Research Services Limited who conduct the NRS) and opened nineteen overseas offices.

The next wave of US agencies came after the Second World War. The US agency's main strategy was mainly to buy up existing British agencies; in 1959 Ted Bates bought Hobsons; in 1960 BBDO bought 60 per cent of DDWS; in 1962 Grey Advertising bought Charles Hobson and Partners. By 1964 eight of the top eighteen agencies in the UK were controlled from the USA. And later, Chicago-based Leo Burnett bought London Press Exchange in 1969, O&M bought S. H. Benson in 1972. In that year US agencies held 86 per cent of the declared billings of the top twenty British agencies. In the biggest move of all, Interpublic bought the largest UK agency, Unilever's Lintas, in 1976.

This wave of acquisitions and mergers in the 1950s and 1960s had led to a shake-up in advertising agency business, and a large amount of restructuring. But between 1969 and 1979 there were only seventeen mergers of agencies (Reed 1992: 33) but dozens of start-ups. The market became saturated (on the back of the commission system). The mergers of large agencies brought conflict. A newly merged agency might now have two large confectionery accounts, so one would move. In the 1970s many clients moved into newly established agencies: often account people and creatives from one of the merged agencies took a major client with them. This is one of the main reasons for the large number of start-ups in agencies. Though the larger agencies offered volume buying for clients, this was not such an important consideration for clients in the 1960s and 1970s, when there was less media around and less of a volume market. The larger agencies also demanded higher fees for their services. Operating on

15 per cent commission, the only way advertisers or clients could show disaffection with the burgeoning extra costs the big agencies were slapping on was to move their business to new start-ups.

However, by the 1990s this had changed. Clients wanted and needed volume and were prepared to go with networks that could secure most cost-effective solutions. The big-spending clients in the late 1980s switched from using medium- and small-sized agencies into larger groups. In the 1980s and into the 1990s there were forty-two mergers in ten years.

In the last decade of the twentieth century several key advertising agencies were bought by the big networks including Simons Palmer and Gold Greenlees Trott which were bought by Omnicom's agency, TBWA and Young & Rubicam bought Rainey Kelly Campbell Roalfe. There were also consolidations of bigger agency groups with WPP buying Y&R and Publicis buying Saatchi & Saatchi in 2000.

The deregulation of London's financial markets in 1985 meant that advertising agencies could raise money by floating on the stock exchange. The problem for a lot of these publicly quoted companies was that they made themselves vulnerable and increased the need to expand. Because agency businesses could not grow organically – due to client conflict – many agencies were forced to expand abroad, either by being swallowed by a larger group, or by acquiring overseas agencies.

In the late 1980s and early 1990s, advertisers began to prepare for the opening of European markets after the Single European Act came into force in 1992. The agencies clamoured to develop European networks to service pan-European campaigns. By 1999 all the top thirty British agencies had access to a European network. The smaller and medium-sized agencies also needed to expand from their narrow national base to link up with European networks. The main reason is to make sure that, at least with a network tie-up, they will not be excluded from appearing on a pitch list.

It is cheaper and more efficient for an international advertiser such as Ford to do a pan-European deal with Hachette (publishers of *Elle* magazine among many others) through a single buying point, rather than to negotiate on a country-by-country basis.

Unfortunately for many agencies, once the hype around Single Europe had diminished and it was clear that pan-European advertising would not be as extensive as everyone first believed, many agencies found themselves with European networks and no clients to service. Most of the large international accounts had already been cornered by agency conglomerates and media buying. These deals have been done solely to maintain control of the media buying market and to offer clients global economies of scale and volume buying.

World-wide agencies also developed triple networks. The double or triple network uses the same principle as a multiple brand advertiser: if you have more brands you control more of the market, especially in terms of research and media buying. Because of client conflict, the agency networks have been forced to develop separate largely independent operations. This happened with

Interpublic, which is the holding company of McCann-Erickson, Lintas, the Lowe Group and True North, British-owned WPP, which owns O&M, JWT and Young & Rubicam, and Omnicom which owns BBDO Worldwide, DDB Worldwide and TBWA.

The aim of using triple networks is to prevent brand clashes. Interpublic's Lintas bought Kevin Morley Marketing in May 1995 because it had a £100 million Rover Car account. Interpublic's other network – Lowe Group – had competitor GM Vauxhall across Europe. If one of an agency's networks had another large soap manufacturer, it is unlikely that Procter & Gamble would use your network, so the networks developed parallel agencies. At first they grew in tandem, then they also started to develop third networks. Interpublic expanded, with the Lowe Group forming a third network. In 2001 Interpublic bought another network, True North, which owns agency FCB. Omnicom, which owns world-wide agency networks DDB Needham and BBDO, bought Boase Massimi Pollit in the UK to form BMP DDB Needham, and later bought a 50 per cent stake in UK-based agency network Abbott Mead Vickers. WPP bought Young & Rubicam in 2000 to develop a strong third agency network, but also to shore up the global advertising account for its major car client Ford which had been giving business to Y&R for the launch of some of its new car marques.

The major agency networks, Omnicom, WPP and Interpublic, offer advertisers the chance to realise true economies of scale is to use one of the three big agency networks.

Advertisers need not only agency networks that can deliver volume deals with media owners but also ones that can specialise in their area. The highly regulated and specialist area of pharmaceuticals is one problem for the big networks. Saatchi's and WPP have both developed healthcare divisions to accommodate this. In the future there may well be the emergence of super-agencies that will have conflicting clients in the same group. In the first phase of internationalisation, agencies grew simply to service big-spending clients. In the second phase (Mattelhart 1991: 1–30) they centralised and concentrated. The third phase will probably be one of fragmentation – it is already beginning with the development of healthcare divisions.

Over thirteen years the share of multinational agencies has risen from 14 per cent to 30 per cent of worldwide billings (Kanso 1991: 134) (Table 6.1). Those that were independent in 1981 were by 1995 either largely or partly owned by a bigger group or have merged part of their services with other agencies.

The new international markets, with their new international media networks, are comparable to the domestic markets of the nineteenth century: a limited number of agencies who have access to all aspects of a new and burgeoning (international) mass media system. As in the late nineteenth century, client conflict is no longer such a problem for advertisers who need agencies with buying clout and the resources to stretch over continents.

The recession of the early 1990s and the separation of media buying have made medium-sized and smaller agencies especially vulnerable, and many sought the safety of mergers with other agencies to try to protect their share

Table 6.1 Top ten advertising agencies in the UK (1981), ranked by declared UK
           billings (£m)

Rank	Agency	Declared billings	Base	Group
1	Saatchi & Saatchi	101.20	UK	
2	J. Walter Thompson	96.10	USA	
3	DMB&B	88.00	USA	
4	McCann-Erickson	76.54	USA	Interpublic
5	Ogilvy & Mather	71.40	USA	
6	CDP	60.69	UK	
7	FCB	56.00	USA	
8	Young & Rubicam	52.36	USA	
9	ABM	50.23	UK	
10	Dorland Advertising	46.00	UK	

Table 6.2 Top ten advertising agencies in the UK (2000, year-end September),
           ranked by UK billings (£m)

Rank	Agency	MMS billings	Group
1	Abbott Mead Vickers BBDO	399	Omnicom
2	BMP DDB	321	Omnicom
3	J. Walter Thompson	285	WPP
4	McCann-Erickson UK	271	Interpublic
5	Publicis	256	Publicis
6	M&C Saatchi	244	–
7	Saatchi & Saatchi	235	Publicis
8	Lowe Lintas	233	Interpublic
9	Ogilvy & Mather	219	WPP
10	Young & Rubicam	214	WPP

Source: AC Nielsen

of the market. BMP was bought by DDB Needham; AMV by Omnicom (equal
partners). TBWA merged with Holmes Knight Ritchie, only to be bought by
Omnicom as its third network. TBWA later merged with Gold Greenlees Trott
and Simons Palmer.

Interpublic's Lintas bought Still Price Twivy Court D'Souza to become Still
Price Lintas in the UK. Lintas later bought KMM to form Lintas i. Interpublic
then merged Lintas with Lowe Howard Spink. Horner Collis & Kirvan combined

with Colman RSCG to form Euro RSCG. Miller Leeves & WAHT was taken over by Bainsfair Sharkey Trott.

There has been a polarisation in the agency world. The only smaller agencies that have managed to keep hold of global accounts, or big-spending ones, are those that have offered creative services as 'boutique' agencies, such as BBH who created highly successful advertising campaigns for clients such as Levi's. BBH's ads for Levi's were distributed by McCann-Erickson. But many clients have taken their media buying elsewhere, to keep volume. The agency either tries to be bought up by a conglomerate (as with BMP) and benefit from their media buying resources, or it becomes a creative boutique/production company, remaining an advertising agency in name only, hiving off its media buying into an independent, or with a media buying tie-up. In 1997 US advertising giant Leo Burnett bought a 49 per cent stake in BBH. At the time BBH said that Leo Burnett would provide the smaller London agency with a 'global media delivery system'.

Regulating industry practice

Advertising agencies are covered by the same legislation concerning employment and conditions of work as other businesses. However, there are some unique rules covering the industry. Agencies are legally the first principals in business transactions. They are not only agents. They control the client's finances and are liable for payment. This legal role places them in a unique position in the business relationship. Because of this, agencies give details of their financial status to publishers as part of the financial recognition system.

In France a bill to make dealings between advertisers and agencies and the media transparent went through in 1992. The original bill called for remuneration to go directly to the client and the return of all media discounts to clients. It also placed a ban on 'bonuses' to agencies for volume deals. The Sapin Bill proposed that agencies should act as agents and not as first principals, that their income should come from clients, not from media owners. It proposed a ban on broking, that media owners should publish rate cards and discounts on offer as well as sales terms, and that the name of the client, not the agency, should be written on invoices with all the terms included.

The Sapin Law came into effect in 1993. The advertising industry won a number of concessions: amendments allowed media buyers to secure multi-client volume deals (but they had to pass the discounts on to the clients, rather than keep them themselves). The proposal to scrap the commission system was also dropped. The amendments allowed media owners to pay agencies 'special commission', which would appear on the invoice sent to clients and on rate cards (the principle of transparency).

Even though these concessions were made, French media buyers, who had to pass on all discounts to clients, saw drops in profitability of between 30 per cent and 50 per cent. Media owners tried to get the government to include below-the-line work in the law to try to stop media buyers moving their advertising this way in order to recoup lost profits. The British clients' trade body, ISBA, approved of the Sapin Law in France, because it forced media owners to give payments directly to clients, rather than from the agencies, to avoid the conflict of interest.

With the large concentration in British media buying on agencies such as Zenith creating a volume-led market similar to France, clients made a drive to tidy up buying practices. Advertisers increased their use of auditors as the hidden practices of agency media buyers came to light. It became clear that many British media buyers do not declare all discounts to clients and keep a percentage for their agency. British advertisers have called for transparency in response.

Examples: five agencies

The following agencies are by no means 'typical'. They are a cross-section of differently sized and shaped agencies. What follows shows the types of clients they work for and their structures.

J. Walter Thompson (JWT)

JWT first came to London in 1899 as a sales house to encourage British advertisers to advertise their exported goods in US newspapers. In 1923 it acted as advertising agency for US client Libby, McNeill & Libby (food canners) and in 1927 set up a formal advertising agency to sell General Motors cars when the latter set up factories in the UK (Mattelhart 1991: 3).

In the 1930s it repositioned Horlicks as a bedtime drink aimed at preventing 'night-starvation', and advised Rowntree to brand their lines and produce Black Magic dark chocolate assortment. In 1986 JWT's profit margins were far lower than the industry average and it was bought by WPP in 1987. WPP also bought the Ogilvy group in 1989. In 1992 JWT's size of billings was £190 million (Register-MEAL 1992). In the 1920s JWT in London had a staff of eighteen; by 1961 it employed 918 people, but by 1992 the staff had fallen back to 425, including seventy-seven account handling, seventy-five media (eight full-time media researchers), 104 creative, twenty account planning, thirty-eight finance, ten JWT Direct and five JWT Healthcare.

welcome to jwt.co.uk

Despite JWT's size and reputation, only a quarter of its clients have been with the agency over thirty years. Among the companies on its client list are Barclays Bank, Esso, Brooke Bond Foods (part of Unilever), Lever Brothers (part of Unilever), Findus (part of Nestlé), Lyons Maid (also part of Nestlé), Nestlé Rowntree, Gallaher, ICI, Jaguar, Kellogg's, Kodak, Kraft (merged with Suchard 1992), Warner Lambert Healthcare, Scott Limited.

Because many clients began to use media independents and separate media buying from creative work, JWT lost a large amount of clients' media buying to other agencies. Though JWT's clients continued to use it for creative work, they bought media through other sources. In 1990 it restructured its media buying and won back two key clients, Rowntree and Kellogg's, who centralised their media buying through JWT, rather than through an independent. JWT managed to win back £170 million worth of business in the early 1990s by separating its media planning and buying functions. The problem is that if an agency cannot guarantee the volume to gain large discounts from media owners, large clients will often move their media buying elsewhere.

In 1997 the WPP Group merged the media planning and buying operations of JWT and sister agency Ogilvy & Mather to create Mindshare. The combined operation included the media buying clout of clients such as Ford, Glaxo Wellcome, IBMUK, Kellogg, Kimberly-Clark, Kodak, Mattel, Nestlé, Shell, Telewest, Telegraph Group, Woolwich plc, Britvic Soft Drinks and Eagle Star.

Though JWT was one of the first agencies to introduce research into agencies in the 1930s, it was also one of the first agencies of the 1960s to hive off research and develop the account planning system. JWT started up Lexington PR and the British Market Research Bureau (authors of TGI). It uses account planners and no longer has a separate research department, but the company uses research to give it an advantage. Using a computer-based media planning system (IMPART) shows how TV day-part changes can increase coverage of any given target group. SESAME shows how changing the weight of advertising, week by week, will affect sales. JWT has long been one of the most diversified agency groups, offering PR, design, market research, promotion and video communications. Nearly half its revenue came from these areas in the 1980s. JWT has also moved into TV sponsorship.

JWT's head of sponsorship said in 1992, 'Had we not opened the door to sponsorship, someone else could potentially have taken as much as 10% of our business away' (Byles and Walford 1991: 43). Clearly JWT had learned its lesson from the loss of business to media specialists in the late 1980s. Between July 1992 and June 1993 JWT (London) spent £147.92 million on its clients' behalf. Of this, £125.66 million was on TV, which reflects the large number of FMCG clients, £10.63 million on national press and £6.11 million on consumer magazines. The rest was spent on outdoor, cinema and radio.

In 1999 JWT launched a new Internet advertising arm called Digital @JWT.

In January 2000 JWT USA launched a new marketing unit called (©) JWT which was a strategic alliance between the agency and Hollywood company Basic Entertainment to develop sponsorship, celebrity endorsements and product placements for their clients in the Hollywood company's shows. Basic Entertainment was responsible for hit shows such as *The Sopranos*, *Just Shoot Me* and *Politically Incorrect*.

Carat

The Media Department started up in 1969, to do media for agencies. Because of the recognition system it used recognition of Kingsley Manson and Palmer (KMP). In 1972 it combined the media departments of seven agencies under the KMP banner. In 1974–1975. The Media Department left the KMP Group and became an independent by default.

In 1975–1976 it became TMD. It became the largest media independent and in 1985 went on to USM and sold 20 per cent of the equity. They used the money to buy a Manchester agency, other media independents and an outdoor poster specialist which became known as Harrison Salinson.

In 1989 the French Carat group Aegis bought 29.9 per cent of TMD and bought the rest in 1991 to become part of a European network. The UK company became TMD Carat in January 1991. It established Carat Research in 1991 and amalgamated direct marketing divisions into TMD Direct. TMD Direct searches for lists and introduces clients to clients with similar customer profiles so that they can swap lists. It also amalgamated all of the business press buying into Carat Business.

In 1998 it dropped the TMD prefix.

By 1999, Carat was the second biggest buying point in the UK after Zenith with estimated billings of £519 million (AC Nielsen). The agency buys campaigns and develops strategic plans. Because the TV buying market relies on volume, Carat has a specialist TV buying department which buys on behalf of all its clients.

The agency's clients include Abbey National, American Express, Bird's Eye Wall's, British Gas, Dell Computers, EMI Records, Guinness, Lloyds TSB, Reckitt Benckiser, Procter & Gamble, Rothmans, Saab, Peugeot and UDV UK. Because of the activity in recent years, 68 per cent of Carat's clients have been with the agency less than five years.

Carat has a sister agency which is also part of Aegis called BBJ Media services. Its clients include Bass, NTL, Renault, BMW and Coca-Cola.

The biggest problem that TMD Carat had was its image as an unwieldy media buying outfit which offers just volume rather than skilful media planning. It has tried to do the latter with Carat Research and the smaller services. Carat developed its own research system for quality of TV viewing (Forte), a section examining 'quality'-press surveys (Quasar), and magazine ad positioning research (Magpie). Carat spends more than double its contribution to industry-wide data (NRS, BARB, etc.) on its own research. *Media Week* commented in September 1993 that one of the aims of the research was to get rid of the image of TMD as 'gorillas with calculators' (Izatt 1993: 25). The agency has also tried to woo medium-sized full-service agencies who cannot compete in the volume-led buying market to do joint ventures, offering media planning and buying to them, but there have been problems with client conflict.

In 1996 it set up Carat Interactive. It started by designing and building web sites and in 1999 narrowed its focus to planning and buying online advertising. It began being web-based but moved its activities into interactive TV and hand-held devices.

Gold Greenlees Trott (GGT)

Since the first edition of this book GGT no longer exists. GGT was formed in 1980. In 1986 the agency floated on the stock exchange and used the money to buy Option One, a sales promotion company, and formed a partnership with Coba-MID, management consultancy. In 1988 GGT purchased BDH in Manchester and expanded into the USA, buying agencies in Atlanta, Minneapolis and Texas. In 1993 GGT formed a joint venture with GGK, giving access to agencies across western and eastern Europe. The group had companies which specialised in sales promotion, direct marketing, sponsorship and event management, audio-visual production, design and management consultancy. The agency had a planning department.

In 1992 the estimated billing for GGT was £54 million, and it had a staff of 115. The agency's clients included Holsten, Marlboro, Taunton, Cadbury (creative and planning); former clients include Toshiba and Farley's.

GGT has traditionally been seen as a creative agency, largely because of the number of awards it has won and the reputations of its creative directors, Dave Trott and later Tim Mellors. Though it was a full-service agency, its medium size has meant that it struggled to retain clients. The first problems came in the run-up to 1992 when clients demanded a European network. GGT responded by tying up with the Swiss-based agency, GGK's European network.

The second problem emerged in 1992–3, when many large clients began centralising their media buying business. GGT had a number of problems trying to secure a media buying outfit that did not have clients conflicting with its own. GGT lost out to a number of competitors and lost several clients, such as Crookes pharmaceuticals, Farley's (part of Boots) and Cadbury's, because of the small size of its media buying operation. At one point it even tried to tie up with two other agencies to retain its client Cadbury.

Option One, the sales promotion arm, worked through the line for KP. But different elements worked for conflicting groups. GGT Direct worked for the *Daily Telegraph*, Option One for *The Times* and GGT Advertising for the *Daily Mirror*: these were kept apart because of client conflict.

Between July 1992 and June 1993 GGT spent £44.78 million on its clients' behalf. Of this, £33.39 million was spent on TV and £7.91 million on national press.

In 1997 GGT was bought by the Omnicom network and folded into its TBWA agency in London. In 2000 the GGT name was removed from the name plate in London.

Howell Henry Chaldecott Lury (HHCL)

HHCL was formed in 1987 one day before the stock market crashed. It has a strategic management consultancy with Adam Lury (Lury Price Associates), and also went into sales promotion. The agency is extremely strong on reputation: it managed to woo big-name clients such as Fuji, Midland and Thames TV soon after it started. Its 1993 client list included Britvic, Mercury, Lego, Automobile Association, Ronseal woodstain, Mazda, Tango, Pot Noodle, Golden Wonder, Danepak, Molsen and MTV.

hhcl and partners *

HHCL is a small agency. HHCL has one of the most effective PR operations in advertising. Its controversial style usually guarantees that it will be the first stop for trade journalists wanting a quote. In 1989 it lost Thames TV's account because it attacked the industry standard research, BARB, with a trade press campaign illustrating what people do in front of TV sets. It has supported the views that advertising should be about challenging social issues, that it should be about trying to talk directly to consumers and should be impact-full. Famous campaigns by HHCL include the First Direct bucket commercials, Pepe Jeans (realism) commercials, Citrus Spring's marketing director talking to camera, Fuji's disabled supermarket worker. HHCL is against lifestyle advertising and argues instead for product-based advertising which does not patronise the consumer. But it follows a very old and simple 'stand out to grab attention' model as displayed by its famous Tango and First Direct campaigns. It has also been involved in writing the Automobile Association's mission statement as an extension of its relationship with the senior management – chairman and managing director rather than marketing director.

The agency's strategy has changed to one of working on high-profile national advertisers, rather than trying to play in the big league of pan-European networks.

The agency responded to the growth of centralised buying and potential loss of business by forming a joint venture media buying company with The Media Business, called Bullet. The deal meant that HHCL could use the resources of The Media Business and reduce costs and overheads to the agency, as well as offering The Media Business buying and research facilities. In 1994 it established its own media planning and buying agency Michaelides & Bednash.

In November 1994 HHCL re-launched as a '3D' marketing communications company, calling itself Howell Henry Chaldecott Lury and Partners. That year it had hired thirteen staff from a sales promotion company, IMP. The move helped secure the Automobile Association's advertising account. In recent years it has developed innovative ad campaigns for clients such as Internet bank Egg and Iceland retail chain.

In 1997 HHCL was bought by PR company Chime Communications and WPP Group which took a 29 per cent stake. WPP is the parent company of JWT, O&M and Y&R. A year later HHCL sold its 50 per cent share of Michaelides & Bednash back to the media agency's managing partners.

Ogilvy Interactive

This interactive agency began life in 1995 as NoHo Digital and built up a number of high profile clients such as Virgin, Microsoft, Sony Playstation and Unilever. It grew from a staff base of four to thirty and was soon snapped up by WPP and rebranded in 1999 with the name of one of the group's advertising networks to become Ogilvy Interactive.

In 2000 the agency significantly increased its client base and employed over 120. It focused on both online and interactive TV advertising and developed a seminal iTV ad for Chicken Tonight and later a Dove interactive ad for Unilever which sat in Sky Digital's shopping platform Open. The agency set up a viral marketing department at the end of 2000 after it developed a campaign for cat food brand Felix. The agency's declared turnover in 2000 was £8 million.

Summary

The recognition system, introduced in 1932, dominated the advertising industry for almost fifty years. It privileged the 'full-service' agency and contributed to increases in media costs. The fall of the recognition system led to the fragmentation of the agency business, and the separation of services such as creativity, media planning and buying and research. One of the consequences of the liberalisation was that multi-brand clients could now centralise their media buying into a single buying point to force better deals from media owners. The drive towards centralised media buying and the concentration among advertisers (see Chapter 1) contributed to a concentration of agencies via merger and acquisition with a handful of international agency networks handling big brand clients. Because of their privileged position in the advertising industry, agencies have been able to maintain a monopoly on professional knowledge and set the terms of business. There are few formal regulations governing internal advertising industry practices.

7 Advertising and the media

···

The economic dependence of media on advertising affects the media in different ways. It is both as source of extra revenue for media owners but also of extra costs. The costs of gaining advertisers in a publication can be prohibitive to a new medium.

Hiring a salesforce, advertising to advertisers in the trade press, producing documents such as media packs and running conferences and exhibitions and awards, as well as a separate production team to produce the ads – these are all substantial costs to media owners.

In the case of the *Telegraph* the sales and marketing and circulation department's salaries account for around 40 per cent of the group's total salaries bill. The increased promotional spends of News International and most of the national newspaper groups acted as a disincentive for new entrants because they would need spend enormous amounts on advertising to compete with the established players.

One such failed new entrant was the *Sunday Correspondent* which launched in 1990. It was unable to keep spending money to keep up with the rest of the field and closed after several attempts at refinancing.

TV companies also need to promote heavily to keep ratings up. TV has increased public relations and on-air marketing of programmes and tailored programmes to generate tabloid newspaper interest. In November 2000 Granada Media put together an evening of programmes which all generated sustained tabloid interest. It included a special edition of *Coronation Street*, *The David Beckham Story*, *Who Wants to be a Millionaire?* and the terrestrial TV premiere of Oscar winning film, *The Full Monty*. Every show had had lengthy on-air promotion and sustained PR activity in the tabloid press. The *Financial Times* concluded that Granada appeared to have learned lessons from US networks that, 'talked about television commands premium advertising rates' (*Financial Times*, 20 November 2000: 26).

Some media are more dependent on advertising than others. The most dependent are outdoor media, commercial radio, free newspapers, and commercial

TV (though extra income is generated from the sale of production and merchandising).

Such dependence on advertising has consequences for editorial content.

Though advertising occupies 'separate' slots on TV and does not directly affect editorial judgement, the need for editorial content that gains a specific type of audience for the advertiser helps to delimit the kinds of programmes that are put out (Curran and Seaton 1988: 199). In the 1960s the strength of the mass brands and the unique position of ITV as a commercial monopoly meant that there was a tendency to promote mass programming in buying ads.

One buyer from the 1960s said: 'If ITV put on anything cultural, we avoid it like the plague, simply because of the high capital cost maintained against a vastly reduced audience' (Pearson and Turner 1965: 206). This kind of approach has changed in recent years, where cultural programmes, and those watched by AB audiences, have become much more valuable to advertising buyers than mass programmes which offer coverage rather than targeted audiences.

Because of competition for advertising revenue, TV programming has been structured by what people consume rather than by demographic group: travel, motoring, consumer affairs, food and drink programmes.

The TV industry also focuses on certain genres that become popular and continue to produce the 'winning formula'. A consequence of the success of TV detective series *Inspector Morse* was that BBC and ITV brought out me-too programmes featuring worldly-wise anti-hero detectives. Similarly, the success of Channel 4 fly-on-the-wall docu-soap *Big Brother* in 2000 brought a raft of imitators.

Another more crude tactic to keep ratings up is to increase the number of times a programme is shown in a week. *Coronation Street* increased from one to six nights a week: this helped to bump up ratings and pull in more advertisers in the face of increased competition from satellite TV.

However, some commercial TV is hardly dependent at all on advertising. Pay TV arrived in the UK in 1989 via cable. In 1992 Rupert Murdoch introduced Pay TV to most of News Corporation's BSkyB in the UK to offset losses and low advertising revenue. The use of subscription reduced the TV channels' reliance on advertising and delivering ratings (Snowden 1993: 34).

The print media also have varying levels of dependence on advertising. Many trade and professional magazines are almost totally reliant on advertising revenue for income. *General Practitioner*, for instance, is a tabloid weekly controlled-circulation magazine which is distributed via direct mail to over forty thousand general practitioners, medical students and pharmaceutical companies. It is highly dependent on advertising revenue from just three drug companies who have a large influence on where editorial and advertising will appear in the magazine.

In 1999 the net revenue per copy of a popular daily was 37p, of this 21p was derived from the cover price and 16p from advertising. The quality Sunday newspapers, however generated 236p per copy, of this 63p was derived from sales and 173p came from advertising revenue. These figures reveal that Sunday quality newspapers are much more reliant on adverting revenue than the popular dailies.

Reliance on advertising can make the media extremely vulnerable to the fortunes of company profits and to recession. Some media are also highly dependent on certain advertising sectors. Regionals are very reliant on local classified advertisers and retailers. In the north-west advertising by retailers accounts for nearly 50 per cent of regional newspaper display revenue.

The number of titles in the women's press has risen by 40 per cent since 1985, but ad revenue and pagination declined during the recession. Advertisers have responded to these decreases by trying to encourage other sources of income, such as 'advertorials' (see below), sponsored supplements, covermounts and competitions.

In 1992 the volume of advertorials and sponsored editorial pages rose by 47 per cent in one year (Waldman 1993b: 24). Other media – newspapers, TV and radio – also developed advertorial and sponsorship divisions to sell their editorial to clients. Advertorials include: advertisements for a single brand disguised as editorial; features mentioning or recommending brand-names; special features, or 'adgets', where advertising is sold to accompany editorial copy (profiling cars, for instance).

The level of dependence on advertising revenue also affects the availability of media. The fortunes of media such as national and regional newspapers, consumer magazines and outdoor media have been highly influenced by the emergence of commercial TV in 1955 and the expansion of new electronic media in the 1990s. From the first year that TV started to 1999 the shares of advertising expenditure have changed considerably: see Table 7.1 (this excludes direct mail and below-the-line work and is only based on rate cards).

The ITV monopoly effectively created the use of single media campaigns. Advertisers switched so much of their advertising resources to above-the-line advertising campaigns, because of the cost of TV. They had to compete with their rivals on TV and the established media had to make responses to the erosion of their share.

The regional media – regional newspapers and local radio – responded by focusing more clearly on local advertising markets. Though regional newspapers are the second largest advertising medium in the UK, gaining 19 per cent of all advertising revenue, their share of national advertising money is only 3.5 per cent. The rest is local classified advertising revenue which is much more vulnerable to recession. Many paid-for titles have turned into free newspapers delivered direct to the door with almost exclusive local advertising from car dealers, estate agents and local businesses. Because of problems with national advertising revenue, local commercial stations began to market their products much more aggressively to local consumers. They increased promotional spend, and successfully lobbied for the relaxing of restrictions on sponsorship and the number of ads per hour. The result has been that regional newspapers and local radio have been in direct competition for local advertising revenue. This problem will increase with the emergence of local cable TV. However, because of the increased number of radio channels and new national commercial stations, the radio industry was expected to reach 4.5 per cent share by the end of the twentieth century.

Table 7.1 Share of advertising expenditure (%)

	1959	*1999*
National newspapers	20.1	14.8
Regional newspapers	23.8	18.6
Consumer magazines	11.9	5.4
Business and professional	11.9	8.9
Directories	0.7	6.2
Press production costs	5.1	4.8
TV	20.9	32.2
Outdoor and transport	5.9	4.8
Radio	0.4	3.8
Cinema	1.5	0.9

Source: *Advertising Association Yearbook* 2000

In 1955, national newspapers responded to TV by keeping their advertisement rates low and increasing commission to 15 per cent. Their profit margins were eroded. As a result of commercial TV six major papers closed between 1958 and 1962 despite a combined readership of 22 million, and three mass-circulation pictorial magazines closed. Partly because of the general recession, by 1975 popular newspapers were making a loss on their advertising revenue (Curran 1986: 313–316). In the new environment newspapers, magazines and other media needed to deliver something extra to get on advertisers' media schedules.

They needed to offer specialist markets that TV could not provide in a cost-effective way, because it was a mass medium. The other media have become highly reliant upon certain sectors of the advertising market.

'Quality' newspapers moved into classified advertising, brought colour into the newspapers to attract food, fashion and drink advertisers, increased classified, personal finance, travel, motoring, TV listings and lifestyle sections. The saturation, concentration and segmentation of markets (see Postscript) meant that multi-brand advertisers needed cost-effective media to target repositioned branded products.

New markets such as magazines for teenagers (*Smash Hits, More!, Just Seventeen*), and for lifestyles or special interests such as gardening, cars and music, meant that advertisers had new media at which to target specific segments of their new markets. In the late 1980s and early 1990s magazine houses launched titles on the basis of attitudinal and lifestyle groups such as 'innovators' and 'the avant-garde'.

Men's magazines *Arena, GQ* and later *Esquire* repositioned their titles along lifestyle lines to segment the market and to attract advertisers of lifestyle brands (Nixon 1993: 489).

In the 1990s Channel 4 television also offered targeted lifestyle programming to deliver lifestyle audiences to specific types of advertisers.

The emergence of digital TV, the growth of channels and the increase in availability in other media; more radio channels; increased newspaper pagination and more specialist magazines – these have also had an effect on traditional commercial TV ad revenues.

Faced with a declining market share, TV companies needed to find cash to pay for production of programmes, and have turned to alternative sources of income. One such method is 'barter' which involves the TV or radio station swapping advertising air time for a programme produced by an advertiser. The seller of the programme may be an advertiser wanting to use the air time to advertise its own goods, or a media buyer who wants to use the airtime for its own range of clients (broking). Cash barter involves both cash and air time going to the advertiser; producers include Pepsi, Unilever and Coca-Cola. Unilever's agency Lintas made an English-language soap opera with French channel TF1 which was half financed through pre-sale agreements outside France. The bartered soap was shown on British TV in the early hours of the morning in 1993 and 1994. Advertiser-owned media may be a thing of the future: in 1994 four major record companies were trying to form a TV channel to rival MTV.

There have also been successful cross-over promotions. Toy companies barter TV programmes and based toys like Pokemon, X-Men and Action Man. These linked in with merchandising and were bought by the TV companies who needed cheap children's programming. Hollywood films such as *Toy Story*, *Star Wars* and *Batman* have merchandising backing up. TV shows also sell merchandising on the back of their programmes such as the BBC's *Teletubbies* and *Tweenies* and US network's WWF wrestling and *PowerRangers*. Film and TV companies often sign deals with other advertisers – e.g. Scooby Doo and Burger King in the UK – to use characters in promotions, and in toy merchandising, to support the release.

TV also began to segment. The new channels started to offer specific kinds of programmes offered at different groups. Channels on satellite such as the Lifestyle Channel, the Children's Channel and MTV aimed at younger audiences, Sky News and Sky Sports aimed at men and the Lifestyle Channel aimed at women.

The emergence of digital television via cable and set top boxes in the late 1990s also led to an enormous growth of segmented channels offering channels aimed at different age groups and at different lifestyle/interest groups such as science and technology channel, the Einstein Channel.

ITV also began to offer programmes such as *Inspector Morse* and *Cracker* aimed at the university-educated high-income brackets, which provided advertisers with older and younger ABC1s respectively. Soaps also segmented: *Home and Away* was positioned as teenage and *Brookside* also had to redefine its audience because of low ratings, to offer advertisers more upmarket viewers.

This included consciously using characters in more professional jobs such as doctors, advertising agents and middle-aged high-income characters.

Though advertisers no longer want mass audiences per se, they do want the right types of audiences, and in sufficient numbers. One hit of a highly concentrated group is much more useful than having to spend on several programmes that offer varying hits; an even spread of viewers waters down the target group. To reach the group, an advertiser needs to buy other media as well, increasing the cost of reaching it. Because more money can be made from delivering media to those most likely to buy certain brands, programme makers and newspaper and magazine publishers had to tailor their programmes more explicitly at these audiences to offer concentrated levels for advertisers. Media owners have been left trying to keep at the threshold in which they are not too 'mass' and not too 'niche' (with a relatively small audience and high cost).

Some claim that advertising acts as a hidden subsidy to the media. It has made media (such as newspapers) cheap. The real hidden subsidy, however, is in the goods that we buy. When we buy a hair colourant for £6 we may not be aware that £2 of that money went to pay for advertising the product to us. This figure only includes the cost of media advertising; it doesn't include the cost of public relations, sponsorship, sales promotions, salesforce and retail trade deals (or the additional moneys retailers take for the sales). If these were included, our figure of £2 would more than double. In effect, by subsidising advertisements, the consumer pays more to independent TV than (in the licence fee) to the BBC. It is not advertising that subsidises the media, but the consumer.

Controlling the market

Media concentration has increased during the post-war period. Between 1947 and 1985 the three leading corporations' share of national daily newspapers has increased from 62 per cent to 75 per cent, and of national Sunday circulation from 60 per cent to 83 per cent (Curran and Seaton 1988: 84).

In TV, by 2000 the TV market had concentrated to such an extent that of the fourteen regional ITV licences eleven were owned by Carlton, Granada and SMG controlling the entire ITV network. In the 1980s there had been fifteen.

In the regional press The Newspaper Society in 2000 estimated that the top twenty publishers account for 84 per cent of all regional and local newspapers and 95 per cent of the total weekly audited circulation.

In the outdoor advertising market, there are over 180 outdoor adverting contractors: six of them accounted for around 82 per cent of Britain's outdoor sites in 1993 (Harrison 1993: 26). The largest contractor, Mills & Allen, has 29 per cent of the market and has regional strengths in certain areas. In Hull, for instance, it has 61 per cent of all 48-sheet sites. But the outdoor scene is not as cut and dried as other media sectors. In Colchester, for example, a local contractor has 56 per cent of the sites and Mills & Allen has only a 5 per cent share (ibid.).

The concentration of the other main media environment – retail – is also significant for advertisers. In the 1990s 52 per cent of packaged groceries were sold through only four retailers: Sainsbury's, Tesco, Safeway and Asda (Nielsen 1993: 80).

Figure 7.1 Telegraph Magazine: this ad for the Saturday publication appeared in the marketing trade press in 1995 and positions the paper against weekend rival the *Sunday Times* (see p. 255). © *Daily Telegraph*

The increased reliance on advertising revenue and the need to restrict media choice has fuelled the merger and concentration of media owners. It gives the media owners greater power in negotiating advertising rates with advertisers.

When the British Government issued its communications white paper in December 2000 – which paved the way for the possibility of a single media owner for ITV – the editorial in *Marketing Week* magazine expressed the fears of many advertisers. It said: 'Advertisers fear that a single ITV company will be able to hike advertising rates, and that they will have little protection . . . a single ITV threatens to squeeze out the smaller advertisers and make those that are left pay more' (*Marketing Week*, 14 December 2000: 3).

Though advertisers are opposed to greater concentration in media ownership the agencies are not, because it makes their job of volume-buying easier. The IPA even suggested to the government that ITV should be streamlined into six mainland regions and Ulster. ITV's monopoly on airtime advertising has been eroded by competition from Channel 4, and Channel 5 satellite TV from the merged BSkyB and from cable companies as well as competition from new digital media. The effect has been that ITV now only commands about one-quarter of TV audiences. Sales contractors amalgamated and concentrated in response to this fragmentation. In the past the fifteen ITV sales companies sold advertising individually. Different sales houses amalgamated and realigned their sales to form large buying points. By 2000 there were only two ITV selling points for agencies to deal with.

Part of the concentration process has been to offer segments and branded packages, such as macro-regions. Because outdoor advertising has a fixed supply (like TV), contractors attempt to control the market through packages. Packages are put together by contractors and offered to clients across the country to aim at certain target groups, such as upmarket commuters. Often they include very good and also less good sites which are very difficult to sell individually. In 1992 there were sixty packages on offer (Harrison 1993: 26) which accounted for around half of available sites which are not able to be bought individually. The packaged sites usually have strong rates and restricted availability. These packages are heavily marketed to agencies and clients.

Media owners also offer packages to woo advertisers away from the more popular and successful media. Regional newspaper groups offer packages to try to woo national advertisers. The basic rate card of the package is about 65 per cent less than the individual rate card for the title (Bailey 1992: 38), and the minimum investment was around £150,000.

In radio, in 1992 there were 120-plus services and six national selling points. The national sales houses offer packages of stations. Agencies argued that the group-sell restricts the local choice of radio versus TV.

Because of heightened competition, newspaper and magazine publishers have also restructured their sales operations and group-sold, mainly to bolster their weaker titles. The magazine publisher IPC Group sells its women's weekly titles, as well as others in its portfolio of women's monthlies.

The concentration of sales points helped to cut costs during the recession: it involved the centralisation of information and technological resources, reduced the salesforce and brought the increasingly fragmented media under one roof. It also offered one-stop shopping packages to buyers, helping to control the market. Concentration can also help to squeeze better deals from clients via packages. A simple one-stop approach reduces overheads for the client in dealing to many points. If a single buying point controls all the business of a major mid-market retailer, it would be more sensible for a newspaper group (with some weak titles) to make one deal across all titles than to try to secure separate deals or try to haggle over price on an individual basis. But it also restricted choice for the advertiser.

Media owners do not tend to cross-sell between media. Organisations such as Emap (which has interests in consumer and business magazines, regional newspapers and radio) and News Corporation (which has interests in satellite TV and national newspapers) could have the potential for developing cross-media sales. In the USA multi-media deals through conglomerates are common-place; in the UK they have yet to become established.

The centralisation of buying and selling points is turning the whole national UK media market into a volume market. In the future there may no longer be the possibility of offering your medium as the sole medium to advertisers. The future may see cross-media sales between different media and tie-ups between, say, regional papers and outdoor sites, or national newspapers and local radio. These may be done within an organisation, such as News International, or as a tie-up between companies. Cross-media sales are already occurring. This is where a media company which has interests in magazines, newspapers and TV, such as Rupert Murdoch's News Corporation, can offer a single package across its media for an advertiser (such as Mars) at a special rate. The attraction for an advertiser is that it does not have to spend money making hundreds of deals with different and diverse media and can cut costs with a single deal. The media owner is also able to reduce costs with single deals, and spread revenue more evenly across the entire group. News Corporation has already begun to offer such packages.

Regulating media availability

Availability is the most important consideration for media planners. If the client is a tobacco manufacturer the regulatory environment means that it will be restricted from some media and have to use others such as sponsorship and posters. The vast majority of state regulations governing advertising availability are in time-based media. TV companies sell air time and collect revenue, but the length, frequency and contents are regulated by a 'separate' body, the ITCA.

Because advertising air-time on ITV, Channel 4 and Channel 5 is restricted, they are not able to boost income by increasing advertising minutes. There is a fixed supply, so sellers have to try for other incentives to add costs to air-time, such as peak rates and seasonality. In response ITV companies have sought to restrict the supply of available air-time to keep the price rigid by increasing the amount of on-air promotion for their programmes. This increases viewing figures and limits the amount of commercial air-time available.

When commercial TV came to the UK in 1955 the new commercial channel was not allowed to carry sponsorship. Newspaper proprietors had lobbied hard to only allow spot advertising on the new medium. Ad agencies such as JWT and S. H. Benson backed the move to allow spot advertising as a concession to the newspaper groups.

At the beginning of commercial TV there was an 'advertising magazine' format, whereby a period of time would be given over to commercials in which a fictional story would take place in a pub, for instance, and various brands would be referred to or puffed. In 1959 Labour MPs had tried to introduce a TV (Limitation of Advertising) Bill to reduce commercial time from 8 minutes an hour to 6. Though the move failed, there was widespread support for limiting advertising on TV (Pragnell 1986: 301). Advertising magazine programmes were banned in 1963 following recommendations in the Pilkington Report, because they gave the impression that they were editorial programmes plugging products.

Because of this the 30-second commercial became the pre-eminent form of British TV advertising for over forty years.

British governments also singled-out television advertising for sectoral bans because it was perceived to be more persuasive. Sectoral bans included political parties, charities and religions, professions and areas like sanitary protection products ('sanpro'), condoms and, from 1965, cigarettes.

Since the 1950s global advertisers (especially US-based ones) have lobbied hard to increase the number of commercial TV minutes across Europe. The 1989 European Directive on television broadcasting set the parameters on minutage and sponsorship. Advertising lobbyists managed to influence the final draft of the European Convention on broadcasting, overturning proposals that feature films should be interrupted only once by advertisements and that TV documentaries, drama series, etc. lasting longer than 45 minutes could have only one break during each 45-minute period. British advertising interests produced research (conducted by Young & Rubicam in London) to claim that the legislation would cost commercial channels around 15 per cent of advertising revenue (ITV and Channel 4 would lose 17.4 per cent) (Palmer 1990: 25). The draft convention was severally modified, allowing up to three breaks in feature films and in TV films and documentaries lasting over 110 minutes. Other forms of programming would be allowed an ad break every 20 minutes. The British practice of having ad breaks after 15 minutes in half-hour programmes ended, except during News at Ten (curiously as it is a news bulletin) – another concession to the advertising industry. Other half-hour programmes would have breaks after 20 minutes, not 15 minutes. The only significant effect on ITV in the UK was the removal of the Hamlet cigar campaign. The directive also allowed member states to change the rules if they could guarantee that the broadcasting did not cross into other EC states. In May 1995 the ITC agreed to accept commercials from alcoholic spirits companies who had previously been restricted to posters and cinema. The important element affecting satellite TV was that the originating country reserved the right to control advertising broadcast from its territory.

Advertisers successfully lobbied the ITC to relax its own restrictions which had prevented advertisers from exploiting the programme in their off-screen marketing campaigns. Advertisers use the plot and style, the title and stars of the programme in press, posters and at the point of sale, as part of the sponsorship deal. Sponsorship guidelines were relaxed in 1991. TV sponsorship now allows a 15-second opening credit, 5-second break bumpers, and a 10-second end credit. Sponsors can use movement and graphics and voice-overs.

Sponsors therefore got up to 45 seconds of air time for their sponsorship in addition to programme trailers during the week. Programmes where sponsorship is not permitted include news programmes, business and financial programmes, and current affairs analysis programmes. One of the reasons why weather sponsorship is so popular among advertisers is that it comes at the end of news items and gets the ABC1 viewers. Cadbury, for instance, used its sponsorship of *Coronation Street* as part of its off-screen advertising and promotions.

Outdoor advertising was generally unregulated in the late nineteenth century. Posters from national and local advertisers were stuck on top of each other, plastering most buildings in British cities with advertising paper inches thick. Despite the implementation of some self-regulation in 1890 by the Bill Posting Association (founded 1862), to censor offensive and misleading advertising,

Figure 7.2 Cadbury: The confectionery company's sponsorship of *Coronation Street* began in 1996. It signed a deal to sponsor ITV's highest-rating programme for a record £10 million a year. In April 1997, the Independent Television Commission relaxed the rules on the use of branded strapline on sponsorship credits. This allowed Cadbury to add a series of product specific messages to its on-screen branding, changing them as appropriate for different times of the year, such as Creme Eggs before Easter. © Cadbury. Artwork: Aardman Animations.

opposition grew. In 1893 the Society for the Checking of Abuses in Public Advertising was formed, a pressure group to restrict outdoor advertising in rural areas. By the turn of the century SCAPA had managed to ban bill sticking. The Advertisement Regulation Act 1907 gave local authorities powers to regulate billposting and protect local amenities (Nevett 1982: 127). The effect of the new restrictions was that outdoor advertising costs were forced up and mass advertisers became the main users of the medium. The outdoor advertising industry also standardised poster sizes at this time. Posters are measured in sheets; sizes today range from four sheets in bus shelters to ninety-six sheets in 'super-sites', often seen on major roads and railway lines leading into cities.

Because of regulations, outdoor (like TV) advertising has fixed supply. To increase revenue, the companies can try either to change the regulations (which radio has successfully done), or to squeeze the maximum revenue out of their existing supply. The latter is done through either upgrading them by using super-sites and illumination or trying to buy up the opposition to increase market share. The outdoor industry has had three MMC investigations in the 1980s and early 1990s. Concentration in the industry forced the MMC to step in and force Mills & Allen to sell poster contractor Dolphin in the early 1990s. However, outdoor advertising has benefited enormously from the TV ban on cigarette advertising in 1965. The transferring of cigarette advertising to outdoor media helped to maintain the outdoor advertising industry's income at a time when advertisers were allocating more of their spending to TV.

Advertisers also lobbied hard in the 1980s for new media such as satellite and cable TV. In 1984, the Cable Bill set up the Cable Authority to award franchises to set up local cable TV networks. There are two types of cable TV: broadband and narrowband. Broadband is where many channels are broadcast and other services, such as telephone, are also available on the cables.

Narrowband allows a limited number of channels and does not offer interactive services. The majority of cable companies run narrowband channels carrying satellite programmes, but without their own dedicated programming.

Radio deregulation in the 1980s resulted in an increase from nineteen local commercial radio stations to over 120 in the 1990s. Deregulation also allowed established local commercial radio stations to split their frequencies. The bigger markets all got second ILR (Independent Local Radio – commercial radio) service. New stations also emerged delivering more narrowcast channels such as jazz, dance music, programmes aimed at Greek and Asian listeners, etc. The audiences are more highly defined, like magazine readerships. Deregulation also brought the national commercial radio stations: in 1992 Classic FM and in 1993 Virgin. In 2001 the UK had four national commercial radio stations, ten regional stations and more than 200 local stations. Before the 1990 Broadcasting Bill, radio stations could carry only 9 minutes of advertising an hour. There is now no limit on the amount of advertising radio stations can carry. All programmes are allowed to be sponsored except news bulletins. Sponsors are allowed to contribute to the editorial content (except news, current affairs, business, financial, political programmes and those concerning current public policy issues);

but not allowed to endorse their own products in the editorial. They are allowed to use advertising slogans, copylines, brand and corporate names; and at least one credit every 15 minutes. Sponsors are also allowed to buy advertising around the sponsored programmes as long as the advertisements are distinguished from the programme and its credits. Companies who are normally not allowed to advertise on radio (producers of cigarettes, alcohol, etc.) may be allowed to sponsor if they obtain permission from the Radio Authority. Promoters of anti-AIDS or anti-drugs messages, or of sanitary protection, pregnancy testing or contraceptives, are not allowed to sponsor children's or religious programmes.

Deregulation has increased the number of advertising opportunities: advertising now appears in hospitals, schools, as sponsorship on TV, and on parking meters and train and bus tickets. Advertisers sought to replace government regulations with the regulations of the market. This would make media more dependent on advertising for survival, providing more media for privileged sections of the community – high-income consumers – and squeezing out alternative media.

Another form of government regulation is taxation. Media advertising remained untaxed until 1961. The then Conservative government imposed on TV advertising a 10 per cent tax (later raised to 11 per cent) called TV Ad Duty. The main reasons why it was acceptable were the enormous profits generated by TV contractors. The biggest TV companies passed the tax to advertisers. The effect was an increase in the costs of advertising for the big advertisers.

The government also stated that agency commission would be allowed only on air time rates which excluded the tax. This meant that the agency commission was reduced from 15 per cent to 13.5 per cent, squeezing its profits. Only the big agencies who could negotiate volume deals and discounts were unscathed. This move helped to concentrate the advertising business further. The tax was changed in 1964 to cover revenue, and in 1974 it was based on TV contractors' profits, thus removing the principle of taxing advertising. The tax system was also changed to reflect the different sizes of ITV companies and the proportions of advertising revenue they received.

The onset of interactive television in the late 1990s allowed advertisers the opportunity to get much more involved in programming. New digital channels such as ONdigital, NTL, Sky Digital and ADSL allowed advertisers the opportunity not only to develop interactive advertising with immediate response – enabling the consumers of Domino's Pizza, for instance, the ability to order a pizza via the TV set – but also the chance for sponsors to 'own' an entire channel. Two examples of this are Granada's joint venture digital health and beauty channel with Boots and Carlton TV's link-up with Sainsbury's.

Media-advertising relations: The *Daily Mirror*

In the inter-war period US advertisers in particular needed mass working-class media as a target for their cheap international brands. The *Daily Mirror* in the 1930s had a disproportionately high middle-class readership but a circulation below 800,000. Lord Rothermere sold it. The advertising agency JWT carried out research for the *Daily Mirror* into readers' preferences, advised on layout and provided its own members of staff to become part of the new advertising team on the paper, using it as a vehicle for its own advertisers (Curran and Seaton 1988: 62). It cut political, social and industrial news by half, and increased sports coverage, crime, sex and human interest and entertainment stories. Thus JWT had a new medium for its mass-brand clients such as Kellogg's, Rowntree and Sun Maid. JWT had made one of the first steps towards developing a mass working-class newspaper that was left of centre and friendly towards business (other mass working-class newspapers like the *Daily Herald* were anti-consumption and socialist). The *Daily Mirror* included entertainment features and consumption-oriented editorial. By 1939 it was selling 1.5 million copies. One of the intentions in the relaunch of the *Daily Mirror* was to try to open up media channels for advertisers to target working-class consumers on a daily basis. The reposition was essentially to take on the *Daily Herald* as a left of centre paper, but with fun articles on entertainment, sports, etc., focusing more on consuming, less on industrial and public affairs, and more on the private and domestic sphere. In 1948 the *Daily Mirror* had reached a circulation of four million.

Examples: media owners

The *Guardian*

The *Guardian* started as a regional paper, the *Manchester Guardian*, in 1821. It became a national newspaper in the 1950s when it moved to London. The paper is now governed by a non-profit-making trust called The Guardian Media Group which includes the group's cash cow, the *Manchester Evening News*, which achieves high levels of income from retail and regional advertising.

The *Guardian* suffered circulation and reader losses (as did *The Times*) when the *Independent* was launched in 1986. In response, it relaunched with a complete redesign, as much to please advertisers as for any change for the readers. The intention was to jettison the *Guardian*'s old image as a newspaper for social workers, teachers and other low-spending consumers, and refocus it as a progressive young urban professional's newspaper. It developed sections in media, European affairs, health and education to transform the economic base of the paper to be more reliant upon classified recruitment advertising. Its display sales do less well than other broadsheet papers', largely because of the image of the paper's readership. The paper increased lifestyle coverage promotions and sponsorship of arts and media events, developed sections on food,

drink, travel, property and motoring to pull in ads and launched brand campaigns to give the paper a more modern consumerist image.

The *Guardian* increased coverage of travel, music and the arts, and developed lifestyle weekend sections, all designed to pull in extra advertising and change the reader profile. It also ran trade press campaigns aimed at showing advertisers how desirable its readers were and transforming its image among media buyers. It has always maintained a middle-class liberal editorial position.

The most significant developments were its increased investment in the Saturday paper in 1991 with the expansion of *Weekend Guardian* and local listings, and the purchase of the *Observer* in 1993 from Lonrho. Both these moves more clearly targeted the paper's main rival, the *Independent*.

The *Guardian* in the late 1990s launched a Friday supplement called *The Editor* which collated news stories of the week and re-presented them in an easy to read format. It also expanded the Saturday paper and added new culture and lifestyle sections.

The *Guardian* has a much bigger classified sales staff than display. The paper's advertising revenue is roughly divided between 60 per cent classified to 40 per cent display. Advertising income accounts for 60 per cent of the total. The company has set up a separate magazine team of agency sales executive who sold the *Weekend* magazine and later the *Observer Magazine* and special supplements. The sales team encourage the sale of space across both titles.

On-the-run colour (a new and cheaper process in which the colour is added in one printing rather than four) has brought in 'style' and packaged goods clients. But the main advertisements for the *Guardian* are recruitment, entertainment and arts, drink, government, social and political organisations, cars, travel, retail and financial. The *Guardian* also sells ad promotions (advertorials) in certain products. However, the *Guardian* gets very little advertorial revenue. Business, city and corporate campaigns do not put the *Guardian* on their schedule because they don't believe that the paper delivers business audiences, especially city audiences. It claims to offer advertisers 'well-educated upmarket adults who enjoy art, culture and being informed'. The paper offers targeted regional advertising in different editions of the *Weekend Guardian* and inserts and accepts group bookings.

In the period February 1993 to January 1994 the *Guardian* had a total NRS of 1,458,000 which is a penetration of 3.2 per cent of the total adult population: 812,000 (57 per cent) were men, 646,000 (43 per cent) were women. It had an ABC1 readership of 84 per cent; 62 per cent of the readers were aged between fifteen and forty-four. By 2000 the paper's NRS had fallen by 25 per cent to 1,100,000 (December 1999–November 2000. However, its proportion of ABC1 readers had increased to over 90 per cent.

The cheapest parts of the paper to advertise in are the features pages and pages in the magazine sections, the most expensive are the main news sections. The paper also offers special advertising rates for arts and charities advertisers. The paper also uses its own commissioned research when selling.

The Guardian Media Group has also expanded into film and TV production, radio broadcasting and launched online recruitment site Workthing.com. However, the most significant move for the newspaper's the launch of *Guardian Unlimited* in 1999.

Guardian Unlimited

Guardian Unlimited (http://www.guardian.co.uk/) launched in 1999. It is a network of Internet sites which is currently free to users and sells banner advertising.

The site includes a dedicated shopping site, sport, personal finance and film sites and sites which focus on certain readers jobs which gain a large amount of recruitment advertising in the main paper, specifically public sector, education and media.

In 2000 the sites expanded to include dedicated news teams covering areas such as the media industry (Media Unlimited) providing daily news updates on the media industry, re-enforcing the *Guardian*'s pre-eminent coverage of this market. According to *Guardian Unlimited*'s own research different sites offer advertisers different demographic groups. For instance, the film site's users are the youngest on the network with an average age of 32 and 72 per cent of *Football Unlimited*'s users are male. The site also offers advertisers advertising opportunities on WAP and PDA sites (this is where WAP phone users and PDA users are able to download news and other information).

Guardian Unlimited sites are audited by the Audit Bureau of Circulations. In March 2000 the ABC audit showed that the network received 12.3 million impressions in one month.

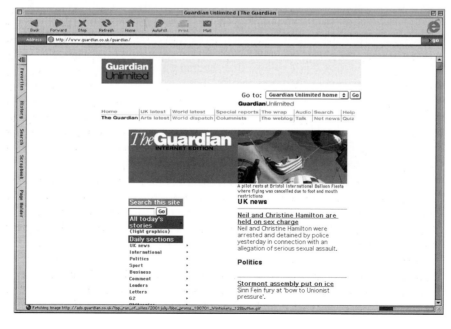

There are three main reasons behind the launch of *Guardian Unlimited*. The first is the possibility of promoting the *Guardian* itself to Internet users who may not buy or read the *Guardian*. The second is to fit with the branding of the *Guardian* as a young, modern newspaper for the technologically literate. Finally, and most importantly *Guardian Unlimited* was launched as a way to protect the *Guardian*'s classified recruitment revenue which accounts for an enormous proportion of the paper's income. GMG stated in its annual report, 'Eventually, most classified advertising will move from paper to on-line, with a consequential effect on the economics of newspaper production'.

Liverpool Echo

The regional evening newspaper the *Liverpool Echo* is owned by Trinity Mirror. Trinity which had been a solely regional newspaper publisher merged with Mirror Group, publisher of the *Daily Mirror*, in 1999 in a deal worth £1.7 billion.

The *Liverpool Echo* has the fifth biggest circulation of a paid-for evening newspaper. In July 1993 Trinity was cleared by the MMC to buy its main rival in Liverpool, Argus Press (publishers of weekly free market leader, *MerseyMart*), for £23 million.

Advertising revenue is split 65 per cent display and 35 per cent classified: this is largely due to the drop in recruitment advertising, especially in recession-hit Liverpool. The group restructured between 1978 and 1988, halving the number of staff in the Liverpool office from 1,280 to 690.

The biggest problem that the *Echo* has in selling the newspaper to national advertisers is the image of Liverpool as a blue-collar low-income city. Their sales presentations concentrate on the spending power of Liverpool consumer spenders, particularly in food, drink, tobacco, clothes, household goods and services. The sales brochure for the *Echo* in 1994 stated: 'For anyone with goods and services to sell, the *Liverpool Echo* is the prime medium to reach some of the UK's top wage earners. Merseysiders are consumers by nature, paying out £1.4 billion a year on food products. Of 702,000 households in the *Echo* circulation area, 73 per cent are privately owned, and home-loving Merseysiders spend £350 million a year on household goods.' The brochure also sells research that shows that 60 per cent of the paper's readers are car owners and 53 per cent of prospective car buyers use the *Echo* when looking for a car.

The *Echo* also competes with national newspapers for retail advertising revenue. For information on national stories the main competition is the early evening TV and radio but also the morning newspapers, especially the tabloids. The paper claims that a quarter of its readers are solus (read no other paper): '62% adult penetration in Liverpool, compared to 51% for the *Sun* and *Mirror* combined' (ibid.). The main competitors for the paper for local advertising revenue are the free newspapers and Radio City (as well as Granada).

The areas of Merseyside with the highest proportion of working-class residents, Liverpool and Knowsley, have the largest numbers of *Echo* readers:

75 per cent of all adults in Liverpool and 72 per cent in Knowsley. In the more affluent areas of Sefton and Wirral the figures are reduced to 50 per cent and 39 per cent. The biggest circulation day of the week is Thursday (jobs and housebuying). The weakest day of the week is Saturday because people are not at work. The Saturday paper is also in competition with local radio for sports coverage.

The main future competition for the local newspapers will be from cable TV, which will be able to offer not only local news and sports coverage but also the main listings information, and features such as car dealer ads.

The circulation of the *Echo* in 1991 was 195,845. In nine years its circulation has fallen 20 per cent to 155,848 (ABC December 1999 to June 2000). According to the NRS, the reader profile is heavily biased towards older readers: 30 per cent are aged fifteen to thirty-five.

National advertising sales for the paper are conducted by sales house AMRA (owned by Trinity Mirror) in London, and the provincial sales are conducted by the provincial office in Manchester. When Trinity took over Mirror Group it closed the Mirror's thirty strong regional sales force and transferred its clients – forty-five Midlands regional titles to AMRA. The move increased AMRA's share of the regional press advertising from 20 to 27 per cent.

Radio City

 Liverpool based Radio City was launched in 1974 as one of the first metropolitan commercial radio stations.

In 1988 it split frequencies along with other stations with '96.7 City FM' and 'City Talk' on AM. City Talk failed to reach a high enough audience to stay on air. It fell into severe financial problems, causing the group to be bought out by regional newspaper and magazine publishers EMAP in 1990. The City Talk service was changed to a 1960s music station, 'City Gold' and more than doubled the City Talk figures. The strategy of the 1980s was to brand the station heavily – Radio City (Sound of Merseyside) – through marketing and advertising promotions and to increase the amount of local advertising revenue to supplement the low revenue from national advertisers. EMAP changed the station's DJs and increased the use of on-air promotions and sponsorships.

The biggest problem that ILR had with national advertisers was the low coverage and predominantly very young, C2DE, listeners. Advertising collapsed by 25.5 per cent in the first year after EMAP took it over, and pre-tax profits fell by 80.6 per cent in 1991–1992 on the previous year. Average weekly hours per listener dropped from 14.7 (1988) to 11.1 (1990) and 9.7 (1991). The station's percentage share of all listening in the area was 27.6 (1988), 19.7 (1990) and 16.9 (1991).

But by 2000 Radio City was the biggest local commercial radio station outside of London. Its marketing activity had grown considerably in the local area including the launch of compilation CDs.

It had changed City Gold to Magic 1548. EMAP used the Magic brand for stations across the UK which have an older profile of listeners.

Advertisers pay for the number of times listeners will hear the ad. The highest rating programmes (breakfast time) demand the highest rates per unit. The main advertisers in radio are car dealers, retailers and fmcg brands. The main competitor to Radio City for local advertising is the *Liverpool Echo*. But Signal Radio in Cheshire and Marcher Sound in Wirral and North Wales, as well as Atlantic 252 (broadcasting from Ireland) and Virgin, have encroached on Radio City's commercial audiences.

The sales director of Radio City oversees and co-ordinates three sales areas. First, local sales include all business in the transmission area that does not use advertising agencies. Second, a regional salesforce is aimed at all business outside London through advertising agencies. Third, the national salesforce based in London deals with advertising agencies. The national sales house EMAP On Air. The fourth area of responsibility covers sponsorship and promotions and accounts for 20–25 per cent of all sales.

EMAP sells sponsorship packages across its radio stations. For instance, in 1999 it sold sponsorship of its sports coverage across North West stations to Ford. The stations included Radio City, Key 103 in Manchester and Rock FM in Preston.

Radio City FM targets young listeners and advertisers, Magic targets the thirty-five to fifty-five-year-olds. The split in the audience profile is even male to female and predominantly C2DE and the station claims to have an equal proportion of local and national advertising. The group successfully defended its franchise in 1995.

In 2000 Emap Digital radio won the local digital multiplex licence for Liverpool with the aim of broadcasting eight programme services in the area. The new services would include EMAP's other brands Kiss and Capital's Xfm. In 1999 EMAP launched a series of websites for its big city radio station brands including Radio City.

Granada Television

North West TV company Granada Television is owned by Granada Media, one of the biggest media companies in the UK which also owns five other ITV franchises including London Weekend Television, Yorkshire Television, Tyne Tees Television, Anglia Television and Meridian Broadcasting.

The Granada region, which was established in 1956, covers Merseyside, Lancashire, Greater Manchester and Cheshire.

The north-west gets around 12% of the total share of recorded viewers for adults, 'housewives' and men. This is after London on around 16% (Carlton and LWT), and the Midlands on around 15%. Granada has an ABC1 profile of 39%, whereas the network average is 42%. The proportion of DEs in the Granada region is 39%, whereas in the whole network it is 33%. The region offers higher penetration of housewives under twenty-five and between thirty-five and forty-four as well as DEs, and a higher proportion with children between the ages of four and nine, and ten and fifteen.

Granada Media owns 50% of digital terrestrial pay television operator ITVdigital, and 50% of electrical retail chain Box Clever. Granada also has equity investments in ITN (20%), GMTV (25%), London News Network (50%), Scottish Media Group (18.1%), Granada Sky Broadcasting (50.5%), Liverpool FC (9.9%), Arsenal FC (5%), TV3 in Ireland (43 %), Ask Jeeves UK (25%), a joint health and beauty venture with Boots (40%), Seven Network (10.4%) and Village Roadshow (18%) in Australia, and Powerchannel Europe (23.5%).

The division which looks after the commercial side of Granada Media is Granada Enterprises. This division was responsible for generating advertising revenues of £1bn in 2000. This represents half of ITV's and nearly a third of all the total UK television advertising market.

Airtime sales for ITV represents over 90% of its revenues. Granada Enterprises is separated into four areas; ITV sales; Channels (which sells advertising on the digital and satellite channels); Commercial Ventures (which provides licensing and merchandising opportunities, negotiates sponsorship deals, and provides product placement and international programme barter across Granada Group); and Interactive sales (which sells advertising on Granada Media's web sites).

ITV sales sells the Granada region as an area in its own right but also sells it as part of a North macro region which combines Granada, Yorkshire Border and Tyne Tees. In 2001 a 30-second ad between 8.00 and 10.30 p.m. would cost £30,000 on Granada. As part of the North macro region, the same length ad would cost £67,500.

When booking a spot for Granada, the rate cards are set on the basis of audience size and profile. Granada offers packages which can be placed anywhere throughout the week and are sold in blocks of ten spots. A peak-time package (8.30 to 10.30 p.m.) in 2001 for a 30-second commercial would cost £30,000. A 10-second slot at this time is worth £18,000.

If the advertiser wishes to book a fixed spot an additional 30 per cent of rate card is charged.

Granada also has Premier and Platinum rates for very popular advertising slots.

Granada offers volume discounts if the advertiser spends over a certain amount of money each year.

Regional advertisers are offered lower rates but there is less likelihood of discounting. Granada also offers special packages to retailers, motor dealers and leisure industries to script, direct and produce a commercial for first-time advertisers. One package for a leisure company includes commercial production of basic live action including a half-day video shoot on location or in studio, edited with digital video effects, voice-over and library music with five peak and ten off-peak spots at 30 seconds.

Granada also offers additional services to advertisers such as: a test marketing service called G-Start which monitors the effects of TV advertising at the point of sale; a salesforce support service through G-Force; an advertising support service on Teletext called G-Text; a service which announces forthcoming TV campaigns to retailers called G-gram; and a conference venue service for product launches called G-Launch.

In addition, Granada also offers a tracking service, called G-Track, to measure audience response to advertising in the Granada regions. This service tests attitude, awareness, recall and usage, product concept and placement testing.

Granada Media is also involved in international programme barter and product placement in its films and videos. For instance Coronation Street's special Las Vegas video included product placements from mobile phone manufacturer Motorola. This programme also appeared on TV.

It also exploits the commercial interests of its parent, Granada Group of companies to support its advertising interests. Granada Media offers advertisers product launches, on-site promotions, sampling and competitions at its parent group's restaurant and hotel companies, Forte Hotels, Granada Motorway Services, Travelodge and Little Chef.

Granada Enterprises has also been involved in advertiser-funded programming and worked with IBM, Elida Fabergé, BUPA, P&G and B&Q. The programmes were developed to 'transform a simple marketing brief into a programme vehicle that can both communicate brand propositions and be traded as a media asset'.

Good Housekeeping

Good Housekeeping came to Britain from the USA in 1922 as a monthly magazine for middle-class 'housewives'. National Magazines, part of the US-based Hearst Corporation, had only seven titles in the UK: *Cosmopolitan*, *Esquire*, *Company*, *She*, *House Beautiful* and *Harper's & Queen*, until 2000 when it paid £30 million for Gruner & Jahr's magazines *Prima*, *Best* and *Focus*.

The vast majority of National Magazines' employees are involved in sales, merchandising and promotions. Wider competition for advertising includes the colour supplements, and TV programmes on food and home interest.

Good Housekeeping has managed to differentiate from most other home and women's interest titles which are either too downmarket in their reader profile or much younger. The only comparable ABC1 and older age profile to *Good Housekeeping* is *Sainsbury's Magazine*. Other competition comes from *BBC Good Food* which has an ABC1 profile of 69 per cent. Fifty per cent of its readers are over 44, the same as *Good Housekeeping*. But it has a much smaller readership.

Sainsbury's Magazine's circulation is around 330,000 and *Good Housekeeping*'s is around 380,000. However, *Sainsbury's Magazine*'s readership is much higher at around 2.1 million compared to *Good Housekeeping*'s 1.7 million. The primary reason for this and the fact that Safeway's magazine, *A Taste of Safeway* achieve higher readership levels is due to the fact that supermarket magazine's tend to be prominently placed in supermarkets and tills and read/flicked through while shoppers are waiting.

Nevertheless, these relatively new titles have provided problems for the title.

ıce 1993 *Good Housekeeping*'s circulation has fallen 19 per cent. Between ınuary to June 2000 *Good Housekeeping* sold an average of 380,062 copies an issue, of which 236,875 (62 per cent) were sold on the news-stand, and 128,597 (33 per cent) on subscription which is very high. *Good Housekeeping* lost 26 per cent of its total women's readership between 1982 and 1992 and lost a further 22 per cent between 1993 and 2000 to 1.7 million readers though it was a good performance in a market that was saturated by new competitors.

It has been estimated that for every £1 of cover price revenue, advertisers contributed an extra £1.30, reflecting the importance of advertising income. The main areas in which *Good Housekeeping* seeks to attract advertising are food, cosmetics, fashion, and furnishings.

The magazine produces cookery books – over forty titles. The *Good Housekeeping Classic Cook Book* has had its forty-third reprint. The Good Housekeeping Institute, established in 1924, tests new products such as cosmetics and food. It can be commissioned for testing and producing information leaflets; it can arrange mailing, point-of-sale material and showcards. Inserts in *Good Housekeeping* cost £26 per thousand loose and £36 bound-in.

A basic full-page display advertisement in *Good Housekeeping* cost £15,075 in 2000. A premium position cost £21,105 and the cover cost £22,610. The cost of an advertorial included single-page promotion at £15,230. The promotion includes production costs for studio photo shoots.

The magazine also has an enterprises division which allows advertisers the possibility to do product licensing, book and stationery publishing, home shopping and telephone services.

Carlton Screen Advertising

Rank Screen Advertising (RSA) was originally formed to sell time for Rank Odeon. It fought its main rival Pearl & Dean by winning MGM/Cannon cinemas and the UCI contract.

It was bought by Carlton Screen Advertising in the mid-1990s and by the turn of the century controlled 70 per cent of the cinema admissions. The rest is controlled by Pearl & Dean.

Special packages include: all screens in the ISBA areas; film packages after individual releases; Disney; children's films; art advertising in art houses; and individually bought advertising in individual screens. A multiplex screen with over twenty shows a week and large audiences will be costed at a different rate from a cinema with smaller audiences perhaps only open at weekends.

CSA also sell six-sheet posters in the foyers of the cinemas to complement the ads that appear on screen. As CSA is part of the multi-media group Carlton Communications which also has broadcasting interests.

When an advertiser is buying a spot on a film release, RSA gives projections based upon similar film releases. So *Wayne's World 2*, released in 1994, was based on the demographic profiles of *Wayne's World* which had 3.8 million admissions. The age profile was 7 per cent for 7- to 11-year-olds, 12 per cent

12 to 14, 29 per cent 15 to 19, 27 per cent 20 to 24, 19 per cent 25 to 34 and 6 per cent over 35. The social grades were 51 per cent C2DE and the gender difference was 58 per cent male, 42 per cent female. *Dangerous Liaisons* (15) had a CAVIAR age profile of 6 per cent 15- to 17-year-olds, 11 per cent 18 to 19, 25 per cent 20 to 24, 19 per cent 25 to 34 and 39 per cent over 35. It also had a social grading of 67 per cent ABC1 and 55 per cent male. The total admissions for *Dangerous Liaisons*, however, were 0.82 million, a much smaller base than *Wayne's World*.

In 2000 CSA's brochure to advertisers pointed out that one of its sales packages, the Millennium Kids packages offers advertisers the ability to target kids with their parents. It claimed that there is an advantage in advertising to children who are accompanied by their mothers. It said: 'Reaching children in the company of others can benefit advertisers when peer pressure determines what is in and out of fashion. Advertising to children in the presence of a parent has a dramatic sales advantage, and cinema is one of the only media that can offer access to this mutual viewing opportunity.'

Summary

Advertising creates extra costs as well as extra income for most media which need sales teams and additional marketing to attract advertisers. The growth in competition between media, especially after the arrival of commercial TV in 1955, created extra pressures on media owners to gain new sources of advertising income. Media owners began to sell their audiences and readers more vociferously to advertisers. Many media tailored their products to advertisers' requirements to deliver the right kinds of consumers with consumption-oriented programmes and features. Some sold editorial space in the form of 'advertorials' to gain extra revenue. Advertisers have successfully lobbied to increase the availability of advertising air time. The deregulation of TV in 1990 placed ITV in a similar position to other media. As a result, the media have concentrated to reduce costs and keep advertising income up in the face of greater concentration for advertisers' money through single buying points.

8 Media planning and buying

T en years ago clients had a different media buyer to the main creative agency, the latter often tried to co-ordinate the media planning and research and to tell the media buying agency where the media should be bought.

As the advertising business placed such a premium on control of knowledge the media planning and research functions were often the most hotly contested functions.

However, by 2000 all of the main London ad agencies had separate media buying and planning functions and virtually all media planning and research was conducted by media agencies.

Media planners work with the client, and media researchers use research to gauge effectiveness and size or spread. The media planner's role is to convince the client that the media buying strategy will hit the right consumers in an effective and cost-effective way. The media planner tries to combine media research and consumer research along with knowledge of the client's communications problem. This means that the separate discipline of account planning has increasingly become restricted to the areas of consumer behaviour and effects research.

The media target

When targeting consumers, advertisers generally use four targets. The first two are the marketing and advertising targets: the total target for their marketing (e.g. all 'quality' and mid-market newspaper readers), a strategic target for an advertising or promotional campaign (e.g. 'mid-market risers', rival brand users, light users of their own brand). This is developed because the manufacturer identifies certain targets who are more susceptible to switching than others: the strategy usually measures their predisposition. The third target is the creative one (see Chapter 10).

The fourth target is the media target. The main purpose of research is 'to eliminate waste in advertising by objectively analysing the media available for promoting products and services' (Chisnall 1992: 218). Because of this, media planning is part of a matching exercise. It attempts to match media and advertising markets by matching the maps or texts of audiences, to the maps or texts of consumers as closely as possible.

If the marketers of Mellow Birds coffee wanted to target lapsed users of their brand of drink (women between 30 and 60), there is no media which perfectly fits their target market. There is no magazine, TV or radio programme for lapsed users of Mellow Birds between the ages of 30 and 60. Any medium that the advertiser chooses to use will have a degree of wastage.

The point of developing a media target is to reduce wastage. Media targets therefore tend to be broader than strategic ones, because generally media consumption does not follow the same lines as brand consumption. The media target tries to focus on all users but with minimal wastage. Mellow Birds, then, may want to target itself as a mid-morning drink and focus on all women coffee users by advertising during TV programme, *This Morning*.

The strategic plan: which medium?

The strategic media plan is decided between the media planner, the client, the creative and the account planner. The planner decides on the budget split between different media (e.g. 50 per cent TV, 30 per cent direct mail, 20 per cent posters – or 40 per cent national press, 30 per cent radio, 30 per cent local press), draws up an outline schedule showing where, when the advertising would appear, and estimates how much the campaign will cost. At the planning stage no formal order will be made, just verbal commitments or options. Though a media schedule is drawn up on the basis of rate cards, a media planner or buyer would know whether and by how much different media are willing to discount: they may also inform the proposed media that they may well be dropped altogether from the schedule if bigger discounts are not offered.

In deciding which media to use, the first questions that the media planner needs to ask must be: who are the target consumers, what is the brand's competition up to and what will be the most cost-effective buy for the brand, delivering the greatest amount of coverage at the lowest price?

Money is the ultimate limiting factor for advertisers. It determines media availability and sets limits on such areas as coverage and frequency of the campaign. Advertisers want to achieve the greatest coverage and most frequent impacts of their target audience at the lowest cost. To guarantee national coverage advertisers need to reach a certain threshold of advertising spend. In the early 1990s that threshold of spend was around £700,000 for a TV campaign, and £200,000 for a national poster campaign (this is after discounting on the rate cards). For the best spots and positions, however, the sums would increase substantially.

Costs of production, especially for TV and cinema commercials, can also be a factor, as can the availability of technology, such as colour reproduction, movement and sound.

The media planner also needs to be aware of current campaigns and media use of the brand's competitors. The choice of media can also be determined by the objectives of the campaign. If there is a need to stimulate action, for instance, direct mail and direct response, with freepost envelopes, or cut-out coupons in newspaper ads, are easier facilitators of action than cinema ads. Or to stimulate trial, door drops for free trial or money-off vouchers may be used. But if the objectives are image building, maybe cinema ads, posters and TV would work better. If it is a new product that needs to be demonstrated, such as a new type of hair grip that styles hair in a particular way, it may be necessary to show how it works on TV (as a convenience product). Another campaign may be based on the sound of a screw cap twisting off a bottle, which may work best on radio. Or, as with food advertising, a full colour print ad may work better.

It may also depend on the type of consumer the advertiser is after and whether there is available media for them. If an advertiser wants to target all divorced women it may have to use the mass media, if no niche media are available: this will directly affect the budgeting strategy. A manufacturer of consumer durables may need a medium that can convey detailed information and PR support, whereas an FMCG manufacturer may need to put more into sales promotion. Also, a new product launch may need media that can deliver greatest coverage, whereas a brand leader may want to use media that can easily remind consumers. An advertiser may also have different sets of consumers in mind: a computer manufacturer, for instance, may want to launch a brand campaign to stimulate the interest of non-users, and a specialist press campaign to target users and enthusiasts.

Though there are occasions when a sanpro advertiser may develop different campaigns for a young women's magazine and an older women's magazine, this is still quite rare. Most advertisers, for reasons of cost, will produce one or maybe two executions of the ad which will adapt the size and length to different media. But 'Often no attempt is made to adapt the advertising approach or advertising language to different audiences; identical ads appear in popular and "quality" publications, in publications of different regional circulations, and in publications of specialised and general interest' (Leech 1966: 63–64). Leech's comment is still as valid today as it was then.

Media plans are usually constructed to cover a year-long campaign. They are made with the client to discuss timing and make sure that the campaign fits in with the rest of the marketing mix: especially to make sure the supermarkets and retail outlets have sufficient stocks (see Red Rock in Chapter 4).

The media planner is given information on the advertising target consumer: this would include who uses the brand, who uses competitors' brands, who buys it, who influences the purchasing decision – parents, friends, experts, scientists, doctors, dentists, pharmacists and hairdressers (this also influences the creative brief). The media planner would then draw up a map of media audiences which would achieve the greatest coverage of the advertising target at the lowest price, based upon media research.

Several plans are usually devised which approximate to the overall sum involved. If the budget is overspent, the media planners can reduce the size of the ad, or the length; the number of commercials could be reduced, or the campaign period cut down. A final solution is to drop one of the media off the schedule. This happened a great deal in the early 1990s as the recession began to bite: certain media, in particular newspapers and magazines, were being dropped from schedules so that advertisers could keep up their presence on TV as their budgets were being cut back.

Coverage, frequency and media availability

Coverage is the number of the target market reached, frequency is the number of times they are reached. Media planners have to balance the two to achieve the objectives of the campaign; create awareness, shift attitudes, etc., within the constraints of costs.

Coverage is usually measured in Average Issue Readerships (AIRs) in print and in TV Ratings (TVRs) in TV. A TVR is the predicted size of a programme's audience as a percentage of the relevant population size. Advertisers add up the total ratings for their ad slots to give their total TVR: for instance, a commercial in the middle of a programme might achieve twenty rating points, but would have to repeat the number of spots to reach its target TVRs. If a programme achieved only five or ten or up to forty rating points the buyer would have to calculate how many times it was needed to transmit to achieve the coverage necessary. The buyer would need to know how many times the target audience would need to view the commercial for it to be effective. Ratings for ads are given in the minute for which the ad started and are given in minutes. Media buyers are perceived to have performed well if they achieve their target TVRs at low cost. But this is not a measure of effectiveness, only buying performance. Ratings are acknowledged to be inappropriate tools for measuring advertising effectiveness, only for buying effectiveness.

Frequency is often measured in OTS (Opportunities to See). If you go past an outdoor site every day on your way to work over a four-week period, you would have twenty OTS that advertisement (presuming that you cannot see the ad on the way back from work). Frequency is not just about getting the prospective consumer to see several of your commercials but also to get them to see the press ad, the poster, to hear the radio commercial and see the point-of-sale material. For this reason media buyers purposely buy space in media that overlap. Many women buy two or three weekly magazines. A media plan would try to target this type of multiple buyer by having the same ads in each, increasing the chance of hitting the consumer. If a magazine has very low dual purchase, this means that the readership is much more exclusive: a media planner may put it on the schedule to increase penetration, rather than keep hitting the same readers. The main factor limiting repetition is cost; the *Daily Telegraph* bought TV air time in only six regions because it was not economically worth its while to advertise in all fifteen (see example in Postscript).

For years big advertisers such as Procter & Gamble put out the same ads on the principle that dominating the market with repetitive advertising encouraged people to believe in the omnipotence of the brand. The Mr Shifter commercial for PG Tips was in the *Guinness Book of Records* for the longest-running single commercial (this is largely because the ad was seen as lightly humorous and pleasurable to watch). The longer-lasting commercials tend to be those that include children and animals. However, even for advertisers who need to repeat, it is important to have fresh executions – new treatments of existing themes – so as not to bore audiences. Most repeat purchase advertisers provide new execution within a repeat campaign. One of the most famous repeat campaigns which reiterated the main themes was Heineken, with its humorous variations on 'Heineken refreshes the parts other beers cannot reach'. The main principle of this is to maintain consistency with difference. In 1998 Heineken changed the strapline of this ad to 'How refreshing, how Heineken' but retained the same humorous theme of the advertising: that drinking Heineken makes unusual things happen. One TV ad featured building workers who were being polite and one poster campaign which featured at Christmas and was withdrawn after protests featured Joseph with his head sticking out of the stable door shouting, 'It's a girl!'.

Different media are understood to have different levels of coverage and frequency. If an advertiser had a fixed sum of £2 million and wanted to target all adults, it might get a TV coverage of 80 per cent with a frequency of 3.5X, whereas with newspapers it might be 85 per cent with 4X frequency, with posters 60 per cent coverage and 20X frequency, with radio low coverage of 50 per cent with high frequency 16X, and with cinema low coverage 20 per cent and low frequency 2X.

Frequency is not always a consideration. Apple Computer made a one-off ad during the Superbowl which was intended to gain maximum impact and media exposure, and to generate media chatter. In this context the single ad reached a large audience, increased by newspapers covering the ad as an event. A series of ads would have had less effect.

The problem generally, though, for media planners is trying to pick up those viewers who did not see the commercial the first time. Several repeats are necessary for this reason, especially when targeting light viewers of TV. Housewives are the easiest to target (because so much media is geared towards them); young men are difficult to target (not big media consumers). Advertising textbooks recommend that the first priority of a campaign should be coverage, and that the threshold for targets that are easy to reach should be around 75–80 per cent of the total population, whereas for more difficult groups the coverage should be around 65 per cent and then the campaign should increase in frequency (White 1988: 101). Media planning is difficult in a recession because of the level of discounting and special deals. When an advertiser is offered a specially targeted medium at the same price as a volume-led medium which actually offers more coverage and is cheaper, the advertiser finds it extremely difficult not to include it in the schedule.

National newspapers are 'nationals' only in terms of availability. Their sales tend to be concentrated in certain areas of the country: the *Sun*, for instance, is primarily concentrated in the south of England, whereas the *Daily Mirror* is strongest in the north. The *Independent* is concentrated around London and the south-east, and the *Financial Times* around London and financial cities across Europe. Newspapers tend to offer high levels of coverage (based on average issue readership – see Chapter 9) and high levels of frequency.

Outdoor advertising offers high OTS, but its coverage is very low among the housebound and in rural areas and cathedral towns (where outdoor ads are sometimes banned to preserve the 'picturesque' appeal). However, they are good for reaching ABC1s in certain areas, and those who are not big consumers of the broadcast media (TV radio and cinema) – this includes financial executives and managers. Two of the biggest users of outdoor media in London are *The Economist* and the *Financial Times*. The problem with a poster is that though it generally has high frequency, its cover may be limiting, the same commuters seeing it every day. To get round this problem contractors rotate the campaigns around different sites to increase cover.

In 1946 cinema attendances were 635 million. In the early 1950s they reached more than one billion, but by 1984 had fallen to 54 million. This was due partly to the increased availability of home entertainment, TV, radio and video, but also to cinema outlets that were badly maintained and low in number. With the development of satellite, cable and computer games, the industry should have collapsed altogether. Hollywood, and cinema chains fought back by massively increasing promotional budgets and controlling the home video market, with home video and cinema cross-promoting releases (Butler in Kent 1994: 181). The cinema chains consolidated and merged and launched multiplex cinemas

Figure 8.1 The Economist: The campaign plays on the instantly recognisable font and colour of *The Economist* masthead. It uses gentle humour that highlights the cache of the brand as well as emphasising that the magazine is read by top decision-makers. © *The Economist* newspaper. Agency: AMV BBDO.

across the UK which by 2000 accounted for over 60 per cent of the total. By 2000 cinema attendances had also increased to around 140 million a year. The result has been a wider use of cinema advertising, though restricted to certain markets such as spirits (gin, liqueurs, etc.) and local ads.

Audience figures are highly dependent on film reviews, the amount of marketing, the time of year and the weather. TV programming can also affect films: the World Cup and programmes aimed at the core of the audiences (fifteen to twenty-four-year-olds pre-family) can also hit attendances.

Extremes of temperature can keep audience levels down. Children's films are deliberately targeted for release during the school holiday period to gain greater admissions. Though the gender balance is roughly fifty-fifty with cinema audiences, in terms of age it is very different. Whereas the total population has 17 per cent aged 15 to 24, the cinema audience has 55 per cent from this group, and whereas the population has 64 per cent over 35, the cinema audience has only 21 per cent.

Most local commercial radio stations aim at young working-class listeners, C2DEs aged 15 to 25. Older people are progressively less likely to listen.

But the launch of 'Gold' stations, which feature easy listening and 1960s music for 40–50-year-olds, in the late 1980s contributed to a change in the profile of audience delivery, 57 per cent coverage for those between 35 and 54. Radio offered agencies the possibility of reaching light viewers and readers. The problem with ILR was that it delivered low coverage (local medium, largely young C2DEs) but high frequency. In 1992 there were 120 stations delivering 22.5 million a week (3.2 million listeners a day). By 2000 the growth in new national stations and the emergence of targeted local stations helped radio increase its share of advertising revenue from 2 per cent to 4 per cent of the total.

ILR's benefit is that it is local, not regional; retailers (especially car dealers) often want certain conurbations, rather than whole regions. Radio competes head-on with local evening papers for news stories. Regional evening newspapers have extended their use of multiple editions into the afternoons, to try to compete with the more up to date radio news. Sports coverage, live match commentaries and sports personality interviews, as well as up to the minute scores, have kept high male audience figures and helped to close many local evening papers' pink newspapers on Saturdays.

Between 1978 and 1992 the total circulation of daily morning newspapers fell by 20 per cent, evenings by 23 per cent and paid-for weeklies by 40 per cent. The main reasons why sales have fallen are demographic changes (people moving away from the traditional catchment areas) and competition from frees for regional paid-fors, as well as price increases. Free newspapers came from nowhere in 1970 to take 36 per cent of regional press advertising by 1991.

Local free newspapers can offer precise targeting with inserts in their papers placed in key estates and villages. Directories and databases have also started to eat into the local classified market, but an even greater threat comes from local cable television.

Media use and technology

Media planners need to consider the technological possibilities of each medium, and how consumers make use of them. National and local newspapers and consumer and business magazines are space-based media. They have the benefit of a physical presence. People can re-read articles, cut things out, collect them for reference. They can also be read and consumed in many places: on the train, in the bath, in the toilet and at work. They are not dedicated information or entertainment media. Consumers often buy them when they are looking for a new house, job, car or second-hand furniture. This has the advantage for advertisers of more predisposed consumers. However, sectionalisation in newspapers and a decline in brand loyalty have led to a decrease in the number of people who read the whole paper, and an increase in 'grazers': those who read only certain sections of a paper and completely ignore others. Readers can skip through items in space-based media and completely ignore whole sections, such as sports or business.

For years magazines benefited from having full-colour reproduction, thus keeping key advertisers such as food, drinks, cosmetics and fashion advertisers to themselves. When colour came to TV in 1969 commercials began to focus on high production values and began to eat into the colour magazine and poster advertising markets. 'Appetite appeal' – using full-colour moving pictures of chocolate pouring over caramel, or roast lamb being sliced – was now a TV asset (Bernstein 1986: 271). National newspapers first extended their brands into glossy colour supplements in the 1960s, and later in the 1980s all the national Sunday newspapers developed full-colour glossy magazines to attract these key advertisers from magazines and TV. The use of on-the-run colour, however, has meant that glossy colour supplements have increasingly become redundant and an expensive way of keeping colour advertisers in the paper. The *Observer* folded its colour magazine into a newsprint tabloid in April 1994.

The magazines industry has responded to this technological onslaught on its market by convincing media buyers that it is 'common sense' that women's monthlies have more loyal readers than colour supplements and TV. They have convinced media planners and buyers that magazines have a 'special relationship' with their readers by using qualitative research. Similarly, radio sells itself as an intimate medium, often listened to when people are on their own (in the car, doing housework, getting ready to go out). The industry sells to advertisers the idea that it is a friend or companion to the listener, and that they can share in this intimacy – though it has been less successful than other media in attracting advertisers on this basis.

Improvements in printing technology and lower print costs after the defeat of the print unions in the mid-1980s meant that newspapers could also produce highly regionalised editions and allow inserts in the papers, eating into regional newspaper markets. The resulting increase in newspaper pagination also allowed some nationals to expand their classified coverage to eat into the circulation of trade magazines (the *Evening Standard*, the *Guardian* with *Media Guardian*, *Education Guardian*, etc.).

Methods of distribution also affect media use. A newsstand circulation is perceived to be most valuable, because the consumer actively goes into a shop and buys a paper or magazine to read. A subscription copy, on the other hand, is mailed to the consumer, and although it is paid for (often at a discount) there is less chance that it is always read. The least liked and trusted distribution method for advertisers is unsolicited controlled circulation. This is most common among business magazines. Though it offers tighter targeting of consumers (e.g. all GPs), the magazines generally have a much smaller readership than their circulation, because they may be seen as junk mail and never opened. Controlled circulation magazines gain revenue from advertising, not from sales.

Time-based media such as TV and radio are generally consumed for information and entertainment. They were not traditionally consumed for advertising messages. Because of this, commercials can be much more intrusive because they break up the programmes. Cinema and TV commercials have the advantage of movement and sound, allowing the product to be demonstrated and providing more impact. Time-based advertising can also be repeated to achieve greater impact and increase memorability, as well as reaching a wider audience.

Traditional time-based media have less potential interactivity than space-based media.

The emergence of digital TV in the late 1990s and the growth of the Internet allowed an unprecendented degree of interactivity with consumers that broke down traditional space-time issues for advertisers. Consumers were able to access commercials whenever they wanted, not only when sat at the PC or digital TV but also via mobile phones using WAP technology or mobile phone text messages.

The most important effect on media consumption is how it fits in to work and leisure patterns. The most important and expensive TV spots are during peak time when the greatest number of people are watching (between 6 p.m. and 10 p.m.). Other important times of the day are breakfast, before people go to work or school, and daytime when 'housewives' and women with babies are at home. Radio can be background noise. It can be listened to almost anywhere (in the bath, in the car), while at work (at hairdressers, at home in the day), on building sites and in shops. Radio's peak time is the morning. Morning radio audiences have been eroded by breakfast TV.

The cinema is a dedicated entertainment environment. Viewers are considered to be in the right frame of mind to view entertaining ads. Though they have come to watch the film, there is less media and information clutter. Feature films are not interrupted by intrusive ads.

Though outdoor advertising is space-based, it is often seen only for a fleeting moment while passing in a car. The main communications messages have to grab attention rather than elicit concentration (like a cinema ad). At bus shelters, train and underground stations and airports people are waiting and have more time to study ads, so the copy tends to be longer. Poster audiences are affected by hours of daylight. Because of this the cheapest months for outdoor advertising tend to be January and February; the most expensive May, June and July. Only the illuminated 6-sheet bus shelter sites and neon signs keep their price in deepest winter (Harrison 1993: 25). With TV the opposite is true: people tend to stay in on the darker nights and watch TV. A co-ordinated seasonal campaign may use TV in the winter months and switch to posters in the summer to maintain coverage. Posters are often combined with TV, cinema and press campaigns because this offers continuous presence. Because posters are often near to shopping areas, they provide one of the last links for advertisers to the buying decision.

According to advertising folklore two-thirds of purchasing decisions are made at the point of sale. This is the only media environment in which advertising does not depend on the consumer remembering the ad the following day or week, but recognising it immediately. In-store media include end-of-aisle displays, brochures, catalogues, leaflets, packaging, window stickers, posters, trolley ads, videos, radio jingles, wire stands, banners and dummy packs, instruction manuals; together with beer mats, towels and ashtrays in pubs. Aeroplanes are also a selling environment, with in-flight videos and magazines selling goods to holidaymakers.

Traditional media act as surrogates for advertising. The media audience for TV, newspapers and radio generally consumes these media for editorial content first and foremost. For this reason, the media audience for these surrogate media will always be distinct from the brand's target audience. With direct mail there is far less wastage. It goes to selected homes, often personally addressed to the consumer, or to certain select groups using geodemographics. However, it generally has a very low response rate, largely because of the perception that it is junk mail. Much of it is thrown-away unopened (though such consumers may not be the ones that direct mailers want anyway).

Advertisers also create their own media. Exhibitions and conferences can be used as a platform to demonstrate goods to potential consumers. The consumers are generally in the frame of mind to look at the goods. They also tend to get editorial coverage. Advertisers will target appropriate exhibitions and events such as the Annual Boat Show, or the Ideal Home Exhibition, to associate the brand with them. Merchandising material such as pens, balloons (for the kids or for exhibition purposes), badges, calendars and wall charts is also produced to support exhibitions and other events. With T-shirts, sweatshirts, baseball caps, pullovers, umbrellas and sun-visors, people become the medium for the advertising message.

Weight and timing of advertising: burst versus drip

Once the media planner has decided upon the coverage, frequency and most appropriate media technology, she or he then has to decide upon the weight and timing of the campaign. The schedule may depend on seasonal sales, for such things as ice cream or chocolate bars, garden furniture or holidays. Or if everybody else in the market throws their advertising weight into the pre-Christmas period, an advertiser may get an advantage by advertising earlier in

September or October, or even in the summer months to gain high awareness before the Christmas push.

Traditionally, demand for television advertising rises rapidly before Christmas and drops rapidly in January. One sector where this occurs is alcoholic drinks. According to AC Nielsen MMS research for 1999 to 2000 drinks advertisers spent a total of £28 million on TV advertising in December 1999. In January 2000 this fell to £6 million and in February to £7 million (*Media Week*, 4 August 2000: 35).

Advertisers tend to stagger their spend over different media and to increase or decrease it seasonally. There are two terms used to describe the weight of advertising impact. 'Burst' campaigns are often used for new products with high coverage and frequency; 'drip' campaigns are for a more staggered effect, achieving low coverage and frequency.

Bursts involve concentrated spend in one short time period (say two or three weeks) using a range of media with high frequency. Drip campaigns are staggered over a number of months, building up coverage and using fairly low frequency, to remind consumers of the brand's attributes. Drip advertising is often used for reminder campaigns and for trying to change longer-term attitudes. This helps to chip away at resistance to the brand and establishes its dominance by its long-term presence in the market. Generally, advertisers admit that most advertising messages are extremely forgettable. Because of this, advertisers tend to select a heavy burst of advertising for a short period of time to raise awareness and give a dominant presence to a new brand, new improved formula, or new promotion. Bursts can also generate media chatter.

Most advertisers hedge their bets and do a combination of the two, bursting occasionally and dripping in between. Media planners work on the principles that the greatest effect of the advertising is just after it is seen. Advertisers are generally unsure about how advertising works; they only have highly selective case studies to base their media planning judgements on. The Prudential, for example, often runs mixed media campaigns, using posters after every burst of TV. After the TV burst, the awareness of the brand often falls away dramatically. Media planners call this 'decay'. Posters were used to sustain awareness when the TV campaign was not running.

Media planners can vary the campaign by using different sizes of ad at different times in the publication. In outdoor advertising this is done frequently with 6-sheet, 48-sheet and 96-sheet ads. TV commercials are also varied in length, or may use top-and-tailing (coming at the beginning and end of the break) for impact. Top and tail ads, such as for the Renault Laguna, are used to help the advertisement stand out, they dominate the whole break, and are intended to use media buying to raise awareness. They are also very expensive. Constantly changing ads and executions adds to their 'newsiness', and gives the impression that the advertiser is constantly changing and on the ball. The size and length of the commercial can also be used to dominate; 96-sheet posters and 60-second commercials can make an announcement, launch a brand

and impress retailers to stock the product; then the advertiser will revert to smaller sizes. Sometimes the reverse is done, as part of a 'teaser' campaign with the dominant advertisement left until the end.

The implementational plan: choosing between media

Once the media strategy has been decided, the media buying schedule can change substantially from the original. The implementational media plan, which involves decisions between media, is decided by the media planner or buyer. Agencies like to have people who can plan and buy campaigns as they are negotiating because the media advertising market changes so quickly. A new media launch, a sharp decline in readership or circulation, or a new package deal by a media owner can change the plan substantially. Most media plans are made with contingency money in reserve in case a new opportunity arises or something newsworthy happens that the brand may want to associate with. The competitive nature of the market means that others can pre-empt on TV and a competitor may pull ads or start an unexpected campaign at the last minute. The media planner or buyer needs to be able to know whether a space in one magazine or paper would be better somewhere else if the buyer were prepared to make a bigger discount.

Separate plans would be drawn up to include specific publications or stations, any special positions, the cost and number of insertions or spots required and the dates of appearance. A separate TV schedule would show the region the length of commercial (10, 20 or 30 seconds, possibly 60 seconds) and the time segments (time of day and programme); it would also include the cost for each transmission and the total cost and transmission dates (Davis 1992: 256).

The cost of space and time is determined by a number of factors: first, what the rest of the market is paying; second, the size and nature of the audience; third, where the ad will appear (at the beginning, middle or end of a break, in between programmes or during a programme), whether it is facing relevant editorial copy in a print ad, etc., how much time and space are bought, and whether it is included in a package. In some cases the media owner may offer lower rates for larger ads because they want to encourage more use of the medium.

Media planners or buyers traditionally compare the relative costs of delivering audience of each publication or station on the basis of its cost per thousand members of the target audience. This approach works best where delivering the greatest volume of the target market is important, rather than the appropriateness of the environment. It is calculated on the basis of the rate card price divided by the projected numbers, divided by 1,000. In 2000, the cost per thousand for *Cosmopolitan* was £8.44, *She* £11.41, *Prima* £13.40, *Company* £14.27 and *Harpers & Queen* £18.67. These are only rate card figures and do not reflect the real cost per thousand (CPT). They are also based upon the total readerships, not on the possible target market of, say, 18- to 25-year-old women, in which case the CPT would be much higher. Similarly in ITV, London TV programmes cost more for every thousand viewers than Border TV or Ulster, because there are more high-spending ABC1 viewers in that area.

Advertisers try to minimise wastage by using media with higher levels of concentration of target audiences. The *Sun* is a mass circulation paper, the *Financial Times* is a low circulation, high AB profile paper. The latter had only 2.9 per cent of the total ABC1 readership in the UK in 1993, but the ABC1 profile of the paper was 90.4 per cent. The *Sun*, however, has 12.7 per cent penetration of the entire ABC1 population, but this is only 29 per cent of the *Sun*'s total readership. Financial and corporate advertisers would use the *FT* rather than the *Sun*, because the *FT* offers the right environment (AB people read the *Sun* for entertainment, not for personal finance information). Also, a financial company would be wasting a large amount of its money. In 1994 the cost of a full-colour page in the *FT* was £37,200; in the *Sun* it cost £34,500. Though the *Sun* offers much better coverage and penetration of the ABC1 market, the low ABC1 profile means high wastage and an inappropriate environment for ABC1 advertisers.

Some costs per thousand include not only the value for money at cost, but also qualitative 'media weights'. This may mean colour availability, or quality of editorial. Advertising planners enumerate these extra values to produce a Valued Impressions per Pound (VIP) rating. This is based on a numerical estimation of value (including quality of editorial, production, etc.), multiplied by the media audience divided by the cost. The *FT* on this basis would come out ahead of the *Sun*.

The cost of a larger and or longer commercial has to be considered in terms of its extra effectiveness. According to research done in the early part of the century into response rates for print advertisements, for every one hundred replies to a full page ad (next to editorial), a half-page ad elicited sixty-eight replies, a quarter-page forty-nine, and a double-page 141 (Bird 1993: 140). This research has been repeated since with similar results. If this is so, then a quarter-page advertisement is twice as useful for direct response as a full page. The cost would suggest effectiveness of 175 per cent, whereas the results from direct response ads show that the actual effectiveness is only 141 per cent. On this basis advertisers are losing out by 35 per cent by buying a double-page spread. According to this rule, the smaller the ad in national newspapers the more cost-effective it may be. Two half-page ads giving 65 per cent coverage each may be more cost-effective than a full-page ad giving 100 per cent.

Because of perceived decline in effectiveness as the ad size gets over a certain level, the cost per square centimetre tends to decline as the ad gets bigger (White 1988: 131).

The mechanics of buying and selling

Media sales representatives are given certain sectors and agencies to work on. Display salespeople go to agencies to make presentations on behalf of their publication or media. Classified salespeople do virtually all their dealing over the phone. Sales reps need to keep aware of which advertisers are starting campaigns and who will want to get on schedules. In TV the sponsorship seller lets the buyer know about the marketable features of the programme and would try to sell those valuable to the client. A buyer described how the programme is sold: 'For the drama series, . . . ABC1 working women are the market, and the drama will emphasise female independence and sexual aggression. Those are the values on sale: the likely sponsors are in perfume, cosmetics and fashion' (Holliday 1993: 16).

The sales department may also have field reps, for instance in the regions or internationally, or a division which sells advertorials and supplements or special features. Many sales departments now have sections dealing directly with the client rather than just through agencies. This cuts out the middle agencies, who miss out on commission.

The rate card is usually set at the start of the year. The rate card price will be set on the penetration of particular markets, the profile of the paper and also whether there are extra values such as high brand loyalty, prestige and authority. The advertisement director or manager would have the ultimate decision about the kinds of discounts allowed to advertisers.

Discounting will be low if there is strong demand (pre-Christmas) or if there are only a few alternative places to advertise. For nearly thirty years ITV had no commercial TV rival: this helped to keep prices high.

Newspapers offer discounts for a variety of reasons: to attract new types of advertisers (such as perfume advertisers) to the medium, to try to undercut competitors, to bring in big prestigious brands (building profile), or simply and most often because they are desperate for the advertising revenue in a buyer's market. This occurred a great deal in the late 1980s and early 1990s when some very famous and established national newspapers were known to be offering discounts of between 65 per cent and 80 per cent to advertisers to fill space. If a newspaper has to cut back on the amount of advertising in its columns, it is obvious to anybody in the industry that they are having difficulties: the effect is spiralling ad rates, as further dealers try to force them down even more.

Advertising is bought in different units. Newspaper advertising is sold by the single column centimetre; the length in centimetres is multiplied by the number of columns. Magazines on the other hand are sold by fractions of a page (half page, quarter page, full page, etc.), TV and radio are sold by time and Internet banner ads are sold by estimated page impressions. With publications, invariably the editorial will be made to fit space created by advertisements (ads pay for more pages to be printed). The advertising people and production on senior editorial agree a flat plan which demarcates the amount of advertising in the next issues. Orders include the size, position, cost and discounts for the booked space, checked against the flat plan to see if it is available. In TV the sales reps have time registers showing booking positions for commercial breaks.

When ads are booked on a run-of-paper basis, it is left to the media to decide where the ads go. The more expensive, special positions are right-hand columns, front half of publication, inside back cover, special sections and supplements, front page, right-hand page, or for facing matter, where the ad faces editorial copy: the reader is supposed to spend longer reading the editorial and cannot skip over the advertising pages. As White pointed out in 1988, media buying in magazines is subject to many dubious myths: 'rate cards charge premiums for specifying certain propositions of this type and many advertisers subscribe to the various myths' (White 1988: 140). This is still true. Newspapers generally charge up to 80 per cent extra for special positions.

Many advertisers agree to buy space or time across a series of issues. A series rate is lower than the sum of the ads together. Series bookings are good for media owners because they save in costs of hiring salespeople, and having a more concentrated number of agencies to deal with helps to reduce overheads. In 1992 Channel 4 managed to negotiate six top car advertisers for campaigns in 1993 for about 25 per cent of their 1993 budgets up front. Group bookings (where the ads are booked across a group of titles) are also used by the media owner, as are volume bookings (where a large amount of space or time is guaranteed to the media owner in return for a discount (this occurs especially in TV). Volume deals are usually over the year or longer in TV, and are based on spending over a certain amount. Series deals are based on number of ads, volume deals on the amount spent. Advertisement sellers have two basic strategies for selling. The first is to gain volume through series bookings and volume deals with discounts to maintain market share; the other is on a yield basis, which is to deal 'line by line' (individually), to gain the greatest amount of money for each ad.

Because TV has a fixed supply (fixed by licences and regulations), the imperative for TV is to deal on the basis of volume and share. A TV company will negotiate with a major advertiser such as Unilever to get a bigger share of their total advertising budget. This is often done on the TV company's overall share of the market. If the company had, say, 9 per cent of the total ITV share for a major FMCG company, and the latter said that it would increase that TV company's share of the advertiser's overall ITV spend to 10 per cent of the ITV market, the advertiser would expect a reward in the form of a discount from the ITV company for the increase in share. Where advertising deals (series, groups and volume) take place, they often involve top-level negotiations between the media owner and the client because of the sums involved (e.g. Ford and Hachette; Unilever and TVS).

The ITV companies are forced to compete against each other for share. London-based Carlton TV would expect to get the biggest share of most big-brand advertisers' budget, whereas a smaller station such as Border would expect to get a smaller proportion than its overall ratings would suggest, because of this system. This type of dealing makes rate cards in TV fairly obsolete.

Rates are only ever fixed when special rates are introduced for events such as the World Cup.

Demand for ITV in the 1980s led to the short-term pre-empt system, where another advertiser can take over a commercial slot at short notice with a higher bid. This helped to force up the cost of TV air time. But it was also costly in terms of the resources of the sales staff and overheads, etc. in negotiating deals. As mentioned above, it is far easier to fix long-term deals and cheaper on staffing and costs than to be constantly renegotiating.

In TV rate cards are usually published twice a year, and the day is divided into segments. The day is divided into all-time (6 a.m. to 5 a.m. the following day), breakfast (6 a.m. to 9.30 a.m.), pre-peak (9.30 a.m. to 6 p.m.) peak (6 p.m. to 10.30 p.m.) and late (10.30 p.m. to 5 a.m.).

Stations offer Guaranteed Home Impressions (GHIs), which involves the station placing the commercials where and when they like to reach the required TVRs. Media buyers can also take selected spots. The term 'spot advertising' denotes that the advertiser occupies a spot in the commercial break and is bought on a station(s)-by-station(s) basis rather than via a network. Peak spots – those at the beginning and end of a commercial break during peak-time viewing – generally command the highest prices. Start breaks and end breaks of ads are very important to buyers. For instance, between *Emmerdale* and *Coronation Street* on a weekday evening, the start break (first commercial in the break) would pick up a larger proportion of *Emmerdale* viewers, but by the end of the break (the end break) a commercial would be picking up a larger proportion of *Coronation Street* viewers. Obviously a large proportion of TV viewers would continue watching, but many would switch over to another channel, or switch to *Coronation Street* from another channel. Whereabouts the ad appears in the break affects the TVRs it receives. Advertisers have to pay more for special positions or for 'top and tailing' at the beginning and the end of an advertisement break.

Special rates are often offered to local advertisers and first-time advertisers. Special discounts are offered for volume dealing and for booking early. TV contractors also offer special packages for test marketing along with sales promotion and merchandising support. Because there is so much demand for TV advertising, air time tends to be booked well in advance. Cancellations are usually not allowed later than eight weeks before transmitting or the agency or advertiser is liable. If an ad has to be cancelled, the agency can transfer the air time to another agency.

Media owners also offer discounts to advertisers in return for exclusivity. In the early 1990s the Office of Fair Trading investigated several famous media owners, including London's Capital Radio, after complaints that it had offered discounts of up to 25 per cent if other London stations were left off clients' schedules. Several national newspaper groups and magazine houses were also known to offer such deals.

Most media, especially radio, cinema, regional newspapers and regional TV, have separate production departments which produce ads. They also have merchandising departments to provide cheap below-the-line support for advertisers. Sellers also commission their own research to try to change the way buyers view their media. These extra services increase the costs of attracting advertisers to the media.

Once ads go in they have to be checked in case they are not in the right place or have gone in back to front, otherwise the advertiser is entitled to a rebate. The final check should also make sure that there is no bad positioning against editorial such as an ad for airlines next to a plane crash – Zenith made this mistake when it bought time for British Airways during an aeroplane disaster movie on Carlton TV (*Campaign*, 17 September 1993: 3). The media owners then invoice the agencies, specifying the discount and the size and position of the ad booked. The agencies obtain voucher copies of all the magazines and newspapers to check that their ads appeared correctly. If the printing is not right or a poster has been damaged, the media owner will be expected to pay back some of the money. In the past agencies used to have their own team of poster monitors who would check sites across the country. However, this has been cut back, and poster contractors monitor their own sites.

Evaluation

Different media take different lengths of time to be consumed. TV is instant, newspapers over several hours of the day, weekly magazines any time over a week, and so on for monthlies, etc. The product may be regarded as a medium in itself for the brand's attributes, being seen more frequently than the media. Media are also consumed in different environments: TV in the home, cinema in a hall, newspapers at work, on the train etc., radio at home and in cars. They also take different forms – visual, audio, movement-based, etc. Because of this it is extremely difficult to make a comparative evaluation.

As part of the control process, media planners evaluate likely results of their campaigns. Media buyers develop theories of media use which help to evaluate likely outcomes and future projections. Evaluation involves estimating OTS, TVRs and penetration levels and inferring from past experience how these will translate in terms of impacts. TV has an information advantage over the press. Actual spots will have breakdowns of audience size and share eight days afterwards. For newspapers the NRS has monthly breakdowns. This difference is largely because consumption of TV is confined to the home, whereas newspapers are consumed in many locations and are harder to monitor.

Agencies use computer systems to evaluate the likely outcomes of campaigns. The systems work by using past data from BARB (see Chapter 9) for seasonality to predict the size and structure of the audience. To plan for January 2003, it would use January 2002 data.

The computer selects the best spots and prepares a schedule on the back of it. Before this had been calculated by the planner. The schedule would be based on cover, frequency and the target audience, using BARB data. The systems also use other factors because of the differences between audiences for certain programmes year on year. A planner also needs to be aware that ratings may increase for one week if the plot of *Coronation Street* changes, or as happened with *Emmerdale* when half the village was wiped out by a plane crash.

The planning systems give a best guide to the spots that would be 'most likely' to provide the required coverage for the target audience. Forecasting is a very inexact and cumbersome process which needs some level of professional or skilful knowledge on the part of the forecaster. Advertisers have access to broadcasting schedules considerably in advance, so that ads can be, and often are, booked and prepared to appear in specific programmes.

However, the unexpected can occur. Better programmes on the BBC will affect viewing figures for ITV. Just as in the 1950s, media planners or buyers have to study the BBC schedules to see which BBC programmes might reduce audiences on the date in question. The weather is also a significant factor.

A great deal of media buying is done on the basis of an intuitive under-standing of the media: buyers do not know how long an ideal advertising campaign should run for – they use established practice or case studies as evidence; they do not know how many times a commercial should be shown to be effective – though three times is the general guide; they do not know what makes consumers buy goods, or form opinions – though since the Second World War they have used psychology, cultural studies, econometrics and soci-ology to try to find out. To address the unmeasurable aspects of their business all media planners use past information to plan campaigns. Media planners have to guess whether the programmes they have bought space for will have the same viewing patterns as last time, or as similar programmes. They employ folklore beliefs in the use of consistent logo or brand-name, the same colours and pack design that produce synergism or familiarising; keeping the brand familiar to consumers. There is no evidence to suggest that this influences buying decisions or makes people feel more favourable towards the brand. The principle of dominance is similar. Dominating the market or the media space is an intuitive guarantee of success. It works in one sense by crowding out the opposition, but is also seen as having a pseudo-psychological effect on the consumer: say it big, say it loud and say it often.

Summary

The main purpose of media planning is to reach the maximum number of target consumers at the least cost. When a media planner makes a decision on which medium to use she or he should take into account the different costs; techno-logical possibilities; the campaign objectives; the environment in which it is consumed; the coverage and frequency of the medium and individual station or publication; the required weight of the campaign. Advertising agency media planners play a key role in the advertising relationship as the gatekeepers of market knowledge. They classify and systematise knowledge in a powerful way to reinforce the role of the agency with advertisers. The use of technical language, and advertising jargon such as OTS, DPS, TVRs, CPTs, also sets up this exclusivity and idea of manageability. The advertisers' trade association, ISBA, has tried to demystify the media planning and buying process, explaining the jargon, practices and knowledge of the agency business to its members and producing a series of 'Best Practice' guides. This is part of a wider challenge to advertising agency legitimacy in recent years (see Postscript).

9 Media research

Controlling media research: the JIC principle

Media research, like all forms of research, needs to have the confidence of its users. Although the methodology of the collection of data may be flawed, and many of the figures and statistics inaccurate, as most are, a consensus needs to be reached that the measurement is fair and objective.

The first Joint Industry Committee (JIC) began in 1956 after the collapse of the Hulton Readership survey, a regular readership survey of national newspapers and magazines providing readership data for agencies. A year before, the survey had been taken over by Associated Newspapers (publishers of the *Daily Mail*). The methodology was 'changed', resulting in a huge over-reporting of newspapers. The average readership of dailies increased by 30 per cent, Sundays 13 per cent, women's weeklies were down 5 per cent and monthlies down 20 per cent. The following year the advertisers and agencies decided to set up a joint funded body to oversee the methodology and pay the running costs of the industry currency.

Similarly, the Joint Industry Committee for Radio Audience Research (JICRAR) (established 1974) was entirely funded and controlled by commercial radio companies. JICRAR and the BBC had competing research surveys with wildly conflicting listening figures. The JICRAR method of researching listening patterns for commercial radio involved the use of stimulus cards.

Respondents were asked if they had listened to any of the specified radio stations within a given period of time and for how long they listened, etc. Commercial radio stations, unlike BBC ones, were allowed to put their own logos on the cards. The logo might include slogans such as Radio City FM's 'The best music mix', to help increase recognisability. The heavily marketed and branded radio stations did particularly well with this system; because people recognised them, they said they had listened to the station even though they often had not.

In 1991 the BBC and the commercial radio companies came together to form a true joint industry survey. The new system was called Radio Joint Audience

Research (RAJAR). The new RAJAR reported a change in total listening for ILR from 36.3 per cent for the second quarter of 1992 to 31.2 per cent for the final quarter. According to the RAJAR figures, Liverpool-based Radio City dropped 45 per cent of its audience share on the previous year, compared to JICRAR figures.

Research bodies

Though media research was conducted in the inter-war years, it was not used as a trading currency. Advertisers bought space on the basis of circulation and estimates of reader profile rather than on total readerships. The growth in media after the Second World War meant that a new regulatory system was needed to provide a currency for trading. Price would still be set on availability and demand, but demand would be shaped by the new regime of knowledge about the market, rather than ad hoc research or intuition about audience profiles. The post-war period saw an explosion of audience research bodies developing to appeal to advertisers, including Exhibition Audience Profile (EAP), the drop letter industry (Association of Household Distributors – AHD) and a research body for bus advertising (BUSADS) covering London buses.

Circulation

In 1931 all national and regional newspapers were bound by agreement to publish audited circulation figures. Consumer magazine and trade and technical publications joined only in the 1960s. The Audit Bureau of Circulations (ABC) is a non-profit-making organisation, limited by guarantee, a joint industry committee including business magazines, consumer magazines, national newspapers and regional newspapers. Until the early 1990s, distributors provided circulation information for magazines regardless of the month in which they were sold. Changes to ABC in 1992 meant that distributors had to give information only for the month to which it was meant to apply. Free newspapers and controlled circulation papers also duplicated names when sending them out, or sent them to family members of the firm, or as complimentary copies and registered them as targets. Because the magazine industry would not pay for a retail audit system, to check how many actual sales occur, the ABC still relies on distributors, which many of the publishing houses themselves control to give the market information necessary.

In 1999 ABC faced the biggest challenge to its legitimacy when Trinity Mirror revealed that its regional newspapers in which had been audited by the ABC Birmingham had been illegitimately boosting circulations by between 10 and 17 per cent and that ABC had failed to detect it. The crisis was largely resolved by the fact that media owners and advertisers had to agree to do nothing in order to sustain ABC's credibility ('Can ABC stem loss of industry's trust?' *Marketing*, 18 November 1999).

Readership

One of the reasons why readership research was introduced in the 1930s and after the war was because of the growth in promotions. Publishers had used sales promotions to boost sales of publications for many years. One of the worst offenders was Lord Northcliffe. He promoted his penny weeklies, *Answers* and *Home Chat*, by running a competition for 1,000 guineas. Consumers were encouraged to buy as many copies of the magazine (which had entry coupons in them) as they could in order to make as many entries as possible. Northcliffe then used the increased sales figures to sell space in his magazines at higher advertising rates. Advertisers were being deceived. The level of sales was much higher than the number of people reading the magazines (and therefore seeing the ads) (Hindley and Hindley 1972: 62). This is one of the reasons that advertisers wanted readership data after the Second World War: there had been heavy promotions in the inter-war period.

The Hulton survey introduced 'housewives' as a currency classification in its first survey in 1947. Other classifications included heads of household, gas and electricity users, people with gardens, regular or occasional drinkers of beer, ownership of bicycles or cars, use of cosmetics, cinema-going and cigarette smoking.

The survey was replaced in 1956 by a joint industry committee after the *Daily Mail* affair. The new initiative, the National Readership Survey (NRS), included the IPA, ISBA, the Newspaper Publishers Association and the Periodical Publishers Association. It included national and regional newspapers, consumer and consumer specialist magazines. The body provides information on readership, interviewing around 3,000 people a month, and includes around 250 titles in the survey. It was the originator of the ABC1C2DE categories for social class.

NRS information includes readership penetration, readership profiles for the different titles, and also readership duplication for those who buy two or more of the titles. Subscribers get more detailed information: this includes demographic breakdowns, regional distribution, TV viewing, cinema attendance, commercial radio listening and special interests. The NRS measures the Average Issue Readership (AIR), that is the average of numbers of readers a publication has per issue. The figures also indicate how many 'readers per copy' a publication has by comparing this to the circulation figures. In 1992 *Vogue* had 8.8 readers per copy, *Cosmopolitan* 4.4, *Country Life* 12.3 and *Classic Car* 19. 'Reading' for the NRS is defined as looking through for three minutes or more. This can mean flicking through in a newsagent's or reading in a library or in someone's house on the coffee table. Design-led magazines (flick-through magazines) and 'coffee table' publications tend to have better NRS figures than wordy magazines and newspapers .

Until 1990 the regional press was measured only on the basis of circulation. The NRS covered only a selection of regional papers. The cost of producing a single readership survey similar to the NRS for regional newspapers has been estimated to be between £6 and £10 million. Agencies and advertisers were not willing to contribute and it has never been set up. However, the new JICREG was launched in October 1990 and was based upon predicted readership data from circulation and distribution figures of around 1,600 regional newspapers and groupings. However, despite the crude nature of the research (estimating readership profiles based on circulation), the IPA and ISBA decided it was better than what had gone on before even though it comes out only once a year.

The free newspaper industry also has Verified Free Distribution. This survey covers three main areas: free local newspaper distribution and magazines; free directories; and magazines such as in-flight and in-house magazines. Other readership surveys include NOP's Financial Readership Survey (FRS), and the European Businessman's Readership Survey (EBRS). The business and technical press have been unable to form JICs because of the diverse nature of the business. One exception to this is the medical publishing market which has a joint industry body called JICMAR. There are six weeklies, a number of fortnightlies and several monthly titles in this market. JICMAR was set up to give the small number of pharmaceutical advertisers some indication of how well read the relative titles such as *Pulse*, *BMJ*, *Doctor*, *Medical Monitor* and *GP Magazine* were. Pharmaceutical companies spend around £25 million a year on ads which target doctors.

There is often a great deal of infighting over research between different groups in the business press: because the margins are so tight in many sectors, poor results in a survey could halt advertising to a magazine.

Viewers and listeners

The first joint industry body for commercial broadcasters was the Joint Industry Committee for Television Audience Research (JICTAR), founded in 1957. It included the ITCA, the IPA and ISBA. In 1968 a regular panel of households was developed and jointly funded by the ITVA which paid 57 per cent of the costs, the IPA which paid 29 per cent and ISBA which paid 14 per cent. The Broadcasters' Audience Research Board (BARB) was set up in 1981, four years after the Annan Committee recommended that a joint BBC/ITV system of audience measurement should be set up. Though the advertisers and agencies are not represented on the BARB board, they are represented on BARB's technical committee. BARB is the single most important arbiter of television programmes' success and failure. Its figures not only act as a currency for the sale of airtime but help evaluate every programme and scheduling decision.

Commercial radio has had a poor image in research for many years. Its Joint Industry Committee for Radio Audience Research (JICRAR) was notorious for being inaccurate and biased towards commercial radio stations (see above). RAJAR was formed in July 1992 and is still paid for almost entirely by radio stations, but including the BBC. Payment is based on station size. The IPA and

ISBA pay nothing towards the costs of RAJAR but, as before, only for research results (£30,000 in total); the ILR stations pay £1.2 million a year. As a result, radio stations pay a far higher proportion of their revenue for industry research than TV (ten times more) and the press (twenty times more). Because of the low coverage, radio offers average weekly hours per listener as a benchmark and sells advertising on the basis of weekly reach. Cinema research is conducted by audience research survey called CAVIAR (Cinema And Video Industry Audience Research). CAVIAR was launched in 1980. It conducts research to find out what proportion of the population claims to have ever gone to the cinema. For a number of years this figure has been around 60 per cent of the population. It is carried out for the cinema trade association, the Cinema Advertising Association.

CAVIAR is solely funded by the contractors, and because of this appears annually. Cinemas send in admissions information each week, from 70 per cent of UK screens. It includes mainstream and independent cinemas, giving audience profiles for feature films based upon field research. Cinema attendances are still very low: only around 7 per cent of the population go to the cinema once a month.

OSCAR (Outdoor Site Classification Audience Register) is a quantitative measure of data in the UK owned by members of the Outdoor Advertising Association and run by the Joint Industry Committee for Poster Audience Research. It was launched in 1985 and measures the number of OTS a week: an index based upon visibility is formed. The data are based on audience counts conducted in September 1983 by a market research company, AGB. Figures for only 10 per cent of existing sites are updated each year. The estimates do not allow for seasonal variation, and are based upon the judgement of the field workers. This has led to severe criticism of OSCAR from media planners. OAA respond that, if they want anything more accurate, the agencies should contribute. OSCAR publishes a six-monthly digest. Outdoor advertising is a very difficult medium to research because it is consumed so passively, and it is possibly the least interactive medium. People walk or drive past; at the most they look at it (they don't open it, or switch it on). OSCAR uses a minimum sample of thirty-five sites and measures the OTS; it does not measure individual sites' coverage, frequency and cost per thousand. OSCAR's problem is that buyers cannot buy a campaign on the basis of its scores. All the highest scoring panels may be along a single street. If planners bought all of them they would have a big OSCAR score, but little coverage or presence around the town. Of the gross audience for posters 80 per cent are in cars, buses and trains or on bikes. One of the problems with measuring road traffic is not knowing the routes of drivers into work. One answer to this is to monitor individual drivers as they go to work with the aid of computerised navigation systems. OSCAR began offering coverage and frequency data in 1990. Its data is also heavily modelled (as is JICREG data). Media planners are sceptical of heavily modelled systems, which include minimal field research, because they widen the chance of statistical error and are supposed to be less accurate.

Research methods in crisis

The four basic methods of research are interviews, diaries and push-button or scanning, and modelling. The industry research bodies employ different methods on the basis of where and when media is used and of cost. The National Readership Survey is based upon interviews. Radio research is based upon a diary method which relies upon the respondent's involvement and has to account more for human error. TV audience research uses push-button or scanning to record the person's presence in the room while the TV set is on. It also employs the diary methods for qualitative answers. Regional newspaper and outdoor media use modelling, that is the use of econometric probability modelling to estimate the size and nature of the readership or viewers.

'People meters' and other scanning or push-button methods claim to record what people are watching, not what they recall having watched. The National Readership Survey method still relies on people recalling what they have read, rather than recording active reading. The NRS uses Computer Assisted Personal Interviewing (CAPI) which is aimed at stopping the respondent learning how to avoid answering further questions: people know that answering yes means there will be more questions, so they tend to answer no. CAPI varies the questions.

Radio research uses a sample of 14,500 adults each quarter. The methodology involves each informant filling in a self-completion diary. Radio cannot be measured at the moment by a people meter because much of it is listened to out of the home, in a car, at work or in personal stereos or battery radios. The scanning device may counter this problem. All these systems involve sampling, that is, taking a sample of the population and recording their media habits. For this reason they are all estimates. Because of the nature of the joint industry approach and the need to keep methodology and research principles simple, the basic assumptions about research remain unchallenged. The most basic assumption is about reading, viewing and listening as an activity. There are enormous problems with the JICs' assumptions that reading is an activity lasting three minutes or more, or that watching a TV programme is simply being present in the room when the set is on.

Most of the research bodies are examining new technological methods. Experiments have been done with passive 'peoplemeters'. These include a hidden camera in the TV which comes on automatically and records what you are doing in front of the TV screen. Readership researchers are also looking into the possibility of developing a wearable passive people meter, but there are other systems, such as using light pens to record bar codes on covers, or having a microchip inserted into the page of a publication: the use of the magazine or newspaper would generate a signal which would be measured and recorded. Transmitters can be built into the spine of magazines or inkdots on a page, or even just using the bar code with a miniature scanner. A single device could measure the exposure of individuals to a number of different media including signals built into TV and radio. People will use the device to record when, where and how much media they consume.

Audience research acts as a regulatory mechanism in the advertising world. The various industry bodies set the standards for measurement and the success or failure of the different media rests upon the regulation through research. The legitimacy of that research is important to making the regulations effective.

Having the set on, or spending three minutes with a magazine or newspaper, is an extremely easily measurable viewer or reader act. From these simple acts, advertisers and media planners try to form a behavioural pattern. The individual elements of consuming the text are reduced or eliminated, and the simple acts of 'viewing' and 'reading' are reduced to such an extent that it is so easily measurable. The more valuable questions of how or why advertising media is consumed remain unanswered. Advertisers are aware of the fact that a viewer being in a room when the set is switched on is inadequate, and that the term 'in the room' covers both watching attentively and glancing casually while doing something else.

In the 1960s JWT conducted readership research to see whether there was much difference in the amount of attention readers gave to right-hand pages and left-hand pages. Special positions were originally based on intuition about how newspapers were read. JWT conducted research to examine whether these special positions justified the extra cost, since in newspapers they cost up to 80 per cent more than basic rates, and larger sizes cost between 10 and 25 per cent extra. JWT research claimed that 20 per cent of readers will not even look at the whole page, 50 per cent look at the page but not the ad, and only 30 per cent would look at both (Pearson and Turner 1965: 191–192).

If, as these figures suggest, only 30 per cent look at the ad, let alone read it fully, then the number of people actually examining the advertisement is tiny, and the standard data on readership figures is meaningless. This was known by creatives, and so advertisers needed to develop advertising that grabbed attention, rather than using subtle communications techniques (see Chapter 13). JWT also commissioned research into TV in the 1960s. This showed that at peak times on a winter weekday evening only 37 per cent of commercial TV viewers (defined as people in the room when the TV is on) were giving undivided attention and at off-peak times on a winter weekday the figure would be 14 per cent. The rest would be doing housework, out of the room or doing something else such as eating or talking (Pearson and Turner 1965: 192).

Other research by JWT in the 1990s showed that only 6 per cent of radio viewers and 66 per cent of newspaper readers gave undivided attention (Ring 1993: 113). To record merely that a TV set is switched on, without trying to measure attentiveness or interest or interaction with the programmes, is far easier and less problematic than trying to develop a consensus around 'viewing' and 'watching', which anthropologists, sociologists and psychologists all disagree on. It is also a very costly method. In the case of industry standard research, the benefits of easily measurable data – their simplicity, ease of understanding and general acceptability – far outweigh the costs.

Most of all, quantitative data are useful to the industry because media owners can only do well from them. Media owners would not agree to funding a system which consistently showed that the media are not as implicitly powerful as the advertisers first thought; that they did not inject messages into consumers and that the relationships between media and audience were far more complex. Many qualitative approaches to audience measurement must, by definition, increase the complexity of the viewing moment and reduce the power of the media sustained through simplistic quantitative research. For this reason, media owners who have an interest in keeping the industry research going have consistently resisted the use of qualitative data.

Until recently, audience measurement by the joint industry committees has only ever been a measure of opportunities to see or hear advertisements: it never tried to find out how or why the media are used. The reason for this is that it is a currency on which advertisers trade. For a currency to work it must be accepted by all parties. If the media industry used qualitative criteria to measure advertising, not only would the methods used be in dispute, but also the underlying assumptions (psychology, sociology, anthropology, behaviourism, etc.) to the research. By measuring opportunities to see, the industry has an accepted currency which bears no relationship whatsoever to the reading, viewing or listening event. But it is a basis on which to trade.

In the 1980s and 1990s, the whole basis of the research was thrown into question because of the growth of media and changes in the media environment. The growth of home computing, the Internet, digital television and mobile telephony meant that all the industry currencies had to change their methodologies.

In the 1980s, a crisis emerged in TV audience research. Agencies led a concerted campaign through trade bodies and the trade press against standard industry research. The problems involved video recording in homes, the use of remote control and the growth of new channels. With TV's Broadcasters' Audience Research Board (BARB), for instance, it was impossible to measure the remote control zapping with the written diary method because respondents would have to keep recording it each time. The industry responded with more sophisticated and technologically elaborate methods of measurement to try to meet the challenge of new technology. Peoplemeters – push-button meters recording who is in the room, linked to the TV to record which channel is used – were introduced in 1983 by AGB. They had an immediate effect on media buying decisions and made a vast difference to the BARB viewing figures. BARB failed to measure the number of video-recorded programmes, which were calculated to add an extra 2–3 per cent to live programme audiences (and around 1.5 per cent to advertisement viewing because of fast-forwarding through commercials, 'zipping') (Roberts 1992: 20). When the ill-fated BBC soap *Eldorado* was launched in 1992 it achieved a rating of 8.4 million and a 2.2 million video playback because a more popular soap, *Coronation Street*, was on ITV.

BARB also recorded the number of people watching, including guests and their demographic profile. Under the old BARB there were eleven target groups

Figure 9.1 HHCL: This ad attacked media research in the 1980s. It is directed at marketing people in the trade press, pointing out that certain media research is flawed because it assumes that people watch TV exclusively, whereas people actually do far more in front of the TV set. © Howell Henry Chaldecott Lury. Agency: same.

available to advertisers; in the new one there were 103 used as currency and 209 potential ones. New categories used in 1992 included business spenders, motorists, pubgoers, shoppers with dogs, and later, shoppers and cat owners, and children according to gender. Costs to agencies and broadcasters rose 15 per cent. Satellite also provided a problem for BARB, as the video recorder had done ten years earlier. Satellite companies disagreed with BARB's estimate of its audience. People meters are fixed to the home TV set, but many pubs and clubs carry satellite TV, boosting viewing figures, especially of events such as the World Cup.

The availability of more channels via satellite TV has introduced the problem of 'channel cruising', that is, viewers flicking from one channel to another without spending much time on each.

In the 1990s fresh threats emerged to research with the growth of multi-channel television and digital TV providing Internet access in the home via the TV set the old research technologies were unable to satisfactorily adapt.

To cope with these new technological threats to television audience research BARB announced in 2000 that a new system would be in place by 2002 which would include a research panel of over 5,000 metered homes.

The new research methodology included a new people meter which could identify all analogue and digital channels, as well as videos and DVDs, videogames, teletext and other information sources, the Electronic Programme Guide, many interactive services and other uses of the television.

In newspapers and magazines, the increase in supplements and sectionalisation has brought problems for the industry currency, as have the changes to the weekend papers. Some of these problems have still not been resolved. In newspaper research the joint industry system almost collapsed in 1990 when News International and Associated Newspapers conducted a rival survey to the NRS and threatened a national newspaper breakaway. National newspapers complained that the information was not accurate or efficient enough because of the increased number of magazines on the survey. The NRS reacted to this threatened breakaway by reforming the NRS and changing its structure. A breakaway was avoided and a new NRS emerged: the title 'JIC' was removed because of the bad publicity it had received. The NRS overhaul included faster and more frequent reporting, new topic and interest questions and separate Saturday newspapers data.

In 2000 the NRS was extended to include fifteen paper sections including business, personal finance and entertainment.

Fused data

Fused data bring together data on brand and product consumption with research on media audiences and readerships. The NRS offers some fusing of data such as car ownership with readership of car magazines. However, it does not offer analysis of readership of car supplements or sections in newspapers or watching of car programmes on TV. It also does not offer brand breakdowns; for this kind of analysis there is the bigger but more cumbersome TGI. Media planners and researchers use TGI to match the product users with the media use, such as TV programmes and magazines. To make it less cumbersome, advertisers combine the brand data in the TGI with media research data in BARB to produce Target Group Ratings (TGRs). However, TGI is conducted only once a year, and does not take seasonal differences into account.

Other problems are its length – an inch-thick book of questions for respondents to fill in – and the fact that it uses a diary method (the respondents ticking off a diary) which produces claimed rather than 'actual' information. However, it is used as an authoritative guide to brand usage and media consumption and offers advertisers some insight into the media habits of heavy, light and medium, sole, primary and secondary users. TGRs may reveal that brands may have other discriminating trends in terms of media consumption, for example that consumers of one soft drink may be more likely to watch *Blind Date* than *Stars in Their Eyes* on Saturday evening.

Environment and context

The perennial problem for the industry currency is that it will never tell an advertiser how effective the advertising will be in the different media. Media owners often supplement the industry research, especially if they do comparatively badly in research (as with magazines), to give qualitative reasons for using their medium.

Media planners and buyers try to target people who are in the right frame of mind, who are most predisposed towards the advertisement: someone who is looking for a car who will want to read the motoring section, someone who may be predisposed towards a personal computer. The mood of the consumer is adjudged to be an important influence on the effectiveness of the ad, and ultimately on the position of it in the editorial. These sections in newspapers and in magazines centre on the practice of consumption and are intended to create the right editorial environment for the advertising to work.

When you turn to an arts review section you are perceived to be in the right frame of mind to be sold theatre tickets or encouraged to buy books or go to the cinema. The same goes for personal finance, food and drink, motoring and travel and property, all of which have had special sections and supplements created by newspapers to gain advertising revenue. These sections of newspapers talk about buying and consuming things, and are perceived to be an ideal environment to place advertising.

The environment that other ads make is also important. Many big-brand advertisers will not use national newspaper colour supplements because they carry mail order ads and Dateline ads (personal introduction services) which are perceived to be downmarket and make their own ads look cheap. Similarly if brands such as Harvey Nichols and Harrods advertise in a medium, expensive cosmetics firms like Elizabeth Arden might want to be associated with those kinds of brands.

The idea is that your ad stands out more if it is placed next to a programme which directly relates to it, such as a Heineken Daffodils ad where Wordsworth struggles to find the lines for the 'Daffodils' poem during *Dead Poets Society*, and a Heineken Midas commercial which featured King Midas drinking the brand in a break for *Goldfinger*. The idea is that viewers notice the link or clever puns between the ad and the programme it interrupts. Viewers congratulate themselves at noticing a clever placement. Another reason is the newspaper chatter (PR) it generates, such as the *Daily Mirror* running a story about Tango soft drink doing an ad in the break for *Last Tango in Paris*. The main reason, though, is that the clients think such ads are very clever and will spend money on them because of this.

Though advertisers do not research context of advertising in great detail, or on a regular basis, they carry with them views about the mood and state of mind of consumers when they read ads – whether they are relaxed, tense or in the mood for information or entertainment (especially a factor in cinema commercial). Car magazines, gardening titles, computer titles and the *Financial Times* are all specialist and supposed to deliver the appropriate mood of the audience looking at ads. In TV campaigns direct response advertising is supposed to be most effective at off-peak times, when it is not having to compete with big-brand advertisers in glamorous locations. Advertising in off-peak times is less spectacular, because it does not have to compete with the big advertisers and peak-time TV programming. With late night and early morning programmes on radio and TV, people are less resistant, and the programming is generally dull (fewer distractions), so they may have little else to occupy their time than replying to ads (Bird 1993: 154). In-home media are perceived to be more useful than out-of-home. In 1990 Millward Brown ran a survey of out-of-home reading of magazines, and found that 41 per cent of quality home monthlies were read out of home (in hairdressers', waiting rooms, etc.) but only 11 per cent of TV listings magazines were. It also found that those who read out of home read a far smaller proportion of the magazine than those who read it in-home (Macleod 1992: 16).

Media buyers judge the right mood of a TV programme for advertisements by the Appreciation Index score, supplied by BARB. This includes two measures: enjoyment and interest. 'Interest' is a measure of the educational and informative value of the programme, and 'enjoyment' is intended to measure the amount of entertainment and pleasure, sometimes shared with fellow viewers, during a programme. The amount of enjoyment has traditionally been the most popular criterion for creating the right environment; game shows, comedy and light entertainment have consequently done well for advertising. However, in a study by researchers from Leicester, it was found that the viewer's involvement with the programme was a much more effective measure of positive attitudes towards the commercials than enjoyment and entertainment. They found that though there was lower memorability, viewers of programmes in which they were involved (such as dramas, current affairs programmes and documentaries) had more positive attitudes towards the brand (Norris and Colman 1994: 41). However, advertisers who wanted higher memorability worked better with low involvement, light entertainment programmes. Reminder ads may work better here.

AIs are supposed to be a qualitative panel which work in parallel to ratings. They were intended for the use of programme makers to gauge the success of programmes, and were funded (£3 million a year) by the broadcasters, BBC, Channel 4, ITC and ITV companies. The assumption was that, if the programmes were more liked, the audience would be more receptive towards the advertising. Audience appreciation was demanded by Channel 4, who saw this 'quality' of viewing research as a way to give Channel 4's low rating programmes a competitive advantage by claiming that they were more liked or appreciated than volume-delivering programmes with better ratings on ITV. Appreciation assessment asks respondents how interesting they found the programme. These scores from one to six are then changed into a score out of 100, and the index is calculated by dividing the total score by the number of respondents for the programme. The respondents are also asked ad hoc questions about the specific programmes. In 1994 BARB introduced a new electronic system called Barbara for audience appreciation data: audiences record their appreciation of a programme (one to four) electronically (Dawkins and Samuels 1994: 70).

Another scale is an impact scale, used not by TV programmes but by advertisers, which measures motivation (did you have to watch the programme because someone else in the room wanted you to?). These are all behaviourist measures. In a buying situation, a buyer might point out to media sellers that they have qualitative research which shows that elements of their editorial have low involvement and appreciation by the audience, and for this reason discounts should be offered. Information is used in this way to try to establish an advantage. Agencies want to undermine the media in order to get lower rates for their clients and force them to discount. But they also they want to support above-the-line media more, because this is the most expensive part of the business and means greater income for the agency.

Summary

Media planners want to know whether their target market is more likely to use one medium or watch one programme than another. Media are bought and sold on the basis of data. Therefore, reliable and trustworthy research is needed as a trading currency. Because the competing groups – advertisers, agencies and media owners – could trust each other to run the research, they formed joint industry committees to oversee it. The committees are in a constant state of struggle about the terms and control of research and in recent years have all faced difficulties in terms of emerging technologies and the reliability of the information they provide. Joint industry research has to remain as simple as possible to sustain a consensus. Because of this, acts such as watching the TV are reduced to the most simple form such as having the set switched on. However, media planners also want to know the how and why of media consumption. They want to know what happens in front of the TV set: whether people are interested, paying attention or doing some other activity. For this reason agencies are constantly trying to seek an advantage over competitors and the media owners by gaining access and producing qualitative research to inform buying decisions.

10 Principles of persuasion

Advertising is neither a science, art, nor manufacture. It has no general standard, no root principles, no hard and fast rules, no precedents, no foolproof machinery. What man can be expert in a subject without end or beginning, a subject as full of controversy today as it was fifty years back?

> (W. A. Alexander of Nash and Alexander
> in Bradshaw 1927: 140)

Successful advertising appeals both to the head and to the heart, to reason and emotions.

> (Beatson 1986: 265)

By the early twentieth century key consumer markets such as confectionery, soap and tobacco had already become saturated. Though advertisers had developed strategies such as expanding consumer spending through increasing credit, they also turned to advertising messages to help increase sales. As early as 1908, when *The Psychology of Advertising* by Professor Walter Dill Scott was published, advertisers began to turn to psychological theories to try to unlock the consumer's mind (Leiss *et al.* 1990: 138). Agencies began to formulate theories of human behaviour and motivation which could be unlocked by persuasive treatments. New approaches to persuasiveness were categorised and systematised in the 1920s into 'reason-why' and 'atmosphere' advertising techniques.

'Reason-why' was designed to stimulate demand by constructing a reason for purchase, such as helping to save time, being modern, or being socially acceptable. Reason-why ads were used to differentiate the product from others on the market, as in an example from the 1960s: 'Make sure it's Cadbury's. Because no other chocolate can possibly give you the proper, creamy, Cadbury taste.' The premise was that consumers were essentially rational and made consuming decisions based upon reason. In an expanding market, there is no

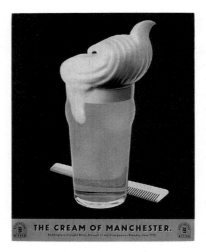

Figure 10.1 Boddingtons: a campaign launched in 1990, an example of the USP – Unique Selling Proposition. This ad uses a visual pun to demonstrate the product's USP: its creamy head distinguishes it from other products on the market. The tongue-in-cheek campaign plays on the brewer's Northern working-class origin. The ad ran from 1990 to 1999. © Boddingtons. Agency: Bartle Bogle Hegarty.

other reason to try to make appeals other than reason-why, because consumers continue to buy, but once competition rises and the market flattens, advertisers need to find new appeals. 'Atmosphere' advertising, on the other hand, appealed to the emotional side and was meant to evoke non-rational responses such as sexual desire and patriotism from consumers. Irrationality became an issue when the market became saturated and advertisers needed a competitive advantage.

The debate illustrated that advertising was trying to set up a professional, rational, discipline. It was the first sign of agencies trying to maintain social control over the discipline – that they 'knew' or had the knowledge about ads, and that amateurs did not.

These approaches tried to get to the essence of what advertising is all about and consequently solve all of the problems of advertising. In reality, advertisers used combinations of the two. New products, for example, at the turn of the century had to be explained and the reasons for using them developed in the advertising. However, new inventions could not rely just on reason-why ads, they also used suggestion and atmosphere. One technique of advertisers of new products was to associate the new brand with traditional and familiar settings such as nature, nationhood and the family.

A later version of the reason-why advertisement of the 1920s was the Unique Selling Proposition (USP) developed by US agency boss Rosser Reeves in the 1950s. This too was based on 'rational' consumer decisions, but more explicitly tried to find an essence to advertising. Rosser Reeves specified that 'Each advertisement must make a proposition to the consumer . . . Each advertisement must say to each reader: "Buy this product, and you will get this specific benefit . . . one that the competition either cannot, or does not, offer." It must be unique – either a uniqueness of the brand or a claim not otherwise made in that partic- ular field of advertising . . . The proposition must be so strong that it can move the mass millions, i.e., pull over the new customers to your product' (Reeves 1961: 51–52). A USP has to be original, differentiating a product from the competition. It is determined purely by market imperatives, the need of the advertiser to compete.

A USP can be achieved through the packaging, such as a unique bottle shape, or a lime segment in the top of a beer bottle (Sol). These differences in the product (the look, shape, size, colour and market position (the biggest/ best/leading) are less to do with the advertising and more to do with the manu- facturer. The manufacturer may decide to design the product in a certain way to provide the USP, such as an unusual pack design. Creatives in agencies would go through the different benefits of the product until they could find something that was different about it – 'melts in your mouth not in your hands' (Minstrels), and, for a boiled sweet, 'double-wrapped to keep in the freshness'. Whether the consumers were interested enough in these USPs to make them want to buy the product was of little relevance. This imperative for differenti- ation came from the companies and the competitive market, not from any predilection towards the consumer. The greatest strength of the approach was that it re-emphasised the basic communications principle that to be effective advertising of brands must emphasise difference; it did not matter for what rational or irrational reason it was differentiated, just that it was differentiated. The only element of 'rationality' in some of the classic USP advertising was the fact that there was a 'reason' for it, it did not rationally matter which reason it was. It was therefore the discourse of rationality, rather than actual rational- ity, that motivated it.

In the 1960s advertisers attacked the reason-why approach of rational persua- sion. One of the reasons for this was 'the purely technical one of the vast shift to the TV medium, which, of its nature, is better able to communicate in pictures than words, images than arguments; biased, some would say, against under- standing' (Tuck 1976: 40). The shift from the perception of rational consumer to one of an irrational consumer came hand in hand with the development of the broadcast medium, at first radio then TV.

Reason-why and USP are still used today in different settings, especially for new products. However, the speed with which goods lose their difference means that the straightforward explanation of the goods' use, and the appeal of product difference is lost and other ways are needed to differentiate the product, such as the emotional sell and the advertising brand image.

If there is a new product to launch and the advertiser needs to explain to the consumer how the product or service works, and why it is better than the tradi- tional way you did things – such as the convenience and ease of using a dish- washer versus scrubbing lasagne off cooking pots – then the next brand that comes into that market is wasting its time telling people the same reason for using the product. The new brand has to differentiate through a separate and distinct product feature or benefit, or, more usually (if there is no difference), to develop a separate personality so that the brand is remembered as quite distinct. It is not so much the appropriateness of the brand's personality to the consumer market as the distinction and therefore memorable nature of the brand's personality that is important.

David Ogilvy asserted that products could be differentiated on the basis of brand image and advertising, though the term 'brand image' had been used for decades before (1983: 15). The distinction for the product is made on brand attributes (softness, strength, German engineering, Australian macho culture), its Emotional Selling Proposition. The personality of a brand is used to replace the selling proposition. If advertisers were convinced that consumers bought goods on the basis of the brand image and values, rather than because it was simply the cheapest or most available, advertising agencies would maintain a powerful position in the communications efforts of firms. Ogilvy was one of the biggest exponents of the power of the brand to influence consumer buying decisions. The attributes are formed by making associations, which provide an identity, which engage with the fantasies or aspirations of the target market. Building brands is as much about establishing familiarity, authority and legitimacy as it is about establishing difference. Any new brand that comes on the market has the weight of this to fight against. What Ogilvy may ascribe to the power of persuasive brand advertising may equally be ascribed to the size, scale and familiarity of the brand's campaign, its availability and product-led modifications. Even if you are not a Coke addict, you may turn to Coke in a store because you are so familiar with its design and its names and packaging. One of the reasons why the brand leaders do not need so much brand advertising is because they have already established that credibility and legitimacy.

The rise of lifestyle advertising in the UK in the 1980s was also a response to the saturation of markets: it has also been attributed to the success of the account planning discipline in advertising agencies. This type of advertising 'draws on the planners' interpretation of the nature of the target audience but fails to talk about the product' (Skorah in Cowley 1989: 9). It focuses on an activity engaged in by the target 'type'. It may be set in a club, at tennis courts, at an exclusive country club or golf club, on a type of holiday. People don't have to be using the product, just doing the kinds of things that people who use this product do such as driving fast cars, or ice skating. The product became secondary, something to be emphasised at the end of the story. Gold Blend was like this: the stories focused more on the story or narrative than on mentioning the product. One ad combines the function of the brand with the lifestyle, Tampax's 'It's My Life', which shows women roller skating, wearing short skirts and doing sports, the idea being that you aren't constrained by your period, and when you aren't constrained the kind of people who use Tampax do all these interesting things.

The brand image, the USP and lifestyle are basically about the same thing; differentiating the brand. The USP differentiated through the product itself, the brand image emphasises the unique values and attributes of the brand, and lifestyle ads differentiate the product on the basis of consumer lifestyles and psychographics.

Research and creativity

Creatives often conflict with the rational and scientific authority of planners and researchers in the advertising industry, especially when their creative ideas are rejected on the basis of empirical tests. However, research findings inform a great deal of creative decisions. Research is conducted to suggest to copywriters, layout artists, photographers and film-makers what the most effective form and content of messages are. Many assumptions about effective communication come from such research, which includes attention research, eye movement, memorability, comprehension and persuasion shift research. This kind of research deals with the most effective use of colour, layouts, typeface, sound effects, use of techniques of suspense and tension. Creatives are told that the first thing readers are supposed to look at is the picture, then the headline, and then the bottom right-hand corner to see who the ad is for. Emboldened quotes, captions, drawings, graphs and charts all attract the eye. When constructing a page, creatives traditionally designed the ad to gain attention and impact by following eye movements from top left to bottom right. Creatives also work on the fact that the average reader spends around 1.5 seconds on most news-paper and magazine advertisements (Crompton 1987: 62).

According to research from the USA, the average US child will have seen around 350,000 commercials by the age of 18 (Law 1994: 28). Research has also suggested that of the 1,500 opportunities to see advertisements that people have each day, only between seven and ten are remembered by a consumer. Advertisers try to increase opportunities to see (using a selection of media, PR, sponsorship), to grab the attention and raise the awareness of the reader; to stand out against editorial matter, against competitors in their own market, and against all the other advertising messages from many other different markets that the target consumer has the opportunity to see. This is in addition to trying to break down the defences of the consumer. Creatives also use psychological research findings from planners to inform creative work. In an article in *Admap* Judie Lannon pointed to research from the British Association which showed that 'young children will eat all manner of foods like spinach and broccoli, providing the authority behind them is someone they admire rather than mother' (Lannon 1993: 19).

The creative target

At the creative briefing stage, the planner gives the creative person information about the aims and objectives of the advertising (such as stimulating trial, reminding or reassuring), whom the ads are aimed at, a breakdown of the targets and their demographic or lifestyle patterns and attitudes. Who uses the brand? Who buys it? Who influences the purchasing decision (parents, friends, scientists, doctors, dentists, pharmacists and hairdressers)? The 'desired' consumer response, or the preferred reading of the text, may include an immediate response: 'a credit card is really handy in emergencies', followed up with 'I need one that is reliable and can be used abroad', 'Barclaycard is widely accepted' or 'I'll go to the bank tomorrow'. Statements and detail of the competitors' work are also outlined, and a phrase pointing to the main proposition of the ad: 'Carlsberg. Probably the best lager in the world'. The briefing also includes a rational reason for buying the product such as providing information on the benefits of using it, and an emotional reason, possibly to do with family or status which involves a role for the brand such as bringing people together. The form and style of the advertising, such as a challenge, demonstration, image or atmosphere or lifestyle, also has to be considered.

The first thing that creatives have to know is how much time they have to make the commercials, the commercials' time length: 10, 15, 30 or 60 seconds, where the commercials will appear (which slots), which magazines and newspapers and the sizes and shapes of ads. The creatives should also familiarise themselves with the editorial environment in which their ads will appear. They may want to stand out from a particular environment or feature somebody who would work best with a specific magazine. The ad may run in a section appropriate to the product market (car section, fashion, beauty). The date the ad will appear is also important: if it is two days before Valentine's Day or Easter or Bonfire night, it might mean a special anniversary for the target consumers; or it might be timed to coincide with an exhibition for the target consumers. Though these may all be important factors, very often ads are created to run for longer periods than the immediate booking time. It may not always be appropriate to tailor the ad to a specific environment.

The creative person then uses information and research people to find out as much as possible about the product: details of how it works, previous ad campaigns, who the competitors are, what campaigns they have run, what the Unique Selling Proposition is: whether it is the biggest, smallest, slimmest, widest, cheapest, most expensive, the same as all the other products. Most importantly, how is the product used, and what do people use it for? What is the purpose of its use, what is the ultimate objective (the satisfaction) that consumers who may use this product are looking for? What are the most desirable brand values and image that differentiate it from others on the market? Account planners and creatives develop a brand personality which is intended first to differentiate it from other brands on the market and second to attach attributes that the target consumers find appealing and desirable. If designing a lifestyle ad, the lifestyles, values and attitudes of the target market are important.

Some creatives use the findings of qualitative research to look for the language and imagery used by the target market. The creative target is the fourth main target in the marketing process (see Chapters 4 and 9): this is a much tighter definition of the target market. Some creatives try to narrow the field even further by constructing a mythic individual to personalise the evidence provided by the researchers. Creatives try to get closer to the consumers to understand the way they supposedly think, their loves, hates, prejudices and aspirations. They construct 'typical' consumers, such as a 'typical' coalminer's housewife: 'she has always voted Labour, believes in capital punishment, and thinks multinational firms are manipulating the world; likes reading romances, does the pools regularly, and watches *Coronation Street* every week' (White 1988: 65).

Modes of address

Two basic modes of address are the direct address – talking directly to you the consumer – and the indirect address, in which the consumer eavesdrops either on a conversation in a TV commercial or on a print image of a slice-of-life advertisement (see Chapter 12). Direct address often takes the form of a presenter or personality (testimonial) talking directly to you, like a salesperson. You are positioned as the potential sales customer, either in the shop or about to use the service, and the advertisement tries to place you in the right frame of mind for the sale.

Indirect address includes monologue and dialogue. A monologue does not address the consumer directly but usually represents the thoughts of a person in the ad. In the Werther's Original ad, grandad sits on the chair and reminisces in a voice-over, 'I remember when my grandfather gave me my first Werther's Original . . .'. You are invited to eavesdrop on his private thoughts; although you are not mentioned, you are brought into the story as privileged observer. The person delivering the testimonial monologue often appears in the commercial as a personality, an expert, or an 'average' consumer (Leech 1966: 45–46). Celebrities endorsing a product are supposed to sign a form saying that they actually do prefer it, before the ad can pass the ITC, though there are probably numerous cases where they don't. In a dialogue situation, the activities in the commercial or the print ad are taken from 'real life' (Oxo, Nescafé Gold Blend). Indirect address can also be without dialogue, but with a sound track over it, such as the Levi's ads, or Wrigley's gum.

The common denominator is direct address. Pure indirect address advertising, which focuses only on an event, or sets of images, is very rare. The Daz commercials with Julian Clary move from indirect dialogue (Julian interviewing a 'typical housewife'), to Julian Clary talking to you ('So there you have it, Daz really does . . .'). All ads need to talk directly to the consumer, even the 'indirect' slice of life ones; there is usually a narrator, or actor's voice and/or a piece of text with the slogan and brand which delivers the endline to the consumer. Though this may not often say 'buy X' or 'get Y' the intervention of the actor's voice at the end anchors the meaning of the text and relates the story directly to the consumer. Endlines are often spoken and accompanied by text on the film (also called 'supers') to add emphasis, as well as the pack shot and/or logo. Indirect commercials have to use an endline, to bring the viewer into the advertisement. Because advertisers are struggling to stand out amid all of the information clutter, direct advertising demands your attention, involving you in the ad. When someone says, 'Hey you!', you cannot avert your attention. So, when Julian Clary turns to camera and says, 'So there you have it . . .', you are now involved in the ad; previously you were merely a spectator watching an incident. This is a basic method of sales technique.

People are supposed to be much more susceptible once their attention has been raised and a dialogue established.

Because mass communications involves one medium talking to many people, and advertisers need to talk to people individually, advertisers employ the beliefs, prejudices, fears and anxieties of the group to which you are supposed to belong. Hailing the consumer involves recognising the language, classifications and metaphors of the 'target' or positioned group of consumers. Rather than describe the working of the internal combustion engine, the wheels, interior and metal surround, we simply say car; to describe different categories of car we talk about sports, saloons, hatchbacks; and to talk of different features we can say fuel injection, turbo, catalytic converters. As our classifications get more specific we close meanings off to more people. Often the commercial may use language that speaks only to people who are meant to understand, such as the Audi commercials which include references to Sigmund Freud and Coco Chanel.

Metaphors and stereotypes

Metaphors are the common denominators of advertising. 'The skill of the agency . . . lies in doing two things: finding a metaphor that is appropriate for the brand; and ensuring that the metaphor means what it is intended to mean to buyers' (Ring 1993: 160). One of the reasons why advertisers use metaphors, apart from the fact that it is an easier method of quick communication, is that we use and understand metaphors in everyday language. Metaphors are part of our everyday speech. We 'chew over' and 'iron out' problems. Metaphors also work by bestowing meanings on goods. In this culture, sending red roses to somebody on Valentine's Day can mean only one thing. At some point red roses came to mean love and passion. Once this was established, advertisers could play upon the metaphor.

Advertisers also try to establish their products and brands as metaphors. A high-performance car can become a metaphor for success. Advertisers try to make their brands omnipotent. In doing so advertisers try not only to attach meanings to the brands, but to attach brands to meanings, so that when you think of softness and strength, you think Andrex, when you think sex you think Häagen Dazs ice cream, and when you think sunshine you think Kellogg's corn flakes.

Advertisers want to get consumers to think in these metaphorical ways, to think in images and pictures in which their brands play a leading role (Williamson 1978: 9–14). Williamson argues that the association of the product with the cultural references causes a transfer in meanings and that the cultural reference becomes the product. Love and sharing mean Rolos rather than Rolos mean love and sharing. The problem is that with all of these brands competing for metaphorical status, many things come to mean love, power, status and passion.

Metaphors work by transferring the feelings, emotions and images from one set of objects, such as things that go fast (trains and weapons), and adding them to, for instance, fast food chains, Pizza Express and Chicken Bazooka. Or they work by associating certain objects with the brand: milk chocolate and silk and bread 'morphing' into a wooden log in a lozenge commercial. Advertisers place different things together to suggest that a connection exists. It is not obvious that Roses chocolates should be given to someone in gratitude.

Saying 'Thank you' with Roses chocolates is an attribute added to the brand. The same could be said for Lucozade, which repositioned its added values in the mid-1980s from a drink to revive the sick to an energy-provider for athletes and club ravers. Associating qualities and settings with products and services is the oldest metaphorical device: ads for nuclear energy, petrol and cars tie in with the countryside and the environment; shampoo ads such as Timotei, with a woman washing her hair in a stream, tie in with natural herb extracts.

Often advertisers will create puzzles and metaphors that people will recognise, and the joke will be that we understand it but others do not; it reinforces social cohesion. A TV ad for Carling Black Label shows an English tourist beating a group of German tourists to the sunbeds by throwing his Union Jack towel down to the swimming pool; after bouncing on the water a couple of times the towel unfolds on a sunbed, beating the clutch of German holidaymakers who are running to the pool. This ad plays on a number of metaphors which English people are meant to share in a common bonding. The most obvious is the holidaying myth that German tourists always get up early to claim the sunbeds around the hotel pool. This has been a popular anti-German joke in Britain for some time. Second there is a metaphor about British war films, specifically the bouncing bomb (dambusters), and third there is a reference to a previous commercial by Carling Black Label which copied the war film and had two well-known comedians in an aeroplane dropping bouncing bombs and a German sentry parrying the bombs like a goalkeeper (references to the 1966 World Cup final). At the same time music from the film *The Dambusters* played in the background.

These metaphors and cross-references are meant to indulge viewers around consensual values, to make them share in a communality, a shared understanding of the meanings.

Analogies are sometimes used when the message cannot be realistically portrayed. One ad which appeared in the UK was a hammer going through a peach, which was trying to represent what a car hitting a child is like.

Figure 10.2 Carling Black Label: the 'Dambusters' ad ran in 1989. It was part of a campaign theme which pitched the Carling lager brand against rival German lagers. This ad included a popular image from the war movie *The Dambusters* and tied the metaphor into recent football confrontations between Germany and England. In this ad a British plane drops bouncing bombs to blow up a German dam. The bombs are 'saved' by a German goalkeeper. The ad ends with, 'I bet he drinks Carling Black Label'. © Bass Brewers Limited. Agency: WCRS.

Advertisers who use people in advertisements often face problems with the interpretations of meaning by different groups in society. Our understanding of human categories of gender, ethnicity, age, class and sexuality makes it more difficult for the advertiser to convey a simple linear message to the viewer. An advertiser could not simply grab any teenager off the street to be in a jeans commercial, because the person would have to conform to certain sets of meanings and metaphors that would not alienate, put off or offend sections of the target audience. The meanings we attach to each other are overdetermined, they overlap. Gender, ethnicity, religion, class, education, hobbies, age and sexuality may all contribute to our identities. All these elements contribute to the construction of our identities and carry complex cultural meanings. Representations of people convey many more meanings than objects, animals or pets because people are much more culturally overdetermined. Advertisers, especially mass market advertisers, get round the problem by avoiding including people altogether. They often include animals instead, for instance PG Tips and Pepsi use chimpanzees, Sunkist used an orang-utan, Andrex use the puppy, and Esso a tiger. Guinness also excluded people from their ads from the 1930s to the 1950s (Schudson 1993: 213–214).

Metonymy involves the substitution of an aspect of a product, thing or person for the thing itself, such as crown representing the Queen. To say, in trying to establish the brand, 'The *Sunday Times* is the Sunday Papers' is a form of metonymy, trying to get the brand to stand for and represent the entire product group. Metonymic ads often feature a specific product attribute: Benson & Hedges the gold cigarette box, Silk Cut the use of purple, Marlboro the use of red, Cadbury the use of purple for the wrapper, Body Shop the use of green, McDonald's red and gold.

In 1993 Marlboro ran an advertising campaign which showed black and white pictures of the American West but with red for different symbols of America, such as Harley Davidson bikes, and the lights on an American police car. The ads were playing on two sets of metaphors: first metaphors that we in Britain are familiar with from US films and TV series, and second the metaphor of Marlboro cigarettes being represented simply by the colour red. There was no reference whatsoever to the brand, apart from the government health warning at the bottom which was intended to give the reader an indication of the product area. The reader was left to deduce that this was a cigarette ad, and that the most familiar brand on the market for cigarettes associated with red is Marlboro. The other connections with America, part of the global campaign (with cowboy, etc.), were also meant to resonate with the readers. The main aim of the campaign was to appeal to existing users of Marlboro, who would make the connections with the brand more easily than others.

When a creative director chooses a personality or an actor for a commercial or a photograph, they are chosen to best match the brand, or the message as it arises. The part stands for the whole, some signs stand for authority, others for pleasure. A particular pen may stand for a certain type of person, clothes also stand for the type of job. The creative has to calculate whether the meanings surrounding that person, hair colour, eyes lips, body shape and size are appropriate for the market the ad is aimed at, or whether it may alienate some consumers; or if the extra meanings of a familiar face or personality are also appropriate. For example Jack Dee's age, sex and appearance were judged to fit with the brand for the John Smith's commercial, as his image was as a sarcastic, cynical comedian. A feminist comedian like Jo Brand might not have worked with this brand. Stars no longer have to endorse a brand: they have only to appear with it or use it to help create meaning.

Stereotypes that we construct about other people, places and cultures are convenient ways of understanding things which we are distant or remote from. When advertisers use stereotypes, they are using our shorthand notions of what people and places are in order to communicate. Mothers are always strong metaphors for homeliness, warmth and strength, and are usually worldly-wise (an important part of self-image: look at the Oxo Mum, where mother knows best). They are always positioned as practical and knowledgeable; this helps to reinforce their role in the domestic sphere and also to establish them as the centre or the heart of familial relations. Just as advertisers stereotype people, so they also stereotype settings, such as people's homes and workplaces – for example a Levi's ad set in a garage where a mechanic is sweating carrying a tyre. Each object must fit in with the stereotype and use elements of the setting which we can all understand (all of us who are not mechanics, in this case). Our culture is composed of thousands of stereotypes and metaphors: the advertiser selects those which will anchor the meaning of the texts. Stereotyping is a convenient and inadequate way of understanding. Unlike the original definition of stereotyping, however, it is not permanently fixed. Stereotypes do change over time.

There is a gap between the world of commodities, products, industry and commerce, and the world of real-life consumption. However, as Davidson (1991: 28) points out, 'Advertising bridges the gap; it communicates not just an airline, but global mobility; not an anti-perspirant, but a release from the anxieties of body odour. This is the source of that particular breed of corporate speak that IBM uses when they sell us "not computers but solutions". This is a continuation of a traditional advertising dictum; "sell the sizzle, not the steak" – selling feelings, emotions and cultural values, rather than simply the product – is carried on in many areas of advertising. Though the original dictum may be true of some brands, most advertisers try to "sell the steak and the sizzle".' This is largely because the added cultural meanings are not fixed and are much more highly contested and constantly changing. It was selling the cultural meanings over and above the product which was seen as a primary problem of lifestyle advertising in the 1980s.

Examples

Coca-Cola

As the market for soft drinks in the USA started to mature, Coca-Cola changed its advertising sales messages from reason-why to atmosphere. By 1916 it was running full-colour posters with two women (one with a tennis racket, the other with golf clubs), drinking Coca-Cola, lots of white space and little copy (Prendergrast 1993: 148). By the 1920s Coke had to reposition to try to target the take-home market. It also tried to encourage consumers to drink Coca-Cola in the winter months, with the 1922 slogan 'Thirst knows no season' (ibid.). Ads from December to February used this slogan and portrayed the drink in snow scenes. The unique selling personality of the brand was pleasure and enjoyment, consumed by good-looking, contented and active people.

Oxo

In 1959 Oxo launched a new TV campaign featuring a 'housewife' called Katie. The intention was to shift attitudes towards the brand to get rid of the view following the war that Oxo was a cheap and poor substitute for beef stock. The campaign had given it a more modern feel as well as associating it with aspirational groups (Katie's husband wore a tie and was constructed as a bank clerk). The packaging change had also played a role: Oxo was available in tins before then, and the new individual foil-wrapped packaging stressed convenience and freshness. The ads were primarily lifestyle commercials intended to reflect the kind of people who use Oxo, rather than the product itself: the persuasion was implicit, rather than explicit.

Nike

In 1992 Nike ran an ad campaign on TV for its brand, with Arsenal striker Ian Wright performing on the field with slow-motion action shots and a popular song 'Can you kick it' playing over the top. The ad not only associated the brand with him as a top-class footballer but also played on racial stereotypes of black men as 'cool', stylish and athletic: associating black American soul and street music with a black British footballer helped to reinforce the racial stereotype that all black men share the same characteristics. The meanings associated with the brand are meant to associate with those meanings – not Ian Wright's footballing prowess but the extra meanings that Ian Wright stands for: black, cool, stylish, masculine and desirable. The ad managed to select-out those metaphors of black masculinity and football which would be most usefully associated with the brand. The ad also shows him being successful on the field, conveying obvious messages about success, competitions and winning.

Summary

The persuasiveness of advertising became an issue only when markets became saturated in the 1920s and advertisers wanted to know why sales did not increase. Agencies began to develop theories of advertising persuasiveness to provide a rational basis for creative treatment. Though they all have a different focus, all the theories attempt to differentiate the brand. The Unique Selling Proposition differentiates through a unique feature of the product (packaging, shape, smell, taste), brand image through the distinct emotional values of the brand; and lifestyle, which takes its cue from the marketing concept, focuses on distinct lifestyles of its consumers. Though these approaches claim to be distinct, in reality advertisers often mix appeals. Creatives employ industry folklore and past research when determining the style, design and content of ads.

Creatives use familiar metaphors to target consumers, which can deliberately include or exclude certain groups. Most creative treatments try to involve consumers in the ad by hailing them with a direct mode of address.

11 Persuasion techniques

··

Advertisers have used models of behaviour to frame their messages since the inter-war years. They have sought to define and understand their target market, and develop models of consumer behaviour to construct advertising which produces the desired response; usually stimulating consumers to buy or use, or to change their attitudes and opinions. For many years, creatives have worked to a behavioural model known as AIDA: Awareness, Interest, Desire and Action. The purpose of advertising in this model is to raise awareness, then stimulate interest which would lead to desire and eventually action. The action would often not take place until the next day, week, month or even year (in the case of car ads, for instance). This meant that advertisers had to multiply their number of messages in the same and other media and retail outlets to reinforce the salespeople's job.

This model has been criticised by sections of the advertising community because there is no evidence to show that people behave in this rational, linear way. Advertisers have also criticised mass media advertising in general for its failure to stimulate desire or action. Because of these criticisms, most modern advertising strategies have focused on the two main behavioural responses: raising awareness and stimulating interest.

Raising awareness

··

Advertisements have to compete with other advertisers in the media, often with editorial, and with the resistance of consumers. Because of this, creatives see the most important job as grabbing the consumer's attention. Some creatives assume that because interests and social life are so heavily gendered you can most easily raise the attention of women through using animals, royalty, weddings, babies, fashion and astrology; to get through to a man you use sport, sex, cars, politics, wars and disasters.

This is often done by involving readers in the ad, or shocking them to take notice. To do this advertisers use similar communications values to news journalists. News is an extremely powerful discourse in advertising. The constant product modifications, relaunches and redesigns reflect a need to be constantly seen to renew, be up-to-date and be modern. Established brands use 'new improved' to maintain brand loyalty and to make existing users feel that the product is improving all the time, and encourage trial purchase. In the 1950s and 1960s advertisers needed constantly to relaunch established brands to maintain reason-why appeals for consumers. The most popular words in advertising became 'new' and 'improved'. There is a promise with a news story that you will find out something not already known, and you are kept informed (socially included). The general dictum is that 'new information works best'. People like facts; they give the reader a reward for reading.

Two other linked news values are prominence and proximity. Proximity includes elements of the message which directly affect the target market's lives. The classic example of this in journalism is Budget Day, when national newspapers translate the Chancellor's statement into data that tell us how our own income and expenditure will be affected. Advertising copywriters tend to use the word 'you' in copy much more than 'we' or 'I' to try to relate the message more closely to the reader: 'How to reduce your income tax by half' (Crompton 1987: 86). Advertisers take familiar features of life like weddings, family albums, getting a first job, and you are invited to relate your own experiences to those occurring in the ad, such as, 'Do you remember our wedding day?' Weddings are also generally the source of positive emotional memories. Prominence involves using a personality, event or object that the target market collectively recognises and understands. It is part of a shared cultural knowledge; famous personalities, and prominent events grab the attention of the consumer because of the familiarity and other associations. For instance, Leslie Nielsen in the Red Rock commercials is associated with *Police Squad* and the *Naked Gun* films by the target market, who would recognise him as a prominent figure.

A much more common news-value criterion because of the over-mediation of modern life is co-option (Bell 1991: 159). Co-option is where an advertiser uses a major media or news event or other advertising campaigns for their own advertising. This forms part of the principle that 'News breeds news' (ibid.). It involves the over-mediation of events and trades on the growth of consumer information. Advertisers perceive readers' interests and knowledge to have been raised by an issue or event and will cover every possible angle in it to try and appeal to this constructed interest. Marketers co-opted elements of the green movement in the 1980s; no CFCs (carbofluorocarbons are gases emitted from many household products which are claimed to destroy the earth's ozone layer), no additives and preservatives. Wants are not fixed, but change with changes in knowledge. In December few people would dream of buying a tennis racket, but in the spring with Wimbledon approaching, people develop more knowledge of the area because of extra media coverage, and people start to talk about it more. Advertisers have also come to co-opt other advertisements as media events, parodying commercials; Carling Black Label parodied Old Spice, British Rail parodied numerous car advertisements, and Peugeot parodied a successful Heineken ad.

Co-option also works with the use of stars: for instance, celebrity cook Jamie Oliver who starred in the Sainsbury's commercials is associated with his TV show *The Naked Chef* and is aimed at the target market of young women. If the stars have a current TV series or a recent feature film, or even appear in other ads it helps to reproduce the media connections. Whereas actors strongly associated with specific ads usually avoid ads for other products, stars are recognised as themselves and the problem does not arise.

Advertisements also co-opt other genres such as news programmes, quiz shows, consumer information programmes and feature films. When Radion was launched in 1989, it used an anchorman to announce the new product and showed a screen with a woman sniffing clothes. Vaseline produced an ad in 1994 with ex-newscaster Fiona Armstrong talking about the scientific values of using Vaseline before going to bed, again in a studio. Ford launched a range of cars in 1994 which copied BBC science programme *Tomorrow's World*. Film genres such as James Bond spy films and westerns (the Milky Bar Kid) are used. Advertisers also borrow from other genres of communication: school reports, criminal records or files, and medical reports: 'Her name: Elizabeth Eldon. Symptoms: constant tiredness. Cause: night starvation. Recommendation: Horlicks. Horlicks guard against night starvation' (Leech 1966: 100).

Because of the growth in media and the perception that the advertising environment is highly competitive, advertisers seek to gain advantage over competitors by generating media chatter – that is, trying to get consumers talking about the brand outside the immediate advertising environment. This technique is not new: 'Beecham's Pills, worth a guinea a box' and 'Good morning, have you used Pears Soap?' entered the everyday conversation of the Victorians at the turn of the century. More recently, slogans like 'I bet he drinks Carling Black Label'; 'Ssssh . . . you know who', BT's '. . . it's for youhoooooooo', Budweiser's "Wassup?", jingles such as 'Everyone's a Fruit and Nut case', 'Nice one Cyril' and 'Just one Cornetto' stay in the popular repertoire long after they have gone off air.

The Budweiser 'Wassup?' commercial managed to gain the involvement of the target market by subverting an everyday social occurrence – making a telephone call – and invited people to live the commercial by repeating the phrase to friends whenever they made a phone call.

In the 1970s agencies used pop songs to give their campaigns extra legs, as with the famous Coke commercial 'I'd like to teach . . .'. Saatchi's campaign for Brutus jeans with a backing track ('I pull my blue jeans on') aimed at 14- to 18-year-olds went to number one in the 1970s. This use of pop songs which gain radio airtime on non-commercial stations was a form of free advertising by association. It has been used extensively, most notably in the 1980s and 1990s by Levi's.

Similarly the Nescafé Gold Blend couple and the Oxo family, which were supported by press PR activity. A novel was also produced about the Gold Blend couple, and Yellow Pages' fictional *Fly Fishing* by J. R. Hartley went to the top of the bestseller list in 1990.

Another PR tactic is to make ads that are controversial to get maximum press coverage. Hennes in 1990, Wonderbra in 1994 and perfume brand Opium in 2000 produced advertising poster campaigns which showed half-naked women, guaranteed to gain more publicity, as were the Benetton posters, which have to be one of the cheapest, most cost-effective, discussed and well-known poster advertising campaigns of the late twentieth century.

The media environment can also be very important in grabbing the attention of the reader. Using media in an unusual way, such as different shapes and sizes of ads and 'top and tailing' (the beginning and end of commercial breaks), adds to the stand-out. Using new media, such as 96-sheet posters, satellite TV and interactive media, is another way of standing out.

Arousing curiosity to involve the reader by posing questions is a common technique. A question can automatically single out the target consumer: 'Looking for help buying a home?' (TSB home buyers' video), 'Chesty cough?', 'Headache, tense, nervous headache?' Using 'why' in a headline demands an answer. 'The inch war. Why Ryvita helps you win', 'Why I drive a Porsche' (Crompton 1987: 66). Or the 'why' can raise your curiosity: instead of 'Orange juice is made with real Spanish oranges', say 'Why our orange juice is made with real Spanish oranges'. 'Why' phrases work better if there is some contradiction, if people who wouldn't normally do this do it, for example 'Why Nigel Mansell drives a Robin Reliant' or 'Why Delia Smith goes to Burger King' (neither does, by the way). Curiosity can be aroused by promising to reveal a secret, or making a headline which is totally unexpected, as with Black Magic's

Figure 11.1 Wonderbra: a deliberately controversial ad which the agency claimed generated extra publicity worth £50m in advertising. This additional publicity was a consideration in the making of the £500,000 ad campaign. © Wonderbra Agency: TBWA Holmes Knight Ritchie.

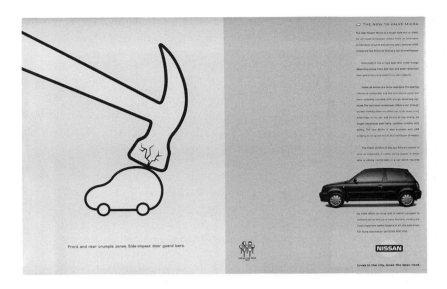

Figure 11.2 Nissan: this ad emphasises product difference. A series of poster ads emphasises the features of the product, using minimal design to catch the attention. People automatically identify this emblematic symbol as a car, then the visual pun is built in: (a) emphasises safety, (b) roominess. © Nissan. Agency: Holmes Knight Ritchie.

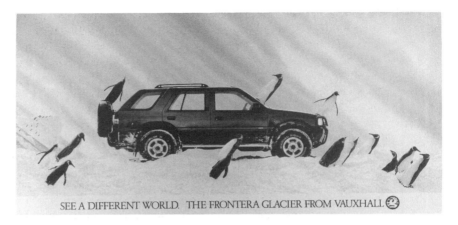

SEE A DIFFERENT WORLD. THE FRONTERA GLACIER FROM VAUXHALL

Figure 11.3 Vauxhall: this is both a demonstration ad and a puzzle. It demonstrates the utility of the Frontera, a four-wheel drive vehicle which can be taken anywhere in the world. Here it is on a glacier. The visual pun is that the car is on the side of the glacier, where penguins are sloping. On the left the horizon is shown as diagonal. © Vauxhall. Agency: Lowe Howard-Spink.

'Find out the secret of the Black Magic box'. The purpose is to let people feel that they are part of a select club. An ad for Birds Eye Fish Cuisine had an actress whispering throughout, to let the consumers in on a secret about this new range of fish dishes from Birds Eye; the consumer is included in the secret and more importantly, involved in the ad.

A familiar journalistic form in women's magazines is the 'how to . . .' feature: get a boyfriend, find out if he's cheating on you, deal with the office lech. They provide advice, information and entertainment, inviting you to read on. It is also used to explain a complicated product to the consumer. How chewing sugar-free gum after a meal helps clean your teeth; 'How does Persil get the plates so very clean'. Sainsbury's also use the how-to format in demonstrating food recipes with famous people.

Challenges and contests also involve the consumer. These are often aimed against the competition when launching a new product to encourage trial: 'It shaves as close as a blade, or I'll give you your money back'; 'We challenged three chefs . . . to wash the dirtiest dishes' (Sun Micro liquid for dishwashers).

Unusual, amazing and entertaining advertising is used to attract the reader and fight against the advertising clutter. As Leech said in 1966, advertisers perceived consumers to be advertising-weary and tried to find new ways to grab attention: 'The growth of 'off beat' advertising styles may reflect the increasing thickness of the public's armour of defence against conventional sales language, and the need of the ad profession to experiment in new and more sophisticated methods of attack' (Leech 1966: 200). This is still true.

A final area is where there is very little to say about the product or brand. Crompton identified these sectors as beers, petrol and oils, steam-baked breads, canned fruits, most cigarettes, butter, margarine and most shampoos, deodorant and hairsprays. Because of development in technology you could equally put cars, hi-fis and many consumer durables in this category now, as well as confectionery, soaps and detergents, toothpaste, banks and some sectors of retail. Crompton's guide in these circumstances is: 'When you have something to say, say it, when you have nothing to say, use showmanship' (Crompton 1987: 36).

Advertising gives brands spectacular and magical qualities over and above their simple functional product use. In the magical world of advertising, animals talk (the Sunkist orang-utan, the Pepsi chimp, the PG Tips chimps), objects talk and have personalities (Trebor's Bertie Bassett, Kellogg's Tony the Tiger and Niblets sweetcorn's Jolly Green Giant). This is a familiar technique used in folktales and storytelling, where inanimate and natural objects talk to humans or do human things. In advertising it elevates products, and gives them added values as brands. The production and consumption process can be mystified through the use of animation, computer graphics and camera tricks to make flames come out of thumbs (British Gas); entire cities lift up and fly over the water (British Airways); the ingredients of chocolate bars magically conjoin (Mars) and sore throats, headaches and coughs magically disappear.

When making ads, creatives exaggerate reality, rather than simply mirror it. There must be a distance created so they use make-up, music and lighting camera techniques to give us the feeling of a magical world of the brand, to lift it above the world of everyday practices; more than real.

We are meant to be dazzled by the superhuman and supernatural characteristics of the show person who manages to perform feats that we are unable to do, such as one ad for BMW which had a car balancing on the windscreen of a convertible car, to show how strong it was, and an ad for Continental tyres which demonstrated the grip of the tyres by conducting a test on the flat roof of a tall building, with the car doing screeching handbreak turns along the edge. We are meant not only to marvel at what has been done but also at the mystery of how it was done, for example, 'How did they do that shot?' We are left asking the same kinds of questions after watching a commercial as we would ask after seeing a magician. One ad, for Rover, placed the car on the top of a thin rock, with the endline, 'How did they do that?'

Creative work in the 1980s relied more on technique, using computer animation and styles lifted from pop music videos. Viewers were meant to be in awe of the wit, glamour and grandiose elements of the commercial, showing a car morphing into a horse (Volvo), faces which blended into other faces as they spoke (the Employment Training ad), computer-animated sweets rolling through a computer-animated assault course (Smarties).

Sustaining interest and winning consent

Though the mass media provide coverage, the existence of editorial makes it difficult to grab attention and interest. Advertisers believe that consumers are

Figure 11.4 Babyface: this ad demonstrates the 'Ah' factor. Tesco used the image of babies in a commercial. It appeals to mothers and reinforces the image of itself as a caring and responsible company. © Tesco. Agency: Lowe Howard-Spink.

in the wrong frame of mind to receive advertising messages, and that many have become immune to the persuasive form and content of advertising messages. Creatives try to make ads stand out by having better production than the editorial, using unusual and entertaining storytelling, humour and self-parody to break down the perceived consumer barriers.

One famous stand-out campaign of the late 1980s was Midland Bank's First Direct two buckets commercial, which bore no relation to the product or brand but succeeded in being talked about. Established brands also had to come up with consistently new ways of grabbing attention. In the 1970s it became very important for ads to be liked. Instead of warming to the sales messages, consumers were meant to warm to the clever advertising; this took other familiar forms: the use of humour (Carling Black Label, Heineken), stylish filmic commercials (Levis), sexy models (Flake), and advertising sagas (Gold Blend couple, Oxo).

Advertisers try to win consent through personality endorsement, puzzles and humour. Prudential used humour in its TV commercials ('I want to be a tree/slug/in goal') to try to disarm the perceptions of banking and insurance as dry, materialist and untrustworthy. Basic selling technique dictates that humour helps to break down people's suspicions; get the punters to relax and let the defences down. The use of humour in advertisements is intended to attract readers into agreeing with the cultural meaning in the ads. Babies, weddings and animals are supposed to have a similar effect, the 'Ah' factor. The advertisers soften the message and struggle with consumers' hostility by using familiar and pleasurable images. This is a process of cultural leadership that Gramsci termed 'hegemony' which wins the reader's active consent.

The other form of this is flattery, trying to make the person you are selling to think that she or he is too clever to be conned. Cynicism was used in advertising by John Cleese in ads for Sony in the early 1980s and also more recently by Jack Dee for John Smith's Bitter and Bob Monkhouse for Sekonda. These comedians pointed out how cheap and nasty advertising is and tried to give the impression they were not selling products. Advertisers try to dampen the opposition from the comedians and from the public by appropriating it. Co-opting is a way of securing the consensus, trying to make the opposition like 'one of us' or at least to nullify it. The sheer number of cynical and alternative comedians who have appeared in TV commercials attests to this: Dawn French, Rowan Atkinson, Jack Dee, Lenny Henry, Paul Merton, Julian Clary, John Cleese, Angus Deayton, Ruby Wax, Harry Enfield, Rik Mayall, Alexei Sayle, Mel Smith and Griff Rhys Jones, Billy Connolly, Danny Baker, Chris Evans and Chris Tarrant. They are used because they have established their hard-nosed, cynical reputations on TV; it co-opts opposition to advertising.

At a less obvious level advertisers co-opt from popular culture to add legitimacy to their brands. In 2000 the highly popular TV game show '*Who Wants to be a Millionaire?*' generated an enormous amount of media chatter. McDonald's launched a marketing tie-up with the game show and produced a radio commercial to support it. The ad included familiar catchphrases from the show which had become popular household phrases. By co-opting the phrases, McDonald's exploited the shows popularity and attempted to win consent by association. Listeners were invited to share the joke.

SFX:	Church organ playing quietly. Occasional cough
VICAR	Do you, Sue Brown, take this man to be your lawful wedded husband?
WOMAN	I do. [*Pause*]
VICAR	Confident?
WOMAN	Yes.
VICAR	You don't fancy the best man?
WOMAN	No I'll stick with, er my fiancé.
VICAR	Final answer?
WOMAN	[*sighs*] You've got me thinking now. Can I ask the congregation?
CHRIS TARRANT	From March 20, everyone will be playing 'Who wants to be a millionaire?' At participating restaurants while stocks last. No purchase necessary. See rules in poster restaurant.

Advertisers now perceive the media-wise consumer to be the biggest problem for getting sales messages across; in response they use parody ads. Parody commercials make safe attacks against certain genres of advertising such as

Figure 11.5 Imperial Leather: an example of a parody ad. It parodies a demonstration commercial characteristic of traditional soap manufacturers, showing two types of product, one superior, one inferior. The presenter is comedian Paul Merton. The woman on the left has been washing her face with a scrubbing brush, and this is what she looks like. Her twin on the right has washed her face with Imperial Leather. Merton is wearing a white coat, parodying the 'scientific' product test. © Cussons. Agency: Gold Greenlees Trott.

demonstration ads – Paul Merton's parody ad for Imperial Leather in which he uses people in white coats and pulls down the dividing line to show tests – or heavy sales ads – Jeff Goldblum in Holsten Pils – and word play or language games, as demonstrated in an ad for Quavers, in which two copywriters are trying to come up with a playful or silly slogan for the snack, or Barr's Irn Bru commercial, which parodies Coke commercials with young Americans having fun: here being American is mercilessly attacked for being phoney. These are examples of advertising trying simultaneously to distance itself from the tired and drab image of traditional advertising formats and to win the confidence and support of advertising-literate viewers.

The point is not to appear to be selling at all. Many of the lifestyle ads which use humour or simply add the message discreetly at the end work in this way. The idea is that consumers are left thinking that they are not being manipulated and that they are free to make up their own minds; to make consumers feel that they have decided of their own volition to buy, rather than been persuaded by advertising (Evans 1988: 26). These types of ads invite people to try the product, to test drive. 'We are simply telling you what we think, you can make the decision for yourself by trialing the product.' Consumers then feel that they have some degree of autonomy and that they have been left to make up their own mind, when really the suggestion has been placed there already by the advertiser. The difference has been established; that all tooth-pastes, coffees, teas and shampoos are not the same.

This involves presupposition, the assumption that the brand is already estab-lished or that there is a positive feeling towards the brand. 'Why more and more men are turning to Flora' (Vestergaard and Schroder 1985: 26) presup-poses that they already are, and 'Which of these continental quilt patterns will suit your bedroom best?' (ibid.) presupposes that all of them already suit your bedroom; you have only to choose one which is best. An advert for Ford showed three cars with the line, 'Which one is right for you?' The debate is closed off, you are unable to deny that any men are not turning to Flora, or that none of the quilt patterns suits your room, only to take it on board. The difference has been established: either you can think that it does not taste as good as your current brand, or it tastes better: either way you cannot say that they taste the same. Another technique is to play on expectation (ibid.). When Fairy asserts that its washing-up liquid is 'kind to hands' it implies that other washing-up liquids are not.

Distraction is also used to break down the resistance of the consumer (Evans 1988: 26–27). This is often done through strong visuals and moody imagery (especially music) in commercials, but also though the use of graphics and photographs in print ads. Sex can also be used in this way, especially erotic images, which can distract the target audience. Before Häagen Dazs, ice cream had not been sold on sex. In the late 1980s the media were talking abut sexual experimentation with partners and adventurous sex more as a way to stop sleep-ing around (keeping to your man or woman): the Häagen Dazs print ads co-opted this by producing ads linking sex to ice cream. The erotic images sug-gested new uses for the brand as well as distracting the consumer from the fact that it was an advertising sales image. Similarly Colgate responded to the emer-gence of a new brand of baking powder toothpaste – Arm & Hammer aimed at young adults – with a sexy ad for a new brand extension, Colgate Bicarbonate of Soda, showing couples kissing in various states of undress (1994).

Creatives believe that the basic desire in people to complete or unify things is a psychological phenomenon (Evans 1988: 29). It involves some degree of interaction on the part of the consumer, whether in willing a conclusion to take place or in solving a puzzle. The consumer is forced to participate and drop resistance by the need to see the message or the story unified and complete. It is also believed that the message will be better remembered because the consumer has been involved in completing it. Silk Cut is the same – just use purple silk and a cut – as is the *Independent*'s famous 'It is. Are you?' campaign. Incompleteness can also be shown visually: ketchup not hitting the plate is supposed to leave the consumer to imagine it happening (Drake in Hart 1990: 111). Consumers are also meant to marvel at the clever, stimulating advertising.

Criticising other brands is meant to reassure existing users that they have made a wise decision. The Daz ad, with Julian Clary, plays on prejudices about

E.ILF

Can anyone make sense of it?

IE.LF

Can anyone make sense of it?

FLE.I

Made sense of it yet?

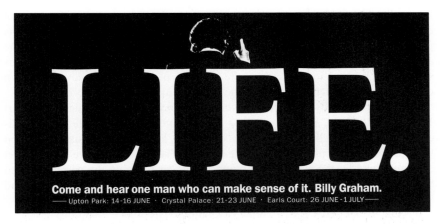

Figure 11.6 LIFE: an example of a puzzle ad. Parts of the ad were released in a poster campaign over a four-week period on the London Underground. Incomplete in themselves, these ads made up a puzzle which stimulated interest. The pieces of the puzzle finally came together in the complete ad for a Billy Graham tour. © Billy Graham Tour. Agency: Foote Cone Belding (FCB).

own label products. This type of strategy plays on the consumer's common sense; as with Stella Artois and 'Reassuringly expensive'. A great deal of advertising is aimed at telling people what a good product they have already bought to encourage them to do so again; especially if the brand is almost exactly the same as others on the market. Similarly brands with image problems for certain sectors of the market, such as Babycham, will use trendy and sophisticated characters to reassure doubting consumers. Inoculation aims to modify or reinforce attitudes. If there is an element of shame and embarrassment in buying certain goods, advertisers try to portray the purchase as natural. BT did this with their first share issue in 1984. They used vignettes of different people (people like me) sending off for BT shares. Or, if they want to portray unconventional activities, like eating corn flakes in the evening, as consensual, they try to make the behaviour appear natural.

Narrative technique

Successful narrative involves the reconciliation of conflict, the solving of mysteries and the resolution of contradictions. Advertisers often set up mysteries that conflict with the proposed consumer's world-view to make the person uncomfortable. The story then unfolds, the brand comes to the rescue and the consumer's world-view is reaffirmed.

An ad can set up an ambiguity or conflict. In an ad for Volkswagen, the song 'Your lips are better than hers' is played, the man is being ogled by numerous predatory women at work, including the female boss. The women are seen to fawn over him, and one actually gets down on her hands and knees in front of him. In the end the man gets into his car with his wife and two kids: this underlines the fact that despite these changes, the family stays natural, the same and constant. The pleasure of the advert and the stylistic shots, the melodious song in the background, as well as the cleavage of the woman who went down on her knees are intended to make the advertisement attractive to men.

The stories usually take certain stages (after Labov and Walesky in Hart 1991: 181–182): the scene is set, then a problem occurs, and there is a complication in the story, the complication turns into a crisis, the crisis is resolved with the aid of the product, brand or service. The events and the intervention are underlined by the assertion of brand values, or bringing the narrative up to the present, or back to the beginning of the ad with the problem resolved, and life back to normal again, as if nothing had happened.

Yellow Pages have run a series of commercials which feature a crisis or predicament resolved with the help of the product. In one ad an old man is trying to track down a book, *Fly Fishing* by J. R. Hartley; he searches for the old book in antiquarian bookshops but cannot find it. He uses Yellow Pages to try and track it down and locates a bookshop that has it. It transpires that his name is J. R. Hartley. The old man is happy and content and the real crisis – that the book he wrote is long forgotten – is resolved. The ad finishes with the line, 'We're not just there for the bad things in life.' This theme, and use of narrative, have had numerous executions, another example of which is given later in the chapter.

Another example is a Ford Fiesta ad which tried to get across the idea that the new Fiesta is roomy and stylish, whereas the old one was not. The orientation is a yuppie couple; complication, his car has had to go into the garage; crisis, he has to pick up some overseas clients at the airport; resolution, he can use the wife's (she sat at her laptop); he sets off and picks up the three Japanese businessmen at the airport. The problem is that there aren't three, there are four (a further complication), but no worries; the new Fiesta can fit all of them comfortably (resolution). The ad ends, 'Can I use it tomorrow?' 'No, get a taxi', emphasising brand loyalty, and again a twist to the traditional formalist ads.

Another form of ad is to structure it as subject, object, giver, receiver, helper and opponent. In the narrative structure the object is usually something like pleasure, security, happiness or status; the subject is usually the person or family in the ad. There is also a giver (the authority figure), a receiver (society/ everyone), a helper (usually the brand) and an opponent. In one RAC commercial, there are the subjects, the yuppie couple, specifically the woman, who is seen most; the object is safety or security; the opponents are the criminals/ underclass; the helper is the RAC knight of the road. The receiver is society (safe streets), the giver is the hero figure (the RAC). The purpose of the RAC ad was to tell the consumer that you need security and safety on the road, and the RAC can help you to attain that.

A representative of the product or service can be the helper, and the brand or company the giver. In one Harp ad, a man and woman go into a women's underwear shop and she is in the changing room changing, she has to have a different size (complication), he goes to change it, he is embarrassed. The object is to escape embarrassment, so he goes to get a Harp: the pint is his helper, the brand in the pub is the giver. Brands can help you overcome problems, they can help you win the Inch War; they will not tell you that Ryvita is tasty, so buy it; they will look at what the target market desires (weight loss, to be attractive) and provide Ryvita as a helper in this. If advertisers were truly altruistic they would try to help large people by instilling self-confidence rather than guilt.

This 'helper' function doesn't challenge, it reinforces the consensus about weight. It asserts that problems and anxieties are inevitable, what you need are little helpers; brands and commodities. The products are there to help you achieve your object: 'Nationwide. We'll help you take a step in the right direction.'

Once consumers are familiar with the happy ending genre of advertising, an advertiser needs to be different. One answer has been parody, but now every advertiser is parodying others.

Fear, guilt and insecurity

Some ads play on anxieties – problems with spots, keeping your boyfriend or girlfriend, fears about career failure, not fitting in, loss of respect, esteem and status, loss of face, loss of material wealth – and then come in to resolve them through the brand. At the turn of the nineteenth century, advertisers increasingly began to focus on guilt and fear of low social esteem. Magazines and periodicals increasingly acted as coping mechanisms providing advice and information for people who no longer had the social networks to give them help. Advertisers too exploited the anxieties of the new mass consumer by the use of nostalgia for rural life and the creation and invention of tradition in advertisements.

One US company advertising in the UK, Cuticura, advertised its Cuticura soap in *Woman* magazine in 1895 thus: '"Disfigured for life" is the despairing cry of thousands afflicted with unsightly skin diseases. Do you realise what this disfiguration means to sensitive souls? It means isolation, seclusion. It is a bar to social and business success ... Cuticura works wonders, and its cures are simply marvellous' (de Vries 1968: 57). Here we can see the juxtaposition between the private sphere, the isolation and seclusion associated with it, and the public sphere of business and social life. This ad was aimed at the new middle-class woman, who is able to get out of the domestic environment but needs a friend to help her. That friend is Cuticura soap. Sounds familiar? Though Biactol and Oxy 10 target the teenage market, the reliance on the brand to help you be successful and assertive in your social life is still predominant. The anxieties of modern consumers, especially about their bodies, were and are a useful focus for advertisers. One ad in the *Illustrated London News* of 1890 has a before-and-after picture of an obese woman with 'Too Fat!! Dr Gordon's

Elegant Pills cure stoutness rapidly and certainly' (ibid.: 15). And from the 1920s the famous 'always the bridesmaid, never the bride' was an advertising slogan used by Listerine.

Heinz Weight Watchers' Pizza ad, 'Pizza without the guilt' actually encourages guilt in the readers (McCracken 1993: 265). An equivalent example in the UK is Ryvita's 'helps you win the inch war', which was also aimed at reminding women that they needed to lose weight and that they should count the inches down. The indication that the tape measure gives is the ideal size that a woman should be: 24-inch waist. If they are not the ideal size, then they should be. And Ryvita can 'help' them reach this goal. The ad functions to contribute to guilt and to provide a 'helper' function: 'Ryvita helps you win the inch war.'

Creatives try to answer the fears and anxieties of their target consumers in creative treatments: loneliness (answer: make friends and be popular); insecurity and lack of self-esteem (answer: security and confidence); tension and stress (answer: relax and wind-down); oppressive or restrictive morality (answer: freedom, liberty, self-indulgence, excess); oppressive relationships, family, partners, work relations (answer: freedom, rebellion); distrust of business (answer: caring or serving capitalism and corporate charity).

One campaign which did not offer a resolution of fears was the government's first set of anti-AIDS information commercials in the mid-1980s. According to one creative director involved in government advertising, 'They just told people to stop having casual sex. The viewer was left feeling, "Oh my God", there was no get-out, no escape, other than abstinence. The fear was treated as being so great that many viewers just rejected it and shut it out of their minds. People wanted an alternative but the ad did not provide it' (interview).

Fantasy, escape and nostalgia

Advertisements use fantasy and escapism in advertising, as with Bounty Bar commercials ('A taste of paradise'), Flake commercials with sexy self-indulgence, and ads for Walls' 'Too good to be true' fat-free ice cream (lounging on a tropical island eating ice cream while a naked hunk washes the dishes). However, the purpose of these ads is not to invite consumers to imagine themselves in the commercial being waited on by a naked man; the commercials are intended to associate the myths, metaphors and stereotypes surrounding our views of 'paradise' (tropical beaches, palm trees, relaxation) with the brand. The familiar elements in fantasy and escapism are more important than the unfamiliar. In the Bounty Bar commercial the emphasis is on the coconut taste in the chocolate bar, in the Flake commercial the emphasis is on the luxury status and self-indulgence that goes with the brand, and in 'Too good to be true' the commercial hangs around a visual pun, 'Too good to be true' and a naked man doing the dishes. People don't fantasise about being in commercials, they bring their own fantasies to the commercials.

Nostalgia ads take away the brand's recent history and make it timeless. They try to make the brand appear natural. Sometimes brands do this by inventing tradition. Bailey's Irish Cream (invented 1985), Ploughman's Lunch (invented in the 1950s), and Hovis's nostalgia for a bygone Arcadian industrial past. The past is a place where people lived in communities, food tasted better and life was better. Though Oxo used the Beefeater as its symbol for many years, it didn't actually come on the market until 1910. It used the timeless British symbol of the Beefeater to challenge the established brand of Bovril. Pears also did this in the 1880s by reproducing a fake advertisement from the 1700s showing a wigged woman bathing her child in Pears soap. Nostalgia ads also play on a fear and distrust for modern living, summed up in cider brewers Gaymer's slogan, 'Give me something Old'.

Music is a popular way of evoking the past. In some agencies it is held that the best way to stir emotions among an older target group is to use a song which was in the charts when they were seventeen. Another use of nostalgia is to evoke another era when things were better, or people were more 'cool'. The Levis' 'Heard it through the grapevine' ad was aimed at teenagers primarily; the nostalgia ad also made those who were 17 when the song was in the charts feel better about their era. Ovaltine re-ran their wartime radio commercial of children singing the Ovaltiney song during the 1980s; the image conjured up warmth and childhood memories, people bought the brand to give them access to a slice of the past. Ovaltine became a memento like an old photograph.

Consistency, familiarity and authority

Sales and advertising people operate on a simple principle that people like to do business with people they know. Advertisers try to establish their brands as familiar and trustworthy. Most of the job of the advertising agency is to gain the consumer's confidence. The oldest and strongest brands often have variations on the same theme. They perform new executions but stick consistently to the same idea: PG Tips and the Chimp family, Tetley Tea folk, the Oxo family. Though the Oxo family was dropped in 1999, for 30 years its commercials were based around the kitchen, with the Mum providing family meals. The family meal setting was perceived to be outdated and no longer relevant to modern family life. Martini is the music, 'Any time, any place, anywhere'. Such rhetorical devices as use of music and voice-overs to add consistency give a feel of sameness and permanence to an ad.

Consistency makes communication easier and less expensive. People should be able to recognise an ad or a leaflet from a certain company without having to read it. When products are modified, advertisers try to convince consumers that it is the same as it has always been, only improved. Completely scrapping a product such as Coca-Cola in 1985 can have dire consequences (see Chapter 13).

Brands need to carry consistency and authority. When advertisers make claims about their products, there is an obvious problem of credibility. Advertisers can seek authority by sheer dominance, as do Heinz, Kellogg's, Coca-Cola and Marlboro. Another answer to this is to get a famous person or an authoritative or 'neutral' figure, such as a journalist, to endorse the product. Many manufacturers also seek to place scientific claims in their copy to give authority and credence: 'Zanussi, the appliance of Science', 'scientifically tested/proven', 'scientists at our laboratories'. 'Skin science update' from Vaseline Intensive Care Hypoallergenic, or 'Hydra renewal' (this means the product contains water), is used to give the impression that it is a product of a laboratory, not a factory. 'Experts' in advertising include scientists (skin care, washing powder, washing machines), hairdressers (shampoo, hair gel), mothers (floor cleaners, washing powder, cooking), designers (nappies, sanitary towels) and, the most common of all, friends (spot cream and dandruff, deodorant).

Memory and action

> If you expect her [housewife] to have your message in her mind, two or three days (or perhaps two or three months) after she last saw your ad, and she's pushing the baby round the supermarket where a million other claims are being made on her attention, then please – say something simple.
>
> (Crompton 1987: 110)

The only direct link between advertising and action can be seen in direct response advertising, where a consumer responds to an advertisement in a newspaper or magazine or on TV and sends off or rings in for an offer. Responsiveness can vary between 0.02 per cent and 2 per cent for most media, but competitions with prizes often get much higher response; rates of between 20 per cent and 50 per cent have been known (Bird 1993: 144–145). But there are other influences on consumers' decisions to respond, such as past experience with products and brands, other marketing efforts and other people's influence.

Many ads finish with verbs as a call to action: try, buy, get, ask, join, cut, save, feel, taste, pick, pop in (or along), write, send, give them/her/him. Because the action usually takes place after the advertisement is seen or broadcast, it is often a call for future action. 'Look for . . .' or 'call in . . .'.

However, saying to consumers 'Hey you! Buy this' is not likely to nullify their resistance to the brand. Asking consumers to send for more information or have a free trial is less obtrusive than telling them to go out to buy it. In this way the advertiser is giving something in return, the consumer is supposed to feel that she or he is gaining added benefit/value from the exhortation to buy. Often it is a matter of changing certain words to soften the tone, especially through the use of 'can' and 'will'. Rather than telling consumers that they should use brand X, advertisers use constructions such as 'Brand X can be used as part of a calorie controlled diet', or 'You'll be amazed what Brand X can do for your waistline'. The action is implied. 'Will' also suggests to consumers that something will definitely happen, 'can' suggests it is possible: 'Milky Way, the meal you can eat without ruining your appetite'.

Some ads don't include a directive, they just have a slogan. The purpose is to put across the brand values and associate the right moods and feelings with the brand. Slice-of-life ads and those which go for a more indirect form of selling tend to anchor the text by using a slogan which finishes it off: 'Pernod. Free the spirit', or 'Carlsberg. Probably the best lager in the world'. The exhortation to buy is implicitly not explicitly made. Rather than assume that consumers react in a predictable way, many creatives produce advertising messages that act as a trigger to individual thought processes and memories that evoke a good feeling towards the brand, rather than directly affecting their behaviour in a linear way. The main aim of these advertisements is to provide positive emotional responses around the brand and influence attitude to create the predisposition towards action, rather than a direct effect.

Because of the time-lapse between seeing the advertisement and buying the goods, mass-media advertising has for years identified memorability as the main behavioural prerequisite for action. This is one of the main reasons why rhetorical devices such as alliteration, assonance, repetition, catchy slogans, rhymes and the use of jingles and associated music have been so common in advertising; one of the reasons why one of the most popular measures of advertising effectiveness is recall (see Chapter 13). Jingles are ritualistic, like children's nursery rhymes, and provide easy memorability. Music is used both to evoke brand values (classical music, jazz, soul music) and to aid memory, especially if a follow-up single is released. However, there is no proven link between memorability and action.

Examples

Yellow Pages

The Yellow Pages campaign (see p. 170) has a strong narrative technique which involves the resolution of distress. A teenage boy wakes up the night after a party at his parents' house. His parents are coming back that morning. He and two others clean the house and he discovers a scratch on his mother's table, but Yellow Pages helps him to overcome the problem by bringing in a repairer. The naughty boy is not allowed to get away with it, though, because his mother's paintings have been defaced. All the Yellow Pages ads have this format, of setting up a problem and Yellow Pages stepping in to help.

Figure 11.7 Yellow Pages. © British Telecom. Agency: Abbott Mead Vickers. BBDO.

HMV

At the end of the nineteenth century HMV used the brand of the pet dog and the new technology to show the naturalness of modern technology. They also targeted parents who could use the gramophone to entertain their kids without having to learn the piano or violin. Whereas middle-class home entertainment had previously been in groups set around the piano using music-hall sheet-music of popular songs, individuals without any musical skills could now listen to their favourite artists wherever and whenever they liked; on their own. Most significantly, the brand image reinforced the sales message, that there was a high quality of reproduction (the dog thought that the gramophone was his master).

Hamlet

For many years Benson & Hedges ran TV commercials for its Hamlet cigars brand which featured men (the target market) getting into embarrassing or difficult situations. The familiar narrative begins with an everyday situation which results suddenly turns into a minor crisis. The cigar was positioned as an aid to relaxation with the endline, 'Happiness is a cigar called Hamlet. The mild cigar.' A radio ad in 2000 continued the humorous theme with a blatantly sexist treatment which was designed to appeal to the male audience. It draws on a situation familiar to men who are asked to comment on their partner's appearance. The humour includes men of a certain age in relationships and excludes women and younger men.

SFX:	Car horn
HUSBAND	Sweetheart, cab's here.
WIFE	Darling, do you think these trousers make my bum look fat?
HUSBAND	No, no, they look alright.
WIFE	Alright, just alright. So you're saying my bum is fat.
HUSBAND	No, no. You said that, I didn't.
WIFE	So you think it looks fat?
HUSBAND	No love, you look gorgeous. Now, come on the cab's waiting.
WIFE	You don't think they look too tight?
HUSBAND	No, maybe you could wear something different underneath.
WIFE	What?
HUSBAND	Well, I mean, your underwear – it's all folded and creased up.
WIFE	I'm not wearing any.
SFX:	Strike match and Hamlet theme.
MVO:	Happiness is a cigar called Hamlet. The mild cigar.

Figure 11.8 Guinness: This 'Surfer Ad' appeared in 1999. It used morphing techniques (featuring horses galloping over waves) and a powerful drum-based musical score. The ad concentrated on Guinness' USP which was that it takes a long time to pour a pint. The metaphor for this was surfers waiting for the best wave. The ad finished with the line, 'Good things come to these who wait.' © Guinness. Agency: AMV BBDO.

Guinness

Guinness' 'Surfer' TV commercial ran on TV in 1999. The ad fixes on the product's USP which is that it takes a long time to pour. Part of the process of consuming Guinness is the long time it takes to pour the pint. The ad features a surfer who is waiting for the perfect wave. The ad was shot in Hawaii and featured a Polynesian surfer. It was filmed in grainy black and white. The camera focuses on the surfer. A voice over says: 'He waits that's what he does. And I'll tell you what. Tick follows tock follows tick follows tock.' Music featuring a heavy drum beat is played. As the waves rise white horses, which are morphed into the scene, gallop over the waves. The ad ends with the surfers on the beach celebrating the wave. The end slogan is 'Good things come to those who wait.' This slogan draws on the history of Guinness advertising – a previous slogan was 'Guinness is good for you' – and emphasises the product's USP.

The creatives who developed the commercial wanted the horses to represent the experience of riding a 60 foot wave.

The ad not only employs techniques of morphing, inviting the viewer to enjoy its filmic qualities (the commercial is estimated to have cost £1 million to produce) but it also intended to position the Guinness brand as young, trendy and sophisticated. Guinness has traditionally been a drink for older men. The ad employs techniques of suspense, drama and closure and combines fantasy escape and nostalgia. It also borrows familiar imagery from popular TV commercials in the 1970s for Old Spice which also featured surfers.

Summary

Most creative treatments attempt to grab attention and sustain interest. Creatives employ news-value criteria such as timeliness, prominence and proximity; they also use different or unusual images, distraction and presupposition to grab the consumer's attention. Once the attention is grabbed, creatives use other techniques to sustain interest, such as the use of suspense, mystery, fantasy and escape and nostalgia. Puzzles are often used, as well as traditional forms of storytelling. Creatives also try to undermine consumers' resistance and win their consent through personality endorsement, the use of stylish commercials, humour and, most recently, parody advertising. The ultimate aim of most advertising is to stimulate people to action, or to challenge or reinforce their beliefs. Some ads contain a direct exhortation to buy, others leave this as implicit. Because many advertisers believe that consumers have short memories, and because ads are seen days, sometimes weeks or months, before a purchase is made, many ads are constructed to aid memorability through the use of rhetorical techniques.

12 Formats, style and language

Three basic formats

There are three basic formats of advertising in commercials and print advertisements. They are presenter, demonstration, and slice-of-life ads.

Presenter

This direct speech form of communication is at the heart of most forms of advertising. It talks directly to the consumer via either a voice-over or a presenter talking straight to camera. A variation on the presenter is the testimonial. This is often done by famous people, but can be done by specialists (hairdressers and scientists), 'top breeders' for dogs, or 'housewives'. The purpose of these ads is to testify and explain the use of the product and to display a range of attributes that go with it. Presenters are also often chosen for their specific features – lips, hair, hands, teeth – which help to show off the product just like a fashion model. This type of presenter is the clothes-peg presenter.

Demonstration

Demonstration ads are the most common. They are not just about showing how a product works, they can also be about showing how it appears. The important thing is to get the consumer familiar with the product being used: the toilet roll being unravelled to show length, butter being curled and spread on bread (to show ease of spreading), cars driving (not static), food being cooked, washing-up liquid working on plates, beer or lager being poured, chocolates being given out or eaten, Oxo being sprinkled into the casserole dish, coffee being poured or drunk in the Gold Blend commercial. Demonstration ads can use visual aids, such as charts, graphics or computer graphics, to show how the product works, such as a razor's double action on tricky hairs, or how double-action lozenges both work on your throat and help to clear your nose (with the help of a cartoon to show how it is released), or how tartar collects on teeth (with plastic models). Cameras can also be used to go into a washing machine and show how the dirt is lifted, or into the washing bowl to show how grease is lifted from the plate, using slow motion. A demonstration ad for Volvo had a driver in a car talking in real time, while the car was crashed into in slow motion. As it occurred he pointed out the features, which included a collapsing central aisle and the strength of the doors from side-impact. Though camera tricks are often used, demonstration ads provide empirical proof of the product's benefits. What viewers can see and hear is justifiable evidence that it is the case.

Demonstration ads can also use showmanship. Unifilla's ad involved boring a hole into the side of a rock in the Grand Canyon. The hole was filled with Unifilla. A hook was bored into the Unifilla and a rope attached. A climber then parascended the rock using the rope, and (surprise surprise) the Unifilla held, demonstrating that Unifilla stays in the hole you put it in. Often such ads involve using a crisis, from soiled carpets to gluing a man to a board above shark-invested water (Solvite adhesive).

Figure 12.1 Daz: TV personality Danny Baker featured in an example of a presenter commercial with a combination of direct and indirect modes of address for Daz. It involved challenging the 'housewife' to compare Daz to branded and own-label rivals. The sequence involved a doorstep interview with a consumer, filmed experts of 'the challenge', endorsement of the brand by the 'housewife' and then Danny Baker talking directly to the consumer about the benefits of the brand. He was later replaced by Shane Ritchie and then Julian Clary. © Procter & Gamble. Agency: Leo Burnett.

The before-and-after commercial is one of the oldest and still very popular. Before-and-after techniques are used in the slimming, anti-dandruff and spot cream ads, all the demonstration ads which involve washing clothes and washing floors (comparison ads). The before-and-after or comparison ad was subverted by a BMP information commercial about HIV which had an attractive young woman in two photographs: 'One of these has HIV' (see Figures 12.2a, b). Another type of demonstration ad is the show-and-tell, which shows the action taking place, not before and after. The Black & Decker Workmate ad did this, with a simple voice-over talking people through a demonstration.

IF THIS WOMAN HAD THE VIRUS WHICH LEADS TO AIDS, IN A FEW YEARS SHE COULD LOOK LIKE THE PERSON OVER THE PAGE.

Figure 12.2a

WORRYING ISN'T IT.

The virus that leads to AIDS is known as the Human Immunodeficiency Virus. Or HIV.

A person can be infected with HIV for several years before it shows any signs or symptoms.

During this time, however, it can be passed on, through sexual intercourse, to more and more people.

There are already many thousands of people in this country who are unaware that they have the virus.

Obviously the more people you sleep with the more chance you have of becoming infected.

But having fewer partners is only part of the answer. Safer sex also means using a condom, or even having sex that avoids penetration.

HIV infection may be impossible to recognise, but it is possible to avoid.

AIDS. YOU'RE AS SAFE AS YOU WANT TO BE.

FOR MORE INFORMATION OR CONFIDENTIAL ADVICE ABOUT AIDS, FREEPHONE THE 24-HOUR NATIONAL AIDS HELPLINE ON 0800 567123.

Figure 12.2b Health Education Authority: this press ad uses juxtaposition and irony to get the message across. At this time it was important to emphasise that HIV infection among the heterosexual population was also growing. The use of repetition is intended to catch the reader's attention. It is also a play on the before-and-after genre of advertising. © Health Education Authority. Agency: BMP DDB Needham.

Slice-of-life

Slice-of-life advertisements show the product in use and the types of people who use it. Slice-of-life commercials and print ads connect brands to the real world of consumption; brands appear natural and everyday. The purpose is to portray the person buying the goods at a showroom or supermarket, or consuming the goods in the most appropriate situation. Slice-of-life commercials can also suggest new or different ways of consuming the product, showing people eating and drinking throughout the day, eating corn flakes at night. It also suggests preferred ways of consuming: people buying Roses chocolates for other people, sharing a pizza with friends, consuming luxury goods such as Galaxy in private.

The three genres of advertising are often mixed in one ad; the slice-of-life ad often includes a demonstration. With Procter & Gamble's Flash, for instance, the mother and son argue over which brand cleans the floor best, they draw a line and challenge each other to a competition. The beginning and end are the 'real-life' situations. Persil, Head & Shoulders and Wrigley's all produce these kinds of commercials.

Form, style and tone

All advertising begins with orientation. In print ads, the photograph, headline and first paragraph establish the scene, in TV commercials it would include the first shots, the background music and sound effects. In radio it would include sounds of the first scenes. If the advertiser uses a traditional narrative structure, the complication is often accompanied in TV and radio ads with louder or faster sound effects; often the ad may have a build-up around the crisis. In the Yellow Pages ad, the music changes to hurried jazz music; when the boy spots the scratch the music stops and then starts again as the problem is resolved, only to shriek again at the end when a new problem is found.

Because the creative is told that most people on average take 1.5 seconds to read each print ad, the style of the copy has to be as short and concise as possible with short snappy sentences, compound words and heavy punctuation: dashes, full stops and semicolons. The main point of the story is indicated by the headline and the picture. Headlines often include 'key' words such as 'new', 'save', 'win', 'try', 'get' or 'buy' to try to hook the reader. 'Free' is the most overused term in advertising, and according to advertisers the most effective. Headlines add emphasis to a certain word by letting it stand on its own in one line, or by emboldening or colouring it. The headline and introduction need to hook the reader, by offering a promise, providing some mystery or setting up an ambiguity that can be resolved only by reading on.

Pictures are easier to read than words: they take less effort and give the eye freer movement. When writing captions copywriters try to bestow meanings on the picture. If the reader can already make out a certain meaning from the photograph there is no point to the caption. The caption should try to explain to the reader what is going on, not describe the picture. Copywriters hardly ever write something that the reader can already see, they anchor the meaning of the photograph. All characters are usually named.

TV commercials may have only 30 seconds to get the story across, hence the need for many short cuts and short sentences. Because of constraints on time, advertisers need to imply events in the story and use metaphor as a form of shorthand. People's attention moves from looking at pictures to listening to the voice-over (or music) to reading text. Where you place these and in what sequence is part of the technique of hooking the viewer. When showing an intricate piece of film, or one in which the attention of the viewer is required, words are often kept to a minimum to keep the viewer's attention. If there is more to say in a commercial, the less action there should be, to enable the viewer to focus on the message. If words ('supers') are used in TV commercials alongside pictures, creatives try not to use images that distract from the text. One Dulux commercial had a series of country scenes with 'wild' flowers to illustrate the names of paints, the music over the top was 'Whiter Shade of Pale' and the scene was framed with a black strip across the bottom. The music begins, each scene is played through, and there is a pause after each picture of the different meadows and orchards to say which paint this stands for. The pause gives the viewer time to look at the picture then to read, look at the picture then read, etc., and at the same time, or while pausing, to focus on the music and its signification that this is a commercial about off-white paint.

Directors of commercials make use of slow motion to give drama and emphasis: drinks slowly pouring into a glass to emphasise luxury, or Ian Wright in the Nike commercial to emphasise skills and analyse movements. Slowing down fast action events (such as athletics, cars going fast) emphasises the movement more and gives the viewer a privileged view of the action. Commercials can also be speeded up for humour (the Kit Kat commercial with the customs man taking a break as cars and elephants quickly passed behind him) or to show the frenzy of day-to-day life, and then slow down into normal speed to wind down. Jewson made speeded-up commercials to show how quick and simple it was to use their DIY products. The time sequence is also important in hooking the reader. The narration may be set in the present but the dialogue may move to the past, then back to the present and back to the past again, as in one Werther's Original ad.

Creatives often leave the product or brand until last in print ads because it is seen to put off the reader. Similarly, TV commercials often leave the slogan and product to the end; if the advertiser goes in first off with the product, the viewer will automatically switch off.

Most designs will have a specific point at which the eye should meet the page. It should be the main point of interest. It may be a model's eyes, a gesture, an object, etc., which relates to the main selling point of the product. When ads are set up by creatives, they are usually constructed so the eye will follow left to right across the page and top to bottom. According to the perceived wisdom, the eye focuses above the centre of the page. The purpose is to follow the grammar of reading a page, because we usually read books from the top left of a page to the bottom right before turning over. Because young people in particular are supposed to be less familiar with book reading and linear forms of communication, preferring instead the zapping culture of TV and video games, advertisers see design for the younger generation as less traditionally structured and more centred on strong images which grab attention rather than tracing 'natural' eye movements. In designing a single-page ad many advertisers include the picture in the top third of the page (with text underneath), or in the top two-thirds (with text underneath). Double-page spreads also tend to have pictures across the top two-thirds of the page. Again the reasoning is that the eye does not focus on the centre of the page but is off-centre.

Familiar design, like familiar language, is used to backdrop something that will stand out. Consistency and familiarity are the keys to understanding advertising, because then you can establish difference by making one aspect stand out. The old principle of design that advertisers followed was that the layout should have balance and unity, that all the parts should be symmetrical or at least balanced in weight. Modern design tends to be less unified and to weight elements to one side of the page, largely because of changes in design and typography since the 1980s.

Many ads use framing devices in order to focus the viewer's or reader's attention. One of these devices, called the mortise frame, is basically a hole through which the viewer is invited to view a slice of life, or the use of a product. Framing is a device which anchors the visual message and indicates a preferred reading to the viewer or reader. The purpose of it is to join the brand to the representations in the rest of the page (Goldman 1992: 61–84).

Advertisers use techniques to keep the eye moving over the page, such as bold, italics and varying the size of the typefaces. Blobs (dots), numbers, underlining, and subheads which break up the text and pull in the reader are also used in newspapers. Characters can be in a lighter shade, or emboldened to add emphasis: colour and size are also important. Large initial letters dropped into the text at the start of paragraphs can also be used to break up texts, and give the effect of magazine articles.

The tone of an ad is set by a number of factors: sound effects and music to denote mood, place and time (train sounds, heartbeats and romantic music) help to conjure up a preferred picture for the viewer. In an ad for RAC: haunting menacing tune, quick cuts and then the RAC Knight of the Road turns up and all is resolved and calm. Advertising music often ascends to a climax which indicates to the viewer or listener that there is a conclusion. The tone of the music, classical or popular, can be mellow, soothing, explosive or thrilling.

The tone of voice of the actors – soothing, authoritative, upbeat – their expression, knowing looks, familiarity or lack of it with other characters, all suggest non-verbal communications in their relationships. Ringing someone up isn't just saying 'hello', it is also adopting different social norms: saying hello to someone you don't know and need to get something from (official), or someone you haven't seen in years (excited), or someone you are very familiar with (matter of fact) or are having a relationship with (intimate).

Colour is also used to set the tone. Blue is supposed to be a cold colour, used to create distance, because of connotations about blue skies. Red is a more intense colour, as are yellow and orange (warm). Black can be sophisticated and mysterious and sinister. Purple suggests luxury (especially silk). Many designs combine soft or cold colours with warm: red and green, yellow and green (BP), red and blue (BT), etc. – or can be nationalistic, using red, white and blue. Colours can be treated as metaphors for nature: green grass and trees, brown earth, blue skies, black night and darkness, red blood and passion, yellow and orange fruit.

Typography can also set the tone: a curly serif script can give the tone of the article a conservative and traditional appeal, a big bold sans serif typeface such as Helvetica or Futura can give a modern, brash tone. There are many families of typeface but the ones most commonly used include the serif old roman style (such as Goudy, Garamond and Bembo). These are often associated with authority and tradition. The transitional serif styles often used in newspapers include Times, Century Schoolbook and Baskerville. The script styles include Vivaldi, Palace Script and Regency (these resemble elegant handwriting and are often used to denote classical and elegant styles – Regency would be good for a luxury fountain pen). The more 'designer' styles include Revue,

TIMES IS A SERIF FACE   Times is a serif face

HELVETICA IS A SANS SERIF FACE   Helvetica is a sans serif face

This is a three-deck headline

This is a three-deck headline

And this here is a four-deck headline

And this here is a four-deck headline

Lynz Font, San Francisco, which like the script styles are hardly ever used in continuous text. Germanic typefaces such as Blackmoor are used in Dracula films and have gothic or medieval connotations.

The tone has to be appropriate to the kind of product. A tone of peace, comfort and warmth may not be appropriate for a sports car, whereas a fast, powerful and dynamic tone may not be right for a cardigan. There is also a tone to the way in which copy is written, whether it is humorous, official, colloquial, dialect, or chatty. Lighting in pictures, and the design of the page – hurried, formal and classical; colourful or youthful – also convey tone.

Ads which go in older women's magazines may take the form of romantic fiction, commercials aimed at young people may use a pop video genre, those aimed at personal finance may take the form of a journalistic piece, those aimed at cinemagoers may have high production values, and a more detailed story line with wide-angle shots, etc. Those aimed at kids in the computer generation may use computer graphics. Creatives watch films that the prospective consumer would watch, and copy their sound effects and filmic techniques; a fight scene might have fast rock music in the background, which stops when the decisive blow hits the bad guy, suggesting resolution.

Persuasive language

Advertisers use adjectives to build up the brand. Adjectives convey mood and emotion; these are the imagistic elements of the brand, these are what makes the brand rise above being a product. Their purpose is to add value to the product and the brand. It is often adjectives which convey the brand's values: young, youthful, fun, soft, strong, warm, traditional, modern. Similarly, adverbs are also important: smoothly, softly, quietly. Adjectives fit appropriately with different types of products: cars may be sleek, elegant, powerful; chocolate bars smooth, creamy; toilet cleaner fresh, fast, hard-working; fast food cafés fun, quick, etc.; clothing smart, practical, warm. The most used adjectives tend to be: free, new, better, best, full, fresh, fine, big (a big bite), real, great, safe, clean, delicious, full, rich (as in coffee). Flowery language can put readers off, as do clichés, double negatives, waffle and jargon (language only a few people understand). In this example from a TV commercial from the 1960s, the words which add to the emotional feel of the brand have been italicised. The purpose of using such descriptive language is to set a mood and tone which creates positive imagery:

> Inside this can is a meal so *tasty* you might have made it yourself. It's the *new* Fray Bentos Steak and Kidney pie. Your butcher couldn't sell you *better* meat. *Prime, lean* steak *tender* kidney . . . in *good rich meaty* gravy – and capped by *lovely, light, crispy* pastry. A meal like this sets a man up! The new Fray Bentos Steak and Kidney Pie.
>
> (Leech 1966: 35)

The content of the copy is straightforward; Fray Bentos steak and kidney pies contain steak, kidney, gravy and pastry. However the form of the copy uses adjectives to add imagery. This type of puffery has been endlessly parodied but is still used today. Advertising adds extra values to the products through the use of adjectives and persuasive language. Adjectives and visual metaphors work together in a powerful combination. Chocolate bars can be visually described as smooth and creamy by placing them next to silk and cream. A sore throat can be represented by a French bread stick morphing into a wooden log.

But overly emotive language in advertising is more of an exception than the rule because consumers are perceived to have become weary of it. Over-exaggeration loses credibility in the eyes of the consumer. Crompton calls for common sense in copywriting: 'Facts presented clearly, sympathetically, and with inexorable logic – and leavened with a little emotion – are best of all' (Crompton 1987: 64).

Verbs are also perceived to work well in body copy: 'see how the . . .', 'look how the . . .', 'fill your tank' give the impression of movement and action. Creatives also use language to emphasise the uniqueness of the brand: 'the' rather than 'a': the leading brand, rather than a leading brand. It excludes other brands and alternative things that the consumer could be doing. 'The best way to unwind your day'. Also phrases such as 'The *Sunday Times* is the Sunday papers', and 'Coke is it' perform a similar function. This radio ad (aired in 2000) for Lurpak Butter uses humour and pastiche of DIY TV programmes to get across a call to action.

PRESENTER	(In pastiche of DIY programme): Before you tackle any job, always make sure you've got the right tools. Now for this one, you'll need a hammer and chisel.
SFX	Chisel chipping away at solid block.
PRESENTER	Not too hard mind, you don't want the whole thing to crack and split.
SFX	Chisel stops.
PRESENTER	Right when you've chiselled away the right amount, just take the oxyacetylene blowtorch
SFX	Blowtorch firing up.
PRESENTER	Be careful with this, always wear gloves and goggles And within seconds . . . the butter should be ready to spread.
PENELOPE KEITH	Alternatively try Lurpak Spreadable. It spreads straight from the fridge.

This ad gets across Lurpak's USP (unlike other butter it spreads straight from the fridge) as well use using the verb 'try' as a call to action.

Language games and rhetoric

Language games are less directly persuasive. They are playful and used to help the brand stand out, disarm or distract the consumer and aid memory. Brand-names can be used to convey the functional performance of the brand (such as Flash), or its rewards (Comfort fabric softener). Some, like Kodak, were meaningless words, made up in the late nineteenth century for easy memorability and because they transferred across countries. In the early nineteenth century Cadbury moved their factory to Bournbrook in the midlands and because French chocolate was so popular changed the name of their chocolate selection to Bournville. Recently Unilever brought out a brand called 'I can't believe it's not butter', and Wall's (also owned by Unilever) one called 'Too good to be true' (a fat-free ice cream). Other examples include 'Chicken Tonight' sauce ranges. The name works with the slogan 'I feel like "Chicken Tonight"'. The main purpose of these brand-names was to help in the advertising campaign and to point to the main selling point of the brand.

In the early days of advertising, grabbing attention meant departing from formal rules of grammar and language, misspelling words, mispronouncing them on TV, or inventing new words. Language games try to make brands in an oversaturated market stand out and be original to stay ahead of the rest.

Making an adjective out of a verb, such as crumble to crumbly, crunch to crunchy, chew to chewy, or out of a noun, such as flake to flaky, meat to meaty, beef to beefy, chocolate to chocolatey, also illustrates the ways that words are changed to convey meaning. Medicines are not just for cold symptoms, but for chesty cough, tickly throat, runny nose. The y-suffix is a more playful child-like use of language: calling something chocolate is factual, calling something chocolatey is intended to evoke extra meanings about chocolate (such as creaminess, sweetness and brownness). Word and phrase invention includes compounding words, such as fast-acting, built-in bedrooms, self-assembly, satin-soft, farmhouse-fresh, feather-light, home-made, sugar-coated, chocolate-flavoured, longer-lasting, ready-to-eat, chicken-in-a-bun, fillet-o-fish. Also compounding two nouns: toothbrush, fireplace, deeppan pizza. Compounding also takes place with the use of the word 'n' to make three words into one: thin 'n' crispy, scratch 'n' sniff, fish 'n' chips, pick 'n' mix. These colloquial forms are combined with the familiar use of I'll, you'll, don't, he's, she's – an attempt by the advertiser to mimic speech and talk more personally and directly to the consumer.

Rhetoric is the technique of using speech and writing to maximise impact and aid memorability. The rhetorical techniques used by advertisers include the use of repetition. Repetition as a sales technique is one of the oldest forms, from the eighteenth and nineteenth century, when it was done in newspaper advertisements, to its use in street markets to catch passing shoppers' attention: 'I'll knock not one pound, not three pounds, not five pounds, not ten pounds, but twenty whole crisp lovely pounds off, just for you missus, there you go, yours for a tenner.'

Figure 12.3 Pepperami: the use of an animated figure and the strapline 'A bit of an animal' make the product come to life as a wild character and emphasise the meatiness of the brand, challenging the health-conscious vegetarian lobby and appealing to consumers who enjoy meat. 'A bit of an animal' is a play on words. © Van den Bergh Foods, Unilever. Agency: S. P. Lintas.

Repetition can include repeating the same sound through alliteration and assonance ('Beanz Meanz Heinz') or a jingle to aid memorability. Alliteration involves repeating the first or last letter or syllables in words. In the nineteenth century alliteration was a very common way of increasing memorability and impact. In the USA medicines had such titles as Botanic Blood Balm, Copeland's Cholera Cure, Goff's Giant Globules, Dr Jordan's Joyous Julep. The name Coca-Cola was also created because of its memorable sound (Prendergrast 1993: 32). Lever copied this American trend by branding his first soap Sunlight Soap. Assonance is also used where words have similar sounds and are easily remembered: 'Get busy with the fizzy' for Sodastream.

Consumers have become so used to repetitive techniques in films, television and journalism that they at least expect a punchline at the end, or they are dissatisfied. To add impact a speech maker will often make three points in delivery; again, this is largely because of convention, as in road safety: 'Think once, think twice, think bike.' Repetition can also work visually, as with photographs of the same product or person in different situations. Repetition adds emphasis and consistency: the different executions of Carling Black Label commercials basically repeat the same gag. Repetition is meant to aid memorability and impact because it deals in and highlights uniqueness. It can also be used in design, having several pictures next to each other, with one standing out as different, or with a different endline, as in the following, where repetition is used and there is an endline for emphasis:

It's new!
It's crisper!
It's lighter!
It's the
New Ryvita

(Leech 1966: 190)

'Widnes car centre 0–5–1–4–2–0–two thousand, 4–2–0–two thousand.' This ad has been on the radio for over ten years said by the same man, the car dealer manager, John Leech, who repeats it consistently with the same banal rhyming tone. It may be irritating, but it is memorable. If you want to buy a 'new or used Nissan Car', you don't even have to look in the phone book.

Sameness highlights difference. That is why there are so many new executions of an essentially similar theme, the same principle in sameness (simile) as in repetition. If we look at similes such as 'red as beetroot', the reason why this simile has worked is because of the difference, not the similarity between the person's face and the beetroot. It is only the colour which is similar; it is the comparison of the person's face and the vegetable that makes the rhetoric more impactful. Using similarity is really about playing with familiarity, taking things which are familiar to us and making them unusual and unfamiliar. As Crompton points out when talking about the 'Inch War', colliding words work better rhetorically and deliver impact. Phrases are also compounded to associate different feelings with products: 'Smell the golden roast', 'Feel the whiteness', 'Eat a bowl of sunshine' (Kellogg's), 'The Inch War. Ryvita wants you to win' (Crompton 1987: 55). A TV commercial for Polo had a girl in a shop telling the shopkeeper that the mints are so 'clean tasting'.

Similarly, juxtaposition occurs where two opposite or competing subjects can be placed side by side. Before-and-afters are the classic example of this rhetorical technique. Clashing words and phrases and clashing cultures are often used, or clashing genders such as men in women's roles, and vice versa. The aim yet again with juxtaposition and contradiction is to highlight difference. Another form is to use 'us and them': the overweight Germans in the Carling commercial contrasted to the handsome and smooth English holidaymaker. The classic juxtaposition is the hip, cool and smooth westerner in a backward, Third World country. One variation on this theme was a cinema ad for Bacardi in 1993: the voice-over featured shots of a young woman in a bikini, a beach and bar in a tropical paradise, and referred to them as 'Aunty Beryl' and 'The Dog and Duck', juxtaposing scenes of tropical paradise with the humdrum of daily life. The implication is that if you drink Bacardi you can buy into paradise, or at least buy into the fantasy.

Parallelism involves juxtaposition of different but related things or statements. A good example is the David Bailey camera ad for Olympus OM40: 'It had to be shot at dusk, or I'd have been shot at dawn' (Evans 1988: 148). Similarly the HIV information commercial discussed earlier, and the Christian Aid ad 'Give a man a fish and he'll eat for a day, teach a man to fish and he'll eat for life' (Crompton 1987: 98).

Just as repeating things and emphasising similarities sets up a familiarity with the reader, so too does setting a familiar scene and omitting a vital element. In 1986 the *Independent* newspaper ran a famous teaser campaign of 'It is. Are you?', which had a number of variations, including posters with wallpaper and 'It isn't. Are you?' on them.

Paradox is used when a statement or evidence is used to conflict with the consensus notions or preconceived ideas of reality: 'These two powders may look the same, but in tests . . .'. This may also take the form of a 'did you know?' rhetorical question. This paradoxical method is used to challenge existing beliefs about products and brands, often using statistics and tests. It is also used to give consumers 'privileged' information, letting them in on a secret. It often takes the form of image versus reality.

Another technique is omission. The vital element – usually the brand image, the product itself, or something directly related to the brand or product – is often omitted. Omission is meant to get people to sit up. It sets up a puzzle for consumers, which they are invited to resolve. Sometimes the omission can be done to suggest that something is going on: clothes and jeans found next to a pool of water, or certain expected sounds being left out, people being left out (the drink driving campaign had a child's photo but no child).

Readers or viewers are left to come up with their own conclusions as to what is going on and why. But their own conclusions should always fall in line with the preferred reading. Omission can also add value to the product, making it appear omnipresent. The Marlboro campaign discussed above is a case in point.

Ambiguity is where the statement or the image has more than one preferred meaning. Signs have many meanings attached to them (see Chapter 13 on effects): the use of ambiguity is the deliberate use of two or more meanings to deliver impact. Double entendres are common as are puns, which pepper everyday English discourse. Words are also deliberately misspelt, some for puns: such as Perrier's H2 Eau, Oh Neau, etc. and Pernod's spelling of Perno, without the 'd'. Puns and double meanings are used to make people think twice when reading the ad, from 'Suck it and vitamin C' in the 1960s to 'Everyone's a Fruit and Nut case'. In the 1960s these word games were commonplace: 'Drinka Pinta Milka Day', 'Unzipp a Banana', 'Schweppervescence', 'Ross Freezum as they Catchum!', 'Gotta Lotta Bottle', 'Wot-alot-e-got' (Smarties), 'Beanz Meanz Heinz', 'For your Blooming Generations' (for Flora margarine). Ambiguity makes the consumer look twice, or listen twice. The actor may add emphasis, or the typography may add emphasis to highlight the double meaning.

Example

Orange

Hutchinson Telecom wanted a brand-name for a new digital cellular phone company that would be bold and memorable and stand out from the technology-driven names of Cellnet and Vodafone. Design and branding consultant Wolf Olins provided 1,400 names. The company decided on Orange. 'It gave us an opportunity to "own" the colour. We can do a lot of things with that. The name by itself is memorable with our little logo', Hans Snook said to *Business Age* (July 1994, no. 46: 58). In 1997 Hutchinson Telecom changed its name to Orange. Throughout the 1990s several other companies established brand names that had utility in other areas and bore no relationship to the product it sold such as the Goldfish credit card, Egg and Smile on-line banking and Monster.com a recruitment website.

Boddingtons

Manchester beer brand Boddingtons developed a TV commercial in the late 1990s which employed juxtaposition as a rhetorical device. The brand needed to attract younger drinkers and give a more appealing glamorous and stylish image.

The first ad was a parody of a Calvin Klein fragrance ad shot in black and white set in and around a house in Malibu and featured half naked men and the then unknown model Melanie Sykes. At the end of the ad Sykes says in a broad Mancunian accent, 'Hey Torquil, are those trolleys (underpants) on the right way round?'. Another ad parodied a Pirelli tyres ad featuring Carl Lewis. It was set in the California desert and included a male sprinter who stops next to an ice cream van. Sykes serves him a pint of Boddingtons and says, 'Do you want an ice cream in that love?', he replies in a Mancunian accent, 'Ta'. The use of the regional accent which in popular culture is the opposite of glamour provides the humour and works as an effective rhetorical device to improve memorability and stand-out.

Summary

There are three basic formats to most advertisements: presenter, demonstration and slice-of-life. The most common TV ad is the demonstration ad, which demonstrates the features, use or USP of the product. Slice-of-life commercials are commonly associated with lifestyle advertising. However, most advertisements feature a combination of these formats. Creatives employ a number of stylistic techniques to grab the attention of the consumer: conventions of design and typography, adjectives, language games and rhetorical devices such as repetition and sameness stand out and act as an aid to memory. Creatives also spend a great deal of time calculating the form, style and tone of the advertisements and use combinations of music, colour, typography, costume, voice, camera speed and lighting to evoke the right atmosphere. The sole purpose of such treatments is to produce the right kinds of reactions in the right target consumers.

13 Measuring effectiveness

···

If you are buying a chair, a good salesman will find out what you want it for and say 'well, if that's where you're going to put it, you're going to watch TV in it. The most important thing is that it should be really comfortable. This chair really is comfortable – don't take my word for it, sir, try it for yourself!' You will indeed make your own mind up about how comfortable it is – but the salesman has neatly diverted you from the fact that the chair is not especially attractive.

(Brown 1991: 35)

Unfortunately, the results of advertising are not discernible, or, at any rate, as traceable to their real causes, as those who have faith in the power of advertising would like to see. ... The weather, the seasons, trade prosperity or depression, the advertising of rival commodities and a hundred other reasons [made it frequently] ... impossible to attribute the change to any one advertisement or general advertisement scheme.

(British advertising agent S. H. Benson, writing
in 1901 in a book called *Wisdom in Advertising*
(Piggott 1975: 26))

The first criterion for effectiveness is that sufficient numbers of the target audience should get to see or hear the ad. This is not as obvious as it sounds: there is a great deal of debate about how much the respondent needs to see before desire and action are stimulated. Some ads are intended for immediate impact, others are intended to remind consumers and take more viewings for effect. It is primarily media research which determines whether TV or radio or press goes on a media buyer's schedule. This is largely concerned with measuring the efficiency of the campaign. Market and advertising research seeks to isolate and measure the effectiveness of advertising messages on consumers and how far the goals of the campaign have been attained to provide a guide for future action.

Pre-testing copy

A large amount of an account planner's time is spent on pre-testing ads. There are two types of pre-tests. The first type is done to influence how the creative will appear, and is often called creative development research. This methodology often involves animatics (cartoons), photomatics (photostories) with selected groups of consumers; these influence the creative treatment before the ad is completed; characters, music, setting and the endlines are frequently changed, as is text. This type of research is done if an advertiser is taking a risk with a new campaign using different messages. The second type of pre-testing decides whether the completed ad will run: 'whereas in creative development research, the advertisement is held to be innocent until proved guilty, in pre-testing it is held to be guilty until proved innocent' (Stewart-Hunter in Cowley 1989: 133).

Pre-testing print ads involves folders which the respondents browse through. The ad is put alongside other ads and editorial. The respondent is first asked about recall and then asked questions about the ads to judge comprehension, mood, liking, feelings and interest of the product. The intentions of the ad will inform the questions.

Filmed commercials are often shown in a hall. Respondents can be asked attitude questions before and after the filming. If the ad is next to a comedy show, documentary or news item, the different contexts are gauged. Usually all the advertiser wants to know is whether the contents mix is right, if the right message is getting through, whether insurance policies should use ease, safety, security, pleasure or entertainment. This kind of testing is based on contents research, rather than context research. Pre-testing is supposed to measure attitude and preference shift (choosing a product differently after being shown the commercial). Sometimes the client may take the advertisement out to a market research company for independent evaluation rather than rely on the agency's own evaluations.

Advertisers hardly ever measure intent to purchase (also known as persuasion shifts). Quantitative pre-testing, where the respondents mark what they have seen on the basis of awareness and interest, is also used called the Awareness Index. Persuasion shift places the emphasis firmly upon the creative treatment in influencing the consumer to go out and buy. It measures change in attitude and intention before and after a commercial is shown. It is a direct and linear measure of cause and effect; part of the hypodermic model. This gave the idea that a single message could be powerful on its own. However, this model has never caught on in the UK (US researchers use a dial which respondents turn to show their interest and appreciation for an ad).

Another measure which also places emphasis on the creative treatment is the emotive aspect of the sell, which measures likeability rather than persuasion.

;umes that if the consumers liked the ad, they would also like the brand.
:his is an indirect measure: some ads, especially for soaps and deter-
ıre not liked, but are supposed to be 'effective'.

The persuasion shift method of judging advertising involves the belief
that 'advertising's role is to impart shattering new information that will immediately change consumers' minds about a brand' (Powell 1994: 33). In the USA
big packaged-goods manufacturers like Procter & Gamble made extensive use
of these techniques, which contributed to the widespread use of reason-why
demonstration ads, rather than image, humour and 'soft-sell' advertising. This
partly reflected a belief in the USA in a direct relationship between mass-media
advertising and sales effectiveness. Simon Broadbent indicates that the 'more
sales' criterion at the heart of the persuasion model is 'a relic of the expan-
sionist era. In some categories, overall growth is now impossible and holding
off competitors is itself an achievement' (Broadbent 1992: 17).

Sales research

In 1927 Coca-Cola conducted sales research to determine where their sales were
biggest. They found that around a third of their sales outlets accounted for about
60 per cent of sales, and the bottom third sold only 10 per cent of the total
(Prendergrast 1993: 166). They also found that many of the high-volume outlets
did not have Coca-Cola signs in the shops or just outside, so salespeople were
dispatched four times a year to deliver merchandising and to encourage more
sales of the drink. Sales research is generally conducted within the company
or with the co-operation of retailers.

Electronic scanners, which are most often seen in supermarkets, carry large
amounts of information from bar codes on products: where, what, when, how,
and in some cases who purchased goods. Bar codes appear on many goods
such as furniture, newspapers, magazines and computers. Scanning allows
advertisers and retailers to know the effects on sales of price reductions and
increases and the effects of advertising promotions, in a tightly defined
geographical space in a matter of days. The advertiser calculates how sensitive
the brand is to price changes, the short- and long-term effect of promotion and
different executions and seasonal variations. Sales promotion information can
be collected the same day in supermarkets. By 2000 around 90 per cent of all
packaged groceries passed over scanners, and market research company Nielsen
predict that this will rise to 80 per cent by 1995. Retail audits let the manufacturer know where the product was placed in the shop (end of aisle, eye level,
etc.) and how well competitors did.

Another way of measuring sales effectiveness of advertising is in direct
response advertising: the effectiveness of the medium, communications message,
etc., can be measured in terms of replies on sales in certain cases, though again
this is not isolatable. For instance the *Daily Telegraph*'s use of direct mail is

important because it is not isolatable from its ad and PR campaigns and much of the internal promotion of the newspaper (see Postscript).

Advertisers are aware that sales and effectiveness are determined by many variables, of which advertising is only one. 'The sales of a product are determined by the mix of marketing variables: the product, the price, the package, the public relations, the merchandising, the salesforce, the distribution. No element of the mix taken in isolation can be a unique determinant of sales ... all the elements must pull together in combination (and in the right sequence)' (Evans 1988: 6). Not only are other aspects of the marketing mix important, but also the placement, position, timing, reach and frequency of the campaign (apart from the contents) inform the 'effectiveness'. The problem is of isolating not only the advertising but also the creative messages from the media buying and planning, the relative effectiveness of each medium and the fact that consumers gain their knowledge from main different sources – friends, family, articles, programmes, education or schools, the workplace, etc. – as well as memory.

Advertisers tend to justify advertising effects in terms of sales because often they have to sell the advertising to their board. Hard sales figures are easier to sell to the finance director and chief executive than increased brand awareness. Agencies and marketers therefore need to convince sceptics by pointing to sales increases. But this is not the main point of advertising, it is an ultimate goal of a marketing campaign, of which advertising is a part. Because of this there is often a conflict and contradiction in what the marketing department wants to measure.

Models of consumer behaviour

Linear models

One of the first models of consumer behaviour was developed in the 1920s by Daniel Starch, who said that ads had to be seen, read, believed, remembered and acted upon (Clark 1988: 106). This was a forerunner to the popular AIDA model of the post-war era (see Chapter 11), and DAGMAR (Defining Advertising Goals of Measured Advertising Results) which was developed in 1961 by R. Colley. Advertisers also know this model as the hierarchy-of-effects model. Like AIDA it is a linear model which assumes that consumers follow rational consuming patterns and decision-making processes. It was seen as an improvement because it took account of the consumer's reactions. Advertising was meant to be planned by selecting goals which could be measured or quantified. The DAGMAR model follows the route of awareness–comprehension (rather than interest)–conviction (rather than desire) and action. Conviction is developed by trying to match the needs of the consumer with the promise of the product.

Both AIDA and DAGMAR models imply that advertising should inject believable and memorable messages, that consumers are rational, and are stimulated by desires and convictions to act. Both models assume that consumers are 'triggered' to act in a certain way to advertisements. If they do not do so then they are either irrational, 'aberrant decoders', or inattentive. But the need for comprehension of the ad, or the understanding of all the codes in it, may not be necessary to get people to buy.

DAGMAR and AIDA assume that consumers have to pass through certain stages before reaching the action stages. They ignore the role of context, environment and mediation in influencing the advertising effectiveness.

Recall: passive victims

The hypodermic model of media effects is a very powerful discourse in society and in the advertising and media industries. The model involves a sender using a medium to transmit a message to a receiver in a linear way. As the term implies, the message is injected into the receiver who passively accepts it without question or negotiation.

The sender–receiver model emphasises the intentions and motivations of the sender; not the unintended effects or cumulative effects such as long-term attitude reinforcement or change. It also isolates the relationships from wider social, historical, economic, political and cultural relations.

Day-after recall was developed in the USA in the 1930s by George Gallup with Procter & Gamble to measure advertising effectiveness (Mattelhart 1991). It measures the memorability of advertising a day after impact or exposure. On average around 20 per cent of a TV audience can remember advertisements they saw on the TV the day before. But this does not measure the sales effectiveness of an advertisement, merely how memorable the advertisement was and the memory of the consumer. There is an argument in the advertising industry that agencies produce advertising work which will gain high memorability and high recall to impress the client with high scores, rather than work which will be persuasive or involve consumers.

Awareness: active victims

In the post-war period US communications researchers also attacked the sender–receiver model. Emphasis shifted to looking at the micro-process of communication and the role of opinion-formers. This was developed by Katz and Lazarsfeld, who rejected the sender–receiver model that implied the injection of advertising messages, and in their book *Personal Influence* developed the idea that communication was filtered and staggered via a 'two-step flow'.

The two-step flow model of communications suggests that advertising messages are not simply consumed and believed by individuals but filtered through 'opinion-formers', and peers who further mediate messages and transform them. Opinion-formers in the group or local community would use knowledge and persuasive information gained from the media to influence others, thus transforming or subverting the message. This model shifted emphasis from the sender to the receiver, it focused on the communications process after the media had been consumed, but was also influenced by the environment in which it was consumed. It focused on group and individual interactions and viewed society as pluralist, with small groups and elites who formed the opinions of others.

This assumes that people are able to select what they want to hear and see according to their pre-given social roles, values and interests. According to this model some people are more active consumers of the media than others.

Advertisers make use of the two-step flow model of communications, especially in campaigns aimed at changing opinions. 'Opinion-formers' are one of the biggest influences on people who are new to the market – usually parents and friends who influence buying decisions at this point. The influence of other opinion-formers, such as dentists, doctors and financial advisers, is also important. Advertisers seek to create and sustain awareness through media coverage (editorial comment, etc.) and through advertising to get the brand familiar to non-users who will be users in the future.

Awareness measures go beyond simple linear models of communication and persuasion shift, measuring not the impact of a single specific ad but the total awareness of the sales message generated by campaign(s). This model of sales technique sees the consumer not as a passive victim but as an active victim.

Awareness is about agenda-setting, delimiting the terms of debate and information for users. 'Consumers . . . discuss brands . . . occasionally, and what they say is very powerful because it seems to be independent' (Brown 1991: 36). The advertising sets the agenda for discussion and helps to sway it in favour of the brand. Even though consumers may resist advertising messages on TV, when the message is confirmed by others (journalists, salespeople, family and friends) then it is supposed to gain more support. This view sees advertising as engaging with the full gamut of cultural practices. It does not see a direct relationship between awareness and sales, but an indirect, agenda-setting role.

The AIDS campaign of 1987 had extremely high levels of awareness, but produced only 5 per cent of respondents who claimed to have changed their behaviour because of the campaign. It used fear, and that put many people off, they did not want to know about things that would kill them (Hart 1991: 195–197). This can have had a number of causes, but it is clear that raising awareness is not the same as changing behaviour. However, just because there is no proven correlation between awareness and consumer effects does not mean that advertising is ineffective. All it means is that no measure is or can be found to link awareness to effectiveness.

Though the emphasis of this awareness research was to move the communicative power from the sender to the receiver, it was still concerned with the effects of the media.

Figure 13.1 BP: an example of a corporate advertising campaign, which seeks to change attitudes. BP presents itself as a caring, benevolent, conscientious organisation, providing electricity so that this young African boy can do his homework. It is trying to change the image of BP as a large, capitalist, exploitative company. In 2000 BP went one stage further and changed its logo to look like a sunflower, suggesting that the Company was environmentally friendly and distancing it further from its main business which is oil and gas exploration and extraction. © BP. Agency: Saatchi & Saatchi.

Attitude

In the 1960s some advertisers broke with the assumption that advertising directly affected sales, especially when so many advertising campaigns did not result in sales success. As White points out, while AIDA was used by most, 'It was still very difficult to see how the process might work, or to account for the fact that some ads worked, and some consumers took action, but others stubbornly did not; or that an apparently good campaign failed to achieve extra sales – for sales were still the only real measure of effectiveness' (White 1988: 52). It had been sustainable in the 1930s and 1950s when there were increases in consumer demand brought about by the welfare state and the rise in real incomes. But by the 1960s this had begun to crumble, and advertising was seen as less effective at directly increasing sales.

New methods of measurement which included usage and attitude arose in the 1960s. Rather than just measuring the effect of a campaign after it happens, attitude research measured attitude before and after the campaign and what attitudes the consumer brought to the text before and after the commercial. Though this did not examine the context, it did shift the emphasis away from the 'power' of the message towards the consumer.

The new method can be summed up by research company British Market Research Bureau (BMRB): 'advertising works by helping to build in the consumer's mind a pattern of beliefs and attitudes relating to specific products' (Chisnall 1992: 241). It is basically an attitude survey, trying to find the area where attitude influences behaviour. This psychological approach measured the consumer's attitudes to brands. Advertisers were able to monitor changes in attitudes over time, and for their own commercial purposes gauge advertising campaigns' effectiveness on the extent of changes which they had instigated.

Attitude research showed that advertising does not have much short-term success (White 1988: 54), and that although attitudes cannot be changed overtly, they can be modified – especially hostile attitudes. The main examples of this are BT and British Rail. Though the latter have not been able to break the hostility of many to its services, they have managed to modify and channel the hostility, emphasising leisure travel rather than the nightmares of a very poor commuting service. Also, rather than trying to change the attitudes towards the brand itself, advertisers try to change and modify people's perceptions about what kind of people use the brand.

Attitudes and usage research is the most expensive because it combines qualitative and quantitative methods. The first survey on attitudes towards the brand or service is done, and then often three to six weeks after the campaign has started attitudes are measured again. The research is conducted in stages, rather than continuously, and repeated over a period of months and years (especially for attitude campaigns which need to be long-term, such as BR's). It can also stress changes in emphasis that may be needed during the campaign.

Attitude research can focus on the brand (I think Sayers cream cakes are attractive, well packaged), on the attitudes towards using the brand (whether you feel guilty about eating full-fat cream cakes, whether you see it as a treat, a sin or an indulgent pleasure), or on general cultural beliefs (towards such things as dieting, fatness, sinful food and pleasure or luxury).

As Randall points out, 'The fact that people have a favourable attitude towards our brand, or that we can change their attitude in a favourable direction, does not mean that their behaviour will change and that they will necessarily buy our brand' (Randall 1993: 40). But one of the biggest problems, and one which has undermined the whole linearity of behavioural models, is that advertising researchers have found that attitude changes can occur after as well as before a brand has been bought.

A basic premise of most effects research is that consumers use their perception to comprehend and learn. This is part of a rational process. Cognitive dissonance is supposed to occur because in certain product areas there is little product difference, and only the false expectations of the advertising and brand image are significant. For instance, with shampoo and beer, we buy the goods, then try to reduce dissonance between the hype and reality by convincing ourselves that we made the right choice. The consumers of beers and shampoos then want to be reassured and would pay more attention to advertisements for those brands. This model again assumes a rational, thinking, 'learning consumer', who constantly needs to rationalise buying decisions.

Dissonant means out of harmony. This view of human psychology supposes that we would like the world to be harmonious and simple to understand (complex issues are easy to understand and conflicts can be easily resolved), and we like to feel that we belong to a group (national, city, town, village, political party, professional group). People need rational reasons for doing irrational things in order to harmonise their world-view. This theory tries to account for irrational action, not asking why people did something (motivation) but examining the justifications for doing it – justifications, for instance, for buying a more expensive brand of lager than a cheaper one that tastes the same.

If we make a choice between brands, and there is very little difference between the two (as with lager); then, to justify our decision, we tend to exaggerate the benefits of the chosen lager over and above the rejected one (better tasting, more body, more alcohol content), making its appeal and interest increase rather than decrease after use. If you bought a car which had similar facilities, colours and features to all other cars in the range, after buying it you would try to find out more about the make (how it works, who else drives it), use the garage facilities of the dealers you bought it from (after-sales service, etc.), and maybe even join a users' club to justify your purchase. The idea is that your loyalty and positiveness towards the brand will increase to help you feel that you made the right decision.

However, cognitive dissonance is based upon certain assumptions about human motivations, that we seek to unify and harmonise the world. Again, this is a generalisable claim, it lacks specificity, it claims to be the same in all times and all ages, and for all people, and it is not testable. Nevertheless, this view has been well supported in the advertising industry among planners (psychologists and anthropologists) and among creatives.

Consumer panels and tracking studies

The tax on TV advertising in 1962 (see Chapter 7) increased costs for advertisers and made enormous dents in agency profits. One result was the 1963 TV consumer audit. It was the first time a major tracking study of sales against TV ads had been done. It gave details of retail sales of clients' brands which were being advertised in the TV region and measured the reactions of competitors, changes in price, ad expenditure weight and marketing strategies in each product category (Henry 1986: 97).

Contemporary versions of tracking studies have subscribers who pay research firms to provide the information on shifts in their market. Consumer panels measure trial, the amount of repeat buying, brand switching and the fall-off from a market; where the extra sales came from; whether existing users bought more; whether people switched brands, whether they trialed the product area for the first time (new users). This gives much more information than the retail audit. With bar-coding surveys can also tell which shop goods were bought from and at what price.

The Nielsen Homescan technique involves a hand-held scanner used in the home; the sample respondents scan the bar code on each item that comes into the house. Homescan tracks shopping day by day and examines how far trialists of a product buy it again afterwards. The problem with this type of data is that it does not tell the advertiser why the consumer made the purchase, or what the connection is between that purchase and the numerous advertising and media messages (including word of mouth, etc.). Scanning research gives data which advertisers use to formulate theories about, for instance, whether changes in sales are affected by price. Manufacturers use retail audits and consumer panels (such as Homescan) to try to match the effectiveness of the advertising campaign to the sale of branded goods in shops. They help to tell marketers about brand switching, changes in consumer behaviour and the frequency of repeat buying. Many studies show a large number of consumers trialing a product for a short time, resulting in high short-term sales, then a substantial fall. This suggests low levels of brand loyalty. Companies also commission ad hoc research if they are about to launch a new brand, or add questions to standard research questionnaires to test recall.

Tracking studies are used to track recognition, recall, advertising and brand awareness, attitudes, and claimed buying behaviour (usage). These surveys are very expensive to run. The sample size must be big enough and random enough to be meaningful. Unlike consumer panels, they do not use the same consumers but select then randomly from the same sample categories. Measures are taken before and after campaigns, and other effects are 'factored' out to find out the advertising effects.

The usage and attitude data try to show how the advertising campaign affected consumers and got them to act in the way that they did. They tend to measure the frequency of product usage and usage occasions and changes in consumers' reasons for buying (attitudes). Usage measures are intended to show how often people buy brands by asking them. However, these hardly ever bear any relationship to the actual buying behaviour of the brand's consumers. In terms of the correlation between people's perceptions of what they buy and what they actually do buy, usage data are useless (Elliott in Cowley 1989: 161). Instead, advertisers use consumer panel data (see above). Attitudes are perceived to shift only slightly in the short term, so continuous surveys are not conducted. Attitudes are usually measured at a specific point in time, but can be affected by seasonal changes (before Christmas, or in the summer), or because a competitor, or related market, has a big campaign on when the research is conducted.

Both tracking and usage and attitude studies are expensive because of large sample sizes and the need to repeat the research (before and after the campaign). The timing of tracking studies is an area of frequent dispute (too early or too late). These factors are all supposed to influence the decision on when to monitor the campaign. Like sales measures, usage and attitude tests are usually conducted and controlled by the client and outside research firms, not by the agency. It is a source of tension and conflict between agency and advertiser if the market research firm employs different methodology and produces unfavourable results. Most marketers combine sales results with usage and attitude tests to give an indication of the reasons for sales changes.

Tracking studies are much more common in the UK than day-after recall. Recall is meant to measure awareness and memorability, tracking is meant to measure awareness and attitudes towards the brand and towards buying. It does not measure buying: this is inferred from the research.

Econometric models and test marketing

Econometrics and area tests are meant to measure the effects of different marketing variables in the marketing mix. This expensive measure of econometrics is favoured by many brand advertisers and uses multiple regression analysis to try to establish causes between advertising and sales (this involves eliminating, or compensating for, other influential factors in the sales process and isolating advertising by a statistical method). A model of the market is created and the brand advertiser assesses the relative effectiveness of burst or drip campaigns, of increasing or decreasing advertising, or of changing creative treatment or media mix.

However, econometric models have been criticised for assuming that variables are held constant and that consumers behave like rational economic agents. They also encourage the view that an advertising message cannot of itself have unique persuasive qualities. One of the reasons why econometrics has been so severely criticised, however, has been because it has indicated to advertisers that marginal price changes can have a much stronger effect on sales than above-the-line advertising. Ad agencies consider that such research is one of the reasons why clients have moved so much of their spend to price cuts and sales promotions rather than above-the-line media spend. You cannot measure the reasons for the persuasiveness of the advertising from these models.

A region or town which is a representative sample of the proposed population may be chosen to test-market. Advertisers can also use split runs in newspapers and on TV (with two transmitters) to test one treatment against another in the same ITV region. This can also be done through the use of test mailings to see which gains the highest response. Test marketing arose in the 1960s as a response to the high costs of TV advertising: advertisers wanted guarantees that the new products would work. Large-brand advertisers such as Beecham's used the new ITV regions to test-market products in the 1960s to help decide whether a product will be launched or not. One famous campaign for a Unilever soap powder, Breeze, in the 1980s was dumped after a test run in the midlands TV region. The agencies argue that test marketing is costly and unrepresentative of what would happen in a national campaign.

Another way of measuring is to have a test advertising campaign in one area and judge the difference between this area and the others. BT used tracking studies and measurement of telephone activity to judge the effectiveness of advertising campaigns in three separate regions of the country by three different agencies. A campaign featuring animals won the effectiveness test. They had used quantitative research to judge effectiveness (Clark 1988: 108). The winning agency apparently did twice as well as rivals.

Involvement

In the 1970s advertisers began to reassess communications models which focused on consumers as passive and active victims. The 'new' audiences that they examined were not victims, but were in control. These active audiences 'deliberately and purposefully select the messages that are of interest to them and "filter out" those that are not' (Wilmshurst 1985: 202). They use advertising messages to satisfy their needs, wants and desires; to resolve insecurities, fears and frustrations; to provide companionship; to learn lessons and gain knowledge; to support and reinforce their identity and their belonging to a social group (national, region, ethnicity); and as a form of escape and fantasy. Consumers actively seek out information which agrees with their views on the world, or with their image of themselves, and avoid those things which do not agree with them.

JWT developed an 'involvement' model of communication for these audiences. The model defines five areas: the sender, the receiver, the medium, the stimulus (message plus emotive language, content and form) and the response (Walford 1992: 30). The advertising in this model works in five ways: 'familiarising, reminding, spreading news, overcoming inertia, adding value to the product. Most advertising will involve two or more of these aims' (ibid.).

The advertising is perceived as one of the many influences affecting the consumer's perception of the brand. 'To modify or re-enforce that perception we send out an advertising "stimulus".' This is different from having a fully comprehended rational message received. The focus changes from looking at the content of the message (the persuasive reason) to looking at the form of the message (the emotional involvement). The receiver is intended to respond to the message, not simply to accept it. JWT's model changes the idea of sender–receiver to one of stimulus and response. The stimulus is 'the combination of what is said, how it's said and who said it'. This means that 'Often the response is very different from the nature or the intentions of the stimulus' (Prue 1991: 39).

According to Prue, the involvement model can work 'by reminding consumers of the brand's relevance to a want or need. This does not have to be a practical need met by a product claim. It can be an emotional need.' This often occurs in markets where there is little product difference, most often for those commercials that use ambiguity and humour. Involvement uses seductive techniques to change attitude towards the brand and suggest likeability. The model helped to give rise to more humorous ads, and to the idea that you needed to involve consumers more in the advertising rather than try to persuade them about the benefits of the product.

Through the use of emotion or entertainment, people are meant to get involved in the ad – the Andrex puppy commercial, the Nike ad with Ian Wright. Puzzle ads also invite the consumer to get involved with the advertising – Silk Cut's long-running pun on silk and cutting, for instance. Parody ads are also part of this: consumers are involved through the recognition of elements of the commercial; cross-references and intertextual references are meant to involve consumers in the advertising more. It is part of a game; spot the reference.

Advertisers identify some products as 'low-involvement'. These include convenience goods and those which are bought with little thought or consideration. The purpose of advertising in these cases is to make consumers more involved in the product by making it more interesting via heavy advertising, giving tea such as PG Tips a 'personality' by using humorous chimps. The CDP planning director and IPA effectiveness awards judge Mary Stewart-Hunter says that ads will be better remembered and be more powerful if the ad is 'watched, read or listened to more carefully'. This happens best if the consumer is amused, entertained, personally identified or 'touched' by the emotional values in the ad (Stewart-Hunter in Cowley 1989: 136).

The difference between the persuasion and involvement models is that the first purports to examine what advertisements do to consumers, whereas the second looks at what consumers do with ads. However, as McDonald points out, each model assumes that there is a 'typical' consumer who will respond to the advertising in a predictable way to fit with the model. 'Even when people are not seen as automata, they are still expected to be uniform: "this ad will put them in involvement mode"' (McDonald 1991: 26). This uses-and-gratifications model provides a different way of looking at the same thing: media effects. It simply turns the problem on its head. Rather than saying that advertising creates needs in consumers, it simply says that it satisfies latent, or existing, needs. Instead of locating the source of power in the media, it locates it in the receiver. The sender–receiver model now becomes receiver–sender. This is an inherently conservative view of communication. It also overstates the 'active' role of consumption. Much consumption is formed by habit and ritual rather than active selection (switching the TV on when you come home from work or school). The model also assumes that the relationship is equal, that we all have equal choices concerning which media we want to select. (But if you are old, poor or sick your range of options is much more limited than if you have a high income and use multiple media.) If advertising reinforces existing values and beliefs, how do you measure reinforcement?

Culture and consumption

Traditional models of consumer behaviour position consumers as rational economic agents who make decisions on buying and using goods on purely economic grounds to maximise their utility and to maximise pleasure. This places human beings outside cultural and social relationships and presents a sterile view of human behaviour as one-dimensional. Anthropologists see goods as the 'vehicles of cultural meanings' which are 'pressed into service in the creation of aspects of the self and the domestic world' (McCracken 1990: 5). This involves the use of symbols, myths and metaphors to add meanings to goods and add to the meanings that the advertiser wants to convey. 'This means surveying the world for the culturally constituted objects, persons, contexts and motifs that make the sought after cultural meanings live in the advertisement' (ibid.). The role for research in this view is to survey and observe the use of meanings in society and how they are culturally constituted, not how information is 'imparted' via historically and culturally bereft vessels (the media).

Researchers examine a range of cultural practices such as ritual, myths and ideologies and formulate a theory of buying behaviour and intentions on the back of it. This usually involves the classification of consumers in terms of different subcultures, classes and 'types'. Like behaviourist research, it uses techniques of observation and imputes that the language systems and rituals of different subcultures affect people's identities and buying and consuming patterns. This moves the level of analysis away from individual practices out towards group practices. It examines shared beliefs, rather than individual ones. It is often in conflict with psychological theories which concentrate on individual motivations and intentions, but also shares many features such as the necessity to find common goals and intention in consumers.

In the 1980s communications researchers began to analyse the extent of reading and viewing patterns by clustering groups and looking for patterns along social or cultural lines (ethnicity, gender, sexuality, etc.). One of these 'ethnographic' studies was of the Nationwide audience in 1980. The principle was very similar to that of audience researchers for TV: identifying typical characteristics of ethnic groups and 'segmenting' the population into 'types'. Though Morley et al. (1992: 75–118) used different criteria from those of the advertising industry (which is primarily concerned with income, status and purchasing patterns), it nevertheless indicated that both academics and advertising professionals were looking for similar things: patterns and structures to viewing. Morley was interested in the ways subcultures and class fractions influence people's ideological viewpoints, whereas the advertisers were interested in the way culture and demographics influence spending patterns. Both approaches downplay the complexity of individual experience, and try to place people into categories for ease of manageability and control. They look at individuals as part of 'subcultural formations' who share sets of values and beliefs (again manageable, controllable and predictable). But, just as there is no necessary connection between people's attitudes and their behaviour, there is also no necessary link between the ideological meanings in ads and the behavioural responses of people. I may like the Gold Blend ad for entertainment value but never buy Gold Blend, I may vehemently disagree with Benetton's advertising campaign yet still use its garments in preference to others. The reasons for our behaviour are overdetermined.

Activity and ritual (e.g. pouring draught bitter from a can in a certain way) is important to heighten the status of the product and add value. The product is a cultural and social good in which you ritualise consumption: watching and interacting with TV, preparing and eating food, social drinking in a pub. Activity and ritual relate the product to its social use. Advertisers combine the rituals of consumption to other added values such as colour, feeling and mood. This form of advertising can be combined with lifestyle advertising (including the self-image of the consumer in the ad, such as the type of person who would drink a beer), or with a USP (in the case of Boddingtons, its creamy head, 'The Cream of Manchester').

Advertisements usually offer something for buying the product: a reward, such as success or wealth, through claims like 'Win!', or 'Free!'; or provide recognition, saying 'thank you' and encouraging consumers to feel good about themselves. They also involve the consumer in the rituals of consumption to add value: special ways of pouring drinks, of eating Creme Eggs, applying make-up, sharing Rolos. Advertising tries to ritualise the consumption moment so that for instance we eat pizza, crisps or snacks in front of the TV, or drink beer in cans while the football is on TV.

The brand plays a sufficient role in the ritual of consumption that there is little need to persuade or change people's attitudes, just a need to remind them. Advertisers try to make their brands part of the consumer's ritual: 'Have a Break. Have a Kit Kat', 'Say Thank You with Roses', 'Go to work on an egg'. This helps to create a 'brand habit'.

As Judie Lannon points out, 'Brands like Heinz, Kellogg, Ariel, Fairy, Nescafé, Persil, Birds Eye and many more have built the kinds of strong brand franchises that have a real utility to people: they form habits; they have time' (Lannon 1993: 19). Marketing and advertising seek to ritualise consumption. They try to demarcate when we should drink cocoa: in the 1930s it was at night, in the 1990s, because of saturation and declining market share, it is throughout the day. The meaning of drinking chocolate changes, from being an 'end-of the day relaxant' to a 'spoil-yourself-break' in the day. Advertising associates the goods and services with social rituals (weddings, births, etc.), and tries to promote new consumption rituals (linked to Mother's Day, Easter, Christmas, Father's Day, Valentine's Day, Grandmother's Day, for instance).

In all the above examples, the model of consumer behaviour shaped the form and style of advertising. Anthropological models of consumer behaviour focused advertising messages on the rituals of consumption; the involvement model in the 1970s influenced the 'likeability' factor in ads, increasing the number of humorous ads and the Andrex 'Ah' factor; the persuasion-shift model in the USA contributed to the number of demonstration ads and reason-why commercials; and the recall model contributed to the number of jingles and the more easily memorable commercials.

Comprehension and negotiation: missing the target

the way in which a message is intended to be delivered may be very different from the way it is received.

(Stewart-Hunter in Cowley 1989: 140)

most of the time, most adult individuals do not perceive themselves to be in the market for the products being advertised. Even when they are, commercials very often 'miss-hit' or 'overshoot' their target. Commercials regularly mis-communicate because the actual audiences they address are quite different in disposition from the hypothesised or targeted audience.

(Keane 1991: 86–87)

Whereas researchers into commercial advertising effects are most interested in direct effects of stimulus material on consumers, academic media researchers have been more concerned with the levels of comprehension of the advertising and the different interpretations consumers put on them (Morley *et al.* 1992: 49–55).

Creatives add meanings and values to objects by associating signs and symbols with them. But culture is far too complex and people's experiences and knowledge far too diverse for them to be able to guarantee that all people will comprehend the advertisement in the same way. Advertisers try to narrow the field by using metaphors and language that the intended majority will understand.

Meaning is produced through the interaction of texts and audiences, not within texts themselves. The meanings are affected by what the texts and the audiences bring to them. John Corner identifies three levels of meaning which audiences may bring to texts, and texts convey: denotation, connotation and preferred reading (Corner 1991: 271–272).

The advertising agency attempts to work on three levels of meaning. First and obviously, they construct denotative meanings; recognising and comprehending words and images for their immediate meaning that we all share (recognising a tree as a tree, etc.). Second, they use metaphors and connotative meanings that culturally specific groups can understand; where a sign or combination of signs may stand for something else that a culture shares, such as a metaphor (red roses meaning love, a tree standing for strength, reliability, nature, family (tree), etc.). And finally, they try to anchor meanings on a personal level by reminding people of eventful or memorable things that have occurred in their lives in a preferred way (the first time you fell in love; images of new born babies, which trigger people's memories of births of their own children; daughters' weddings). People bring their history, values and knowledge to texts.

Corner claims that people choose a genre first, then select the programmes or stories within that genre; whether it is fiction or fact, 'real' or fantasy, the levels of belief and disbelief are important, according to him (Corner 1991:

276). This invites the viewer to agree or disagree, and, in the context of humorous advertising, like or dislike. People recognise textual forms: different people may automatically switch off a religious programme on a Sunday afternoon, or a football match, or a news bulletin, or a pop music programme, or a radio talk show, or classical music on the radio, or ballet on TV; they may automatically reach for a glossy magazine, or a broadsheet newspaper. However, the overemphasis on genre ignores the fact that many people watch different genres of TV (they may like to watch *Blind Date* and the *Money Programme*, or *Noel's House Party* then *Wildlife on One*). There is no evidence that people select only according to genre, rather than according to programme. There is also the problem that many of these demarcation lines have been blurred by the widespread use of docudrama and reconstruction (mixing fact and fiction) and the greater similarities between entertainment and factual programmes such as 999 on ITV. The same goes for advertising genres which are blurred – celebrity endorsement, slice-of-life, comparison and demonstration ads all overlap to make the concept of distinct genres unworkable.

Advertising has its own genres, such as demonstration ads, presenter ads, and slice-of-life. It also uses TV programme genres such as soap dramas, TV news, science programmes, game shows, etc., to play on the 'realism' or 'naturalism', the entertainment or magical imagery of the host texts, and to associate the discourse of the editorial with the brand.

Though the advertisements provide the template for understanding, 'it is the viewer who must complete the meaningful connections' (Goldman 1992: 62). Stuart Hall (1981) suggested that audiences read texts within three basic forms. First, 'preferred'; this is when people understand what has been transmitted (they clearly comprehend the messages). Second, 'oppositional', whereby the messages are comprehended but subverted, opposed and a struggle over meaning takes place. Finally there are those readings in which the reader does not understand the codes that the advertising messages convey, in which case it is an 'aberrant' decoding. Though aberrant decodings do take place (especially in the case of some global advertisements which fail to hit the right cultural mark), most readings in practice are a negotiation with the preferred meanings within the text. According to Morley *et al.*, the objective demographic position of the viewer (age, sex, class and ethnic position) are crucial determinants of the ways in which decoding are made (Morley *et al.* 1992: 55–56).

However, although there are many meanings in texts, advertisers place preferred readings on them, they anchor the meanings of signs in order to narrow the field of choice. The relationship between advertising text and audience is not an equal one. Advertising messages and texts occupy a privileged position to the audience; the agenda is set by advertising, not by the reader. For Hall this is a site of struggle over meanings around the consensus. Advertisers are in a privileged position in the mass media to occupy the common-sense ground. Advertisers set the agenda by excluding meanings and signs, negative statements about brands, negative images, and also certain types of people: poor people, the very old and the sick do not live in adworld.

Advertising texts such as TV and radio commercials and print ads usually combine elements of sound, speech, text, movement and image to give strong preferred readings. However, those ads which are more image-based, such as the Benetton ads, do not anchor meaning very well and leave space for extra meanings to be decoded. The advertiser needs to anchor meanings with texts to enclose the meaning of the text more. In practice, advertisers use a combination of effects criteria, recall, usage and attitude, and involvement models.

Generally, advertising and promotion try to influence the consumer's information about the product on every level: personal experience (you know why it tastes so good); word of mouth information, influencing opinion-formers in the family; the press and TV, heavy PR (car manufacturers give journalists cars, computer journalists are given computers, etc.); schools and colleges, again involved in sponsorship and promotion in these areas. Trying to isolate information sources is like trying to isolate advertising effects. Marketers therefore hedge their bets by appealing to all of the potential information areas.

Examples

Advertising agencies try to use metaphors, signs and symbols that are most easily comprehended by the target market. These are some examples of campaigns which for different reasons missed the target.

Benetton

Benetton's global campaign 'United Colors of Benetton' was launched in 1984. Luciano Benetton came up with the campaign. The first executions were statements of Luciano Benetton's cultural vision, with different races having fun together. In the 1990s, however, Benetton changed tack and ran campaigns with newborn children, nuns kissing, a mercenary holding a human thigh bone, a bird covered in oil, and an AIDS patient. The conventional campaign for a clothes shop would be to show the range of pullovers. According to Evans and Riyait the intended responses to the advertising for the newborn baby (love, the force from which life is born, a baby is the most permanent form of love, holding on to the warmth and security of the mother's womb) were in many instances in various countries completely different to the responses elicited (Evans and Riyait 1993: 291). The report concluded that the ads were open to wildly different interpretation. However, Benetton's other intentions were to provoke people to confront their values, and most of all to arouse controversy and get extra publicity in the press and among the media. One of the knock-on benefits of all this publicity was Benetton's success in managing to improve distribution through licensing arrangements with shops to sell their goods. The newborn baby ad caused offence in Britain, and generated hundreds of complaints to the ASA. In 1995 German retail franchisees tried to sue Benetton

Figure 13.2 Benetton: the death row ad campaign led to the departure of creative director, Oliviero Toscani, after US department store Sears Roebuck, withdrew Benetton products from its 400 stores. In Britain, the Advertising Standards Authority brushed aside 144 complaints that the use of such images for commmercial gain was offensive. The ASA insisted on the advertiser's right to free speech. Benetton claimed that the close-up photographs of the inmates faces, along with the interviews that ask many personal questions, aimed to humanise the death row inmates. © Benetton.

for loss of sales, claimed to be due to the advertising campaign. In Benetton ran a fresh ad campaign featuring the faces of Death Row prisoners. The ads sparked outrage in the USA and were condemned by the families of inmates and the families of the prisoners' victims. US retail chain, Sears, announced that it would stop selling Benetton clothes in its 400 stores. The crisis led Benetton's creative director Oliver Toscani to resign. In 2001 Benetton dropped its controversial advertising in favour of ads depicting young people wearing Benetton T-shirts, jumpers and swimwear.

Guinness

Guinness had been having problems with its stout throughout the 1970s. Its share of the beer market had halved to 5 per cent over ten years as the younger drinkers moved towards lager. Guinness used market research to determine that the target market they were after was the 70 per cent of their consumers who drink Guinness only occasionally. The intention was to encourage them (specifically under-35s) to drink more of the product on a regular basis. The company and its agency, Allen Brady & Marsh, pre-tested seven campaigns and the campaign which tested best was a 'Friend of the Guinnless' campaign. It was a humorous campaign designed to encourage people who had gone too long without Guinness to come back to the drink. The 'Friends of the Guinnless' was like a parody of a phobia group. The campaign tested well, and the £7 million campaign proved moderately successful in its first year: sales increased by almost 10 per cent. The campaign did not prove successful in the following year, though it had a high visibility; the joke wore thin and the negative proposition in the campaign turned consumers off. After two years ABM was sacked and Guinness appointed Ogilvy & Mather, who targeted a similar market group but changed the direction of the campaign completely by using a surreal theme and employing movie star Rutger Hauer, dressed all in black, to come out with witty existential comments such as 'It's not easy being a Dolphin'.

Coca-Cola

One of the biggest flops of the 1980s was the relaunch of Coca-Cola in 1985. The company changed the taste of Coke in response to market research and to the success of their main rival, Pepsi, in whose campaign, 'The Pepsi challenge', consumers revealed that they preferred the sweeter taste of Pepsi. Coke's taste had remained the same for ninety-nine years. Market researchers found that consumers in unseen product tests preferred a new sweeter and less fizzy Coke to the old one. But they did not find out how consumers would react if the new Coke product replaced the old one. This was to be at the centre of the new global strategy for Coke to advertise the new product on the basis of its new taste. Perhaps if Coke had just changed the taste and not told anyone the problem might have gone away. But Coke didn't. The company spent millions of dollars launching the 'New Coke' world wide. Coca-Cola received a barrage of complaints from its regular consumers. At one point Coke's office received eight thousand phone calls a day. The media also joined in on the attack. Within four months the company was forced to back down. The President of Coca-Cola was forced to announce the reintroduction of Coke with the new label 'Classic Coke' to appease its consumers. In 1988 Classic Coke was outselling the new drink by three to one. Coca-Cola later withdrew the New Coke brand and eventually dropped the Classic Coke brand, returning the Classic Coke flavour to the main Coca-Cola brand.

Unilever

Unilever launched a new boxed washing powder brand, Breeze, in the midlands area in 1984 as a test marketing case to see if the company's agency, Collett Dickenson Pearce, could produce radical advertising of a soap product which did not rely on testimonials, or product demonstrations; the USP of soap advertising. Positioned as a soap powder which was kind to coloured clothes, it featured an Arcadian setting, with mother nature, pixies and cherubs. It was pitched as an upmarket soap powder with a more aesthetic identity or brand image. The advertising was perceived to be too obscure. At the same time, unfortunately for CDP, the major soap rivals also launched their liquid soaps (Ariel and Persil), and this helped to scupper the launch of the brand completely. Breeze's sale price was lowered, but sales did not improve. Within a few months the agency was forced to run a new commercial featuring a consumer journalist who gave a testimonial. In 1988 Breeze was withdrawn and CDP was dropped. Unilever used the commercials again, however, in France for its mass-market soap brand Coral which had been in France since 1968. The commercial was apparently much more successful in France.

However, six years later, Unilever took a risk with a new ingredient to their soap powders which was meant to revolutionise the market. It took out thirty patents on a new manganese-based ingredient that had cost £150 million to develop to prevent its rival Procter & Gamble launching a near-copy. The new ingredient allowed cleaning at much lower temperatures and made clothes whiter than white. They launched Persil Power in May 1994. Within days of the launch of Persil Power, Procter & Gamble produced data from six independent sources which cast doubts on the soap's safety. Procter & Gamble ran a spoiler campaign on TV and press, claiming that the new 'accelerator' damaged clothes. Newspapers such as the *Sun* ran stories which featured 'victims' of Persil Power complete with shredded clothes. Unilever responded to the adverse publicity by reducing the levels of the new additive while still maintaining that it was perfectly safe. Persil's share of the £1 billion soap market fell from 27.9 per cent in April 1994 to 20.2 per cent in April 1995 as a result of the PR disaster. In January 1995 Lever Brothers replaced Persil Power with New Generation Persil, a concentrated soap powder which included a bleaching agent but did not include the manganese accelerator. Procter & Gamble's Ariel became market leader in the UK for the first time in its history.

Hoover

An example of a campaign that was too successful was Hoover's autumn 1992 promotion for two free flights to Europe or the USA for people buying a Hoover product costing over £100. The cost of the product was substantially less than the cost of the free flights. When sales promotions involve rewarding a consumer after the purchase is made, the companies try to put as many obstacles as possible in the consumer's way to make sure that only a limited number of consumers will take up the offer. This often involves filling in numerous forms and meeting strict deadlines for replies. Hoover made the classic mistake of offering too big a reward. Over 220,000 customers leapt over the obstacles, forcing Hoover to deliver. Delays in delivering the tickets caused a great amount of ill-will and a public relations disaster for the company for incompetence and its embarrassing attempts to avoid rewarding consumers. They received over seven thousand letters of complaint. Three senior executives lost their jobs and the 'free-flights fiasco' cost Hoover £48 million.

Hush Puppies

In his book *The Tipping Point*, Malcolm Gladwell recalls the story of shoe brand, Hush Puppies. Sales of the brushed suede shoes had slipped to around 30,000 in the USA by the early 1990s and the company which produces it, Wolverine, considered axing the brand altogether. In 1994 ultra-trendy young people in Manhattan started to wear the shoes as a fashion statement. In 1995 fashion designer John Bartlett used the shoes in a fashion show, other designers followed. In 1995 the company sold 430,000 pairs of Hush Puppies, a year later it sold almost 2 million (Gladwell 2000: 3–5).

Gladwell contends that the Hush Puppies' success came from the way in which the early adopters – the ultra-trendy kids in Manhattan – started wearing the shoes in order to make a fashion statement that they were separate from the mainstream was adopted by intermediaries or connectors (Gladwell 2000: 199–200). The connectors adapt the new fashion and tailor it to the mainstream. This is often assisted by advertising and promotions. In the case of Hush Puppies it was the fashion designers who profiled it on the catwalk who helped push the brand into the mainstream. The brand became 'cool' to wear. Many marketers try to get these 'early adopters' to start using their brands before pushing them into the mainstream.

Summary

The success or failure of an advertising campaign cannot be judged solely on the basis of sales. Advertisers need wider measures of advertising effectiveness. All measures of advertising effects carry implicit models of consumer behaviour. The most common model is one which views the message as being intrinsically powerful, and the consumer powerless. This is partly because it is easier to measure what ads do to people than what people do with ads. But it is also because the advertising industry needs to support the belief that getting the message right is more important than simply dominating through the media. Agencies and market researchers use a variety of techniques to test advertisements before and after they are released to gauge their 'effectiveness'; if an advertiser believes that the advertisement can have a direct effect on consumers, the recall and persuasion shift methods of research would be employed; if it believes it does not, the attitude or involvement model may be more appropriate. Effects research exists to help predict and manage future behaviour, to reduce uncertainty, along with costs. However, the purely commercial criteria underpinning much effects research fail to address how meanings are negotiated between texts and audiences, and why so many campaigns often miss their target.

14 Regulating advertisements

At the present stage of our civilisation, the withdrawal of advertising (which some advocates of the Socialist State have demanded) would create enormous unemployment ... the housewife in need of a parlour-maid would be at the mercy of registry offices ... you cannot announce 'Situations Vacant' by wireless! ... parted lovers could breathe their affections in no Agony column ... the lost dog or the pocket book dropped in a train must be mourned in vain ... Everyone of us must acquire an unheard of expertness in the appraisal of commodities. We shall be at the mercy of the shopkeepers ... What is more we must pay dearer for all these desirable objects, for the cost of distributing them without the aid of advertising will have to be borne by all who consume.

(Russell 1924: 168)

Anti-advertising opinion at the turn of the century identified it as an alien cultural form. Advertising represented brash US global expansion and Britain's relative economic decline. US manufacturers had already wiped out the sewing machine market in the UK, key sectors such as soap and confectionery were beginning to suffer and the tobacco industry was engaged in a long, bitter and costly advertising war which would see dozens of UK tobacco companies disappear in amalgamations. US manufacturers' chief weapons in UK markets were advertising and publicity. Relatedly, advertising was also attacked for debasing British cultural life. One of the many examples of this criticism came in the 1930s from J. B. Priestley, who blamed the system of advertising for creating what he called the 'Admass' which created the 'mass mind, the mass man' (Carey 1992: 38). Later, criticism of advertising would emphasise its effectiveness in reinforcing racial and sexual stereotypes and fostering consumption as a way of life.

Responding to criticism: the road to self-regulation

Print media

In 1924 the *Daily Mail* published an article by a Cambridge University chemistry professor claiming that a drug called Yadil was not what it claimed to be and cost sixty times the value of the raw materials. The drug claimed to cure consumption, cancer, malaria, pneumonia, pleurisy and bronchitis (Turner 1953: 259–260). The article helped to put the manufacturers of Yadil out of business. The advertising industry had to respond to the claims that advertising increased costs to the consumer, as well as to the claims that advertising was misleading. The Advertising Association was formed at the end of 1924 to fight against such claims. The first real advertising code, which set in stone the principles of advertising practice, came in 1924 at an international conference at Wembley, a week before the Yadil case. The code included such guiding principles as seeking truth, avoiding exaggeration and misleading claims, and refraining from 'unfair competitive criticism' (Turner 1953: 184). The code was generated to counter criticism and threats of legislation against the advertising industry, as well as to help define what it was to be an advertising agent. The organisation set up a National Vigilance Committee, which became the Advertising Investigation Department in 1928, to investigate claims against advertising. It built up dossiers of fraudulent advertisers and circulated them to members.

Though the AA's ostensible role was to raise and enforce standards, providing some degree of self-regulation, in reality it acted as an organisation to promote advertising in government and cultural life. It is the public relations arm of the UK advertising industry, it produces research reports and PR books for students, as well as reports to parliament to demonstrate how ineffective advertising is. It has lobbied in the USA, Australia and Europe to lobby against regulations on tobacco advertising. It has been very effective in shifting the consensus in Britain away from legal constraints and anti-monopoly legislation towards self-regulation and moving advertising control off the political agenda.

Advertising was also condemned for its more sinister powers of manipulation. During the hysteria of the Cold War, advertising was singled out as an element of the mass media which had the supposed power to brainwash entire populations. In the USA, Vance Packard's book *The Hidden Persuaders* (1957) explored psychological techniques being used by agencies – specifically motivation research – and in Britain there was a subsequent article in the *Sunday Times* on subliminal advertising (showing a shot of a product during a film). The IPA shrewdly condemned the practice of subliminal advertising, which none of its members practised, and managed to shift debates about advertising's effects away from more damaging areas such as alcohol and tobacco and advertising to children. The IPA announced that it would investigate subliminal advertising and recommended that its members should not take it up.

In 1959 the Labour Party set up the Advertising Inquiry Committee to police 'socially harmful' ads, and in 1961 set up an independent commission under Lord Reith which recommended creating a National Consumer Board financed by a tax on advertising. At the same time the advertising industry removed 73,000 shop-front signs and resited 15,000 others (shop fronts were the responsibility of agencies). The AA Conference in 1961 unveiled the British Code of Advertising Practice to pre-empt moves towards government legislation. A year later, the Advertising Standards Association (ASA) was formed to monitor and field complaints about advertising. This produced single guiding principles for the industry and was widely publicised. Threats of legislation against the industry had been made in the wake of anti-advertising publicity.

There were two bodies covering the practices of the industry: the Code of Advertising Practice Committee and the Advertising Standards Association. Representatives of the IPA, ISBA and the media owners were on the committees. The ASA was formed in order to provide an independent veneer to self-regulation. The intention was to expose bad practice on the fringes of advertising, making mainstream advertisers less susceptible to public criticism.

In 1972 the Labour Party produced a Green Paper which condemned advertising for creating an imbalance between consumers and producers and recommended the setting-up of a National Consumers Authority to redress the balance (Nevett 1982: 198). The Authority was intended to test producer claims and investigate complaints and to suggest a statutory code of practice for advertising, but it came to nothing. The proposal was to make half of all advertising expenditure tax-deductible and to finance the National Consumers Authority. The Labour Party had adopted taxation on advertising as official party policy. When the Labour government came into power in 1974 the 'independent' ASA, fearing that statutory regulations and codes would be imposed, was widened to include more non-advertising people, and rewrote the Code with tighter regulation on misleading ads. Copies were sent to every Citizens Advice Bureau in the country, and the ASA launched a public relations advertising campaign to publicise its work, urging people to complain. The ASA also produced regular releases on adjudications and separate sections to cover trouble areas such as medicine and children (Nevett 1982: 200). It was then that a 0.1 per cent levy was enforced on ads which contributed to the ASA and a finance committee was developed to raise money.

Though the ASA has no legislative powers, it does now have the stamp of government authority. The ASA chairman is appointed in association with the Department of Trade and Industry. The ASA deals with public complaints about press, outdoor and direct mail advertising, and the Code of Advertising Practice committee deals with internal advertising industry matters. The British Code of Advertising Practice does not apply to broadcast commercials, government campaigns or prescription drugs (the ABPI is the self-regulatory body administering this). The Code does not cover political advertising because political advertising is exempt from CAP provisions on honesty, fairness and negative comparisons, (at election time it is legitimate for political parties to knock each other's policies). However in the 1997 election the Conservative party ran the famous 'Demon Eyes' ad campaign which depicted Labour leader Tony Blair as a demon beneath his façade. The ad had the strapline, 'New Labour, New Danger' the ASA could uphold complaints against this ad because it portrayed a person in an offensive way, which was covered by the guidelines. However campaign by the Labour Party which had the strapline, 'Same old Tories, same old lies,' could not be regulated.

In 1999 the ASA decided to refuse to regulate political ads altogether. A separate system for political advertising is being drawn up by parliament.

There are twelve members on the ASA. At least one-third of the members must represent advertising interests. The system involves an 'independent' controlling body in the ASA which supervises an executive body – the Committee of Advertising Practice (CAP) – which was formed in 1988 and is exclusively run by advertising interests (advertisers, agencies and the media). It includes the Broadcast Advertising Clearance Centre, the Cinema Advertising Association, the Outdoor Advertising Association and since 1996 the Radio Advertising Clearance Centre. The Director General of the ASA is usually also the secretary of the CAP. This committee regularly reviews the Code of Practice. It also investigates complaints within the business (not from outside consumers, but on practice within the industry). It clears copy for the cigarette advertisers and makes recommendations on areas such as comparative advertising (making reference to competitors), etc. This body has a Copy Panel which gives guidance to advertisers. It covers the press; bodies represented include the Newspaper Society, PPA, NPA, IPA, ISBA and ASA. CAP subcommittees deal with such areas as health and nutrition and direct mail. The sales promotion section of the code covers mail order and includes ads which mislead people into opening envelopes by suggesting that they have won something. The 1995 code states that 'All advertisements should be legal, decent, honest and truthful. All advertisements should be prepared with a sense of responsibility to consumers and to society' (Codes of Advertising Practice Committee (CAP) 1995). It also places an obligation on advertisers to abide by the codes. 'Any unreasonable delay in responding to the ASA's enquiries may be considered a breach of the Codes . . . The Codes are applied in the spirit as well as in the letter' (ibid.).

BCAP also covers complaints about ads which encourage violent or anti-social behaviour (CAP 1995: 10). This became a problem for Tango when their commercials showed a mythical character slapping and popping the ears of characters drinking the fizzy soft drink. They were forced to change the commercial after children began to do it in school playgrounds and injuries were reported.

When somebody gives a testimonial that a product is good, the advertiser is advised not to give the impression that the person giving the testimonial, and being paid to do so, is giving independent approval. 'Advertisers should hold signed and dated proof, including a contact address, for any testimonial they use' (CAP 1995: 11). Advertisers are also instructed not to play on people's fears (without justification). In many European countries comparative

Figure 14.1 Conservative Party: the Conservatives used this poster and newspaper advertising campaign during the 1997 general election to impugn New Labour's 'moderate' policies. Because of the lack of substantive policy differences the Conservatives launched a personal attack on Blair which proved to be unsuccessful. © The Conservative Party. Agency: M&C Saatchi.

advertising is illegal. In the UK comparative advertising is now allowed after the Trade Marks Act 1994 was introduced. 'Comparisons can be explicit or implied and can relate to advertisers' own products or to those of their competitors; they are permitted in the interests of vigorous competition and public information' (CAP 1995: 14). However, the Code also states, 'Advertisers should not unfairly attack or discredit other businesses or their products' (ibid.). Not only do newspapers knock TV and vice versa, but some newspapers like the *Sun* pushed the limits in 1995, by suggesting that media buyers who place ads in the *Daily Mirror* are 'wallies'. Representatives of the media owners such as these sit on the CAP and adjudicate on advertising.

The ASA and the self-regulation system are in a constant state of revision and renegotiation, largely in response to new legislation from government and threats of new legal controls: particular areas concern advertising to children, medical and nutritional advertising and mail order business, all of which have had subcommittees, mainly because they are so contentious. In 1995 the ASA introduced a new code, *The British Codes of Advertising and Sales Promotion*. In response to new legislative threats to advertising of slimming products, alcohol and advertising to children, it introduced new rules, saying for instance, 'Advertisements should not actively encourage them to eat or drink at or near bedtime, to eat frequently throughout the day or to replace main meals with confectionery or snack foods' (CAP 1995: 36). The BCAP is now called BCASP.

Publishers are supposed to refuse publication of ads that break the Code. The CAP and ASA recommend publishers not to accept ads that they rule against. They require substantiation for claims, descriptions and comparisons. One of the biggest problems in recent years has been substantiating claims by advertisers. The committees have to rely on scientific assessments supplied by the advertisers themselves, rather than independent tests. This can lead to misleading claims of test results (the difference between actively misleading and not telling the whole truth, etc.). Though the ASA calls on advertisers to respect the CAP in terms of providing objective test results for product claims, and insists that testimonials should be genuine, it has no mechanism to test whether the testimonials are genuine or not, or whether tests are correct. Such checks were part of proposals issued by the Reith Commission to provide testing of products claims.

The recommendations of the CAP and ASA have been consistently flouted by big-brand advertisers. In the 1980s big-brand advertisers, including BP, Benetton, Hennes, Vauxhall Corsa, Nissan, Sainsbury's, etc. were increasingly criticised by the ASA for breaking regulations. The main reason for this is the intensified competition, with recession and more brands than ever, also a movement against regulation in the UK. Other areas of constant irritation to the ASA are car insurance and slimming products. In one year there were eight slimming product advertisers who had made misleading claims in one month; five of them had been condemned the year before by the ASA (Clark 1988: 134). In 1994 the ASA attacked manufacturers of slimming products, again, claiming that 65 per cent of slimming product ads were breaking the code of practice. When they were told, the majority of advertisers ignored recommendations to change the ads and continued to make misleading claims. In 1995 the code included new rules on slimming ads which included: 'Advertisements for any slimming regime or establishment should neither be directed at, nor contain anything that will appeal particularly to, people who are under eighteen' (CAP 1995: 46). And 'Advertisements should not contain general claims that precise amounts of weight can be lost within a stated period or that weight can be lost from specific parts of the body' (CAP 1995: 47).

This is an example of an ad campaign from the inter-war period that would not pass today's regulations:

Seven good reasons why Guinness is good for you

1 Builds strong muscles for sports.

2 It is good for the nerves.

3 It is good for the blood (also the complexion).

4 It is a splendid digestive.

5 It gives a permanent sense of greater health and strength.

6 It is beneficial to the aged.

7 It helps you to sleep.

A more recent example, from 2001 of an ad campaign that over-hyped its product's abilities was for soft drink Red Bull. The advertisers suggested that the drink would improve endurance, concentration and reaction time.

The Advertising Standards Authority took four years to investigate the claims of the company and conduct clinical trials and found that the quantity of caffeine in one can of the drink could not deliver what the advertising claimed.

The 1995 code also stated that 'Advertisements should not be directed at people under eighteen through the selection of media, style of presentation, content or context in which they appear. No medium should be used to advertise alcoholic drinks if more than 25 per cent of its audience is under eighteen years of age' (CAP 1995: 33). 'People shown drinking should not be, nor should they look, under twenty-five. Younger models may be shown in advertisements, for example in the context of family celebrations, but it should be obvious that they are not drinking' (ibid.). 'Advertisements should not suggest that any alcoholic drink can enhance mental, physical or sexual capabilities, popularity, attractiveness, masculinity, femininity or sporting achievements' (CAP 1995: 34).

Despite the CAP ruling in 1985 that showing politicians and other public figures in ads without their written permission was forbidden, agencies consistently break the ruling, and ads depicting Tony Blair and Bill Clinton have appeared. Chastisement by the ASA has now become a matter of kudos and 'respected' advertisers such as John Hegarty at BBH flout rules and adjudications by having awards for banned ads.

Figure 14.2 Club 18–30: in 1999, package holiday company, Club 18–30 ran a series of poster ads using slogans such as 'Beaver Espana', 'The Summer of 69' and 'It's not all sex, sex, sex, sex, sex, . . . there's a bit of sun and sea as well'. It chose billboards to create controversy to reinforce the proposition that this was 'a holiday your mother wouldn't like'. The ASA banned the posters because they could cause offence to the non-target market and the campaign switched to young adult magazines. © Club 18–30. Agency: Saatchi & Saatchi.

The ASA's lack of teeth and the fact that print advertisers are able to run controversial ads and be sanctioned afterwards has brought a great deal of criticism. In 1995 holiday company Club 18–30 ran a poster campaign featuring a man with a bulge in his boxer shorts and the strapline, 'Girls can we interest you in a package holiday?'. Other headlines included 'Beaver Espana'. The ASA received a large number of complaints about the ad and banned the ads. The day that the ban came into effect was the day that the campaign ended. In 2000 a similar situation occurred with perfume Opium which featured a naked model Sophie Dahl. The ad was banned as the campaign came to a close. The ASA is only able to generate negative publicity. In contrast TV and radio advertising authorities have the ability to impose sanctions against media owners who break advertising codes, for instance the IOTC imposed a £500,000 fine on Granada in 1994 for giving undue prominence to supermarket Safeway and *She* magazine on its *This Morning* show.

Though the ASA has the ultimate sanction of being able to refer persistent offenders to the Office of Fair Trading between 1988 and 2000 it referred only twelve cases and the majority of these were not major advertisers.

For advertisers, voluntary controls are more useful as no legal fees are incurred, and no penalties can be inflicted: the worst that can happen is for the ad to be scrapped, and they have to start again. BCAP has no power to impose penalties; the only sanction is for press advertisers to withdraw the ads. In a time of recession, many are reluctant to do so.

Figure 14.3 Opium: this poster campaign, featuring catwalk model Sophie Dahl, succeeded in generating an enormous amount of extra publicity for the Opium brand. The ad was withdrawn following a ruling by the Advertising Standards Authority that the ad was offensive and degrading to women. However, the Australian equivalent of the ASA refused to ban the ad. © Yves Saint Laurent: Steve Miese.

Self-regulators spend a great deal of time and money informing the public and legislators that they are accountable and effective. The ASA in particular does a great deal of its own advertising in newspapers and magazines (newspapers are expected to give over space to the ASA), as does the ITC in TV. The main purpose of self-regulation is, as one commentator puts it, to 'enable the British agency business to stave off a number of attempts to control advertising by statute' (White 1988: 168). As another points out, 'Self-regulation is a form of PR for advertising . . . the British advertiser enjoys greater freedom than applies in many other parts of the world. Some of this liberality is due to the painstaking lobbying by the trade organisations such as the Advertising Association, IPA and ISBA' (Jefkins 1992: 355 and 376).

In 1995 the ASA extended its remit to cover advertising on the Internet. In 2000 the CAP set up the Admark scheme which is a voluntary membership scheme for Internet advertisers. Members who refused to comply with ASA decisions would be removed from the scheme.

Other self-regulatory bodies include the Periodical Publishers' Association, which started to self-regulate advertorials in July 1992. It announced the setting-up of a voluntary code of practice for advertorials because of criticism

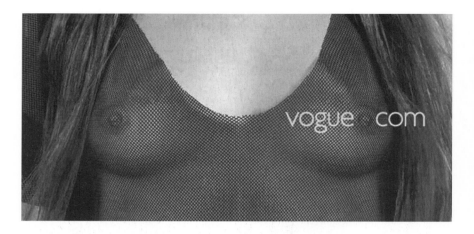

Figure 14.4 Vogue dot.com – Magazine publisher Conde Nast used this poster campaign to publicise the website of its flagship magazine, *Vogue*. The ad in which a women's nipple became the 'dot' in the 'dot.com' provoked eighty-four complaints to the ASA which were all thrown out. © Conde Nast. Agency: M&C Saatchi

from consumer bodies about the deceptive use by established publishers of advertising within editorial matter. The Outdoor Advertising Association adheres to the CAP and ASA and has its own rules, which include the right to refuse ads which are hostile to others, for example anti-smoking posters. The British Transport Authority's code covers the acceptance of ads for bus and rail outside London, forbids advertisements that attack a member or the policies of any government, are of a political nature, or concern public policy, encourage social unrest or conflict with CAP. The cinema industry examines all commercials before screening to ensure that they adhere to the CAP. Those of 30 seconds or over have to go to the British Board of Film Classification to be certified. Cinema has a voluntary system where ads for alcoholic drinks are removed from performances where 25 per cent of the expected audience is under 18. The contractors use evidence from previous films for this.

Television

From the outset TV was viewed as a particularly powerful medium. As the IBA Code of Advertising Standards and Practice stated, 'broadcasting, and particularly TV, because of its greater intimacy within the home, gives rise to problems which do not necessarily occur in other media and it is essential to maintain a consistently high quality of broadcast advertising'. The IBA does not specify what these 'problems' are. However, the implication of this was that TV regulations could not be trusted to a self-regulatory body. The IBA

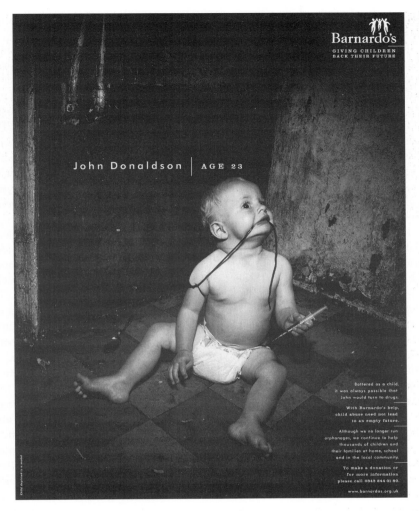

Figure 14.5 Barnardo's: this shocking ad caused uproar when it launched in 2000. Several newspapers refused to carry the ad for fear of offending their readers. The Advertising Standards Authority rejected claims that the ads were offensive; it said that the ad was justified in order to highlight the seriousness of drug abuse. © Barnardo's. Agency: Bartle Bogle Hegarty.

was given the power by parliament to formulate procedures and regulations governing broadcast advertising and ban advertisements where necessary.

However, when commercial TV was launched in 1955 a special Advertising Advisory Committee was formed to propose the Principles for Television Advertising. The AAC was overwhelmingly weighted in favour of advertising industry interests. There was no consumer interest represented (only business trade associations and some professional bodies). The first holder of the position of AAC Chairman in 1955 was the chairman of advertising agency S. H. Benson, R. A. Bevan, one of the most active lobbiers for liberal advertising rules on ITV: he later became chairman of the IPA. The first code was extremely liberal: no mention was made of tobacco or alcohol advertising or children's programmes, documentaries or drama. The IBA also had a body which surveyed audience attitudes to taste and decency, imposing bans on such areas as sanitary products and contraception.

In the 1990 Broadcasting Bill two separate regulatory bodies for commercial TV and radio were established: the Independent Television Commission (covering ITV, Channel 4 and later Channel 5 and the digital channels), and the Radio Authority. The equivalent of the ASA for TV is the BACC, which oversees and adjudicates on broadcast commercials for the ITC. The ITC is responsible to the National Heritage Department for controlling ITV, Channel 4, satellite and cable TV, while the Broadcast Advertising Clearance Centre (BACC) is a self-regulatory body which clears TV advertising. The ITC operates to a Code of Advertising Standards and Practice. The ITC code includes broadly the same principles as the ASA: all advertising should be 'legal, decent, honest and truthful'. It also includes a number of additional prerequisites, for instance: 'An advertisement must be clearly distinguishable as such and recognisably separate from the programmes'. The expression 'News Flash' is not allowed in advertisements. No ad should offend against 'good taste and decency or be offensive to public feeling'. Ads should not exploit superstitious people. 'Advertisements must not claim that alcohol has therapeutic qualities nor offer it expressly as a stimulant, sedative or tranquilliser . . . they must not give any impression that performance can be improved by drinking'. Heineken's advertising campaign, 'Only Heineken can do this, because it refreshes the parts other beers cannot reach', broke this guideline for years. So did the 'I bet he drinks Carling Black Label' ad, which featured people doing extraordinary things. 'No advertisements for a medicine or treatment may include a testimonial or be represented by a person well-known in public life, sport, entertainment, etc.' Section 20 of the ITC concerns car ads: 'No ad may encourage or condone dangerous, inconsiderate or competitive driving practices or breaches of the Highway Code'. This is consistently broken by car advertisers who often portray cars speeding through villages and towns. It is not only the content of the ads that are monitored but the tone and style of them as well. If an advertiser tries to make factual claims in a script it must provide evidence from clinical, technical or scientific tests to back it up. These often go unchecked.

'Advertisement must not, without justifiable reason, play on fear.' The reason why the code says 'without justifiable reason' is because of public information ads such as the anti-AIDS information commercials where it is seen as legitimate to frighten people. However, the vagueness of the clause allows many other abuses to take place with slimming products and spot cream. Those giving a testimonial to a product have to sign a statement that they use or prefer it and have not been paid to say something that is not true. The Annan Committee in 1977 recommended the removal of advertisements in children's programmes, but the government did not take up the recommendation (Young 1990).

Advertisers are allowed to use other products as substitutes in the commercial for production reasons (food melting in light, etc.), for instance mashed potatoes for cream 'as long as they don't give a misleading impression of the product or its performance' (Evans 1988: 77–78). This means that putting glass or plastic film on a floor to give it that extra shine is not permitted, but using chocolate-painted wood in a commercial instead of a chocolate bar is (as chocolate melts in studio lights). In August 1991 the US government fined Volvo and their agency Scali McCabe Sloves $150,000 for rigging a Volvo car with reinforced steel while being run over by a pick-up truck, while other cars in the commercial were weakened so that they would collapse under the strain. The agency was sacked by Volvo. Advertisements which use camera tricks are permissible as long as the trick or fake prop 'presents a fair and reasonable impression of the product or its effects and is not such as to mislead' (Section 27).

The Broadcast Advertising Copy Clearance Centre (BACC) vets every commercial before it is aired. Roughly 20 per cent of the scripts it sees are sent back to be changed (Davis 1992: 274). In 1997 it saw 22,000 TV commercial scripts. It also provides pre-transmission clearance for finished films. In 1997 it watched 17,000 finished films.

Additional codes included the ITC Code of Programme Sponsorship and ITC Rules on Ad Breaks. These allowed charity and religious advertising. Religious ads are still restricted to announcements of events and religious goods and book sales. The overall tendency has been one of deregulation. As the chairman of the ITC, Frank Willis, said in 1992, 'The history of the IBA and ITC over the last few years has been wholly in the direction of removing sectoral bans. Certain kinds of financial services, charities, sanitary protection and dating agencies are all examples of this deregulatory process' (Willis 1992: 39).

Radio

Until 1996 the copy clearance system for radio was voluntary and run by the radio companies themselves, rather than centrally and the BACC was a joint secretariat for radio and TV commercials, and examines and approves scripts for both. In 1996 the Radio Authority set up the Radio Advertising Clearance Centre which was wholly funded by the radio stations. The Radio Authority is able to impose strong sanctions which include forced apologies and heavy fines.

The Radio Authority Code Advertising Standard and Practice and Programme Sponsorship states that DJs and presenters are not allowed to endorse or identify themselves if they do commercials for advertisers on their station, or make reference to any ad while they are in an editorial programme. They are also not allowed to feature in an ad for a medicine or treatment. Ads are not allowed to include car and traffic noises which may distract drivers listening to car radios.

Clients and agencies are encouraged to check commercials at no charge to ensure that they comply with codes. Some categories such as alcohol, medical and charity ads must be cleared by the clearance centre before they are broadcast.

Legislating for sectors

In Britain, unlike other countries in Europe, children are used extensively in advertisements. The rules and regulations in the UK are much less stringent than in other countries, and this is partly because of the success of advertisers in developing self-regulatory systems.

Nevertheless, the lax rules and regulations in the UK have undermined other national legislators in Europe through satellite TV and international media. Children's ads on satellite, for instance, undermined other European countries' ability to set guidelines on viewing. The Children's Channel goes into countries where advertising to children on TV is banned. This illustrates the need for pan-European legislation. This is why advertising trade bodies are organising themselves into pan-European bodies to fight Brussels.

The Medicines Act (1968) prohibited the use of doctors and nurses in medical advertisements. But there is nothing to prevent actors putting on white coats and pretending to be scientists for cosmetic, soap and shampoo ads. And under the 1939 Cancer Act, advertisements are not allowed to claim that medical treatments can cure, only help or relieve.

The Trade Marks Act 1994 made trade mark infringement a criminal offence in some cases. Advertising slogans, such as 'Have a break. Have a Kit Kat', could now be registered, and sounds and jingles could be registered as trade marks. Previously trade marks could be infringed only if they were written down. Shapes and smells could also be registered. The Act also made comparative advertising possible, provided that the ad was honest, fair and not detrimental to the reputation and distinctiveness of the trade mark (Slingsby 1994: 40).

The Lotteries and Amusements Act prevents advertisers and publishers from distributing prizes on the basis of chance; some skill has to be involved. Free draws are supposed to be illegal. Many advertisers and publishers make offers for questions with obvious answers, like 'What is the capital of the UK?' to get round the law. Publishers too have to let readers know that they are able to obtain tokens for a sales promotion by sending off for them and that no purchase of the newspaper is necessary to enter. Nevertheless advertisers do try to emphasise (in an attempt to boost sales), that the newspapers contain the tokens and collecting them can allow entry. Bingo games are also not free draws because they are supposed to involve some skill on the part of the consumer.

Though advertisers are allowed to send unsolicited mail and unsolicited samples, they are not allowed to send goods for which a payment is needed (Unsolicited Goods and Services Acts 1971 and 1975). This was a problem for 'inertia selling' which would guilt-trip people into buying. However some mail-order companies such as book publishers still engage in this practice by sending unsolicited books through the post and demanding payment or return (postage to be paid by the recipient).

Local authorities also have the power under the Trades Descriptions Act (1968) to enforce the law locally and prevent local advertisers (and national ones) from making misleading claims. When you buy a product you are entering into a contract with the manufacturer and distributor. If the ad fails to deliver what it claims by misleading, then the advertiser is in a breach of contract. If an advertisement breaks a law, such as the Trades Descriptions Act, it is usually the advertiser who is liable, and occasionally the agency as well.

Under the Trades Descriptions Act an advertiser cannot claim that a body, organisation or person endorses a product without their approval. This can lead to prosecution for defamation. Defamation does not need to be intentional: an advertiser could inadvertently defame somebody by inventing a name and a real person of that name could sue for defamation if it had lowered their esteem. As the result of a number of famous cases in which people sued newspapers for being represented in their advertisements, in 1935 publishers managed to secure a legal obligation from advertising agencies to pay for the costs of any libel action in which the advertisement libelled somebody. The clause still operates today.

Advertising claims such as 'Melts in your mouth, not in your hand' are not legally binding, because they are perceived to be part of a sales message, and not meant as wholly true. The same goes for 'Heineken refreshes the parts other beers cannot reach': this cannot be proved or disproved. However, terms such as 'Guinness is good for you' could be held to be misleading, as could an ad suggesting that this aftershave will make you successful with women. Advertisers imply this, rather than say it outright.

The Business Advertisements (Disclosure) Order 1977 obliges advertisers to declare who they are and what their motives are. It forced publishers and advertisers to publish the word 'Advertisement' above copy which pretended to be editorial. According to this law, advertisements should have the appearance of advertisements, and advertorials should not pretend to be editorial. Advertising is also covered by laws governing slander, libel and copyright and conditions of employment and contractual obligations between businesses which cover all business practices.

The 1980s and early 1990s were a time of deregulation for advertising. Charities, religions and high-alcohol spirits were allowed to advertise on TV, professionals such as lawyers, accountants and architects were allowed to advertise, sponsorship was allowed on TV and radio, and new advertisers came on to the market as over-the-counter drugs became available, and restrictions on financial advertising were lifted. The government's privatisation programme of telecommunications, gas, electricity and water also boosted advertising industry fortunes. The government has also protected the advertising industry by staunchly preventing EC legislation against key sectors such as alcohol and tobacco advertising.

At the same time, advertisers pushed the boundaries of existing controls, and were more outlandish (see Benetton in Chapter 13), helping to shift the agenda of acceptability. This is one of the main reasons for the growth in 'reputable companies' being brought before the ASA. Part of the contradiction of Thatcherism was that it championed deregulation at the same time as championing the rights of the middle-class consumer. This has meant that in some areas such as 'green' labelling, the government has enforced legislation.

The Consumer Protection Act 1987 made it legally necessary for retailers and advertisers to recall defective products. This happened with beef, Perrier water, Austrian wine and numerous other branded goods in the late 1980s. Food labelling laws covering the nutritional claims of products, vitamins and slimming were also introduced. The declaration of food contents was also made compulsory, as were breakdowns of calorific content, and fat content as well as ingredients including additives and preservatives. Claims for 'naturalness' also need to be substantiated.

Legislators and reformers have proposed a number of ways of dealing with advertising in public policy. The first is to use taxation. This can be done either punitively, to discourage market distortions, or as a progressive anti-monopoly tax. Restricting levels of advertising spend may not be a viable policy option. There is no direct link between increased spends on advertising and increases in consumption. Some very famous campaigns have done well at lower costs than competitors', such as Häagen Dazs and Homepride. It is not a matter of how much is spent on advertising, but of how much access to the media and channels of communication big business has. Advertising closes off communications to consumers.

One area that has been tried and suggested is to provide consumers with alternative information, such as government-sponsored consumer reports and guides to buying goods. If consumers wanted to buy a car, for instance, they would have an impartial source of information, not a car magazine where the journalists have all been 'loaned' cars for a year. Though this may never match the ability of advertisers to provide entertainment-based sales messages on TV, it would act as an independent resource for shoppers. The problem that such an approach would have is that, as advertisers fully recognise, most people do not make planned rational decisions in buying things, they are mostly governed by ritual and time constraints. An alternative may be to force advertisers to say certain things or to indicate competitors, or to force them not to puff up their products. In the USA the government has the power to order advertisers who use deception to admit deception publicly, and pay for publicising it.

The most common direct means of legislation is the sectoral ban on socially harmful products such as tobacco and alcohol. The problem with sectoral bans is that they assume that advertising has a direct and singular effect on the business and consumption environment. The power of advertising lies in its relation to other elements of the business mix and in its privileged position in the mass media; if a government bans tobacco advertising it would also need to ban its use of sponsorship, merchandising, sales promotion, packaging and branding, and curtail the ease of availability of produced goods.

The advertising industry depends upon the belief that advertising is effective. To be effective, it needs to have a single cause, or combination of identifiable causes. Legislators tend to have a clear view that advertising has a clear effect on consumers, especially in relation to children and the 'more vulnerable' members of society. However, legislators have been unable to identify exactly what those harmful effects are, or specify those elements in advertising (contents of message, availability of media message, context, attitude and psychological make-up of consumer) that are most effective.

Even though advertising may not increase the total demand for goods and services in saturated markets, it does help to skew demand patterns within markets heavily (towards fizzy soft drinks and away from still drinks, for instance). We are encouraged to eat too much chocolate and too many sweets, drink too much alcohol and smoke too many cigarettes.

The advertising industry has tried to convince governments that it has only a benign influence on consumers. It does not make people buy things they do not want. However, advertisers' ultimate aim is to stimulate demand. In the case of generic ads – such as for sugar, milk and meat, and wool in the 1960s – the aim of advertising was to try to raise the overall market for consumption of the goods. But in individual markets advertisers generally want to stimulate demand for their products; either by encouraging trial and brand-switching from competitors, or by getting their consumers to consume more by changing their behaviour (e.g. Kellogg's). In panel data from 1962 research showed that 'half of beer drinking households consume 88% of all beer, half of Cola drinking households drink 90% of all Cola, half of cake mix households consume 85% of all cake mixes, half of shampoo using households consume 81% of all shampoos' (Schudson 1993: 26–27). Though overall consumption may not increase, individual consumption may increase dramatically. Between 1959 and 1978 the volume of beer consumed per adult rose by some 52 per cent, spirits by 132 per cent and wine by 268 per cent. The effects of this kind of activity – overeating, over-smoking and over-drinking – are more damaging on an individual level than on an aggregate level.

Sectoral bans: tobacco

In 1962 the Minister of Health, Enoch Powell, delivered a speech to the House of Commons on a report from the Royal College of Physicians making a direct link between smoking and cancer. The cigarette industry immediately claimed that it was not proven, and that there were psychological benefits to smoking. They also claimed, without any proof, that 'Cigarette advertising was designed merely to get people to smoke one brand rather than another, and not to increase the total consumption of cigarettes; a suggestion which would raise a horse laugh from any experienced advertising man' (Birch 1962: 124). The ITA attempted to forestall a total TV ban by imposing tighter rules on timing and content of tobacco ads. However, in 1965 the Postmaster General overrode the IBA code and imposed a sectoral ban on all cigarette advertising on TV. The logic for banning cigarettes on TV was that it was the most powerful medium because it went into the home.

The tobacco industry responded by increasing its advertising and sponsorship spend in posters, magazines and cinema (until it was banned in the latter). Another tactic of tobacco advertisers was to sponsor major sporting events, such as motor racing, cricket and snooker, which would gain coverage on advertising-free BBC TV. Benson & Hedges also managed to flout the rules for over twenty years by advertising their Hamlet cigars on TV (advertising of cigars and pipe tobacco was allowed on TV). Benson & Hedges used the Hamlet commercials to promote B&H corporate brands: 'Happiness is a cigar called Hamlet, the mild cigar, from Benson & Hedges'. At the same time, Benson & Hedges' cigarette brand Gold was heavily branded as a corporate brand on billboards and magazines. As Tim Bell points out, 'what the cigar commercials were saying was that its tobacco is like a drug. When there is a disaster, you light a cigar and all your cares go away, you can forget any cares about the world and be "happy". The ads made smoking seem humorous and fun' (Bell 1986: 446–447).

However, the ban on TV advertising did not decrease the opportunities to see of key groups in society. Children were just as likely to see tobacco ads in magazines, newspapers, on billboards and most of all on newsagents' shop fronts where they went to buy sweets. Though the British government still refused to ban tobacco advertising, it pledged to spend £4 million each year for three years on anti-smoking advertising. However, the tobacco industry still manages to spend £50 million on average each year on advertising, despite being banned from TV, radio and children's media.

In 1997 the British government announced the future ban on tobacco sponsorship of sport and a year later it announced that it intended to make a complete ban on tobacco advertising which would remove advertising from posters and magazines.

The main argument of the advertisers is that tobacco advertising does not have an effect on overall demand for tobacco, it merely fights for brand share. As advertising executive Frank Convery says: 'The task of most advertising is to keep the product on the market or increase its share from someone else. This is share-oriented advertising, pushing brands. Most, even for tobacco, is brand oriented – it doesn't make people smoke' (Leiss *et al.* 1990: 40). Adam Lury, managing partner of HHCL, reinforced the advertising view, first articulated in the 1960s by the tobacco industry in response to government legislation: 'Advertising predominantly encourages switching and it's only one part of an environment that says it's all right to smoke' (Martin 1993: 25). However, this is not a commonly held view. Chris Powell, chief executive of BMP DDB Needham and former chairman of the IPA, said: 'I'm sure advertising encourages people to start smoking. Of course children are influenced – you can't just ghettoise a target audience. In almost all advertising markets I know, the aggregate spend increases the market's size' (ibid.: 24). And Adrian Vickers, deputy chairman of AMV.BBDO, said, 'I wouldn't work on cigarette business again because cigarette advertising does influence children. It is a fact that the four most popular brands among the young teenagers are the four most heavily advertised' (ibid.: 25). Research by academics has shown that children have greater brand awareness of those cigarette brands that sponsor sporting events such as snooker and motor racing (Young: 1990). Children apparently recall the more heavily promoted brands and the imagery of them more than least promoted (this fits with the AIDA behavioural model). But 'there is no direct evidence that such tobacco promotion influences the consumer behaviour of the child' (ibid.).

Though no link between behaviour and recall was proved, this does not mean that it does not exist. Advertisers would argue that the most important thing about advertising to the young at this stage is to make sure that they have are knowledgeable about the brand before they became consumers, so that they are able to differentiate when they decide through peer pressure or whatever to take up smoking. The task of advertising in this context is to try to make tobacco acceptable and to influence attitudes to it as being 'common sense' to smoke. An advertiser would be more interested in attitudes to smoking at this age than recall, because attitudes are seen as one of the most important influences on the buying and using decision. The role of a tobacco company is to intervene on as many promotional levels as possible; from sponsoring football annuals to sponsoring snooker; from advertising in newsagents' shops, on posters and billboards to influencing journalists; from running sales promotion campaigns to advertising in young people's magazines and appearing in films, on TV shows, in books and on shelves and in machines in pubs. Constantly repeating and dominating in this way helps to get tobacco talked about and play an authoritative cultural role in society.

Hardly any tobacco advertising directly exhorts consumers to brand switch; most tobacco campaigns are aimed at encouraging their existing consumers to consume more of the goods and sustain high brand awareness among non-users, especially the young. The main preoccupation of advertisers is to keep their market share, but it needs a steady stream of new consumers to keep sales up; hence much of the tobacco industry's targeting of young people. They want to encourage trial and to encourage repeat purchase. Those who stay smokers are therefore encouraged to smoke more, while at the same time new smokers are needed to replace those who give up, or die of lung cancer.

Summary

The advertising industry has had to respond to severe criticism from various groups in civil society and the state: the medical profession, consumer groups, political parties (particularly the Labour Party), sections of the media and the establishment, as well as from within the business community. But it has successfully managed to resist legislation and controls by setting up a system of self-regulation and lobbying heavily for its own interests. Advertisers have managed to confine public policy issues towards sectoral bans, such as those on tobacco, alcohol, medicine and advertising to children, rather than legislation for the whole system of advertising. The aim of most advertising in most mature, saturated markets is not to encourage new consumers as much as to encourage existing consumers to consume more. Ironically, in trying to resist sectoral bans, advertisers and agencies have been in the position of claiming that advertising is ineffectual at influencing consumer behaviour.

15 Postscript: Advertising in crisis

·····

Brand advertising emerged in the nineteenth century as a means to stimulate consumption because the technology-driven factory system caused over production. Using the mass media, manufacturers were able to circumvent retailers and develop a relationship with consumers via the mass media which reinforced their ability to command prices and distribution.

In the twentieth century the advertising industry had become a stable, regulated industry with clear professional status and a clear, defined role in the business community. However, by the 1990s the advertising industry had reached a state of crisis. The fundamental ability of manufacturers to control the market had been undermined by the more powerful retailers, the mass media had fragmented and advertising agencies desperately searched for new roles as manufacturers switched to alternative forms of promotion.

Retailers fight back
·····

By the late twentieth century, retailers had begun to concentrate. Sainsbury's launched the first supermarket in Croydon in 1950. Between 1971 and 1985 supermarkets increased their size and decreased their number from 11,000 to 4,500 and increased their share of the total grocery business from 44.3 per cent to 70.1 per cent. In 1985 the top 10 per cent of shops held 80 per cent of all commodity turnover in the retail grocery trade (Smith in Hart 1990: 14). Now only four companies dominate: Tesco, Sainsbury's, Asda and Safeway.

By the late 1970s supermarkets had begun to advertise themselves as brands. They managed to transform the consumers' question of what to buy into where to buy. Sainsbury's, Safeway and Tesco managed to establish their own-label brands as high quality and to compete more directly with established brands such as Heinz Baked Beans and Kellogg's Corn Flakes. Sainsbury's even had the audacity in 1994 to launch Classic Cola against Coca-Cola. The cheaper own-label brands were able to undermine the power of the established manufacturer brands by running quality commercials about their stores. Throughout the 1980s and 1990s the top ten advertised brands have been dominated by retailers. In 1992 in the top twelve advertised brands, eleven were retailers: Texas Homecare, MFI/Hygena, Comet, B&Q, Woolworths, McDonald's, Curry's, Sainsbury's, Boots, Safeway and Dixons. Many of these produce own-label goods which would benefit from this heavyweight brand advertising. Retailers accounted for 14.7 per cent of total advertising expenditure. By 1999 retailers accounted for 19 per cent of the total. According to research company AC Nielsen by 1999 own-label goods in UK supermarkets accounted for 45 per cent of total grocery sales (*Marketing Week*, 6 July 2000: 'Shelving own label').

Retailers have also sought to re-inforce their control of the market by launching loyalty card schemes such as Tesco Clubcard and the Shell Smart Card. They have also sought to offer customers extra incentives to stay loyal such as cheap insurance, banking and utility supplies.

Retailers will allow shelf space only to leading brands, other big-ad-spending brands and their own-label products. Some long-established, big-name brands such as Quakers have been removed from the shelf by some supermarkets. Most manufacturers have tried to influence consumers at the point of sale by sales promotion and by offering special incentives to retailers to get shelf space for their brand. In these ways manufacturers are having to secure distribution not through the power of their brand (as happened in the nineteenth century) but through special trade deals and financial investment.

Manufacturers have tried to fight back through direct marketing. With the help of deregulated telecommunications, companies try to build up databases of consumers and deal with them directly via telephone, mail, fax or computer. The deregulation of TV has also opened up the possibility of home shopping, circumventing bricks and mortar retailers altogether. New retailers have emerged such as Amazon.com and Lastminute.com but the traditional retailers have fought back opening their own home shopping channels and online retailing (e-tailing). Manufacturers have proved unable to use the web and other new-media technologies to circumvent retailer power. Brand loyalty to retailers who provide customer service and a degree of independent advice when selling products has proved more powerful than brand loyalty towards individual products.

Brands in crisis

The second reason for advertising's existence – the ability to stimulate consumer demand – is also in crisis. The first crises came in the 1960s, as it became apparent that advertising was unable to increase sales in saturated markets, and so agency pundits shifted from claiming that advertising was powerfully persuasive and had the power to increase sales, to claiming that it created the 'environment' to improve sales. Advertising agencies claimed that advertising's power lay in building long-term brand loyalty which is unquantifiable. As Simon

Broadbent points out, 'How can we say what it is worth to improve the morale of a salesforce? To help get distribution? Even to keep a price relatively high? (Broadbent 1993: 37). If you buy one particular brand of washing powder (for whatever reason) on a regular basis the advertiser would term you a 'brand-loyal' customer.

But a great deal of evidence points to the erosion of brand loyalty in recent years. One of the main reasons why 'brand loyalty' has eroded has been because the saturated markets have provided more choice for consumers. The 'power' of the brand was eroded by the increase in the number of brands and greater choice. Advertising agencies were quite happy to cash in on the idea that they had been the cause of loyalty among customers, but when it was found that loyalty was not so great as they imagined advertising agencies blamed sales promotion for eroding the power of the brand. Agencies promote the idea that sales promotion, competition and coupons 'erode brand loyalty'. And they spend large amounts of money trying to prove this is the case. The awards ceremonies also celebrated the success of campaigns without taking into account other elements of the marketing mix which helped sales: the fact that there were money-off coupons, sales promotional activity and PR effort to back it up.

Ehrenberg's study in 1972 discovered that in mature markets with segmented brands and wider choice, people will not remain loyal to one single brand of goods. They will, inevitably, 'repertoire buy' – that is, buy a repertoire of brands, such as Mars Bar, Galaxy and Dairy Milk, rather than stick to the single brand of Dairy Milk. In other words, the consumer would have a select repertoire of preferred brands to choose from rather than stick to one. Advertisers would try to become one of the repertoire, rather than become the sole brand that the consumer purchases. Most goods are bought infrequently, even fast-moving consumer goods. Ehrenberg revealed that, in the USA coffee market, 40 per cent of the buyers of Maxwell House bought it only once a year, and that other brands like Nescafé and Maxim had even larger proportions of light buyers (Ehrenberg 1991: 290). These findings led Ehrenberg later to claim, 'Brand loyalty is merely a continuing propensity to buy' (Ehrenberg and Barnard 1994: 13). The idea that advertising could create and sustain brand loyalty was also broken down. 'Advertising is a weak force (which is why we need so much of it), and mostly reinforcing rather than strongly persuasive' (ibid.: 13).

Advertisers have traditionally perceived consumers to be 'loyal' towards a single brand. This was largely because they operated in markets in which there was a relatively small number of brands in a product market and a relatively small number of advertising messages in limited media. This has changed in recent years, where consumers have a greater choice of brands.

Advertising tries, and on the whole fails, to stop the long-term slide in sales of individual brands. Though many advertisers still try to maintain brand loyalty with consumers, there is a greater realisation of the need to encourage brand switching, by price cuts and promotions to defeat competitors, especially the shop's own label, rather than develop the so-called brand franchise with

consumers. Because of the decline in new users of brands and the acknowl-
edgement of repertoire buying, advertisers seek more and more to increase the
weight of buying of existing users, or encourage brand switching from rival
brands.

Consumer markets in decline

The greatest boon to advertising in the twentieth century was the growth of the
welfare state. Rationing ended in 1952–1954 and restrictions on hire purchase
were lifted. The huge post-war housing boom in the major cities also made
possible a boom in the household goods market and the birth of the do-it-your-
self industry. Working-class consumers were able to spend less on basic welfare
and more on consumer goods. Gradually cookers, inside toilets, fridges, washing
machines, TV sets, cars and foreign holidays came within the scope of consumption for unskilled workers. There were also thousands of new white-collar jobs
created in health, education, social security and the civil service generally. Mass
media also cashed in on the consumer bonanza fuelled by imports from overseas manufacturers, primarily in the USA, who continued the trend set in the
1930s by bringing their agencies with them to London. By the 1960s consumer
markets had begun to saturate again. Key manufacturing industries such as
cotton manufacturing, shipbuilding and steel had begun their terminal decline.

However, since the 1970s more new brands have been launched than in the
history of marketing (*Marketing*, 14 August 1993). Despite this, there is a
massive failure rate. Estimates by market researchers put product launch failures at around 80 per cent in advanced consumer markets. In the confectionery
market, for instance, most of the lead brands were launched before the Second
World War: Cadbury's Dairy Milk (1905), Crunchie (1929), Milk Tray (1915),
Rowntree's Fruit Pastilles (1881), Fruit Gums (1893), Black Magic (1933), Kit
Kat (1939), Aero (1935), Dairy Box (1936), Smarties (1937), Mackintosh's
Quality Street (1936), Mars Bar (1932), Milky Way (1935), Maltesers (1936).

In the 1960s manufacturers responded to the saturation of markets by
segmenting brands and encouraging changes in behaviour, encouraging their
existing consumers to consume more goods more often. In the 1960s Ford ran
newspaper ads for Anglia cars, encouraging people to have two-car households,
Colman's suggested mustard with chicken – 'English Roast Chicken . . . It's
nicer with mustard' (Birch 1962: 179) – and Jacobs suggested serving cream
crackers with honey or marmalade as a breakfast snack – 'Soggy toast hasn't
a look in with Jacobs Cream Crackers around'.

In the 1980s the wilful destruction of the welfare state by the Thatcher government restricted consumer goods markets further. Manufacturers tried to cope
with the crisis as they had in the 1930s by extending credit to widen consumer
markets. But the various attempts to encourage changes in behaviour became
far more widespread in the 1990s. Kellogg's ran TV commercials in 1994
encouraging consumers to eat corn flakes at night, and BT's desperation showed

in the same year when actor Bob Hoskins was recruited to tell people blatantly that they should use the phone more often and for longer periods of time. Marketers realised that the single most important objective in saturated markets was to try to encourage changes in behaviour. The way they do this is to try to get you to eat turkey throughout the year (Bernard Mathew's), eat Mars Bars in the summer (after putting them in the fridge), drink Ovaltine, Horlicks and drinking chocolate throughout the day (at the turn of the century this was actually usual; it was only in the 1930s that the cocoa drinks industry tried to switch consumer behaviour to drinking it at bedtime). Advertising suggested new rituals of consumption such as family meals at McDonald's or Christmas in front of the TV.

Manufacturers' ability to differentiate a product in terms of technology has been greatly reduced. Because of the speed of technology, there is less product difference between brands than ever before. As soon as a modification is made to a product a competitor can copy it. For instance, in the car market the first cars to launch catalytic converters were differentiated, but they soon became standard. Then came ABS brakes, sixteen-valve engines, side-impact doors, central locking. What were additional features became standard to all cars in a very short period of time. However, the manufacturer still needs to convince the consumer that its brand is different; it has a 'new improved formula'. This involves constantly making modifications to brands, to create the impression with the consumer that the product is constantly being improved. Very often this is not a real improvement, merely a change in pack design, product shape or advertising slogan or campaign. Even the so-called classic brands, with an older profile of consumers, need to show that they are taking product development seriously, and are changing with the times. If the competitors are modifying and changing, the brand needs to appear to keep up.

Though many new brands have been launched (see Chapter 1), completely new services or products are relatively rare. These are perhaps the most costly and risky ventures for an advertiser, but they can account for a large amount of marketing activity. When the *Sunday Correspondent* was launched in 1989, all the rival Sunday newspapers, and the Saturday weekend newspaper groups, pumped millions of pounds into defending their market share. The *Sunday Correspondent* collapsed after eighteen months.

Because of the saturation of markets and high levels of advertising by competitors, many advertisers believe that highly advertised brands are unlikely to reach people who have never tried the product category before (Cowan in Cowley 1989: 48). Advertisers try to hold on to as many loyal users as possible in a declining market and encourage brand switching from rivals; they tend to target buyers of the product category, their own brand buyers and light or unloyal buyers of competitors' brands. Advertisers believe that advertising cannot make a lifelong Tory vote Labour. It can, however, sway somebody who is more predisposed (someone who has voted Labour in the past). Knowing, or classifying the probables, is much more important in modern politics than trying to change people from being deeply conservative to being radical socialists. Advertisers try to influence long-term attitudes, emphasising more positive elements and destabilising existing attitudes and beliefs.

Media fragmentation

In the nineteenth century mass media advertising was a cheap means to appeal to consumers over the retailer's heads. However by the 1990s the increase in media availability has provided problems for advertisers. Whereas in the past they could simply gauge the ratings of one programme such as *Coronation Street* to deliver coverage and frequency, they now need to use more media to get the same coverage. In the 1980s ITV was offering around 90 per cent of the market for commercial TV in the UK, but it was predicted that by 1995 this would have reduced to 75 per cent (because of cable and satellite, etc.). Traditional programmes could deliver mass audiences; *Coronation Street* could offer 48 per cent TVRs on an average weekday evening. In 1992 an average weekday evening spot for *Coronation Street* drew 25 per cent (Armstrong 1992: 12). In 1992 there were over two and a half million satellite TV homes with cable, with a dish and with satellite to master antennae TV (i.e. with shared reception). In 1993 satellite was in 14 per cent of homes and cable had only 4 per cent penetration. TV audience shares from 1984 through to 1993 and 2000 for the month of January were as in Table 15.1. In the 1970s and 1980s it was possible to reach 70 per cent of the available audience with two spots on ITV, but with the new TV media environment, and increased choice, advertisers believe that viewers are much more discriminating about what they watch. This gives advertisers the ability to target TV much more. It also means that magazines and other narrowcast media are losing their *raison d'être*.

The prospect for media planners is that people may be watching more electronic media than ever before, but watching many more channels, programmes and forms of electronic media. In the US market, where there is a much wider choice of commercial media, FMCG manufacturers such as Procter & Gamble use TV all year and try for coverage of 50 per cent but with very high OTS in trying to target heavy users and their core market (Armstrong 1992: 12).

Table 15.1 TV audience shares, January 1984, 1993, 2000 (%)

Channel	1984	1993	2000
BBC1	36	32.9	28.6
BBC2	10	9.5	10.7
ITV	49	40.8	30.1
Channel 4	5	11.7	10.7
Channel 5	–	–	5.3
Other	0	5.0	14.6

Source: BARB

The number of new media choices available to advertisers owes more to changes in the traditional media (such as magazines, outdoor sites and newspapers and terrestrial TV) than it does to new technology such as cable and satellite. Old media have been forced to respond by segmenting and offering new forms of media: outdoor advertising offers illuminated sites, revolving sites and mobiles; newspapers offer regionalised editions, on-the-run colour and sectionalised newspapers; magazines offer advertorials and niche targeting with differentiated publications (such as the women's weeklies); and TV offers more tightly defined audiences, sponsorship opportunities and increased daytime and night-time TV audiences. Media costs have increased as the amount of available media has increased. Unilever's Persil had only a quarter of its 1985 exposure on TV in 1993 (Robert Heller, *Observer* Business Section, 26 September 1993: 8).

In 1961 the *Radio Times* had 18.8 million readers; in 1997 its NRS figure was 4.2 million. It has gone from 100 per cent to 27 per cent of the market for weekly magazine listings titles, because of deregulation and changing viewing patterns. It has managed to maintain its strength by having a disproportionately high number of ABC1 readers. But it is also in competition with listings in other magazines and national newspapers who produce weekly listings, as well as Teletext and Ceefax.

Advertisers' requirements of the media have also changed. Target audiences have become more narrowly defined because of over-competition and saturation of markets, and the ability of the traditional mass media to deliver these new audiences has been fundamentally challenged. The result has been that many mass media such as women's weekly magazines have had to redefine their audience to niche age segments of the population rather than 'the mass'. In 1985 there were only four women's weekly magazines, now there are twelve which reach the same number of women. The ability to increase sales through mass media advertising has virtually disappeared for many mass market brands.

Traditional media research has been unable to cope with the changes, and huge flaws have appeared, leading to attacks from agencies (see Chapter 9). Though virtually all the joint industry committees reformed in the face of the onslaught from trade associations and the trade press, the image of mass media advertising had been damaged for advertisers. Agencies had exposed the inadequacies of the industry currency in an attempt to get media owners to reduce rates, claiming that the media did not deliver what they promised: impact and effectiveness. This backfired on agencies; many clients simply moved their money from above-the-line media to below-the-line. Agencies may have a short-term interest in attacking media owners, but they have a longer-term interest in keeping the client's faith in mass media advertising; it is in above-the-line media that agencies make most money. By 1993, much of the criticism had cooled.

The outcome of all these changes in media availability, and the loss of faith in mass-media advertising in being able to deliver, has been that advertisers have switched large amounts of spend to public relations, sponsorship, direct marketing and sales promotions as an antidote to the inflated costs and dubious effectiveness of mass media advertising.

The result has been a redefinition of what advertisers regard as 'media'. Clients are no longer willing to rely on a single medium, or combination of mass media, to deliver sales messages; they have attempted to replace the traditional distinctions of above and below the line with through the line. Advertisers are returning to a pre-mass-media definition of 'the media' which covers all forms of promotional material which a company or organisation relays to the public.

In 2000 Britain's biggest advertiser, Procter & Gamble cut its annual advertising spend on traditional media by 26 per cent from £154 million to £114 million (AC Nielsen MMS). The primary reason given for the drastic cut in advertising spend on traditional media was due to the rising cost of television airtime (*Financial Times*, 11 January 2001: 1).

Crisis in effectiveness

Though advertising has suffered the periodic problem of being unable to deliver sales, giving rise to new methods of effectiveness research, the problem reached crisis points in the 1980s and 1990s as media fragmentation accelerated, costs rose and sales for advertisers continued to decline.

In recent years advertising messages have been preoccupied with grabbing attention and sustaining interest, rather than transferring persuasive messages. This has largely been due to a perception that advertising needs to stand out and perform an aesthetic, educative or entertaining function in order to be received by consumers (see Chapter 11). The agencies who produced these kinds of commercials argued that, because there was so little product difference, advertisers needed to provide difference through the advertising itself, not the product. The desired consumer response for Carling Black Label, according to Jim Ring, was 'That's another great ad for Carling'. It was the ad which was the most important element, its use of humour which helps people to warm to the brand, not the product. The advertising is more important and significant than the brand (Ring 1993: 88). Others attacked this view: 'Advertising used to be about persuading people to want your product. Now the task seems to be make people admire your advertising', said one industry commentator (Wilkins 1988).

Because many of the stylish and humorous award winners did not produce sales success, clients began a backlash. Critics claimed that over-stylised advertising sacrificed content for form; the product is often secondary or incidental, and 'clever' advertising takes precedence over selling. In 1980 the IPA started the Advertising Effectiveness Awards and the Advertising Works case study series of publications in response to clients' pressure for advertising that 'worked' rather than simply looked good.

This kind of debate is not new. When describing the creative work of one agency executive, Bradshaw pointed out that he 'is conscious always of the danger of designing advertisements which are a better demonstration of advertising technique than of a selling instrument' (Bradshaw 1927: 123). And Rosser Reeves called 'art' advertising on TV in the 1950s 'vampire video' which distracts the viewer from the product and makes the commercial's selling message less effective (Reeves 1961: 101–105).

The debate around 'effective' advertising became much more intense in the 1980s and 1990s with increases in media costs, media fragmentation and declining sales. Agencies began to push research people and planners forward as spokespeople who could convince clients that advertising could be effective. Planners identified one of the problems to be a new breed of media-literate 'savvy' consumers who were more impenetrable than ever to sales messages, calling for more sophisticated forms of advertising.

Involvement (see Chapter 13) was a way of overcoming the resistance of the 'savvy' consumer. And, as Judie Lannon pointed out, 'consumers are less naive, more professional and cynical. They are more aware of the processes of manufacturing, marketing and communication, more aware of the manipulation of images ... a conclusion which the viewer has reached himself will last longer and be better internalised' (Lannon 1993: 21).

Agencies have explored new ways to involve consumers in ads. HHCL produced two commercials in 1994 with the purpose of involving consumers in the ads and in the company. The first was an ad for Tango drink which asked consumers to ring in if they had seen anyone pushing a pirated still version of the brand (apparently thousands did, though it did not exist). The second was a commercial for Mazda which ran with the sound down and invited viewers to turn the sound up on their TV sets if they wanted to hear the sales message.

More recently advertisers have become interested in the possibilities of new media technologies, particularly multi-media technologies which increase the level of consumer interaction with the medium, and possibly the brand. Interactive TV via broadband cables provides possibilities for advertisers.

The launch of digital television via cable, satellite and set top boxes allowed a fundamental change of viewing experience which included Internet access via the TV set and interactive TV allowing multiple viewing of live sporting events. It also allowed advertisers the possibility of developing interactive advertising so that they could gain immediate response from viewers to their advertising. However, this type of advertising is still very much on the fringes of the advertising world.

Though agencies have embraced the interactive age, as it 'allow[s] a one-to-one relationship between the producer and consumer', according to Garrett O'Leary, chief executive officer of advertising agency Bates Dorland's interactive marketing division (Halstead 1994: 63), it is still in the experimental stage and interactive advertising remains a side-issue in most agencies.

The rise of the 'savvy' consumer has also given rise to a further model of effects, the 'salience model'. 'In order for advertising to be registered and for it to evoke a response it must be provocative – it must be unusual and

Figure 15.1 Tango: an example of an 'interactive' commercial concerning a fake product scare. The serious-looking, rather grim presenter told viewers that another company was using the Tango name on its still orange drink, and asked Tango consumers to phone an 0800 number if they saw evidence of this, thus involving them in the advertising. Tango ads and commercials identify their consumers as lovers of the wacky and unusual, their ads depicting strange experiences and bizarre happenings. © Britvic. Agency: Howell Henry Chaldecott Lury.

challenge the standard advertising methods. It must stimulate the consumer and not reflect the consumer' (Lury 1994: 99). Standing out involves getting people to talk about an ad and write articles about it. This has been done to great effect by Benetton, Wonderbra and Budweiser's famous 'Wassup?' commercial which also had special e-mail jpeg commercials featuring Marvel comic heroes and Hassidic Jewish men shouting 'Wassup?' (see Chapter 4 examples). In January 2001 *Media Week* magazine made the Budweiser advertiser of the year because of this campaign. It said, 'If there was one campaign this year that cut throught the increasingly dense media clutter and became a fixture in playgrounds, offices and bars around the country, it was the Budweiser series of ads based on the simple premise of a few guys yelling at one another, watching the game and having a Bud' (*Media Week*, 5 January 2001: 15).

The growing use of e-mail technology in offices and in the home also opened up new advertising opportunities and the chance for advertisers to multiply their messages in a virus-like fashion.

In the late 1980s and early 1990s agencies began to produce commercials intended to appeal to these new consumers. The commercials were self-

Figure 15.2 Mazda: an example of an 'interactive' commercial. The features of the car were being extolled, but viewers could hear only by actively turning up the volume on their TV sets. © Mazda. Agency: Howell Henry Chaldecott Lury.

referential, often parodying advertising or sales messages in general. The intention was to get consumers to talk about advertising in its own right. The ads often tried to challenge the conventions of advertising to make consumers sit up. HHCL ran commercials for Fuji which included Asian and disabled actors who are not represented in mainstream advertising. They also ran ads with 'real people' in them for Pepe and did a famous ad for Midland Bank's phone service bank, First Direct, which had two buckets in it. Parody ads include comedian Bob Monkhouse for Sekonda, saying how much he was paid to do the commercial and comedian Jack Dee being offered more money by the advertisers to do a John Smith's commercial.

Some agencies' enthusiasm for the 'savvy' consumer go further. HHCL's Adam Lury declared, 'Today's consumer is active and knowledgeable – an expert in communication and selling techniques. She/he is a long way from the passive innocent victim of the 1950s and 1960s mass production and mass communication techniques' (Lury 1994: 101). However, the problem with most of these approaches is that there is no evidence to suggest that consumers of the past were any less media-literate, or had less understanding of manufacturing processes. What has happened has been the growth in media and advertising, and a change in academic and advertising communication models which bestow more power upon the consumer.

Crisis in advertiser power

In the 1980s consumers started to take a very strong interest in the things that they bought and their ingredients. The 1980s was the decade when the consumers began to get organised. Vegetarianism, animal welfare organisations, health food organisations and the growing strength of established consumer bodies forced marketers to reconsider their marketing strategies. Consumer activism was also a feature of the 1970s and 1980s in the forms of boycotts on South African and Chilean goods and widespread press criticism of the food industry's practices. This problem reached a head in the late 1980s with the revelation of salmonella in eggs and chicken, listeria in cook-chill foods, food additives and radiation treatment of foods, chemicals in Perrier mineral water, BSE ('Mad Cow Disease') in British beef and in the 1990s the emergence of genetically modified foods. Consumers also began to buy low-fat, low-sugar and low-salt goods. Before the late 1980s any environmental concerns and pressure groups were seen as 'fringe', in the late 1980s they had become mainstream. All the main political parties had to parade their 'green' credentials, as had manufacturers.

According to the *Daily Telegraph*, product boycotts were operated by around 50 per cent of the population in the late 1980s (Nava 1992: 197). In each case, consumers sought to assert their power in the marketplace. The consensus had been broken. Consumers were no longer confident that what they were buying was safe and properly tested. The result was a growth in generic campaigns to help rebuild the image of British food production and a concerted PR effort in the press and on TV to restore consumer confidence.

The year of the green consumer in Britain was 1989. The Green Party achieved over 2 million votes in the European elections. In June 1989 Mori published *The Green Consumer*. Aimed at advertisers, this examined the impact of environmental concerns on consumer choices. In 1988–9 42 per cent of people claimed to have selected one product over another because of its environmentally friendly packaging. Whether they were telling the truth or not, advertisers responded. They brought out new product lines with more 'eco-friendly' packaging, and advertising proclaimed their care for the environment. In 1989 the ASA criticised BP, Austin Rover and Citroën for making claims that unleaded petrol was 'friendly to the environment'.

The other area of attack came in the form of legislation from Europe. Though the British government has often acted as the advertising industry's representatives in Brussels to help fight legislation, it has found it difficult to resist legislation on tobacco and alcohol advertising.

The EC issues Directives, which must be obeyed by the member states. The draft Directive on misleading advertisements was first considered in 1972, but did not get through until 1986 because of intensive lobbying by the advertising industry through the European Association of Advertising Agencies and media owners. As one commentator put it, 'The ad industries in Europe have developed efficient lobbying tactics that have seen off what, in the early 1970s, appeared potentially dangerous "consumerist" pressure' (Duval 1990: 11). The EC Directive originally included recommendations on misleading and unfair ads; comparative and corrective advertising were left to individual countries' discretion.

In response to the EC Directive on misleading ads the British government introduced the Control of Misleading Advertisements Regulations in 1988. The law states that only after a complainant has not managed to get satisfaction from the ASA the Director General of Fair Trading may use the High Court to bring out injunctions against misleading ads. Though this gives the consumer more legal redress, it also shows how bound up the ASA is in the governmental system. The EC misleading advertising Directive was implemented by using the Office of Fair Trading, which could refer misleading claims to the High Court. The provisions made by the government ensured that 'action is normally only to be taken where existing measures have proved ineffective or inadequate. In other words, the OFT provides the safety net' (ibid.). In 1991 the OFT received 282 complaints. Most objections were for direct mail followed by newspapers, point-of-sale material and magazines. 'Since 1988 only four cases have led to an injunction or undertakings in lieu of court action' (ibid.).

However, threats of more wide-ranging legislation on tobacco and alcohol advertising promise to be more difficult to circumvent. In 1991 the government was forced to issue statutory regulations on tobacco warnings for all tobacco products, as laid down by an EC Directive in 1989. Previously warnings were self-imposed. In May 1991 the EC published a draft Directive proposing the banning of all tobacco advertising across Europe. The UK, Germany and the Netherlands, which all have self-regulatory bodies, opposed it.

The 1992 Smee Report produced evidence to show that advertising affects tobacco consumption. It found that tobacco advertising bans in Finland, Canada, New Zealand and Norway had all been followed by falls in tobacco consumption on a scale which 'cannot reasonably be attributed to other factors' (Cardwell 1993a: 17). In January 1993 the House of Commons Health Committee produced a report which concluded that a ban on advertising would have a definite impact on reducing smoking, and urged the government to support the EC Directive. At the beginning of 1994 the government agreed to ban future shop-front advertising by tobacco firms.

In 1991 the advertising industries of Europe came together to form the European Advertising Standards Alliance. The intention of this body was to try to circumvent European legislation by developing a European-wide code of practice for self-regulation of the industry. The Director General of the Advertising Standards Authority was the Vice-Chairman of the Alliance. The intention of this body was to restrict the amount of legislation coming from Brussels to try to provide a European-wide framework which copies the British form of self-regulation and minimal government intervention.

Agencies in crisis

The first unbundling of advertising agencies began in the early to mid-1960s. Agencies had grown at an enormous rate in the late 1950s on the back of commercial TV; the commission system and the problems with client conflict meant that the only way they could increase profits was to add on services and costs for their existing clients. They added on huge market research departments, merchandising, public relations and in-house product research and media production facilities from the extra moneys from TV.

The inflated costs and the additional fees that clients had to pay for these services, combined with heightened media inflation, produced a backlash in the 1960s. The abolition in 1964 of Resale Price Maintenance, which had fixed prices, forcing manufacturers to use mass media advertising to compete, meant that advertisers could pump large amounts of money into price promotions, cutting expensive brand advertising.

Large advertisers moved to new creative agencies which did not offer all the 'hidden extras'. The move to the smaller agencies was also caused by resistance to the large takeovers and mergers of the 1960s (see Chapter 6). Large clients went to small and medium-sized agencies, which did not have media buying clout but did have creative flair. The weightier agencies had a shake-out and jettisoned many of these additional services. Between 1963 and 1978 the number of market researchers in advertising agencies had declined by almost 60 per cent. As part of this unbundling, between 1966 and 1974 the number of jobs in advertising agencies declined from 20,000 to 14,000.

The second major unbundling of the agency business occurred in the late 1980s. Intense competition from retailers' own-label goods, new advertisers such as financial institutions, retailers and government advertisers helped to force up media costs in the 1980s. In 1986 TV ad rates increased by an average of 16.7 per cent over the previous year.

The basis of client ownership also changed considerably in the 1980s, from there being many private firms run by boards towards companies being run by financial institutions such as pension funds and insurance companies, which increased ownership of UK companies from 20 per cent to over 50 per cent between 1970 and 1991 (Briggs 1993: 20). Such changes in ownership affected the expenditure decisions of the big firms, who wanted more return for their costs, and had huge acquisition or merger debts to refinance. Marketing departments were now responsible to a board run by a financial institution (which was not from a marketing background) and to investors who wanted dividends: the result was an emphasis on shorter-term tactical campaigns aimed at sustaining sales. An executive from SmithKline Beecham remarked in 1993 that they had spent more on media than on blackcurrants for their Ribena brand (Cook and Waldman 1993: 24).

In 1992 ISBA canvassed a hundred advertisers on their experiences and discovered that 74 per cent of them were 'extremely' or 'very' concerned about press creative and production costs. ISBA's intention was to provide a price guide for its members; previously prices were set by the agency and the client was expected to rubber-stamp them.

Between 1981 and 1991 TV costs rose from £900 million to £1.4 billion, an increase of 55 per cent. Production costs rose from £118 million to £233 million, an increase of 97 per cent. Most of this extra production money has gone on large fees to directors and artists, exotic locations and shots, expensive graphics and technology, travel agencies and production companies. An average TV commercial costs around £150,000 to make. Depending on the locations, actors' fees and props can cost between £30,000 and £50,000. The production company's mark-up is between 30 per cent and 35 per cent. Because of the sums involved, some clients insist on an independent audit to see whether the production company has made profits in excess of its mark-up. The production company budget does not include the costs of fees to artists and their repeat fees, stills photography (which an agency will use for other purposes), music, voice-overs, art work and weather insurance. Other items such as latex dummies, etc. may also be excluded from the production company's budget (ibid.).

Advertisers began monitoring the costs of the full-service agencies. In 1992 Unilever caused a storm among agencies when it brought an auditor, Focus on Film, to act as consultant on seventy commercials for Birds Eye Wall's, Brooke Bond Oxo, Elida Gibbs (toothpaste), Lever Brothers (soaps) and Van den Berghs (margarine) (*Campaign*, 21 February 1992: 3). Clients also began to employ media experts to monitor the media buying performance of their agencies. Cadbury had been one of the first clients to hire a media controller and media consultant. One audit consultancy, Media Evaluation, claimed to have found that in TV buying there were discrepancies of up to 30 per cent, which as it pointed out could mean the difference between paying £700,000 and £1,300,000 on a £1 million budget (Peach *et al.* 1992: 23). Deceptive practices include deliberately underestimating the target so that the buyer has to buy more media to reach it (encouraging the client to overspend), rewriting data to 'improve' a poor achievement, inventing spots and centre breaks, or omitting spots from the reported campaign.

Other consultants started to challenge agencies' research findings and their creative rationales. The new consultants are generally ex-advertising-agency employees and represent both the breakdown in trust that has occurred between client and agency and the increased confidence of clients in challenging the power and knowledge of the agencies. Big names such as Sainsbury's, Renault and Lever Brothers also used these consultancies for special advertising projects.

By the 1990s, for the first time in its history, the advertisers' trade association, the Incorporated Society of British Advertisers, began to set the agenda in terms of its relations with agencies and media. A series of reports on production costs, media-broking, agency kickbacks and failure to rebate clients increased the pressure on agencies.

Media clutter, audience fragmentation, the use of zapping (channel switching) and zipping (fast forwarding on video) meant that fewer commercials were being watched. This, in addition to increases in production costs and the cost of TV airtime, made advertisers increasingly sceptical about the use of TV advertising, and some came off TV altogether. Because the recognition system was now broken, clients could now set up their own advertising departments and not have to worry about recognition.

Companies such as Heinz and Procter & Gamble brought more of their functions in-house and, most importantly, farmed out specific services to specialist consultancies, undermining the control of the agencies. Clients have gradually taken marketing responsibility back in-house, whittling down the agencies' involvement.

The commission system had insulated agencies from inflated media costs and general inflation; as costs went up, so did the agency's commission. The costs were automatically passed on to the client. However, in the 1990s this began to change. Clients began to pay in fee form which would be negotiated between agency and client, and to force down commission rates so that agencies would absorb some of the effects of recession. From 1991 to 1992 full-service ad agency Lowe Howard Spink claimed to have pulled out of six pitches for new business because the clients were asking for commissions ranging from 4 per cent to 8 per cent; all of the accounts went to major advertising agencies, at the reduced rates (Hood 1992: 15). With the commission system broken, full-service agencies had lost their moral authority. Advertisers were able to pick and mix. The 1990s are seeing the re-emergence of the advertising consultants (see Chapter 6), and also the growth of a new breed of communications specialists, marketing analysts, and production companies who would bypass the agency and deal direct with the client. The first two big advertisers to mark this shift were Coca-Cola and Heinz who completely bypassed advertising agencies to use independent production companies to produce their ads. Many more were already using research companies and media buyers. In the USA, Coca-Cola used a talent agency (CAA – the Michael Ovitz Creative Artists Agency) to communicate brand messages. It was revealed in October 1992 that CAA would produce the executions for some twenty-five of next year's thirty ads for Coke (an account normally handled by McCann-Erickson). By 2001, the vast majority of UK ad agencies were paid on a fee rather than commission basis.

The IPA's influence also waned. Whereas in the past it could rightfully claim to speak on behalf of the advertising agencies, and to some extent on behalf of the industry, today it is a shadow of its former self. IPA presidents have come under attack for not standing up for members, it has been involved in costly legal actions with agencies and in ongoing battles with ISBA, the media owners and the Association of Media Independents. Largely because of the recession it has also had financial difficulties. In 1991 it admitted direct marketing agencies for the first time, partly because of the drift towards below-the-line advertising activity but also to help bolster funds. In doing so the IPA has recognised the changing nature of advertising. Whereas in the past the IPA could be said to represent the full-service establishment, the admittance of direct marketing agencies and media independents was a recognition of the declining significance and omnipotence of the full-service agency. It has also admitted media independents.

Agencies were particularly badly hit by the recession of the early 1990s. Many agencies had to pay for the debt accrued from acquisitions following stock market listing. The agencies were now responsible not only to the directors but also to shareholders, who demanded profitability. In 1991 only nine agencies made over £1 million profit. Rather than cut salaries, agencies cut staff to maintain profitability. From the late 1980s there was a wholesale shedding of staff, from around 15,400 employees in 1989 to under 11,000 in 1993 (IPA). This figure remained until 2001. Many of those who were made redundant came from agencies set up in those sectors which agencies had begun to hive off, such as design consultancy, commercials production, media research and buying, auditing and planning consultancy.

The recognition system and monopoly commercial TV had helped agencies to define themselves in terms of above-the-line media. With the recognition system gone, and commercial TV fragmented, many agencies responded to the crisis by returning to being traditional rounded publicity and communications agencies as at the turn of the century.

The former marketing director at Rover Group, Kevin Morley, took the car manufacturer's account out of the Saatchi & Saatchi-owned agency BSB Dorland in 1992 to form his own advertising/marketing agency which would offer 'through-the-line' advertising and marketing to clients. He also attacked BSB Dorland and agencies for not offering wider communications functions such as direct marketing, sponsorship and sales promotion (*Campaign*, 25 June 1993: 5). Rover Group spent 60 per cent of its total marketing budget on below-the-line activities and had to use fifty separate communications agencies.

Kevin Morley Marketing was formed in February 1992. KMM did no media buying; UK media buying for Rover was done through Zenith (the Saatchi & Saatchi/BSB Dorland/CME.KHBB media dependant). Among KMM's functions were direct mail and promotional agencies, in-house sales promotion, database management, event sponsorship and marketing, publications, design, marketing operations studio and media. The agency also had joint venture arrangements with agencies in direct marketing, motivation, training and merchandising, such as direct marketing and sales promotion and PR. In May 1995 KMM was bought by Lintas Worldwide and re-named Lintas i (i stands for integrated). Other agencies such as Bates Dorland, JWT, HHCL, Grey and DMB&B professed their integration credentials. By 2001, all of the major agency networks had global marketing communications arms in non-advertising areas such as PR, direct marketing, sports sponsorship and exhibitions.

Agencies also moved to other areas, such as charities, retail, government, politics, religion, schools and hospitals to try to spread their influence. Agencies, like their client companies, had responded to their saturated markets by trying to create and construct new ones. They helped and persuaded government institutions and other bodies of the need for marketing solutions to their problems. They offered design, packaging, branding and other marketing solutions to their problems of consumer disaffection.

By the turn of the century two further threats emerged to the traditional advertising agency, management consultancies and new media agencies. Management consultancies which also offered international reach began to offer branding advice to clients in the 1990s and by the end of the 1990s had begun to hire key advertising personnel in order to offer advertising services to key clients. Management consultancies, unlike ad agencies, often had board-level links in companies and were generally perceived to be more influential. One further threat were new dot.com ad agencies which emerged in the late 1990s and threatened to take significant pieces of the advertising budgets away from the traditional agencies. The response of the traditional agencies was to buy up the new players and re-brand them as their own.

The leading agencies agencies include Tribal DDB UK (Omnicom), Oyster (Omnicom), Traffic Interactive (Omnicom), Zinc (Havas), Ehsrealtime (Havas), Circle.com (Havas), Ogilvy Interactive (WPP), M Digital (WPP), Saatchi & Saatchi Vision (Publicis) and Initiative Dot Com (Interpublic). Many of these agencies produce banner ads and interactive ads for clients, web-site development and viral marketing campaigns. The new media agencies which are part of traditional agency structures tend to work for the main agency's clients. For instance Saatchi & Saatchi Vision has developed interactive TV ads for main agency clients Procter & Gamble and Toyota.

The new media crisis

By the turn of the twenty-first century a new crisis had emerged in advertising. On top of all of the problems that media fragmentation and a weakening in efficacy had given advertisers, they were now faced with a new medium which threatened to turn their old communications models on their head. By the late 1990s advertisers believed that they were in the midst of a consumer revolution that was being propelled by the new medium of the Internet. Amid much hype many in the advertising industry confidently predicted that this new medium not only threatened the old media environment but that it also threatened the ability of advertisers to reach passive consumers. Advertisers would need to change their approach to advertising to reach consumers who were more actively consuming media. Media owners and retailers launched websites and sold advertising in the form of banner ads (advertising strips which sit on a web page) and flash ads which flicked on screen when consumers used the sites. However, this brave new world of Internet advertising did not materialise. Though Internet usage grew rapidly at the turn of the century, advertisers quickly learned that the Internet offered only limited possibilities for advertising their products. A number of big brand advertisers abandoned plans to develop their own websites and also withdrew funding to develop Internet-based advertising campaigns in favour of traditional media.

Conclusion

The UK is the fourth biggest advertising market in the world (following the USA, Japan and Germany). It dominates virtually all aspects of media financing, editorial and new media technologies, and has achieved political success. Despite challenges from Europe, the British advertising industry had fifteen years of Conservative government, which provided unprecedented deregulation of advertising markets. New media markets in TV and radio sponsorship, cable and satellite TV, radio and telecommunications and new advertising sectors such as the professions, charities, religions, and the financial and pharmaceutical industries, have emerged.

Conservative governments also played an important role in supporting the wider ethos of advertising in the public sector. Social security, education and health have all appropriated ideas and concepts from marketing and advertising. The ideology of the marketplace has been accepted across whole range of areas, adopting 'citizen's charters', 'customer services', and 'targeted services'; at Liverpool John Moores University, for instance, the marketing department took to extremes the idea of students as consumers by producing material showing students in academic robes pushing trolleys in a supermarket and being handed degrees by check-out staff.

Old beliefs in 'brand loyalty', the power of 'persuasion', consumers' media consumption and the power to influence sales have been shattered. So too has the confidence of agencies to manage the business effectively. And, because advertising is also mostly conducted by agencies outside the immediate firm, many businesses view it as the least precise, least manageable and most costly business activity.

Agencies are trying to adjust to the new promotional environment. Most of the large agencies now also offer new forms of promotion and publicity: TV and radio sponsorship, direct marketing, product placement, management consultancy and interactive media. Their aim is to keep control over business communications. Because of this, advertising is returning to its pre-mass-media nineteenth-century role, encompassing all promotional activity, rather than the more narrow definition of paid-for mass-media communication.

Example

The *Daily Telegraph*

Newspapers are some of the oldest brands in Britain and have been engaged in heavy advertising and promotion since the mid-nineteenth century.

The removal of stamp duty and advertising tax in the 1850s allowed publishers to supplement receipts from newspaper sales with advertising revenue and invest profits in new machinery. In June 1855 the *Daily Telegraph and*

Courier was launched, priced 2d. Within months it was sold to a new proprietor who reduced the price to 1d (the first penny daily). The *Telegraph* managed to keep its price at one penny for sixty years, growing from four to twenty-four pages, establishing itself as the clear market leader. Its rival at the time, *The Times*, kept its price at 3d during this time and its sales fell to 40,000. By the 1960s the *Telegraph* had established its clear dominance of the broadsheet market with a circulation of 1.7 million.

The strategy of using advertising revenue to maintain low prices and high circulation has been a feature of most national newspaper publishing in the last 100 years. However, from the 1970s the cover price of national newspapers rose considerably. In the Sunday market, for instance, cover prices rose by 89 per cent in real terms between 1970 and 1992. At the same time sales fell by over 30 per cent. But it is not solely increased cover prices which are to blame. New newspapers such as the *Daily Star*, *Mail on Sunday* and *Independent/Independent on Sunday* cut large chunks out of the existing newspapers' circulations. Newspaper markets have also been eroded by the electronic media. They are no longer the first stop for news in the morning. TV and radio have already transformed the way newspapers cover news events, making them more 'newsanalysis papers'. In the 1980s the reduction of labour and print costs had allowed newspapers to make savings. Instead of using the savings to cut cover prices, national newspapers used them to increase the number of pages – the *Daily Mirror* now publishes 44 per cent more pages than it did a decade ago. But it was the 'quality' and mid-market papers who decided that the best way to compete with the electronic media was to increase their cover price and offer their readers to advertisers as 'quality' consumers. They used the extra capacity to develop brand extensions such as colour supplements, new sections and colour newsprint supplements. The new sections were used to generate extra income from advertising, with consumption-oriented features in fashion, cars, health and beauty, food and wine, property and travel, and business. This ate into consumer magazine advertising markets. Others, such as the *Guardian*, which found it more difficult to eat into consumer advertising markets, switched to business markets by targeting recruitment ads in education, media, and health, eating into trade and business magazine advertising markets.

Newspaper markets were saturated and in decline. New product launches were hopelessly expensive and mostly doomed to failure. Brand extensions such as sections and supplements were the only way the market could grow.

Newspapers have become fairly undifferentiated. All newspapers have news, all have listings and fashion features, business and personal finance sections, travel and property. The speed of technology means that when they do develop something different such as separate listings sections, separate media guides or business sections, the rest can follow very quickly and easily.

Most groups adopted a policy of encouraging brand switching through sales promotions and trial offers. According to one senior executive from a major national newspaper, the strategy was simple: 'The daily market has been contracting every year. Our strategy has been almost exclusively focused on sales promotion to encourage trial from rival papers' (interview).

Like all other products, a national newspaper operates in several markets at the same time. Though marketers put labels on different segments of the market, there is no closed finite area in which markets begin and end. Newspapers are meant to occupy specific markets according to their readership profile. Generally, this has been set in terms of occupational class. Those papers with a high profile of ABC1s tend to be called 'qualities' (and are usually in broadsheet format, though this is changing) those with an above-average proportion of ABC1s are termed 'mid-market', and those with low ABC1s are called 'tabloids'.

The *Sunday Times* and *Telegraph* included children's pages, aiming at parents who read mid-market papers such as the *Mail on Sunday* and *Sunday Express*, as well as horoscopes, fashion and travel features, which were mainly mid-market areas before the mid-1980s.

There has also been a perceived decline in 'brand loyalty'. Newspapers believe that because of the increase in competition from other media for time, and because of the greater similarity between newspapers, readers have become 'grazers'. They buy on odd days of the week and may buy different papers altogether throughout the week and at the weekend, depending on whether there are job advertisements, colour supplements or TV listings included. The *Telegraph* for instance has wide differences in circulation between Monday and Saturday (200,000 more sold on Saturday), and Sunday, where the circulation is half that of the Saturday paper. The *Daily* and *Sunday Telegraph* were bought in 1985 by Canadian newspaper proprietor Conrad Black from the Berry family, headed by Lord Camrose, after losses forced them to sell. In the early 1990s they had around 360 editorial staff and 220 advertising sales staff (50 per cent selling classified, 50 per cent display). Because of the over-competition in the 'quality' market and the decline in circulation, the central strategy of the *Daily Telegraph* was to try to maintain its existing circulation and defend its market share. The principal strategy it employed was to encourage trial from other brands.

Though the *Telegraph* has a large number of ABC1 readers, is in traditional broadsheet format and covers the traditional 'quality' newspaper sectors of business and finance, it has always maintained a mid-market editorial style: human interest stories, clear language and writing style, concise journalism. To advertisers it was happy to be perceived as a 'quality' paper because it meant gaining large spending accounts from financial institutions, car manufacturers and corporate classified advertising.

The main targets for promotions are the top end of the mid-market *Daily Mail* and *Daily Express* readers. There is perceived to be a 'life-stage' progression from the *Daily Mail* to the *Telegraph*. The paper tries to encourage younger readers (in their thirties and forties). The paper's marketing department calls them 'mid-market risers' who are supposed to be younger, ambitious C1s and Bs. The *Daily Mail* also has the biggest number of ABC1 readers of any national newspaper in the UK (13 per cent of the total ABC1 population). It also has a similar political and moral perspective to the *Telegraph* and has a large number of readers over 45 (55.5 per cent) (Table 15.2). The problem with the data is that it does not break down into As, Bs and C1s. This would show that the *Telegraph* actually has more Bs and C1s than *The Times*, which is weighted more towards As and Bs. In 1986 the balance of advertising spend had been 90 per cent on conventional media and 10 per cent on below-the-line. The main reason for this was the launch in that year of the *Independent*, which forced the paper to compete with other newspapers in mass-media advertising. But also the marketing strategy was less concerned with boosting short-term sales in a declining market, and more with refocusing and positioning the brand to advertisers and readers. Its 'Hitchhikers' campaign in 1988 tried to reposition and use image-advertising to change the attitudes and perceptions of the paper among middle-class mid-market readers that it was conservative and reactionary, and put across a more dynamic and modern image.

'Hitchhikers' did not add sales. The *Telegraph* ditched brand advertising. The emphasis of the campaign switched from repositioning the brand to supporting and maintaining sales. The *Telegraph* used sales promotion to encourage switching such as give-aways, coupons, competitions, and appealing to the pocket rather than the image. In 1990 there were six supplements and promotions aimed at building circulation (including Battle of Britain souvenirs and 'You and Your Home'). In 1991 there were twenty-two, from Gulf War to catwalk specials, west-country living and an independent schools guide. Newspapers had to throw so much money into sales promotions and below-the-line activity because they had to keep short-term sales up to stop losing advertising revenue. The market became extremely short-term, concentrating on constant innovations; 'new improved' editorial and marketing products were launched every other week. Between 1930 and 1986 there were only eight major editorial changes to the *Telegraph* (including the launch of the *Sunday Telegraph*). Between 1986 and 1994 there were twenty-seven major editorial changes to the paper.

Table 15.2 Reader profile for the *Daily Telegraph* and its competitors, in sex, class and age of readers (%)

	Men	Women	ABC1	15–44	Over 44
Daily Telegraph	59	41	87	31	69
The Times	60	40	88	49	51
Daily Mail	50	50	65	39	61
Daily Express	53	47	63	39	61
Sunday Times	57	43	87	57	43
Sunday Telegraph	54	46	84	34	66

Source: NRS, May 2000 to October 2000

The repositioning in the late 1980s was aimed as much at agencies as at readers. The revenue base of the paper was split 55 per cent advertising revenue and 45 per cent cover price revenue. The split between display revenue and classified was 75:25. Many agencies perceived the *Telegraph* as grey, elderly, reactionary and conservative, a high-income, but low spenders' paper. In 1989 the *Daily Telegraph* signed a two-year deal to sponsor American football on Channel 4 to attract younger readers but primarily to appeal to advertising agency media buyers associating the brand with a younger, more modern, less stuffy and traditional transatlantic feel. It sponsored a month's coverage of the Tour de France on Channel 4 to highlight sports coverage in the paper and run a two-month series called *Challenge to Sport*.

The bid to win more advertisers helped to shift the strategy of the paper in 1988. The *Sunday Telegraph*, launched only in 1961, continued to sell only half the number of copies of the weekday paper. The main reader and advertising rival on Sundays, the *Sunday Times*, was extremely popular with advertisers keen to target young AB readers. The *Sunday Times* had also increased the number of sections and opportunities to advertise, cornering a huge share of the weekend advertising market. If the *Telegraph* wanted to take on the *Sunday Times* with the *Sunday Telegraph* it would prove extremely costly, especially because of the huge resources behind Rupert Murdoch's media empire. Murdoch had already developed a strategy of pumping vast amounts of promotional money to defend the *Sunday Times* as the broadsheet market leader (1.3 million circulation).

The *Telegraph* developed a concerted advertising and public relations campaign to try to convince advertisers that the Saturday *Telegraph* was the main rival to the *Sunday Times* at the weekend. It also claimed that, because it came out a day earlier, Saturday *Telegraph* readers had more opportunity to go out and buy consumer goods at the weekend than *Sunday Times* readers did. Until September 1988 newspapers sold fewer copies on Saturdays than on any other day of the week. Both the *Independent* and the *Telegraph* launched Saturday supplements in September 1988.

The Saturday product became the main focus of the *Telegraph*'s strategy, by increasing the sale by 200,000 over the weekday sale, adding sections such as the Weekend section, the *Young Telegraph* (against the *Funday Times*) and shifting the *Sunday Telegraph*'s colour magazine to Saturday they added value to the product. The Saturday Business section was the only section which did not add to the sale of the paper. This was launched, however, to try to attract more business readers than more actual sales, and most of all to attract more business advertising revenue. According to the 1992 European business readership survey, the *Financial Times* came out as the top daily with an AIR of 76 per cent, followed by the *Daily Telegraph* with 40 per cent. The *Sunday Times* scored 71 per cent (Cardwell 1993b: 15). The intention was both to win advertisers from the *Sunday Times* and to encourage brand switching from other broadsheet papers and the *Daily Mail* on Saturday.

Figure 15.3 The *Daily Telegraph*: two front pages from 1984 and 1994 show the difference in design over a decade. © Daily Telegraph.

Figure 15.4 The *Daily Telegraph*: an example of product-led advertising, this ad demonstrates the various sections available in one newspaper, giving that much more value for money. © Daily Telegraph. Agency: WCRS.

By 1993 the *Daily Telegraph*'s promotional budget changed to 60 per cent on sales promotions, PR sponsorship and direct mail, and 40 per cent on conventional media advertising. Most of the *Telegraph*'s effort was through direct marketing. It used a mixture of direct mail consumer lifestyle databases which have lists of readers for competitive titles, primarily *Daily Mail* and *Daily Express* readers. Though the *Telegraph* still included traditional media advertising, it was mainly used to support the sales promotions (give-aways and competitions) rather than the other way around.

In September 1993 *The Times* made a price cut which shook the market. Murdoch took advantage of the strength of his monopoly position to try to force other groups out of the market and increase advertising revenue and circulation. The *Telegraph*'s price was 18p above *The Times*.

At the same time the *Daily Mail* (the *Telegraph*'s main competitor) and the *Daily Express* increased their Saturday package by including weekend sections but kept their Saturday cover price down. This added value to the paper was seen as an increased threat to the Saturday *Telegraph* readership. *The Times* also enlarged its weekend sections in October 1993.

Because of *The Times* price cut, the *Telegraph* increased sales promotions to one a month: holiday tokens, cut-price offers, etc. They used to be used tactically to cover any price increase; now they are used to sustain sales. Much of this involved direct mail, which has the advantage of being covert. By January 1994 the *Telegraph* was running more intensified campaigns. In one month it ran three promotions aimed at the 'mid-market-risers'.

By May 1994 the *Telegraph*'s circulation had dropped below one million. So it made its first substantial price cut by offering the Saturday and *Sunday Telegraph* for £1 to *Independent* and *Times* readers. But *The Times* still managed to gain 40,000 readers in the next month. In mid-June the *Telegraph* cut its price from 48p to 30p to make it level with *The Times* which had by this stage gained around 150,000 sales. The *Telegraph*'s cut also put the paper below the price of the *Mail* and *Express*, which were at 32p. But the move was made largely to prevent ad revenue declining and going to *The Times*.

According to observers, the *Telegraph* was able to sell their advertising space at three times the price of *The Times* because of its 43 per cent share of the market. By May market share had slipped to 40 per cent. Advertisers had already begun to switch from the *Telegraph* to the younger readership of *The Times*. Analysts estimated a rise in advertising income for *The Times* of around 50 per cent on the previous year (*Guardian*, 9 July 1994: 40), though it had not managed to push up its advertising rates.

The new strategy for the *Telegraph* proved expensive: a projected £40 million was lost in sales revenue for the year, equivalent to £160,000 a day with the bonus that sales would remain above the one million mark and advertising income could be maintained at previous levels. *The Times* retaliated with a further drop in cover price to 20p and made a guarantee to advertisers that circulation would not fall below 600,000 sales. However, in September 1994 the *Telegraph* changed its focus again by launching a brand-building campaign. Because all other newspapers in the market were competing on price and sales promotions, the *Daily Telegraph* sought difference in its promotions by focusing on the image of the product.

It also reintroduced brand advertising to reassure advertisers. At the time of the switch the paper's marketing director said: 'We put our emphasis on short-term promotions to boost copy sales in '91 and have now realised that it doesn't get us anywhere.' He added that adding brand values would make it easier when the cover price is increased again. By early 1995 the *Times* had failed to push the *Telegraph*'s circulation below one million and had not managed to erode its advertising revenue base, though the *Telegraph*'s costs remained enormous.

By 2001 *The Times* price had increased to 35p and the *Telegraph* had settled at 45p, a price gap of just 10p. The *Daily Telegraph* had managed to maintain its circulation above 1 million and *The Times* had a circulation of over 700,000. However, both of these titles did so by distributing a significant proportion of their newspapers at a discounted rate, either via bulk sales (where a hotel group or airline buys a bulk number of copies at a nominal amount, sometimes as low as less than 1p per copy) or via discounted subscriptions. Long-term sales of individual newspapers continue to be in decline.

In an effort to halt the decline in circulation the newspapers launched subscriptions drives, offering free trials of the newspaper and cheap subscriptions. This strategy locked readers into the paper and minimised the effects of 'grazing'.

Meanwhile, the newspaper group was one of the first to establish its own website, Electronic Telegraph in 1994. ET was intended to raise the paper's profile among the young and relatively affluent. A further part of this ongoing brand re-positioning towards a younger audience was the group's signing as an official sponsor of the FA Premier League, emphasising the daily newspaper's sports coverage which attracts younger male readers. It also launched a new media supplement called dotcom.telegraph and a student magazine called Juice. However, the age profile of the paper has worsened. According to the National Readership survey, the *Daily Telegraph*'s 45-plus readership increased between 1995 and 2000 from 59 per cent to 69 per cent.

It also launched a financial services division in 1996 to sell PEPs and TESSAs to its readers. However, it was forced to pull out of this after objections were raised by its financial services advertisers.

Summary

The *Daily Telegraph* is a fast-moving consumer good. It operates in one of the oldest branded markets in Britain which is saturated, concentrated, segmented, very competitive and in decline. The paper's strategy has been to try to keep its sales and advertising revenue up by using below-the-line promotions and encouraging brand switching from the *Daily Mail* while at the same time pumping promotional money into its brand leader, the *Saturday Telegraph*. The paper has also segmented its brand through sectionalisation and adding new products on to the main paper, while trying to undermine the popular image of the paper as reactionary, conservative and undynamic. Because of new technology and the ability to change the products very quickly, national newspapers offer very similar packages. The market has been unable to offer substantial product difference, at the same time promoting heavily. The result has been a heavy reliance on sales promotion and efforts to keep up the short-term sales of the paper to compete with cheaper rivals.

Workshop suggestions for individual and group work

....

Chapter 1

1 Examine a brand for two of the following products: cereals, low-fat margarine, shampoo, crisps, computer games, depilatory cream, airlines, house insurance, fast food restaurants, launderettes, men's or women's clothes shops, a range of dog foods, banks, charities, petrol, crisps, car, perfume, night clubs, local radio stations, taxi companies. Find out who makes it, which company owns it, which other companies and brands the company owns. Find where the brand is principally distributed.

2 Why might branded over-the-counter pharmaceutical products undermine the authority of the retail pharmacist?

Further reading

Mintel

Marketing Week – www.marketingweek.co.uk

Marketing – www.marketingmagazine.co.uk

The Advertising Statistics Yearbook – published every year by the Association. London: Advertising Association

Chapter 2

1 Examine the market for the two brands. Describe the main features of this market. Where, when and how are the products consumed? What type of good is it? How does the consumption of the product affect the way it should be marketed? Who are the main rivals in the product sector? Are there any other markets that may overlap with these? Do they aim at any particular segment of the market? What is the size of the market, is it local, national, international?

Examine the influences on decisions to buy. Where might consumers go for information? How might these processes influence the advertiser's distribution?

2 Examine the range of available personal soap products and how they position or segment along lines: deodorant, luxury, complexion, simplicity, reviver, no additives, colour, shape, packaging, price, lifestyle (e.g. sporty), lather and scent.

3 What are the benefits and drawbacks of having global brand names?

Further reading

Euromonitor sector reports

Mintel sector reports

Chapter 3

1 Consider the target market for your new products. What do they think about work, pleasure, religion, ambition, family life? Do they cook or like cooking, gardening, hobbies, consumer goods? What type of car would they like to drive, do they like new or traditional things, would they buy antiques or modern furniture? What are their musical tastes, clothes (trendy, avant-garde, traditional)? Are they team players or individuals, materialists or idealists? Spiritual, youthful, peer-oriented? Do they buy the products because their friends did, are they a face, or a follower? What type of media do they watch or read? What life-stage are they at? If you wish, consult Target Group Index or the National Readership Survey.

2 Discuss the different life-stages at which you may need the different services of a bank. How might these 'life-stages' reflect in bank advertising.

3 Discuss the problems of classifying people in terms of age, sex, class, lifestyle and attitude.

Further reading

Target Group Index

National Readership Survey

Cowley, D. (ed.) (1989) *How to Plan Advertising*, London: Cassell in Association with the Account Planning Group.

Maslow, A. H. (1954) *Motivation and Personality*, New York: Harper and Row.

Packard, V. (1957) *The Hidden Persuaders*, London: Penguin.

Chapter 4

1 Your two brands want to launch brand extensions aimed at a specific segment of the market. One is a line extension, using the same brand-name as a variant on the lead brand, or in a different product area. The other is line filling, a fresh brand aiming at a segment of your brand's market. The product differences could be based on price (premium), packaging, consumer lifestyle (see Chapter 5) or a product improvement. Consider how the price, distribution, product or packaging and the promotional campaign would work together. What would be the most important aim of advertising in the markets (creating awareness for a new product, encouraging brand switching, advertising to retailers and surrogates, changing consumer attitudes or behaviour)? Which elements of the advertising mix would be most useful to achieve the objectives for their campaign: above-the-line, or below-the-line, or a mixture of both? How do you expect each of these elements to work? How do they use advertising, to whom are they appealing?

2 Examine the demands on government information for one of the following areas: giving blood, fire safety, safe sex, anti-smoking. What are the characteristics of the appeals, what would be the most appropriate marketing mix to reach the appropriate consumers?

3 Go into a chemist's shop, newsagent, bookshop, jeweller's, fast food outlet, supermarket and clothes shop. How are the different shops designed to keep customers in and how much are they designed to get them to leave quickly. Why might this be? Why do you think all supermarkets have the same layout (fruit and veg first, meat and frozen food and bakery middle and finally snacks, crisps and soft drinks, then alcohol last)? Why do some supermarkets have toys and confectioneries three feet off the ground, and the main or heavily promoted brands at adult eye-level?

4 Vernons Pools and Barclaycard both sponsored *Wish You Were Here* travel programmes, Konica sponsored *This is Your Life*, Ambrosia custard brand sponsored *SMTV*, Cadbury sponsored *Coronation Street* and Nescafé sponsored *Friends*. Discuss the reasons why the different advertisers may have decided to sponsor these particular programmes.

Further reading

Marketing Week

Marketing

Randall, G. (1993) *Principles of Marketing*, London: Routledge.

Chapters 5 and 6

1 Examine the most appropriate advertising agency for your brands. Would you need one with creative flair, one that can delivery big volume discounts for advertisers, one with local market knowledge or the ability to plan international campaigns? Consider issues of client conflict, and the need to have an agency with experience in your product field. Would a through-the-line agency be more appropriate?

2 Examine the ways in which advertising agencies and advertising people are mythologised in our culture in film, on TV and in books. Examine *Campaign* magazine. How does the form and contents of its news and feature coverage construct advertising practices? Is there anything particular or peculiar about its coverage? How does it negotiate with the advertising and marketing industries? How are businesses and personalities treated? What is it trying to convey about itself and the industry it covers? How might these 'myths' of advertising reflect and influence professional practices?

Further reading

BRAD, *Agencies and Advertisers*, Maclean Hunter, London, 1994.

Account List File, Black Box Publishing, London, 1994.

Campaign

Mattelhard, A. (1991) *Advertising International: The Privatisation of Public Space*, London: Comedia Routledge.

Chapter 7

1 Compare the profile of advertising in the following women's monthly magazines: *Good Housekeeping, Cosmopolitan, Tatler, Vogue, She, Marie Claire, Elle, Woman's Journal*. How much of the magazines are advertorials? What are the profiles of the advertisers? Which kind of market might they aim at? Do a similar profile for national newspapers, local commercial radio stations, satellite and terrestrial TV.

2 Discuss how far the modern media industry is influenced by the needs of the advertising industry, with particular regard to advertorials, sponsorship, programming and the need to deliver certain audiences to advertisers.

Further reading

Braithwaite, B. and Barrell, J. (1988) *The Business of Women's Magazines*, London: Kogan Page.

Curran, J. and Seaton J. (1988) *Power Without Responsibility*, London: Routledge.

McCracken, E. (1993) *Decoding Women's Magazines: From Mademoiselle to Ms*, London: Macmillan.

Chapter 8

1 Develop two media schedules for the brands examined in Chapter 1. As your line extension can rely on the existing brand and traditional distribution outlets, examine which media would be most appropriate to target the specific segment of the market. For the second brand-filling campaign, you may need to consider a weighty launch for the new brand. Consider when and where will be the best times to target them – seasonal influences, the weight of the campaign (drip versus burst) how and where the media are used, the environment and the likely 'effects' on the consumers. The second schedule will examine the specific publications, programmes and special positions you may wish to use for environmental effect. Consider which media may offer the greatest profile, and which offer the greatest penetration of your target market.

2 What would be the different media requirements for the following brand advertisers: a local retailer, a business computer manufacturer, a personal computer manufacturer, an established brand of cereal, a dating agency, a whisky brand, a cigarette brand?

Further reading

Target Group Index published by BMRB

National Readership Survey

BARB

Davis, M. P. (1992) *The Effective Use of Advertising Media*, London: Century Business.

Chapter 9

1 Compile a diary of your media consumption in a single day; from getting up in the morning through the rest of the day, everything you watch, read, listen to, including passing posters and bus shelters, direct mail, ads in shops and supermarkets. Record the times of the day you consumed these media. Are these the times of the day you are 'most likely' to switch on the TV, the radio, pass the poster? What was your state of mind, were you paying attention, interested, entertained, involved? Recall the ads you saw (spontaneous recall). Compare with other members in your group. How might these findings influence the media schedules outlined in Workshop 8?

2 What are the problems with using industry-wide research to plan and buy media on? What does it tell media planners about the audience?

Further reading

Ang, I. (1991) *Desperately Seeking the Audience*, London: Routledge.

Morley, D. (1992) *Television, Audiences & Cultural Studies*, London: Routledge.

Kent, R. (ed.) (1994) *Measuring Media Audiences*, London: Routledge.

Chapter 10

1 Consider how you might differentiate your new brand; lifestyle, Unique Selling Proposition, brand image. Consider where your brand is consumed: for instance, a lager might be consumed in a bar, a club, a wedding reception, a restaurant, the home at Christmas, a pub, or at the beach. How might this fit with the brand image, or USP? Suggest an appropriate brand-name and image for your new brand. Consider the brand-names for others on the market, e.g. Ariel, Daz, Fairy, Flash, Sunlight, Milky Way, Snickers, Bounty, Timotei, Citroën AX, Peugeot 206, Volvo 440, Gold Blend, Kestrel, Kaliber, Chanel, Opium, Egg, Cahoot, Smile. Which images do they conjure up?

2 Devise a creative brief for your brand, outlining the rationale for the moves; include the background, a statement about the product (benefits and use, etc. and packaging), why the company is advertising, the target audience, the argument (rational and emotional), the proposition, the tone of voice, the desired consumer response. You need to state the one promise you are going to carry in your product, where it will be consumed, where it will be bought, who will be consuming it, what the attributes of the product are, when the product is consumed, what the consumer's frame of mind will be when seeing the ad. Consider factors such as consumer resistance and media clutter, as well as competition from other brands and supermarket own-labels. Construct a 'typical' individual to aim the campaign at; age, attitude, name, job, family, etc.

3 Which characteristics are associated with the following creatures: bear, swan, snake, eagle, puppy, rabbit, monkey, antelope, spider, tiger, lion, cat, elephant, hippo, shark, seal, fly, rat, butterfly? How might these be used in advertising to associate values and added meanings with certain brands?

4 Examine the Boddingtons print advertisement on p. 138. Which elements stand out, and are memorable? What are the metaphors being used in the ad? How does the advertiser anchor meanings in the ad to give a preferred reading? How are images and writing or text used to anchor meanings? In which ways does the ad play on a supposed knowledge of the consumer? Which appeals does it use?

Further reading

Hopkins, C. C. (1966) *My Life in Advertising and Scientific Advertising,* Illinois: NTC Business Books.

Ogilvy, D. (1983) *Ogilvy on Advertising*, London: Pan Books

Reeves, R. (1961) *Reality in Advertising*, London: Macgibbon & Kee

Chapter 11

1 Develop your brand campaign employing some of the techniques discussed in the chapter: nostalgia, fear, magic. Which personalities might be appropriate? How would you break down the resistance of consumers? Are there any long-term attitudes that may need to be addressed? Do you need to change behaviour in any way? Develop an ad with a narrative structure that presents a conflict that needs to be resolved and the brand comes in as helper.

2 Examine ways in which women, men and children, ethnic minorities and different classes are addressed. Examine different media (TV, radio, magazines, newspapers) aimed at these different groups and compare treatments in advertising. Look for the mode of address, the use of language, the form of narrative, how the fears, anxieties frustrations are appealed to, the concerns with status, ambition and achievement or success. Do the ads suggest that the target groups have opponents (e.g. men for women, or, more generally, failure or shame)? Who are the givers/helpers, and what are the objects of the ads: status, respect, power, wealth and fitting-in?

3 Which appeals would be most appropriate for government advertising examined in Workshop 4? How might a narrative structure be developed for giving blood, fire safety, safe sex, anti-smoking?

Further reading

Cook, G. (1992) *The Discourse of Advertising*, London: Routledge.

Hart, A. (1991) *Understanding the Media: A Practical Guide*, London: Routledge.

Vastergaard, T. and Schroder, K. (1985) *The Language of Advertising*, Oxford: Basil Blackwell.

Williamson, J. (1978) *Decoding Advertisements: Ideology and Meaning in Advertising*, London: Marion Boyars

Chapter 12

1 Construct the tone of your advertisement: the character's age, gender, class, ethnicity and possible lifestyle or psychographic group, hair (is it young, stylish, cropped, does it hide part of the face, is it traditional?) and make-

up, the body (its shape, size, clothed, part-clothed, naked), posture. Are they at work (in an office, at home washing the dishes), at play, doing sports, relaxing, having a meal with friends or family (activities such as eating, drinking, using the product)? Consider body language: will their arms be open, folded, legs crossed, do they look at ease, self-assured and comfortable, or excited, agitated and frenzied? Will they be smiling, laughing, dreamy, excited, happy-go-lucky, pensive, seductive or coy? Are they running, jumping, sitting, do they have their arms around someone (conveying love, warmth, friendship, protectiveness)?

According to Andrew Hart, agency radio production companies colour-code actors' voices with 'deep brown', 'rich golden' or 'silvery' (Hart 1991: 51). He also claims that advertisers evoke different sounds and images according to gender and age. One study by Durkin (1985: 29) claims that children's toy ads are gendered: boys' toys are more active and noisy, girls' more quiet and slow-moving. In indirect, slice-of-life commercials advertisers try to create a slice-of-life feel by including accents, slang and dialect. The endline finishes with a home counties 'received pronunciation' voice-over at the end. The home counties voice represents sophistication, authority and tradition. The actor who speaks the direct address lines anchors the meanings of the tests and tidies up any ambiguities or uneasiness with regional accents (stereotypes of Scousers, aggressive, dishonest, sarcastic and street-wise). Decide which elements of the commercial will be direct and indirect address. Will it be dialogue, monologue or straight to camera? What are the different implications of each treatment? What will be your establishing shot? What will be the backing music (will there be any?) Will it build up, stop, wind down? Where will voice-overs come in? How will the product appear in the ad? Is it being used in the ad, or is it outside the action, separate to it? Will the ad use any genres: filmic, cartoon, romance, TV presentation or chat show, news genre?

2 Remove the sounds from a TV commercial. How might other meanings to these ads be developed without the meanings being anchored? Is image-based advertising less effective? Reveal the sounds to reveal how the meanings of the pictures are anchored. Do a similar exercise with your own advertisements. Examine the denotation, connotation and preferred reading and how the genre might affect consumers. Are there any polysemic meanings in the examples you use? How might a brand of coffee mean different things to consumers throughout the day? Or a chocolate bar? How far does the social setting in which we consume brands affect their meanings?

3 Devise a 30-minute pitch for your campaign, bringing together all the elements of the campaign, using storyboards, indications of market structure, target consumers, media use and creative treatments.

Further reading

Crompton, A. (1987) *The Craft of Copywriting*, London: Century Business.

Dyer, G. (1982) *Advertising as Communication*, London: Routledge.

Evans, R. B. (1988) *Production and Creativity in Advertising*, London: Pitman.

Leech, G. N. (1966) *English in Advertising: A Linguistic Study of Advertising in Great Britain*, London: Longmans.

Chapter 13

1   Monitor the commercials on a TV channel during one night. The following day, do a recall test on a friend of commercials viewed. Try to find out how much of the brand and sales messages they remembered. Find out how many they remember unprompted, then prompt their memory by suggesting some of the others to see how much they reveal. Which ads were best remembered? Can this tell you anything about the effectiveness of the commercial?

2   According to Lannon (1992: 12), unseen tests were done on respondents in tasting and using diet colas. The respondents gave their taste preferences as in the Table. In this test, though the majority of consumers claimed to prefer the product taste in Diet Pepsi, many more preferred the branded taste of Diet Coke. How do packaging, brand image, price, advertising and promotion affect the perceptions of the brands? How would the place and time in which the drink is consumed affect its image? Do you drink it with food (chocolate, crisps, etc.), or on its own, do you consume other things at the same time? TV? Newspapers? Magazines? Would this affect the moods of consumers?

3   BP's corporate TV campaign in 1991 showed a young African boy studying schoolbooks at night with electricity provided by BP (see p. 196). What are the different corporate images the company is trying to convey? Why are they so different? In the 1920s BP (British Petroleum), whose parent company was Anglo-Persian Oil Ltd., ran ads in illustrated periodicals which depicted scenes from ancient Persia. 'In studying this series one catches something of the glamour and tradition of this ancient land. . . . One unconsciously forms an impression of vast enterprises, of pioneering endeavour, and, above all, the connection of a British firm with a land rich in tradition

Cola preferences (%)

	Unseen	Branded
Prefer Diet Pepsi	51	23
Prefer Diet Coke	44	65
Equal/Don't Know	5	12

and bygone glory' (Bradshaw 1927: 324). Why might the image that BP wants to convey have changed in this way? Discuss the similarities and differences between the two campaigns.

4 Do a case study of one of the following corporate campaigns: BT, BNFL, Electricity, British Gas, Water Boards, Shell. What are the attitudes and image implications of these campaigns? How are they seeking to influence consumers? What models of communications do they employ? How might they be said to have an image problem?

5 How do cigarette and alcohol companies try to raise awareness of their brands among young people? Give examples.

Further reading

Katz, E. and Lazarsfeld P. F. (1955) *Personal Influence*, New York: The Free Press.

Schudson, M. (1993) *Advertising the Uneasy Persuasion*, London: Routledge.

Cowley, D. (ed) (1989) *How to Plan Advertising*, London: Cassell in Association with the Account Planning Group.

Gladwell, M. (2000) *The Tipping Point*, Boston: Little, Brown & Company.

Chapter 14

1 Consider possible legislation and regulations covering your own advertisements. Are there any problems with taste and decency, stereotyping or influence on 'vulnerable' members of the community?

2 The BCAP, ASA and ITC codes state that all advertisements should be 'legal, decent, honest and truthful'. How do you draw the lines in terms of decency, for instance? Who should be the arbiters of taste, decency and honesty?

3 One strategy that advertisers have employed in defending against anti-advertising criticism has been to distinguish between manipulation (falsehood and lying) and persuasion (exaggeration and embellishment). Some critics say that 'while advertisers are not to lie, they are not necessarily bound to tell the whole truth and nothing but the truth' (Leiss *et al.* 1990: 44–45). They do not give the whole story, rather than give an untrue story. Are there any contemporary examples of advertising doing this? Discuss.

4 In 1993 Youth TGI was launched, an annual survey interviewing six thousand young people about their consuming habits. This showed concern about the danger of smoking cigarettes. Seventy per cent of seven- to ten-year-olds were very worried, 61 per cent of eleven- to fourteen-year-olds but only 36 per cent of fifteen- to nineteen-year-olds (Read 1993: 24). What happens between the ages of ten and fifteen? Also account for the reasons why children had a healthier, more balanced diet with rationing during the Second World War than they do today. What possible reasons could you suggest for these findings? Can advertising be isolated?

Further reading

Independent Television Commission (1991) *Code of Advertising Standards and Practice*.

Code of Advertising Practice Committee (CAP) (1985) *The British Code of Advertising Practice*, London.

Crone, T. (1991) *Law and the Media*, London: Butterworth Heinemann.

Glossary

....

ABC Audit Bureau of Circulations, audits the number of copies sold for magazines and newspapers.

above-the-line media All media that remunerate agencies on the basis of commission, e.g. TV, radio, newspapers, magazines and posters.

Adget A section of a magazine which is specifically designed to attract advertisements. These often take the form of special supplements in which the feature is written without the involvement of the advertiser, but the magazine's sales force sells space to advertisers who want the right editorial environment, for instance cosmetics companies who want to advertise in a beauty supplement in a fashion magazine, for travel firms who want to advertise in a holiday supplement.

ad hoc survey A one-off research of a particular topic during a particular time.

Adshel A four-sheet poster site in a shopping centre and the name of a poster contractor.

advertisement Paid-for dedicated space or time sequence in which only the advertiser is represented (can be in newspapers, magazines, TV, radio, posters, or in direct mail, retail, etc.).

advertisement appreciation Measures the likeability and interest in advertising. Respondents rank likeability from one to five.

advertiser The manufacturer, government body or organisation which wishes to have advertisements created and placed.

Advertising Association Information and lobbying organisation for the advertising industry, jointly funded by agencies, advertisers and media owners.

Advertising Standards Authority The semi-independent watchdog of the advertising industry set up in 1961 by the Advertising Association.

advertorial An editorial feature that is paid for or sponsored by an advertiser and often includes the product name and company logo; it usually includes 'Advertisement feature' at the top.

AIR Average Issue Readership, the average number of people who are estimated to have looked at an issue of a publication for three minutes or more in a specified time period.

air date The date of broadcast for a radio or TV commercial.

animatic Moving picture illustrations developed from a storyboard used in pre-testing commercials and to give clients an idea of what the finished commercial will look like.

audience appreciation Measure of how much audiences were interested in and enjoyed or were entertained by TV programmes. Conducted by BARB and gives an Appreciation Index score for programmes.

banner ad This is an ad image that is placed on a web page, typically at the top of the page or down the side.

BARB Broadcaster Audience Research Board, run by ITV and BBC; produces TV ratings and audience appreciation data.

Barbara Electronic system for measuring audience appreciation for programmes administered by BARB.

bar code A small block of vertical lines on products which contains information about the product which can be scanned by retailers, manufacturers and consumer panels.

below-the-line media All media that do not remunerate on the basis of commission, e.g. sales promotion, direct marketing, public relations and sponsorship.

BRAD British Rate and Data; provides monthly information on costs and specifications in advertising media.

brand filling Involves filling a gap in an existing market, e.g. Coke launching Tab to fill the clear soft-drink segment, or Colgate launching Bicarbonate of Soda toothpaste.

brand image Term used by David Ogilvy which indicates a unique emotional personality for a given brand.

brand positioning Term used to describe the unique added values and appeal of the brand in relation to other brands in the same market; often describes how it is positioned to consumers.

brand stretching New models, versions and sizes of a brand e.g. Coke, Diet Coke and Caffeine-free Coke.

break ratings The audience rating during a commercial break.

British Direct Marketing Association The trade body of direct marketing companies.

Broadcast Advertising Clearance Centre A self-regulatory body which pre-vets TV advertisements.

brown goods Electrical goods, such as hi-fis, TVs, CDs, video recorders. So named because first generation had brown wooden casing.

burst An intensive period of heavyweight advertising activity, usually repeated during the year.

cable TV A system of direct-to-home cables (some copper, some fibre-optic) which relay TV signals; some also carry satellite channels, and since the late 1980s also telephony.

Campaign Weekly advertising trade magazine aimed primarily at full-service agencies, owned by Haymarket Publishing; takes its name from industry term for period of advertising publicity.

Cinema Advertising Association Trade body representing cinema advertising companies.

circulars Also known as direct mail, sent direct to people's home or place of work via the post.

classified advertising Advertisements which do not usually use illustration, including recruitment, business-to-business, family notices, etc. Usually involve consumer's searching through the advertising columns.

click rate The click rate is the number of clicks on a banner ad as a proportion of the total number of clicks on the page that the ad appeared. For instance, if 10 people clicked on a page and 2 clicked on the ad the click rate would be 20 per cent.

Code of Advertising Practice Provides the guidelines for advertising content. The CAP Committee is the ASA adjudicator on complaints.

commercial impacts BARB viewing figures for commercial breaks.

commission Percentage sum agreed between the media owner and the agency in reward for placing the advertisement in the medium; can be anything between 15 per cent and 2 per cent for some agencies

comparative advertising Ads in which products are compared to those of a competitor.

consolidated viewing BARB viewing figures which take into account video playback.

consumer durable Infrequently purchased products such as electrical goods, cars.

consumer research Research conducted into the characteristics, changes and usage and attitudes of consumers.

continuous research Research conducted constantly to pick up trends and indicate fluctuations in markets.

controlled circulation Publications sent to targeted individuals, usually free and relying on advertisers wishing to target those groups.

convenience goods Goods which are bought with little effort.

cookies Web sites place cookies on users' hard disks so that it can record something about them at a later time. These are often used by advertisers to rotate banner ads and can also be used to customise pages based on the browser type or on user's viewing preferences.

copy date The date by which a publication requires the advertisement.

copywriting Writing text for advertisements.

corporate advertising Advertising by a corporation designed to highlight the full operations of the firm; aimed usually at institutional financial investors, but can also be aimed at consumers. The company itself becomes the brand.

corporate identity A consistent logo and design that is used by a firm to suggest its corporate style and ethos.

cost per thousand (CPT) The cost of reaching one thousand readers, viewer or listeners of a target audience (e.g. ABC1s) or the total audience via a medium.

coupon offer Usually a money-off voucher allowing consumers to gain a discount on the promoted product.

coverage The percentage of the target audience who have an opportunity to see the ad at least once.

creative development research A test of advertisements by planners while advertisement ideas are being formulated to influence the final creative treatment.

day-part TV Advertising is divided into day-parts at different rates to reach different audiences.

demographics Classificatory system of research based upon shared characteristics of people such as age, sex, class and ethnicity. Systems include ACORN, MOSAIC and Superprofiles.

demonstration ads Advertisements that include a demonstration of the product in use and or a comparison of the product with others on the market.

depth interview An informal interview usually between an interviewer and one respondent (sometimes more) which is meant to explore the hidden motivations why consumers buy and consume goods.

desk research This involves using publicly available data and previous datas to examine markets; the cheapest form of research.

diary method Method of research used in a number of media research activities, such as RAJAR; involves respondents filling in a diary of their media and consuming habits.

direct response Enquiries which freepost and freefone consumers can send in via Royal Mail and BT, charged to the advertiser not the consumer. Used to encourage people to contact the company; also uses 0898 numbers.

discount Percentage awarded to an agency by a media owner either for booking large sums of money or booking early, or trying to attract them because of low circulation revenue.

display advertisement Advertising which usually involved an illustration, photograph or image and usually takes up large amounts of space in newspapers and magazines. Its aim is to attract immediate attention, rather than rely on people searching through (as with classified).

double-page spread (DPS) An advertisement occupying two facing pages (usually in a magazine).

drip Long period of lightweight advertising activity.

drop Door-to-door advertising material dropped in designated areas.

early payment discount Given when an agency agrees to pay the invoice earlier than usual.

establishment survey Establishes the demographic profile of homes in ITV regions to gain a representative sample for the BARB panel.

execution A new execution is an new treatment of a consistent theme, e.g. the Andrex puppy in a new situation.

facing matter The advertisements face editorial pages in magazines and newspapers.

fast-moving consumer goods Also packaged goods; frequently purchased goods such as confectionery, toiletries, cereals, etc.

fee payment A flat fee paid by the client to the agency for all work done.

fibre optics Cable system which allows interactive programming via fibre optic cables, multiple channels and quick two-way communication between sender and receiver.

FMCG See fast-moving consumer goods.

focus groups Groups of usually around eight respondents who are invited to talk about the brand and product sector of qualitative research purposes.

forty-eight-sheet A standard poster size of 7×3 metres (20×10 ft); a ninety-six-sheet poster is double this size.

frequency The average number of times the audience will have an opportunity to see the advertisement.

full-service agency An agency that researches, creates, co-ordinates and buys an advertiser's advertising campaign.

geodemographics Classificatory system of research based upon shared characteristics of people and lifestyles according to their neighbourhood and geographic area.

GHI Guaranteed Home Impressions, the number of home impacts guaranteed by the TV contractor for the given TVRs in a specified period of time at a fixed cost.

GSL General Sales List, medicines available in any retail outlet.

head-on site An outdoor poster site which faces traffic.

impressions Used in web advertising to refer to an ad view. Advertising is often measured in terms of impressions.

Incorporated Society of British Advertisers (ISBA) The trade organisation representing clients.

Institute of Practitioners in Advertising (IPA) The trade organisation which traditionally represented full-service agencies but began admitting direct marketing companies in 1991 and admitted media independent TMD Carat in 1993.

interstitial ads These are Internet ads that are between editorial content. It is usually designed to move automatically to the page the user requested.

involvement advertising A type of advertising which attempts to involve consumers by either humour or emotions in the advertising to help them warm towards the brand.

ITC The Independent Television Commission, set up in 1991, is the regulator body covering commercial broadcasting on ITV and Channel 4.

lifestyle Classificatory system of research based upon the shared values, attitudes and personality of consumers.

line-by-line Buying individual sites of posters which are not part of packages.

list broker Someone who trades lists of names of consumers who may be compatible for direct marketing purposes (e.g. insurance companies and mortgage companies).

luxury goods Goods consumed for their symbolic value over their use value.

media dependent A media department hived-off from a full-service agency.

media independent A media planning and buying agency that has no link to a full-service agency.

media plan Recommendation for a media schedule, including dates, publications, TV regions.

media research Research conducted into the relationships between different media and audiences, quantity of media audiences, and the quality of viewing, listening or reading.

media schedule Record of bookings made for a campaign, or a proposal for a campaign with dates, times, sizes and costs.

merchandising Traditional term for sales promotion, use of in-store leaflets and materials.

multi-media Use of space- and time-based media via computers and fibre-optic cables allowing the consumer to control the order, timing and selection of programmes and advertising.

National Readership Survey (NRS) Produces a monthly survey of readers for national and regional newspapers and consumer magazines, run and funded by a joint industry committee. Provides an Average Issue Readership.

Newspaper Publishers' Association (NPA) Trade body representing national newspapers.

Newspaper Society Trade body representing regional newspaper groups.

next matter An advertisement appearing on the same page as editorial copy.

on-the-run colour Colour can be put on to the paper in a single run through the printing machine(s). Before, the paper would have gone through four times to have the yellow, black, red and blue inks printed. This was extremely expensive, time-consuming and prone to breakdowns. Now, the four separate inks are applied on one run of the paper through the machine, quickly and at much lower cost.

opportunities to see (OTS) The number of possibilities an individual has of seeing an advertisement on billboards, on TV and in the press.

OSCAR Outdoor site classification system run by the Joint Industry Committee for Poster Audience Research.

OTC Over-the-counter drugs, those which are available without a prescription in chemists' shops and newsagents'.

Outdoor Advertising Association (OAA) Trade body representing outdoor contractors.

outside back cover The very last page of the publication.

peoplemeters Electronic method of collating research information for BARB on numbers and profile of people in a room while the TV set is switched on.

payment by results Usually an agreed sum (fee) between the agency and the client, plus a percentage increase for achieving the advertising goals.

pay-TV A system whereby consumers can pay directly for programmes viewed, usually in an advertising-free environment.

peak time The time of day when usually the highest numbers of the TV audience are watching; the rest is called off-peak.

penetration The percentage of homes or people reached by a brand in purchase or usage.

Periodical Publishers' Association Trade body representing magazine publishers.

persuasion shift A type of advertising research popular in the USA which suggests that the consumer has been directly persuaded by the advertising message contained in the advertisement to buy the product.

P medicines Pharmacy-only medicines.

point of sale The place in which the goods are bought or sold, usually a place in which other display material is used to reach the consumer before the decision is finally made.

POM Prescription-only medicines.

poster specialists Intermediary media buyers who specialise in outdoor advertising.

pre-empt To buy commercial advertising time at the last minute at a higher rate, thus displacing ads already booked.

premium offer Offering another product or service free, or at a reduced price with purchase of a product, e.g. Hoover offering two free flight tickets for Europe or the USA with every purchase of a Hoover product over £100.

presenter A style of advertisement that either includes a testimonial from a famous person or authority figure, or features an actor or personality talking directly to the consumer.

press date The date a publication is finally printed.

pre-test A test of advertising before it is transmitted among target consumers.

product placement Placing a product in an editorial programme so that it is prominently seen; this often involves a payment to the production company.

product tests Tests carried out to measure the strength of brand values, often disguising the brand name of the product. Other tests include observing the usage of the product for incorporation in advertising and marketing.

profile The breakdown of audience classifications for a medium of each demographic group.

programme schedule Usually issued four times a year to media buyers in TV, from which the buyer estimates the size and profile of the audience.

PR shops Consultancies which deal in public relations, public affairs and corporate promotions.

psychographics Classificatory system of research based upon the shared psychological make-up of groups of people.

public relations Covers non-paid-for publicity such as press or media relations, sponsoring events, lobbying government, donations to charity by which the company promotes its image to the public, government and other businesses.

quota sample Interviewers collect information from a set number of people with specific demographic characteristics to gain a cross-section.

Radio Advertising Clearance Centre Self-regulatory body set up by the Radio Authority to pre-vet radio commercials.

Radio Authority The regulatory body covering commercial and public service broadcasting.

RAJAR Research body jointly funded and run by BBC and commercial radio.

random sample Sample in which each member has an equal chance of being selected from a pre-given list.

rate card Issued by media owners to give an indication of the structure and levels of prices for advertisements. These are hardly ever adhered to by advertising agencies, who usually manage to obtain substantial discounts.

recall Used in research to find out how memorable an advertisement was, for instance after an ad has been broadcast or shown in newspapers ('day-after recall'); also 'spontaneous recall', where the interviewer simply asks respondents to list ads recalled, and 'promoted recall', where the interviewer suggests ads and asks the respondent to give details.

release form Signed by anyone photographed or filmed allowing advertisers to use their image in advertisements.

retail audit A measurement of brands from a sample of retail distributors which indicates the sales performance of brands during promotions.

RTE Ready-to-Eat cereals, which do not need preparation, such as corn flakes, Shredded Wheat.

run-of-month and **run-of-week** Ads which appear whenever and wherever the media owner decides within the time period given, for cheaper rates.

run-of-paper The media owner decides where the ad appears, for a standard rate.

sales houses Representatives of media owners who sell space or time to agencies; these are sometimes owned by media owners or act for independents on their behalf.

sales promotion Also known as merchandising; form of promotion used at the point of sale which includes posters, stickers and stands; also the use of money-off coupons, competitions and other promotions to stimulate trial.

salience A style of advertising which tries to stand out from the rest of the advertising and media messages to grab the attention of the viewer and break down resistance.

sample A scaled-down version of a research universe, used to estimate patterns in the total universe; supposedly, the larger the sample size, the more accurate the estimate.

sanpro Sanitary protection products: tampons and sanitary towels.

sans serif Typefaces without curls or strokes at the end of letters.

series discount A discount offered for advertisers who book a series of advertisements over a number of issues.

serif Typefaces with curls and strokes at the end of letters.

SFX Sound effects used in TV, cinema and radio commercials; can include music or background noise.

shopping goods Goods in which a comparison is made by the consumer before it is bought, often on price/value for money.

single-column centimetre Unit of measurement for advertising in newspapers: a centimetre high and a column wide.

slice-of-life A style of advertising that can be in either print, TV or radio form which invites the viewer to eavesdrop on a situation, usually one in which the product is being discussed, used or consumed.

solus position An advertisement which is placed where no other ads appears; can be in print media or billboards, or in broadcasting breaks.

speciality goods Goods which consumers will travel distances to buy; usually expensive or highly desirable goods, such as cars and luxury furniture.

split run test Test made by placing different ads in the same publication, either split by area (north/south) or in alternate copies over the same area.

split transmission Simultaneous transmission of separate advertisements offered by TV contractors for test purposes within one region.

sponsorship A form of promotion which involves payment by the advertiser for an editorial product (in the media) or for an event in which the company are often allowed to have the brand credited and promoted, and can use the product/event in their own promotions.

spot A single commercial break of 10 seconds on TV.

spot colour A single colour in an advertisement.

spot rating A rating for a single commercial.

staggered campaign A mixture of burst and drip advertising campaigns.

subscription Method of payment for media (publications and TV) which involves a payment of money in advance by the advertiser for media consumption over a period of time, often at a discount.

supers Use of words over a picture.

Target Group Index A survey of product and brand usage and media usage conducted by BMRB over a year, including demographic and lifestyle categories.

telemarketing Use of phones to contact and receive calls from potential customers.

Television Consumer Audit A consumer panel of grocery purchases by TV viewers.

TGRs (Target Group Ratings) The combination of brand and product users in the Target Group Index achieved by TV programmes matched to the BARB figures.

through-the-line A mixture of above- and below-the-line promotion, generally using a combination of mass media advertising, public relations, sales promotion and direct marketing.

tracking study A continuous survey of recall, usage, attitude and awareness of brands which advertisers use to gauge the effectiveness of advertising and promotion.

transmission certificate Sent to agencies by ITV companies to confirm that a commercial has been aired.

TV contractor The company which holds the franchise for transmission in given ITV regions, e.g. Granada in the north-west.

TVRs (Television Ratings) The percentage of target audience (e.g. 'house-wives') achieved by TV programmes.

universe The total number of a target group from which researchers take a sample.

usage and attitude Ad hoc research conducted into the use of products and brands and attitudes towards them by consumers.

USP (Unique Selling Proposition) Term coined by Rosser Reeves in *Reality in Advertising* to indicate a brand characteristic which separates it from competitors.

vignette A short description or character sketch to give a portrait of somebody or something, or a summary of a story in a few lines.

viral marketing This technique is often used on the web or via e-mail and induces users or web sites to pass on a marketing message to other sites or users, creating an enormous growth in the message's visibility.

VOD Video-on-Demand system developed by British Telecom whereby consumers can call up videos of their choice into the home via traditional copper-cable phone lines.

voice-over Spoken words used in relation to pictures on TV and cinema.

voucher A copy of a publication given to an agency to prove that its advertisement ran.

white goods Electrical goods, often kitchen equipment such as washing machines, fridges, cookers.

Useful websites

Advertising Association http://www.adassoc.org.uk/
Account Planning Group http://www.apg.org.uk/
Advertising Standards Authority http://www.asa.org.uk/
Broadcast Advertising Clearance Centre http://www.bacc.org.uk/
Committee of Advertising Practice http://www.cap.org.uk/home.asp
British Design Art & Direction http://www.dandad.org/
European Advertising Standards Alliance http://www.easa-alliance.org/
Institute of Practitioners in Advertising http://www.ipa.co.uk/
Incorporated Society of British Advertisers http://www.isba.org.uk/
History of Advertising Trust http://www.hatads.org.uk

Useful sites for news and information about advertising

http://www.adageglobal.com/
http://www.adage.com/
http://www.campaignlive.com/
http://www.mad.co.uk/mc/
http://www.marketing.haynet.com/
http://www.adslogans.co.uk
http://www.millwardbrown.com/

http://www.luerzersarchive.net
http://www.radio-ads.co.uk/
http://www.raynet.mcmail.com/
http://www.shots.net/
http://www.adbusters.org/
http://www.uksponsorship.com/
http://www.aargroup.co.uk/

A selection of ad agency websites

http://www.aegisplc.com.
http://www.amvbbdo.co.uk/
http://www.bbh.co.uk
http://www.bates.co.uk/
http://www.bmp.co.uk/
http://www.carat.com/
http://www.cdpmedia.com/
http://www.cia.co.uk/
http://www.dfgw.com/
http://www.ehhcl.net:8889/
http://www.initiativemedia.com/
http://www.interpublic.com/
http://www.leoburnett.com/
   splash.html

http://www.lowelintas.com/flash.
   html
http://www.mcsaatchi.com/index_
   mac.html
http://www.mccann.com/
http://www.ogilvy.com/
http://www.omnicomgroup.com/
http://www.saatchi-saatchi.com/
   innovation/launch.html
http://www.walkermedia.com/
http://www.wpp.com/
http://www.wcrs.co.uk
http://www.zenithmedia.com/

Bibliography

....

Advertising Association (1991–2) *Advertising Statistics Yearbook*, ninth annual edition, London

Ang, I. (1991) *Desperately Seeking the Audience*, London: Routledge

Armstrong, S. (1992) 'Dealers of the New Age', *Media Week*, 28 August, p. 12

Bailey, E. (1992) 'Regional Response', *Media Week*, 11 December, p. 38

Beatson, R. (1986) 'Address by the Director General of European Association of Advertising Agencies', *International Journal of Advertising*, vol. 5, pp. 261–266

Bell, A. (1991) *The Language of News Media*, Oxford: Blackwell

Bell, T. (1986) 'The Agency Viewpoint' in Henry, B., ed. *British Television Advertising: The First 30 Years*, London: Century Benham

Bernstein, D. (1986) 'The Television Commercial: An Essay' in Henry, B., ed. *British Television Advertising: The First 30 Years*, London: Century Benham

Birch, L. (1962) *The Advertising We Deserve?*, London: Vista Books

Bird, D. (1993) *Commonsense Direct Marketing*, London: Kogan Page

Bird, M. (1990) 'Why Classify?', *Admap*, December, vol. 26, no. 12, issue 302

Bocock, R. (1993) *Consumption*, London: Routledge

Bradshaw, P. V. (1927) *Art in Advertising*, London: The Press Art School

Braithwaite, B. and Barrell, J. (1988) *The Business of Women's Magazines*, London: Kogan Page

Briggs, M. (1993) 'Why Ad Agencies Must Change', *Admap*, January, no. 1, issue 325

Broadbent, S. (1992) '456 Views of How Advertising Works', *Admap*, November, vol. 27, no. 11, issue 323

Broadbent, S. (1993) 'Advertising Effects: More than Short Term', *Journal of the Market Research Society*, vol. 35, no. 1, January

Brown, G. (1991) 'Big Stable Brands and Ad Effects', *Admap*, May, vol. 26, no. 5, issue 307

Campaign, 8 November 1991

Campaign, 17 September 1993

Cardwell, Z. (1993a) '5 Things to Know about Tobacco Ads', *Media Week*, 12 February, p. 17

Cardwell, Z. (1993b) '5 Things to Know about EBRS', *Media Week*, 23 July, p. 15

Carey, J. (1992) *The Intellectuals and the Masses*, London: Faber & Faber

Channon, C. (ed.) (1989) *20 Advertising Case Histories*, London: IPA

Chisnall, P. M. (1992) *Marketing Research*, London: McGraw-Hill, 4th edition

Clark, E. (1988) *The Want Maker*, London: Hodder & Stoughton

Code of Advertising Practice Committee (CAP) (1988) (8th edn) *The British Code of Advertising Practice*, London

Code of Advertising Practice Committee (CAP) (1995) *The British Codes of Advertising and Sales Promotion*, London

Colley, R. H. 91961) *Defining Advertising Goals for Measured Advertising Results*, New York: Association of National Advertisers

Colwell, J. (1990) 'Qualitative Market Research: A Conceptual Analysis and Review of Practitioner Criteria', *Journal of the Market Research Society*, vol. 32, no. 1, January

Committee of Advertising Practice (1995) *The British Codes of Advertising and Sales Promotion*, London

Cook, G. (1992) *The Discourse of Advertising*, London: Routledge

Cook, R. and Waldman, S. (1993) 'Altogether Now', *Media Week*, 13 August, p. 24

Coopers & Lybrand (1991) *Report on the Advertising Industry*, London

Corner, J. (1991) 'Meaning, Genre and Context: The Problematics of "Public Knowledge"' in Curran, J. and Gurevitch, M., eds, *Mass Media & Society*, London: Edward Arnold (New Audience Studies)

Cornish, P. (1990) 'Demographics Not Standing Still', *Admap*, December, vol. 26, no. 12

Cowan, D. S. and Jones, R. W. (1968) *Advertising in the 21st Century*, London: Hutchinson

Cowley, D. (ed.), (1989) *How to Plan Advertising*, London: Cassell in Association with the Account Planning Group

Crompton, A. (1987) *The Craft of Copywriting*, London: Century Business

Crone, T. (1991) *Law and the Media*, London: Butterworth Heinemann

Curran, J. (1986) 'The Impact of Advertising on the British Mass Media' in Collins, R. *et al.*, *Media Culture & Society: A Critical Reader*, London: Sage Publications

Curran, J. and Seaton, J. (1988) *Power Without Responsibility*, London: Routledge

Davidson, M. (1991) *The Consumerist Manifesto*, London: Routledge

Dawkins, D. and Samuels, J. (1994) '"Barbara' and audience appreciation', *Admap*, February, vol. 29, no. 2, issue 337

Davis, M. P. (1992) *The Effective Use of Advertising Media*, London: Century Business

De Vries, L. (1968) *Victorian Advertisements*, London: John Murray

Dickinson, R., Herbst, A. and O'Shaughnessy, J. (1986) 'Marketing Concept and Customer Orientation', *European Journal of Marketing* vol. 20, no. 10

Douglas, T. (1984) *The Compete Guide to Advertising*, London: Macmillan

Durkin, K. (1985) *Television, Sex Roles and Children*, Milton Keynes: Open University Press

Duval, R. (1990) 'The Regulatory Environment', *Admap*, October, vol. 26, no. 10, issue 300

Dyer, G. (1982) *Advertising As Communication*, London: Routledge

The Economist (1990a) 'The Doctor's Dilemma', 27 January, pp. 69–70

The Economist (1990b) 'The Advertising Industry: The Party's Over', special report, 9 June

Economist Books (1993) *Pocket Marketing*, London: *The Economist* and Hamish Hamilton

Ehrenberg, A. S. C. (1991) 'New Brands and the Existing Market', *Journal of the Market Research Society*, vol. 33, no. 4, January

Ehrenberg, A. and Barnard, N. (1994) 'Justifying Advertising Budgets', *Admap*, January, vol. 29, no. 1, issue 336

Elliott, B. B. (1962) *A History of English Advertising*, London: Business Publications Limited

Evans, I. G. and Riyait, S. (1993) 'Is the Message being Received? Benetton Analysed', *Production and Creativity in Advertising*, London: Pitman

Featherstone, M. (1991) *Consumer Culture and Postmodernism*, London: Sage

Forty, A. (1986) *Objects of Desire*, London: Thames & Hudson

Gladwell, M. (2000) *The Tipping Point*, Boston: Little, Brown & Company

Goldman, R. (1992) *Reading Ads Socially*, London: Routledge

Griffiths, C. (1992) 'Brand as Verb', *Admap*, July/August, vol. 27, no. 7, issue 320

Gullen, P. (1991) 'High Definition Media Planning', *Admap*, December, vol. 26, no. 12, issue 313

Hall, S. (1981) 'Encoding/Decoding in Television Discourse' in Hall, S. *et al.*, eds, *Culture, Media, Language*, London: Hutchinson

Halstead, R. (1994) 'The Boffin as Hero', *Business Age*, July, no. 46

Harrison, D. (1993) 'Case for a Specialist', *Admap*, April, vol. 28, no. 4, issue 328

Hart, A. (1991) *Understanding the Media: A Practical guide*, London: Routledge

Hart, N. A. (1990) *The Practice of Advertising*, London: Heinemann Professional Publishing

Henry, B. (ed.) (1986) *British Television Advertising: The First 30 Years*, London: Century Benham

Henry, H. (1993) 'How Production Costs Have Outstripped Media Rates', *Admap*, January, vol. 28, no. 1, issue 325, p. 446

Hindley, D. and G. (1972) *Advertising in Victorian England 1837–1901*, London: Wayland

Hobsbawm, E. J. (1987) *The Age of Empire*, London: Weidenfeld & Nicolson

Holliday, R. (1993) 'When Negotiations Stop and Talks Start', *Media Week*, 11 June, p. 16

Hood, M. (1992) 'Cutting Ad Rates Doesn't Pay', *Campaign*, 17 July, p. 15

Hopkins, C. C. (1966) *My Life in Advertising & Scientific Advertising*, Illinois: NTC Business Books

Ind, N. (1993) *Great Advertising Campaigns*, London: Kogan Page

Independent Television Commission (1991) *Code of Advertising Standards and Practice*

Izatt, J. (1993) 'Brand and Deliver', *Media Week*, 3 September, pp. 24–25

Jacobs, B. (1991) 'Trends in Media Buying and Selling in Europe and the Effect on Advertising Agency Business', *International Journal of Advertising*, vol. 10, no. 4

Jefkins, F. (1992) *Advertising*, London: Made Simple Books

Jones, J. P. (1990) 'Ad Spending: Maintaining Market Share', *Harvard Business Review*, January–February

Kanso, A. (1991) 'The Use of Advertising Agencies for Foreign Markets: Decentralised Decision Making and Localised Approaches?', *International Journal of Advertising*, vol. 10, no. 2

Katz, E. and Lazarsfeld, P. F. (1955) *Personal Influence*, New York: The Free Press

Keane, J. (1991) *The Media and Democracy*, Cambridge: Polity Press

Kent, R. (ed.) (1994) *Measuring Media Audiences*, London: Routledge

Lannon, J. (1992) 'Asking the Right Question', *Admap*, March, vol. 27, no. 3, issue 316

Lannon, J. (1993) 'Branding Essentials and the New Environment', *Admap*, June, vol. 28, no. 6, issue 330

Law, A. (1994) 'How to Ride the Wave of Change', *Admap*, January, vol. 29, no. 1, issue 336

Leech, G. N. (1966) *English in Advertising: A Linguistic Study of Advertising in Great Britain*, London: Longmans

Leiss, W., Kline, S. and Jhally, S. (1990) *Social Communication in Advertising*, 2nd edn, London: Routledge

Levy, H. P. (1967) *The Press Council: History, Procedure and Cases*, London: Macmillan

Lury, A. (1994) 'Advertising Moving Beyond the Stereotypes' in Keat, R., Whiteley, N. and Abercrombie, N., eds, *The Authority of the Consumer*, London: Routledge

McCracken, E. (1993) *Decoding Women's Magazines: From Mademoiselle to Ms*, London: Macmillan

McCracken, G. (1990) 'Culture and Consumer Behaviour: An Anthropological Perspective', *Journal of the Market Research Society*, vol. 32, no. 1, January

McDonald, C. (1991) 'Intended Response', *Admap*, July/August, vol. 26, no. 7, issue 309

McKendrick, N., Brewer, J. and Plumb, J. H. (1983) *The Birth of the Consumer Society*

Macleod, C. (1992) 'Reading Patterns at Home and Away', *Media Week*, 29 May, p. 16

McQueen, J. (1992) 'Stimulating Long Term Brand Growth', *Admap*, April, vol. 27, no. 4, issue 317

Makin, C. and Dovey, J. (1991) 'Broking Isn't Coming – It's Here', *Campaign*, 6 September, p. 15

Martin, M. (1993) 'Should Cigarette Advertising Be Banned?', *Campaign*, 19 February, pp. 24–25

Maslow, A. H. (1954) *Motivation and Personality*, New York, Harper & Row

Mattelhart, A. (1991) *Advertising International: The Privatisation of Public Space*, London: Comedia Routledge

Mistry, T. (1993) 'Agencies Have to Face Tough Decisions on Media', *Campaign*, 30 July, p. 12

Morley, D. (1992) *Television, Audiences & Cultural Studies*, London: Routledge

Myers, K. (1986) *Understains*, London: Comedia

Nava, M. (1992) *Changing Cultures: Feminism, Youth and Consumerism*, London: Sage Publications

Nevett, T. R. (1982) *Advertising in Britain: A History*, London: Heinemann

Nielsen, A. C. (1993) 'Sales Promotion and the Information Revolution', *Admap*, January, vol. 28, no. 1, issue 325

Nixon, S. (1993) 'Looking for the Holy Grail: Publishing and Advertising Strategies and Contemporary Men's Magazines', *Cultural Studies*, October, vol. 7, no. 3

Norris, C. E. and Colman, A. M. (1994) 'Putting Ads in Context', *Admap*, January, vol. 29, no. 1, issue 336

Ogilvy, D. (1983) *Ogilvy on Advertising*, London: Pan Books

Packard, V. (1957) *The Hidden Persuaders*, London: Penguin

Palmer, M. (1990) 'Advertising Industry – Filling the Lobby', *Admap*, October, vol. 26, no. 10, issue 300

Peach, A., Phillips, N. and Terris, J. (1992) 'Economy with the Truth', *Admap*, April, vol. 27, issue 317

Pearson, J. and Turner, G. (1965) *The Persuasion Industry*, London: Eyre & Spottiswoode

Perris, J. (1993) 'Are the Agencies Too Powerful?', *Media Week*, 12 November, p. 20

Phillips, H. and Bradshaw, R. (1993) 'How Consumers Actually Shop: Customer Interaction with the Point of Sale', *Journal of the Market Research Society*, vol. 35, no. 1, January

Piggott, S. (1975) *OBM A Celebration: One Hundred and Twenty Five Years in Advertising*, London: Ogilvy Benson & Mather

Powell, C. (1994) 'The Client–Agency Relationship', *Admap*, January, vol. 29, no. 1, issue 336

Pragnell, A. (1986) 'An Authority View in Henry, B., ed., *British Television Advertising: The First 30 Years*, London: Century Benham

Prendergrast, M. (1993) *For God, Country and Coca-Cola*, London: Weidenfeld & Nicolson

Prue, T. (1991) 'Recall or Response?', *Admap*, June, vol. 26, no. 6, issue 308

Randall, G. (1993) *Principles of Marketing*, London: Routledge

Read, D. (1993) 'Young Pretender', *Media Week*, 8 October, pp. 23–24

Reed, D. (1992) 'Mixed Marriages', *Campaign*, 14 February, p. 33

Reeves, R. (1961) *Reality in Advertising*, London: Macgibbon & Kee

Ring, J. (1993) *Advertising on Trial*, London: Financial Times Pitman Publishing

Roberts, B. (1992) 'New Directions', *Admap*, September, vol. 27, no. 9, issue 321

Russell, T. (1924) 'An Industry that Makes Industries', *Illustrated London News*, vol. 165, 19 July, p. 132

Schudson, M. (1993) *Advertising: The Uneasy Persuasion*, London: Routledge

Shields, R. (ed.) (1992) *Lifestyle Shopping: The Subject of Consumption*, London: Routledge

Slingsby, H. (1994) 'Distinguishing Marks', *Marketing Week*, 11 November

Snowden, S. (1993) 'Why Satellite's Lift Off Might Add Costs', *Admap*, December, vol. 28, no. 12, issue 335

Tuck, M. (1976) *How Do We Choose?*, London: Methuen

Turner, E. S. (1953) *The Shocking History of Advertising*, New York: E. P. Dutton & Company

Unerman, S. (1993) 'Reader Tendencies', *Media Week*, 26 March

Vardar, N. (1992) *Global Advertising: Rhyme or Reason?*, London: Paul Chapman Publishing

Vestergaard, T. and Schroder, K. (1985) *The Language of Advertising*, Oxford: Basil Blackwell

Waldman, S. (1993a) 'The Top 100 Buying Points', *Media Week*, 3 September, p. 18

Waldman, S. (1993b) 'Branded Editorial', *Media Week*, 2 July, pp. 24–25

Walford, N. (1992) 'How It Works', *Admap*, July/August, vol. 27, no. 7, issue 320

Wernick, A. (1991) *Promotional Culture*, London: Sage

Whitbread PLC (1983) *Thirsty Work: Ten Years of Heineken Advertising*, London: Macmillan (text by Peter Mayle)

White, R. (1988) *Advertising: What It Is and How To Do It*, London: McGraw-Hill Advertising Association

Whittington, R. and Whipp, R. (1992) 'Professional Ideology and Marketing Implementation', *European Journal of Marketing*, vol. 26, no. 1

Wicken, G. (1993) 'Getting to Grips with AB Consumers', *Admap*, September, vol. 28, no. 8

Wilkins, C. (1988) *Campaign*, 16 September

Williamson, J. (1978) *Decoding Advertisements: Ideology and Meaning in Advertising*, London: Marion Boyars

Willis, F. (1992) 'Satellite: The Role of the Regulator', *Admap*, December, vol. 27, no. 12, issue 324

Willott, R. (1993) 'The Latest State of Pay', *Campaign*, 13 August, pp. 22–23

Wilmshurst, J. (1985) *The Fundamentals of Advertising*, London: Butterworth Heinemann

Woodhouse, P. (1986) 'Copy Controls from Within' in Henry, B., ed., *British Television Advertising: The First 30 Years*, London: Century Benham

York, P. (1988) 'Tune In to the Ads of Tomorrow', *Campaign*, 16 September, pp. 34–35

Young, B. M. (1990) *TV Advertising and Children*

Index

....

(NB Page numbers in italic refer to tables and figures)